LONG WARS
AND THE
CONSTITUTION

LONG WARS
AND THE
CONSTITUTION

Stephen M. Griffin

Harvard University Press
Cambridge, Massachusetts
London, England
2013

Printed in the United States of America

Library of Congress Cataloging-in-Publication Data
Griffin, Stephen M., 1957–
Long wars and the constitution / Stephen M. Griffin.
pages cm
Includes bibliographical references and index.
ISBN 978-0-674-05828-6 (alk. paper)
1. War and emergency powers—United States. 2. United States—Foreign relations—1945–1989. 3. United States—Foreign relations—1989– I. Title.
KF5060.G73 2013
342.73'0412—dc23 2012045934

To Starlynn and Christina Griffin,
for their love

Contents

List of Acronyms ix

Introduction 1

1 War Powers and Constitutional Change 11

2 Truman and the Post-1945 Constitutional Order 52

3 War and the National Security State 99

4 Vietnam and Watergate:
The Post-1945 Constitutional Order in Crisis 120

5 The Constitutional Order in the Post-Vietnam Era 153

6 The 9/11 Wars and the Presidency 194

7 A New Constitutional Order? 236

Appendix: Executive Branch War Powers Opinions since 1950 277

Notes 281

Acknowledgments 351

Index 353

List of Acronyms

AUMF	Authorization to Use Military Force
CIA	Central Intelligence Agency
DOD	Department of Defense
DOJ	Department of Justice
FBI	Federal Bureau of Investigation
FCC	Federal Communications Commission
FISA	Foreign Intelligence Surveillance Act
JAG	Judge Advocate General
JCS	Joint Chiefs of Staff
NATO	North Atlantic Treaty Organization
NSC	National Security Council
OLC	Office of Legal Counsel, Department of Justice
OVP	Office of the Vice President
WMD	Weapons of mass destruction
WPR	War Powers Resolution

LONG WARS
AND THE
CONSTITUTION

Introduction

In the aftermath of the terrorist attacks of September 11, 2001, the American constitutional system was shaken by a series of controversies arising out of the aggressive response of the Bush administration. Prominent among these were furious and deeply felt disputes over the use of torture in interrogation, the treatment of detainees, especially at Guantanamo Bay, and domestic surveillance. The Bush administration came under heavy criticism not only for actions initially taken in secret and unauthorized by Congress, but also for the way it led the nation into the authorized war against Iraq in 2003. Many Americans believed that the war had been foisted on the public in a deceptive way without adequate consideration of its costs. As a result of these controversies, President George W. Bush was only the latest in a long line of chief executives accused of acting as an "imperial" president.

The advent of the Obama administration did not lead to a stilling of the waters. To an extent surprising to his supporters, President Barack Obama did not break decisively with all of the controversial policies of the Bush administration.[1] This suggested a factor common to these administrations was at work. The controversies that plagued the Bush administration and the unwillingness of the Obama administration to change those policies were the latest examples of a long chain of constitutional difficulties connected with the unilateral exercise of presidential power in foreign affairs and, more specifically, the use of presidential power to wage war.

Controversies over the use of executive power have existed throughout American history. But they took on a completely new dimension following the enormous expansion in the capacities of government necessary to prevail in World War II and the Cold War. Seen in this light, the deeply problematic aspects of the Bush administration's "war on terror" belong to a family of constitutional crises that include Watergate in the Nixon administration and the Iran-contra affair in the Reagan administration. These crises are part of a pattern of recurrent policy disasters and constitutional problems linked to the war power that run back to the Truman administration and include both covert and overt military operations such as the Bay of Pigs and the Vietnam War.

Scholars have had difficulty analyzing this recurrent pattern, in part because of the influence of persuasive yet misleading narratives such as the "imperial presidency." While presidents have not been blameless in their exercise of power in foreign affairs, neither have they been alone in making decisions or operating entirely outside the Constitution. Criticizing presidents as individuals gone haywire ignores that they have had significant, even sometimes overwhelming, political support for actions that from a constitutional point of view are quite dubious. It further ignores that they have plausibly seen themselves as chiefly responsible for advancing the foreign policy and protecting the national security of the United States.[2]

Americans like to think of their constitutional system as stable and resistant to formal change through amendment. Somewhat paradoxically, they also believe in the "living Constitution," a document that has adapted successfully to changing circumstances. The clashing character of these beliefs has been especially evident in the debate over the use of executive power in foreign affairs. "Presidentialists" argue that increased executive power after World War II was a reasonable alteration of the constitutional system in light of the new global responsibilities and hegemonic status of the United States. "Congressionalist" opponents of this perspective cite the original eighteenth-century constitutional arrangements as their touchstone in defending the traditional powers of Congress. Common to both positions is the assumption that regardless of the degree of practical changes in the responsibilities of government, the Constitution was adequate to the challenge of the post–World War II era.

We can make better progress if we reject this assumption. This is an unfamiliar path for analysis, but one better able to cope with the complex relationship between the reality of changed circumstances and a relatively fixed text and set of traditions. Since the United States assumed a position of global leadership and responsibility after World War II, serious tensions have plagued our constitutional system. They are connected by the near-total reliance on executive power to defend national security.

Relative to the popular yet opposed narratives of the imperial presidency and executive triumphalism offered by congressionalists and presidentialists respectively, the argument I develop in this book is complex and cuts across the standard lines of the war powers debate. With presidentialists, I agree that the new global responsibilities of the United States necessitated a significant alteration to the constitutional order. Against presidentialists, I contend that the transition was anything but a smooth adaptation and was the source of severe and ongoing problems, not only within the constitutional order, but also with respect to policy-making in foreign affairs and national security. With congressionalists, I agree that post-1945 presidents have acted against the eighteenth-century meaning of the Constitution and sometimes abused their power. Against congressionalists, I contend that the historical meaning of the war-making provisions of the Constitution could not be implemented in the post-1945 context, at least not without a formal overhaul of the separation of powers, especially of the structure of Congress, to a degree that has never been contemplated.

So my purpose in this book is not so much to contribute to the still-ongoing war powers debate as it is to reconceive it and change our perspective on what it should be about. Put another way, I offer a novel *internal* critique of the presidentialist position rather than adjudicating every point at issue in the debate. Presidentialists argue that executive leadership in foreign affairs is not only good policy, but is justified by the text and eighteenth-century history of the Constitution, as well as by subsequent practice. While I accept this position in its broad outlines, I insist on a key reservation. War is different. It is marked as such not only by legal authorities that all parties acknowledge as relevant to the war powers controversy, but also by the actual practice of American diplomacy. While historical practice is a source of evidence that presidentialists have claimed for their own, it in fact supports the vital qualification that among the tools of diplomacy and national security strategy, war is special. The original constitutional order, preserved in key respects through the decades until the advent of the Cold War, makes approval by Congress obligatory before the nation goes to war. This order encouraged interbranch deliberation by requiring presidents to run the risk that their proposals for war would be rejected. In the post-1945 period, the unthinking extension of the position that the executive must lead in foreign affairs to the very different situation presented by decisions for war has destabilized the constitutional system and deranged policymaking.

In understanding the differences between the Cold War and previous periods of military conflict, we must consider all three dimensions of executive war making that were prominent after 1945. The Cold War featured new ways of war making in addition to conventional war. For example, covert wars involved paramilitary forces recruited from other countries. These forces were capable of mounting significant military operations, whether considered technically "covert" or not. Likewise, we should not overlook nuclear weapons. The presence of such destructive weapons strongly influenced military doctrine for fighting conventional wars. Perhaps more important, all presidents in the post–World War II period were required to come to grips with their responsibility for ordering U.S. forces to launch a strike that might kill hundreds of millions of people and render large areas of the globe uninhabitable.

One main theme of this book is that the Constitution can influence policy even when it is not enforced by the courts. War powers are an especially timely and relevant example of this phenomenon, which is still too little acknowledged by lawyers and legal academics. The Constitution could not constrain or empower government until it was implemented within an institutional structure which I call a "constitutional order." A succession of constitutional orders has enabled government to function effectively in the United States from the eighteenth century onward. War powers, however, have had a unique history. The Constitution was written to reflect the premise that the nation could go to war only through the meaningful deliberation and consent of the legislative and executive branches of government. A war undertaken solely by one branch would thus risk policy catastrophe. This is what has occurred all too frequently since 1945.

Critics of the imperial presidency have worried about the loss of civil liberties that has followed from the expansion of presidential power. Although I do not wish to minimize the violations of constitutional rights that did occur in the Cold War and after, our chief concern should be the consequences of overthrowing the policymaking process for war established by the Constitution. In particular, what I call the "cycle of accountability" that turns between the executive and legislative branches has not properly operated with respect to foreign affairs after 1945. The cycle is a handy way of capturing what occurs when ordinary interbranch interaction is extended over time. Once a cycle is created, each branch knows that its decisions will be reviewed by the other. A pattern of mutual testing and deliberation results. Having a cycle of accountability means there is the potential to learn from mistakes. The cycle is an ongoing institutional practice in which both branches are held accountable.

Why is the post-1945 context so powerfully relevant for us today? Many commentators have seen the new-style conflict that followed 9/11 as a "long war."[3] Surprisingly, the most outstanding example of a "long war"—the Cold War fought against the Soviet Union and its communist allies—has been relatively neglected in the vast commentary that surrounds 9/11. Indeed, one of the striking characteristics of post-9/11 America has been the failure to engage with the Cold War as a way of understanding how presidential power in foreign affairs is exercised in the context of a lengthy indeterminate struggle. This is both odd and telling.

No one doubts that the origins of the contemporary constitutional order in foreign affairs and defense policy, sometimes called the "national security state," lie in the Cold War. Yet we have not been overwhelmed with comparisons to the Cold War since 9/11. The pattern among legal scholars has been to search for analogies to the "war on terror" in Lincoln's leadership in the Civil War or Roosevelt's decisions during World War II.[4] While it is important to understand the constitutional order in which Roosevelt operated, especially prior to Pearl Harbor, that order underwent a major transformation after 1945. The post-1945 constitutional order with respect to national security established by President Truman at the beginning of the Cold War and the all-encompassing struggle against the perceived threat of communism form the most important baseline for understanding our post-9/11 constitutional and governmental reality.

The constitutional order prior to Pearl Harbor did not have to cope with a strategy in foreign affairs that assumed American responsibility for global security, accompanying global military commitments, U.S. troops permanently stationed in foreign countries, intelligence agencies engaged in covert action, or nuclear weapons. Whereas prior to Pearl

Harbor the U.S. was certainly engaged in world affairs as a naval power, it also adhered to a sharp distinction between war and peace and declarations or authorizations of war as integral elements of diplomacy. The Cold War constitutional order involved apprehension of an existential threat, a perceived danger from an appealing global ideology that mandated increased internal security, assertions that we had to stand ready to violate long-held values and beliefs, and enforced acceptance that we were in totally unique circumstances, never before seen in American history, involving an indefinite war against an implacable foreign enemy. If these elements seem familiar, as of course they should, I hope you will join me in wondering why scholars have not been probing the Cold War more assiduously for clues about the sources of our post-9/11 difficulties in foreign policy.[5]

While war powers are central to my argument, this book is more of an analytical history of presidential decisionmaking than a legal treatise and, apart from parts of Chapters 1 and 2, is not structured as a contribution to the war powers debate. As I stated earlier, I am not so much trying to contribute to the standard debate as I am attempting to reconceive it and change commonly accepted ideas of what the debate is about. In my view, the debate must be firmly grounded in an understanding of U.S. foreign policy and, at the same time, the special issues posed when the U.S. actually engages in a major war. Many people believe, for example, that important questions are at stake every single time the president orders the use of any sort of military force. By contrast, I closely analyze presidential decisionmaking concerning major wars and covert paramilitary actions in the context of U.S. foreign policy. While this presents some issues of definition, there is wide agreement on the most significant wars the U.S. has fought since 1945—Korea, Vietnam, the 1991 Gulf War, Afghanistan, and Iraq. Although I also discuss major covert actions involving the threat of war, such as those against Cuba and Nicaragua, and the deployment of nuclear weapons, the major military conflicts just noted are my central concern.[6] The first two wars caused most of the casualties suffered by our armed forces since 1945 and have been solemnized with memorials on the Mall, one of our nation's most honored spaces. Such wars past and present deserve our special concern, respect, and attention.

Nevertheless, the fact that I cross the path of the war powers debate demands some further comment. The standard debate has been ongoing at least since the Vietnam War became controversial in the mid-1960s. Yet the controversy is unusual in some respects. Consider that there is no scholarship on the history of the war powers debate as such. Was Vietnam in fact the origin of the debate and its vast and intricate web of argumentation? Consider also that there is no scholarly history of key elements of the debate, such as the 1973 War Powers Resolution. It is as if the debate has always been with us, beyond history. Indeed, it is widely believed that the controversy flows from a power struggle between the executive and legislative branches that began in the early republic. One of my key findings is that this sense of a timeless controversy is an artifact of the Cold War itself, something largely promoted by presidentialists. The war powers debate did not exist in its contemporary form, including the broad claims made by post-1945 presidents, until the advent of the Cold War in the Truman administration. This is a strong claim, yet one amply supported by a detailed consideration of diplomatic history.

In order to demonstrate this contention and promote clarity with respect to a debate many legal scholars regard as a stalemate, I have gone to some lengths to situate the debate in the Cold War. This naturally suggests a focus on the distinctive assertions of power that presidents made in this period. Over time, however, the academic debate has focused more on the claims of scholars than of presidents. While this is not entirely surprising, what is startling is how badly many prominent scholars have misunderstood the maximal character of those presidential claims. In turn, because of this misunderstanding, the clarity with which the evidence from the founding period speaks to the contemporary war powers debate has not been appreciated fully. Beginning with Truman, nearly all post-1945 presidents have claimed the unilateral power under Article II to initiate war, "real" war, full-scale war. The underappreciated crux of the war powers debate is that, while this bold presidential claim is inconsistent with the historical meaning of the Constitution, it has an eminently defensible policy rationale.

While I am not sympathetic to this unilateral presidential claim, the standard congressionalist critique is simply too narrow. Considered from the perspective of the executive branch, this claim does not appear extraordinary, because it is encapsulated in a larger perspective, which many have found persuasive, in which military force is one tool among others in advancing the foreign policy and preserving the national security of the United States. By concentrating on whether every presidential military action is specifically authorized, the congressionalist critique has missed the real problem—the absence of interbranch deliberation over time on matters of foreign policy and national security strategy—that is, the lack of a cycle of accountability.

By contending that presidential war powers claims should be understood within the framework of American diplomacy, I urge a bit more sympathy for presidents than congressionalists have managed to display in the war powers debate. The presidentialist position cannot be understood and evaluated appropriately unless we have a firm grasp on the situation the executive branch faced at the beginning of the Cold War.

In order to carry out this contextual task, we must expand the frame of the war powers debate, considering insights that constitutional scholars have generally bypassed from primary and secondary sources relating to diplomatic history and presidential decisionmaking in foreign policy. This book is thus based primarily on a comprehensive survey of the diplomatic and presidential history of the post–World War II period. Inevitably, my sources will not satisfy some historians who expect familiarity with the latest specialized studies. However, my argument is based on a more thorough assessment of the relevant historical literature, along with some key collections of primary sources, than any previous work on war powers with respect to this critical period of American history.

The plan of the book is as follows. Chapters 1 and 2 create the framework that guides the discussion in the rest of the book. Chapter 1 introduces the concept of a constitutional order and describes the order of the early republic with respect to war and foreign affairs. Chapters 1 and 2 contrast this pre–Pearl Harbor constitutional order with the post-1945 constitutional order founded by President Truman, his advisers, key members of Congress, and the foreign policy elite in the early Cold War. Chapters 1 and 2 also establish the historical context necessary to evaluate the arguments in the standard war powers debate. Chapter 2 shows how Truman created the presidential power to initiate war, a key element of the post-1945 constitutional order, when he made the decision in 1950 to intervene in Korea. It concludes by summarizing the elements of the post-1945 constitutional order.

The next four chapters provide an extended analysis of the problems and tensions encountered as policymakers attempted to work within the inherently flawed structure of the post-1945 constitutional order amid three different arenas for war making: conventional, covert, and nuclear. Chapter 3 discusses the Eisenhower and Kennedy administrations and describes Eisenhower's way of war and the increasing use of covert war in both administrations, culminating in the 1962 Cuban missile crisis. Chapter 4 describes the crisis of the post-1945 constitutional order in the Johnson and Nixon administrations, linking the Vietnam War with Watergate.

After Vietnam there was a break in the continuity of the Cold War in that the political parties took different paths with respect to war and foreign affairs. While Democrats increasingly doubted the verities of the Cold War, an attitude reflected in their support of Nixon's policy of détente with the Soviet Union, Republicans bypassed the trauma of Vietnam in favor of renewing a commitment to the Cold War. Chapter 5 thus begins with an analysis of where matters stood after Vietnam and follows the path of the Ford, Carter, Reagan, and Bush I administrations as they attempted to cope with a post-Vietnam environment in which the post-1945 constitutional order was nonetheless still dominant. Chapter 6 carries the post-Vietnam discussion through the Clinton and Bush II administrations, especially in light of the challenges posed by 9/11. Throughout these chapters I focus on demonstrating the recurrent pattern of policy dysfunction and constitutional crisis caused by the friction between the original constitutional order and the post-1945 order.

In Chapter 7 I examine whether it would be possible to build a new constitutional order to deal with the problems caused by the jerry-built structure of the post-1945 order. I do this in two main stages. I first summarize how to reconceive the war powers debate by reviewing what the debate should be about. After commenting on how the Obama administration fits into the post-1945 constitutional order, I then move to a consideration of how altering the structure of Congress is a necessary precondition for addressing our war powers troubles.

In all candor I should say that proposing solutions is secondary to this book's purpose. Why is this justifiable? While I like proposing solutions as much as the next legal academic, it bears emphasis that the solutions offered in faculty lounges tend to assume a judicial *deus ex machina* that is not available for war powers. The most important task with respect to war powers is simply to understand the position we are in. Thus my primary purpose is not to propose solutions to our war powers difficulties but rather to change our perspective on both where the problem lies and how to move forward.

Ultimately, I aim to provide the missing connections between the exercise of presidential power in foreign affairs and a continuing series of policy disasters and constitutional crises. This book connects the dots with respect to the Constitution and national security and explains a recurrent and, indeed, tragic pattern of interbranch relations and presidential decisions.

1

War Powers and Constitutional Change

IMAGINE a world in which there is a robust judicial doctrine of presidential war powers. Legal casebooks would have as many Supreme Court decisions on such Cold War conflicts as Korea, Vietnam, and Central Intelligence Agency (CIA) interventions into Latin America and the Middle East as they do on the commerce clause and the Fourteenth Amendment. All students would be familiar with the series of cases in which the constitutionality of the Vietnam War was finally underwritten by the Supreme Court. They would study the gradual way in which the Court restrained presidential power in the aftermath of Vietnam and how the first and second Bush administrations responded with thoughtful, deliberative efforts to win congressional support for the 1991 Gulf War and the 2003 Iraq War, respectively. They would understand the relationship between the restrictions the Court put on the CIA and that agency's refusal to implement the harsh interrogation regime proposed by Bush II administration hard liners after 9/11.

In such a world, presidential war powers are *legalized* (or judicialized). They are part of the legalized Constitution, those aspects of the Constitution that are typically enforced by the judiciary. In this world, the relevance of the Constitution to war powers would be unquestioned. Indeed, the Supreme Court would be intimately involved in every aspect of foreign policy.

For better or worse, this is not our world. In the real world, there are few judicial decisions relevant to presidential war powers.[1] The use of force in war, circumstances short of war, or covert operations is not adjudicated by the courts. Scholars say that the constitutional provisions concerning war powers are given meaning in "the Constitution outside the courts."[2] Yet this is more of a handy label than a widely accepted theory of how the executive and legislative branches determine constitutional meaning. This creates what we might call a problem of constitutional relevance—whether and how the Constitution is relevant to foreign affairs.

Any constitutional historian can reel off a number of Supreme Court decisions that were related to the Cold War, such as the *Steel Seizure* case, the prosecution of members of the Communist Party, and, arguably, *Brown v. Board of Education,* perhaps the most famous and influential decision of the twentieth century.[3] But how central was the Constitution to the conduct of foreign affairs in the Cold War? From histories of this era, one can surmise the conventional answer that the Constitution was not central at all. One can plow through thousands of pages in comprehensive histories of U.S. diplomacy and the Cold War without encountering a single reference to the Constitution. We have few informed discussions of the relationship of the Constitution to key post-1945 events such as the founding of the United Nations, the Truman Doctrine, the National Security Act, crucial documents of national security policy such as NSC-68, and the Korean War.[4]

Historians and lawyers tend to make the same assumption—the Constitution is not relevant unless the Supreme Court makes it so. Yet there is another sense in which everyone agrees that the Constitution was implicated in U.S. foreign policy in the post-1945 period. It is widely acknowledged that there was a significant increase in presidential power as a consequence of World War II and the new role the U.S. assumed in world affairs.[5] To briefly mention a few events specifically related to war powers: the North Atlantic Treaty led to the permanent stationing of significant numbers of U.S. troops in Europe. After an initial period of demobilization and defense cutbacks after 1945, the Cold War took hold by 1947 and a commitment was made to a substantial military buildup in the wake of the invasion of South Korea by North Korea in June 1950. The executive branch formulated the doctrine of containment to guide Cold War policy, and the capacity of the U.S. to intervene worldwide through means both overt and covert increased.[6] These developments suggest the Constitution was relevant to the conduct of U.S. foreign policy. What we lack is an account of *how* it was relevant.

Focusing on war powers invites us to consider the relationship between the Constitution and some of the most important controversies that dogged presidents in the post-1945 period. Harry Truman's presidency was widely regarded for years as a failure because he could not bring the limited war in Korea to a successful conclusion, a war that was seen as his initiative because he never asked for formal approval from Congress.[7] The massive policy disaster of the Vietnam War adversely affected the historical reputations of presidents from Eisenhower to Nixon. The constitutional crisis of Watergate was set in motion partly because of Nixon's conflicts with Congress over foreign affairs and Vietnam.[8] The history of executive policy in the Cold War had to be largely rewritten after the intelligence revelations in the mid-1970s. The intelligence agencies also figured prominently in the Iran-contra affair during the Reagan administration and the torture controversy after 9/11. Presidential war powers were thus interwoven not only with the conduct of U.S. foreign policy but also with a series of troubling episodes in the post-1945 constitutional order.

Although there was an early skirmish over the constitutionality of Truman's decision to intervene in Korea without congressional approval, the conflict over presidential war powers became a full-fledged public and academic debate during the Vietnam War.[9] Much of the initial discussion was narrow and somewhat unhelpful in that it focused on the legal justification for Vietnam and later on the constitutionality of the 1973 War Powers Resolution (WPR).[10] Although the larger question of an imbalance between the executive and legislative branches was raised, the participants in these debates did not pay close attention to the historical circumstances of the Cold War that had led the U.S. to this point. In fact, the focus on Vietnam and the WPR has skewed a proper understanding of war powers both as a matter of legal interpretation and the larger context in which presidential war powers were used before and after that tragic conflict. To make progress in understanding presidential war powers, we must thus begin not with Vietnam or even Korea, but with the new circumstances the U.S. faced at the end of World War II.

Here we face the problem referred to earlier. While there is agreement in a sense that the Constitution was involved with the conduct of foreign affairs in the post-1945 period, scholars lack a conceptual framework in which to assess the constitutional significance of key events. This is why standard histories of the Cold War keep the Constitution offstage. This is not to criticize historians. Legal scholars and political scientists as well lack a generally accepted theory of how to understand the Constitution outside the legalized sphere of formal amendments and judicial doctrine. We thus need to begin our inquiry into war powers with a better understanding of how constitutional change occurs outside the judiciary.

The Importance of Constitutional Orders

Constitutional change outside the legalized Constitution, that is to say other than through formal amendment or judicial doctrine, has played a substantial role in the evolution of American constitutionalism. The Constitution was not enforced solely by the Supreme Court. It was implemented through multiple independent and distinctive institutions, all of which mediated constitutional meaning. At the same time it provided a textual template for these institutions, the Constitution created an agenda for future change by leaving important questions of constitutional power and structure unanswered. Further, an internal logic of constitutional stability discouraged change through formal amendment that might have answered these questions. Officials found themselves in a system of governance in which they could use the existing text and institutions to implement their preferred visions of constitutional power outside Article V. As the national government developed over time, this led to persistent use of informal means, including creative interpretation, institutional restructuring, and democratic elections to initiate change.

Constitutional orders are crucial to the implementation of the Constitution, functioning as relatively stable patterns of institutional interaction with respect to basic aspects of the Constitution such as powers and rights. They are constructed from the actions and norms of multiple institutions.[11] The working elements of a constitutional order are several and independent. The first is the text of the Constitution, "the supreme law of the land" and an ineluctable source of authoritative rules, standards, and principles nonetheless sometimes not given sufficient weight in accounts that stress the importance of the "living Constitution."[12] A second element is the political and policy objectives of government officials, elites, and the public. A third is the structure and capacity for action of state institutions.

There are *reciprocal relationships* between the elements of a constitutional order. This allows for the possibility that the text can play a paradoxical role in enabling constitutional orders to change. While scholars attached to the idea of the "living constitution" are correct that change does not happen solely through amendment, this does not make the text irrelevant. We might say that the text is imprinted on the structure of government institutions. It can provide authority essential to those seeking to change the constitutional order outside the formal amendment process. Political actors can use powers given by the text to leverage constitutional change. We should therefore avoid an approach that subsumes the written Constitution to the unwritten or "living" Constitution. Powers granted by the text are central to understanding how informal constitutional change can happen. In fact, there is an unavoidable tension between the "written" and the "unwritten" Constitution.

While I am not claiming that the Constitution outside the courts is a kind of political free-for-all, the startling implication of this theory is that the policy objectives of state officials and the public along with new capacities for government action can create a constitutional order that is in considerable tension with the meaning of the text. As the discussion in subsequent chapters will show, government officials were aware of the fragile constitutional foundations of Cold War foreign policy. Yet they so strongly believed that it was necessary that they willingly drove forward and implemented a new constitutional order that was at odds with the order that had prevailed since the early republic.

How could this happen? We should first remember that foreign affairs and war powers are in general outside the legalized Constitution. In the sphere of the legalized Constitution, the judiciary, guided by forms of legal argument influenced by the common law, is supreme.[13] Judicial doctrine as to the meaning of the Constitution *is* constitutional law. Indeed, the idea of a form of "law" within this sphere that does not proceed from the Constitution itself, some other enactment recognized by the judiciary, or judicial doctrine literally does not make sense. But the legalized sphere is effective in enforcing the Constitution partly because it is limited in scope. Regardless of what one may think of individual controversial decisions, over the long run the federal judiciary has exhibited a certain institutional restraint. The Supreme Court has never attempted to take on all possible issues of constitutional meaning or attempted to enforce all norms in the Constitution on the other branches of government.

In the nonlegalized sphere, things are different. New policy priorities and state capacities can create new constitutional powers. I see this approach as the only way to explain what has happened to presidential war powers in the post-1945 period. As the discussion in this chapter and the next will show, presidents acquired a new power to initiate full-scale military conflict—in other words, war. Constitutional change outside the legalized Constitution can thus be influenced by the tide of events, political imperatives, and the structure and capacity for action of state institutions. While we can study change in the legalized sphere through amendments and judicial interpretations, there are no true analogues to these markers of change in the nonlegalized sphere. Without legal markers, the way to track change is by studying the succession of constitutional orders or, put another way, the relationship of constitutional powers and rights to the historical development of policy and state institutions. These institutions may imitate the judiciary and use the forms of legal argument to justify constitutional change, but they are not obliged to do so. The legislative and executive branches swim in a sea of policy and politics. To be sure, they make law, but not *entrenched* constitutional law. By conventional understanding, this power is reserved to the judiciary and the amendment process specified in Article V.

This difference has the further consequence that the norms of the nonlegalized sphere do not, as a practical matter, have the same status as those in the legalized Constitution. Given that they are not (or not typically) enforced by the judiciary, they lack the certainty, stability, and authority of legal norms, creating ambiguity and tension within American constitutionalism.[14] Indeed, I will be stressing that experience with constitutional change arising out of war and foreign affairs has shown that the process of nonlegalized constitutional change is inherently problematic. Some of the norms in the Constitution, including the "declare war" clause, certainly have the formal appearance of legal rules, whether they are enforced by the judiciary or not. That they are not enforced by the judiciary can be a source of frustration for those who take them to be legally binding. There is often a belief, certainly on display in the war powers debate, that they *should* be legally binding.[15] But reality is different.

Like Bruce Ackerman, I believe that theories of constitutional change must be historicist.[16] We must take seriously the reality of historical change and political and institutional development over time. We should not "flatten" history by treating events as if they were strings of legal precedents devoid of context. Without appreciating past constitutional orders in their full historical context, we cannot make sense of the constitutional changes that have occurred in the post-1945 era. The creation and ratification of the Constitution in 1787–1788 and the beginning of government operations in the early republic provide a meaningful historical baseline against which subsequent changes in the constitutional order can be assessed.

The Original Constitutional Order

As one might expect, the original constitutional order was based on the Constitution ratified in 1787–1788. With respect to war and foreign affairs, it embodied what I will call the "interbranch synthesis." The synthesis is an interpretation of the text of the Constitution which accepts that presidential leadership in foreign affairs is underwritten not only by long-standing government practice and judicial precedent, but also by the Constitution itself. Recent meticulous scholarship has established that the vesting of "executive power" in the eighteenth century carried with it the power to conduct the foreign affairs of the nation.[17] At the same time, the Constitution explicitly recognized that war, even when considered in the context of foreign affairs, required special consideration by Congress. The purpose of the "declare war" clause in Article I was to make Congress the gatekeeper over whether the nation went to war. Under this interpretation, there was a de facto sharing of the war power because, setting aside the possibility of civil disorder or rebellion, normally the president is the first mover in foreign affairs. Nonetheless, if the president takes the initiative in deciding for war, he faces a mandatory congressional check. This means that the arrangement of institutions and powers in the Constitution strongly encourages interbranch deliberation before the decision for war is made.[18]

At this initial stage of the argument, what I wish to stress is that this textual command was actually implemented in the constitutional order of the early republic. The Constitution itself provided no capacity to the president outside of that furnished by the legislative branch to enable him to assess whether military action was in the best interests of the country and to implement a decision for war. The road to war lay through the legislative branch and, as the discussion below will show, all of the presidents of the founding era were aware of this.[19]

The Constitution also embodied a "cycle of accountability" based on the separation of powers between the branches. The cycle occurs when conflict and cooperation between the branches with respect to an area of policy like war powers are repeated across time. Each branch knows it will be judged by the other and by the people. Each branch thus feels the weight of responsibility and decision. This creates the potential for learning from experience. Each cycle increases the chance that policy the next time around will be formulated against the backdrop of the "lessons of history." By contrast, the lack of a cycle increases the chance of poor policy, indeed, policy disasters. As subsequent chapters will show, this is what occurred in the post-1945 period.

War is a unique act, whether we are concerned with the Constitution, policymaking, or politics. War places exceptional burdens on a republican and democratic political order. It calls for citizens to sacrifice themselves for the good of the nation. It requires the leaders of the executive and legislative branches to justify that sacrifice to themselves and to the country. War is thus qualitatively different from any other foreign or domestic policy pursued by government. It creates special challenges even for a well-functioning constitutional order. The Constitution recognized this reality by placing the decision for war with the branch the framers believed to be most representative of the people.

Foreign Affairs and War in the Early Republic

A constitutional order is an analytical tool that can help us make sense of a complicated past. But some have doubted whether any sense can be made of the sometimes conflicting evidence from the early republic. In his famous concurrence in the *Steel Seizure* case, Justice Robert Jackson exhibited frustration with the state of founding era materials on separation of powers, especially in foreign affairs. In lines often quoted to show the implausibility of looking for the original intent or meaning of the Constitution, Jackson said he was "surprised at the poverty of really useful and unambiguous authority applicable to concrete problems of executive power."[20] The materials he had to work with were "almost as enigmatic as the dreams Joseph was called upon to interpret for Pharaoh."[21] As William Casto notes in his valuable study of foreign affairs in the early republic, Jackson referred specifically to the 1793 exchange on the neutrality crisis between Alexander Hamilton as "Pacificus" and James Madison as "Helvidius."[22] Like Jackson, many contemporary commentators have assumed that the opinions of the founding generation with respect to executive power in foreign affairs largely cancel each other.[23]

Nevertheless, Justice Jackson chose poorly when he fastened on the Pacificus-Helvidius exchange as an example of enigmatic historical materials.[24] What we obtain from history depends on the questions we ask. It is likely that Jackson's questions were too general and so he thought the materials inadequate. But we should observe that if eighteenth-century materials yielded nothing, then Jackson would have had no basis for knowing what "Pacificus" and "Helvidius" were discussing, let alone whether they were disagreeing and on what basis. If we ask the right questions, there is plenty of evidence available from the founding era in matters of foreign affairs and war powers.

Consider some episodes from the early republic—the 1793 exchange just referred to between Hamilton and Madison on executive power in foreign affairs, the controversy over the 1798 Quasi-War with France, and the debate on how to handle the depredations of the Barbary states in the Jefferson and Madison administrations. Reviewing these episodes will allow us to address three enduring mysteries of the modern war powers controversy.

One mystery, highlighted by Justice Jackson's comments in *Steel Seizure,* is how commentators acquired the idea that the founding generation disagreed about war powers as much as they disagreed about presidential power in foreign affairs generally. While not all commentators have followed Jackson in believing the historical materials to be especially cloudy, many have assumed that the 1793 exchange between Hamilton and Madison was a precursor of a two-sided debate over war powers that has continued until the present day.[25] The second mystery is how the dispute originated over whether Congress had properly authorized the Quasi-War in the face of the multiple legislative enactments supporting the war effort.[26] The third mystery, in some respects the most enduring and misleading, is how commentators came to believe the distinction between "offensive" and "defensive" war was of special significance to interpreting the "declare war" clause.

In 1793 Hamilton's concern was to defend President Washington's Proclamation of Neutrality with respect to the war that had been declared between France and Great Britain.[27] The U.S. had signed a treaty of alliance with France in 1778. The friends of France, a group that included Secretary of State Thomas Jefferson as well as Madison, were discomfited by the lack of support toward France which they felt was implied by the Proclamation.[28] Hamilton wrote seven essays as "Pacificus" to defend the Proclamation in depth. It was the first essay, dealing with the issue of whether the Proclamation was constitutional, which drew Madison's concern and has attracted the attention of scholars.[29]

In this essay Hamilton placed the executive branch at the forefront of foreign policy in the sense of ordinary dealings with other nations.[30] He supported the constitutionality of the Proclamation on the grounds that the executive department is the organ responsible for intercourse with foreign nations, for interpretation of treaties, for faithful execution of the laws (including treaties), and for command of the "Public Force," through the commander in chief clause.[31] Hamilton also made the famous argument that the vesting clause of Article II of the Constitution was a general grant of executive power and the particular powers granted in Article II do not derogate from "the more comprehensive grant contained in the general clause."[32] Hamilton asserted that through the Proclamation, the executive branch was trying to avoid embroiling the United States in an unnecessary conflict: "It is the province and duty of the Executive to preserve to the Nation the blessings of peace. The Legislature alone can interrupt those blessings, by placing the Nation in a state of War."[33]

Given this tightly worked network of arguments, what drew Madison's attention?[34] Madison made it clear that he was concerned, first and foremost, with "the extraordinary doctrine" that he and Jefferson took Hamilton to be propounding: that the power to make war (as well as the treaty power) was an executive power given by the vesting clause of Article II.[35] Madison set about refuting this doctrine in detail, although it is very doubtful that Hamilton actually held such views, instead focusing his attention on the conduct of foreign affairs and not presenting a detailed treatment of the war power. This did not stop Madison from engaging in a lengthy discussion of the power to make war. The reason this discussion is of interest today lies not so much in understanding where Hamilton went wrong (if he did), but rather as a statement of what Madison, Jefferson, and no doubt others thought was plainly the case in the light of the deliberations in the 1787 Philadelphia Convention and the experience of the early republic. It is in this respect that "Helvidius" is quite useful in understanding the constitutional order of the early republic.

Madison began with what public law authorities such as Burlamaqui, Vattel, Locke, and Montesquieu had said on the nature of executive power, only to immediately reject them. He argued that it is of little use to consult such writers, "not only because our own reason and our own constitution, are the best guides" but also because these sources "wrote before a critical attention was paid to those objects, and with their eyes too much on monarchical governments, where all powers are confounded in the sovereignty of the prince."[36] Madison stated that the power to declare war is "one of the most deliberative acts that can be performed," and when performed it constitutes a new rule for the executive, "a *new code* adapted to the relation between the society and its foreign enemy."[37] Madison then moved to the text of the Constitution, asking whether it provides any support for saying "that the powers of making war and peace are considered as of an executive nature."[38] There is of course no clause in the text which directly supports this proposition. By this point in the essay, it is clear that Madison did not understand the "declare war" clause in a narrow way or as a term of art. When he considered whether any of the enumerated powers given to the president in Article II are analogous to the "powers of war and treaty," he brought up the commander in chief power:

> And instead of being analogous to the power of declaring war, it affords a striking illustration of the incompatibility of the two powers in the same hands. Those who are to *conduct a war* cannot in the nature of things, be proper or safe judges, whether *a war ought to be commenced, continued, or concluded.* They are barred from the latter functions by a great principle in free government, analogous to that which separates the sword from the purse, or the power of executing from the power of enacting laws.[39]

So where could "Pacificus" have derived his mistaken doctrine? Madison concluded his essay scornfully: "There is but one answer to this question. The power of making treaties and the power of declaring war, are *royal prerogatives* in the *British government,* and are accordingly treated as Executive prerogatives by *British commentators.*"[40]

This famous exchange between Hamilton and Madison is not well described as a debate, at least if we are concerned with the war power.[41] Hamilton never responded to clarify where he and Madison disagreed. While Hamilton was concerned with justifying the Proclamation, Madison focused on the possible dangers if Hamilton's arguments (as he understood them) were accepted.[42] There is thus substantial reason to doubt whether they actually disagreed over the specific question of the war power.[43] Had Hamilton replied, he might well have urged Madison to calm himself by pointing out that the war power was not at issue. In the "Pacificus" essays, Hamilton never argued that the power to declare or initiate war belonged to the executive.[44] As we have seen, he explicitly acknowledged that the legislative branch had the sole power to place the nation in a state of war. Madison appears to have been somewhat overwrought by what he saw as implied in Hamilton's confident support of the executive power to issue the Proclamation: "a unilateral presidential power to take the country to war."[45] As Madison held, war poses special dangers—it is "in fact the true nurse of executive aggrandizement."[46] But there is no evidence that Hamilton disagreed. As more recent scholarship has concluded, there was no debate between Helvidius and Pacificus with respect to two points—"the Constitution does not give the president power to declare war and does not give the president unilateral power to make treaties."[47]

Far from producing confusion about what the founding generation thought about foreign affairs and the war power, the exchange between Hamilton and Madison strongly supports the widely held intuition that while the president must lead in foreign affairs, war is special. It is a unique category of government action and was explicitly marked as such by the Constitution. Despite Madison's concern about Hamilton's tendency to extol executive power, there was no one in the early republic who even attempted to make the case that the war power was executive in nature. Furthermore, this exchange illustrated very well that some important members of the founding generation had substantially the same concerns about executive power in relation to war as Americans do today. Madison's arguments were brutally substantive and cut right to the heart of concern over giving the executive the power to initiate war. If nothing else, this exchange showed that it is quite wrong to base the interpretation of the war powers in the Constitution on lawyerly distinctions.

Hamilton's career provided many illustrations of the difference between interpretations of the Constitution that were merely proposals or opinions and those that were implemented in the original constitutional order. Some of Hamilton's interpretations of the Constitution while he was treasury secretary, such as his advocacy of the constitutionality of a national bank, won the favor of President Washington and Congress and were implemented.[48] These interpretations and institutions thus formed part of the constitutional order of what we can call the Federalist Republic, however much Jeffersonians may have disagreed. Opposing such Hamiltonian interpretations of the Constitution was not therefore a matter of simply offering a different interpretation, but overthrowing a prior order and replacing it with another, something that helps explain the significance of the Jeffersonian "Revolution of 1800."[49]

Other Hamiltonian interpretations and the policy visions they supported went unrealized. As Gordon Wood describes, Hamilton wanted to put the United States on the playing field with Great Britain and the other great powers of Europe.[50] Historians have described Great Britain as a "fiscal-military" state which harnessed the country's financial structure to serve its global ambitions.[51] Hamilton understood this relationship and wanted to create a counterpart in America.[52] This meant building a powerful national state—"a strong central bureaucratic government directing the economy and reaching to all parts of a united and integrated nation and possessing a powerful army and navy that commanded the respect of the whole world."[53]

But Hamilton's vision was never implemented. It better describes post–World War II America than the early republic. It alarmed Jefferson and Madison and struck them as anti-republican—"the very kind of monarch-like war-making state that radical Whigs in England had been warning about for generations."[54] For the founding generation, the war power was linked to executive (monarchical) authority, but not in a good way.[55] They sought to break this link and, as I will argue in the next section, no doubt thought that they had done so by giving Congress the power to declare war.

This competition between policy visions in support of different constitutional orders played out during the 1798 Quasi-War with France. From the American point of view, France initiated naval hostilities in

1797. In response, President Adams proposed to Congress a two-track policy—a limited military buildup and negotiations. Congress approved this policy and authorized increases in the Navy and militia while both branches awaited the outcome of negotiations. When it was revealed in early 1798 that negotiations had failed, public opinion turned against France.[56] At this point, the nascent political associations of the time split on the proper course of action. Federalists favored an all-out war with France and wanted to take advantage of the situation to build up the military capacities of the national government. Republicans or Jeffersonians opposed the war and, despite the obvious naval hostilities, claimed there was no war because Congress had never passed a literal declaration of war. This claim had some credence because Federalists were divided about the constitutional meaning of the steps Congress had taken to support the war.[57] This was probably the source of later confusion over whether the war was "undeclared."

The question of state capacity, crucial to the construction of a constitutional order, is helpful in understanding what was truly at stake. As the government had little capacity for fighting even a limited naval war, Congress held the central position. It authorized an expansion of the Navy and the creation of the Navy Department, as well as passing numerous other laws in support of the military effort.[58] As we shall see, in the Cold War important officials in both the executive and legislative branches argued that the president had the power to initiate war. While there was dispute in the early republic over the exact legal way the nation should go to war, nothing in the public debate even suggested this line of argument. Officials disputed *how* Congress should act, not whether it had a key constitutional role. No one denied that Congress had authorized a limited military conflict through legislative enactments. But Republicans expressed their deep political opposition to fighting France by repeatedly claiming that there was no "war" because there had been no literal declaration. When the Supreme Court ruled in *Bas v. Tingy* that a state of limited war with France existed, the correct decision in the view of many subsequent commentators, Republicans predictably condemned the decision.[59]

As I discuss below, the ability of Congress to authorize war through legislative enactments that did not have "Declaration of War" written across the top was a fine point of legal analysis that was eventually sorted out. The new issue presented by the Quasi-War was not the role of Congress, but whether the president would be given the capacity to respond rapidly to foreign threats and expand U.S. power globally on the seas through a navy and on the North American continent through a new army. Federalists like Hamilton wanted to go beyond what President Adams had requested in service of their policy vision. At their behest, Congress approved a substantial "New Army" with former president Washington and Hamilton as its leaders. But this innovation failed abysmally and there was no permanent increase in state capacity.[60]

Once Jefferson became president and Madison became secretary of state in 1801, they adhered to the principles they had expressed on presidential war power in the 1793 neutrality debate. There was uncertainty in the executive branch as to the proper scope of presidential power when Tripoli declared war on the U.S. that same year. Jefferson adopted the position that while reprisals were appropriate, the U.S. could not engage in war without the consent of Congress.[61] Never one to take Jefferson lying down, Hamilton rose to the attack and suggested a broader vision of presidential power, one in which presidents could respond with full force once a foreign power had declared war.[62] The issue never came to a head because Jefferson obtained authority from Congress to strike back in 1802.[63] While Hamilton's argument was probably the origin of the distinction later popular with commentators between "offensive" and "defensive" wars, his argument never influenced the government and thus the original constitutional order remained unchanged.[64] While the Second Barbary War (the Algerine War of 1815–1816) involved attacks on the U.S. similar to those earlier perpetrated by Tripoli, President Madison did not treat those incidents as a justification for a presidentially ordered "defensive" war. He requested a declaration or authorization for war from Congress, which was granted.[65]

While Hamilton never argued that the president could unilaterally initiate a war, he steadily worked to increase the capacity of the executive branch to take such action and made legalistic distinctions that would have enlarged common understandings concerning the president's power to act when the U.S. was challenged by foreign states. The original constitutional order with respect to the war power, however, proved quite stable and all of these projects failed to come to fruition.

I labor the example of Hamilton's career partly in response to those who believe that when it comes to the Constitution and its fundamental principles, there is nothing new under the sun.[66] Even significant new developments such as the global responsibilities the United States assumed in the Cold War along with a permanently large standing army strike them as linked with the kind of vigorous national leadership advocated by Hamilton. But this perspective is profoundly distorted in that it cuts us off from understanding our own history. In some respects, our constitutional order in which the executive is not only assumed to have a broad scope for action with respect to foreign affairs, but further has the capacity to strike militarily at the nation's enemies on a global and round-the-clock basis, would have struck many in the founding generation as alienating, threatening, and anti-republican. As I will show in Chapter 2, in order to change the pre–Pearl Harbor constitutional order into what we have today, an enormous effort was required. After that effort, we had a new constitutional order uneasily established, one that still had links to that of the early republic while bearing little resemblance to it on the surface.

At the same time, the eighteenth-century foundations remain. My theory of constitutional change enables us to hold these realities in a productive relationship. We have experienced tremendous changes to our constitutional order since 1789. A few of them occurred through formal amendment, more through the evolution of judicial doctrine, but in foreign affairs and war powers they have occurred largely outside the legalized Constitution. But it should not be supposed that the constitutional order morphs into a new form every few decades in response to national security requirements. Or that we have experienced a succession of self-contained constitutional orders, each with their own distinctive period and name.

Although I am uncomfortable with metaphors, think of a house that is perhaps more common in New England than in the rest of the U.S., originally built in the eighteenth century. From a distance, the house looks much as it did 225 years ago. Once you come closer and go inside, you can see that while the eighteenth-century walls have been retained, it has large additional wings, some of them in a different architectural style than the original. All parts of the house are connected, but there are odd angles and sudden steps where it is easy to trip. The original foundation, including a Jeffersonian wine cellar, still undergirds the main structure. But the newer additions sit uneasily. The roof leaks and there are ominous cracks in the walls. This is the Constitution we live in.

Reconceiving the War Powers Debate

Since the Vietnam War, war powers have been the focus of a seemingly endless debate.[67] Congressionalists hold that presidents have aggrandized war powers that properly belong to Congress under the Constitution, especially since World War II. In the absence of constitutional amendments or judicial doctrine to the contrary, they believe that wars can be initiated lawfully only by Congress. While there are different lines of presidentialist thought, they tend to converge on the perspective that the president must lead the government in foreign affairs, that war powers in the Constitution are shared between the executive and legislative branches, and subsequent practice demonstrates the constitutionality of presidents ordering the use of armed force without authorization from Congress.[68]

The contemporary debate has increasingly had difficulty making progress and is widely seen as a stalemate.[69] One reason for the lack of progress is that both sides approach the debate as if it were occurring in a judicial forum inside the sphere of the legalized Constitution. Despite the lack of legal doctrine, scholars studying war powers tend to use an adjudicative model.[70] They focus on instances of conflict between the executive and legislative branches and treat them as if they were cases. Scholars using this approach are often trying to answer the abstract question of how the Constitution allocates war powers in any situation involving the use of military force.[71] While it can be useful to abstract from reality and focus on hypothetical cases when analyzing a difficult legal question, this is less likely to be helpful when there is no relevant doctrine to guide us. In effect, this approach assumes we could produce a legal treatise on war powers despite the near-total absence of judicial precedents.

Another problem with the debate has been a notable lack of historical perspective and interest in historical context. Scholars on both sides have approached the debate as if it has always existed in its current form. The debate has been conducted as if developments in foreign policy and the capacity of the government to take action subsequent to the early republic make no difference. In the initial stage of the contemporary debate, which ran roughly from the mid-1960s to the passage of the WPR in 1973, it was not even clear the two sides were debating in the same arena. Congressionalists tended to focus on text and original intent and assumed a sharp break between "war" and other sorts of military activity. Presidentialists tended to highlight the leadership role of the president in foreign affairs and viewed military action as one instrument among others in the pursuit of U.S. foreign policy.[72]

The war powers debate is a stalemate partly because of this failure to find common argumentative ground. But the debate has also suffered from a lack of attention to the context of post–World War II diplomacy, especially the consequences of the new position the United States held on the world stage. Since the 1970s, war powers scholarship has become somewhat insular as scholars have tended to engage more with each other than with the positions actually taken by presidents.[73]

We thus have good grounds for reconceiving the debate. To promote understanding about the approach I take here, I should begin with a few general observations. Initially, let's observe that it could be objected I began out of order by discussing the three episodes from the early republic. Some scholars hold that events after the ratification of the Constitution cannot provide legal authority. The purpose of these episodes, however, besides debunking several of the myths that have grown up in the extensive literature on war powers, was to show there is strong evidence that everyone in the founding generation shared the same set of assumptions about the purpose of the Constitution with respect to war powers. It is, of course, possible that figures like Madison had changed their views since the Philadelphia Convention. As we shall see, this is not what happened.

Another fundamental difference between my approach and the standard debate is that my argument is based on examining the claims of presidents considered in the context of post–World War II foreign policy, rather than addressing the viewpoints of scholars. Indeed, by the end of the book we will have reviewed all public (and some confidential) executive branch legal opinions justifying the use of presidential war power since 1950 (for convenience, they are gathered together and listed in the Appendix). These presidential claims created the contemporary war powers debate. Like nuclear weapons and covert paramilitary operations, the war powers debate is a product of the post–World War II world. Scholars have not fully realized that it did not exist in anything like its current form prior to President Truman's 1950 decision to intervene in Korea. It is very much a debate we are having with ourselves, not an age-old controversy continued from the early republic. The debate is still important and relevant today because of the consistent insistence of the executive branch after roughly 1950 that it must have the power to initiate war in order to fulfill the objectives of U.S. foreign policy.

While presidential claims are crucial, we must understand them in context. We cannot discuss issues of war powers meaningfully unless we understand the constitutional order that existed in foreign affairs during the post-1945 era. In advocating the interbranch synthesis that agrees in general that the president must lead in foreign affairs, I could be regarded as taking the side of presidentialist scholars. To forestall misunderstanding, it is not my view that a focus on foreign affairs favors presidentialism. But this is far from the end of the story. Before we can properly critique the claims of presidents, we must be sure we understand their perspective.

Consider that the presidentialists in the war powers debate had often served in the executive branch.[74] Perhaps as a consequence, they instinctively appreciated the link between war powers and the strategies by which the U.S. pursued its post-1945 foreign policy goals. Congressionalists tended to ignore this link and, in some cases, continue today to deride all post-1945 military conflicts as "presidential wars."[75] There is no doubt an element of truth in this view, although it is persuasive mainly with respect to Vietnam. Nevertheless, I will argue that this charge is not helpful because it ignores the contextual link between the wars the U.S. fought and its general strategy in foreign policy.

It is one thing to say that Korea and Vietnam were unpopular wars. It is quite another to claim that the public objected to the general goals of containing the Soviet Union and defeating international communism. Presumably, no one would make such an implausible historical claim. Yet Korea and Vietnam were obviously linked to the pursuit of these broader objectives. You could say that presidents and executive branch officials thought they *had* to have broad war powers in order to meet the challenges of the post-1945 era, regardless of what the Constitution said. It would be more accurate, however, to say they believed that in order to advance the foreign policy and defend the national security of the United States, they needed the capacity to take various sorts of military action. In other words, they did not so much think about *war* (despite fighting several), as about foreign policy and national security. If we want to understand the troubled nature of the post-1945 constitutional order, we need to understand their perspective.

The arguments used by both sides in the war powers debate are thus problematic because they fail to properly relate the Constitution to historical change. Consider the odd nature of the debate. Congressionalists wind up condemning everything that has happened in the post-1945 world with respect to the exercise of presidential war power as a deviation from the way the Constitution has been traditionally understood. They cannot understand how such a drastic change could have occurred in a legitimate way without formal amendments or judicial decisions. For their part, presidentialists simply deny anything of significance happened when presidents like Truman committed the armed forces to fight in a foreign war without asking Congress for permission. No change here! In truth, both sides lack a conceptual framework to analyze what did happen: an amendment-level change to the constitutional order outside the Article V amendment process and beyond the scope of judicial decisions.

Finally, I will maintain that the debate should be centrally concerned with the ability of the executive branch to initiate *war*, "real" wars, major wars, rather than under what circumstances it can use military force to rescue citizens, intimidate the nation's enemies, and cooperate with allies and international organizations in humanitarian endeavors. At the same time, I will take into consideration that warfare in the post-1945 era has had a tripartite structure: conventional, covert, and nuclear. But conventional war is special. By common understanding, the U.S. has fought a number of wars since 1945: Korea, Vietnam, the 1991 Gulf War, Afghanistan (or the "9/11 War"), and Iraq. No one would deny that these are among the most significant military conflicts in American history. Presidents have repeatedly recognized their special character. As President Eisenhower discussed the impact of the Korean War with his advisers, for example, he remarked that "it was impossible to contemplate walking out of Korea. To do so would be to cross off three years of terrible sacrifice."[76] Sacrifice is an accurate description of what major conventional wars require. For the sheer scale of their casualties and costs, the significance of the foreign policy objectives for which they were undertaken, the sorrow and suffering in their wake, the damage they have done to the Constitution and its values, they deserve our special attention. Thus, the issue at hand is not presidential use of any sort of military force. The issue is war.

The 1950 Thesis

Curiously, despite regular scholarly interest on war powers from the Vietnam War onward, not much attention has been paid to the consistent position of the executive branch since the beginning of the Cold War that the president has the power to order troops into combat (in fact, to start a war) without authorization from Congress. It became clear, for example, during the run-up to the 1991 Gulf War that President George H. W. Bush took this position. At the time, legal commentators were incredulous and did not believe Bush's view had any historical antecedents.[77] The late Louis Henkin, an eminent scholar who authored a widely respected treatise on the law of foreign affairs, referred to Bush's "radical view" only to set it aside, noting that in the end Bush obtained a resolution from Congress.[78]

While the Gulf War is discussed in detail in Chapter 5, what is important to emphasize here is that Bush was serious. Bush made clear in his memoirs that while he certainly wanted Congress's *political* support, he and his national security adviser, Brent Scowcroft, were firm in their conviction that Bush had the power to go to war on his own constitutional authority.[79] Like their post-1945 predecessors, members of his national security team believed that war was one instrument among others in the making of foreign policy.[80] When members of Congress grasped the administration's position and objected, historian Julian Zelizer describes that "Bush and his Republican allies in Congress responded by saying that since Truman and Korea in 1950, presidents regularly deployed troops without the formal approval of Congress."[81]

Although commentators were surprised by the claims of the Bush I administration, these views in fact tracked the dominant understanding among Cold War presidents. To be sure, presidents did not often address the scope of their war powers directly, but ordinarily there is little reason for presidents to make abstract statements on the nature of their constitutional powers. Nevertheless, as the discussion in this book will demonstrate, Bush's views about the scope of his war powers had solid support in arguments advanced throughout the Cold War by the State Department and the Department of Justice.

This suggests the plausibility of what I call the "1950 thesis," which has been prominent in the war powers controversy, that Truman's 1950 Korea intervention marked a sharp break in our constitutional tradition.[82] Truman's decision to resist North Korea's invasion, of necessity a major commitment of U.S. military forces to combat, had no parallel in any previous military intervention. For some commentators, this inaugurated a new era of "presidential wars" in which chief executives took aggressive positions about the scope of their constitutional power, especially their power as commander in chief under Article II.[83]

A significant number of scholars who have given full-dress treatment to war powers issues have advanced the 1950 thesis.[84] Louis Fisher characterized the period after World War II as having "a climate in which Presidents have regularly breached constitutional principles and democratic values."[85] He cited Truman's decision as a prominent example.[86] Agreeing with earlier work by Francis Wormuth and Edwin Firmage, John Hart Ely contended that the Truman administration's intervention broke with a "long-standing legislative-executive consensus."[87] In his review of the constitutional law of diplomacy Michael Glennon agreed that "[i]n recent decades, presidents have assumed the power to involve the armed forces in 'full scale and sustained warfare.'"[88]

The 1950 thesis alerts us to the possibility that the constitutional order had changed in order to enable the executive branch to fight the Cold War. The details of this change will be discussed in Chapter 2. What is important to emphasize here is that we can make greater analytical progress if we infer the scope of presidential claims concerning war powers from the general strategy the U.S. has followed in foreign policy. Once we do this, there is a sense in which the 1950 thesis was *more* correct than originally perceived by these scholars. Although attention should be paid to how later presidents claimed Truman's Korea decision as a precedent, broad claims of presidential war power were arguably *required* by the new global role of the U.S. Containment, the global strategy of the U.S. during the Cold War, was not credible unless the president had this power.[89]

As we will discuss in much greater detail in Chapter 2, the executive branch thus responded to the Cold War by articulating a novel doctrine based centrally on the president's Article II powers over foreign affairs and as commander in chief. Typically claiming support from past instances of military interventions, the new doctrine asserted that the president could commit U.S. armed forces to combat without seeking congressional authorization. After Truman, although congressional approval was sought and appreciated during the Eisenhower, Kennedy, and Johnson administrations, the view of the executive branch was that such support was not required by the Constitution. Writing after his service in the Johnson administration, William Bundy, a pillar of the foreign policy establishment, provided insight into the split between the branches in the Cold War. He noted that President Johnson "treated the [Tonkin Gulf] resolution as merely affirming, for the sake of national unity, his power as Commander in Chief. Members of Congress, on the other hand, tended to regard it as a particular-case *delegation* flowing from powers held fundamentally by Congress. It was a crucial and enduring difference of view."[90]

In 1967 Under Secretary of State Nicholas Katzenbach provided one of the most detailed public presentations of the official position of the executive branch on war powers during the post-1945 era.[91] Discussed in greater detail in Chapter 4, his sophisticated presentation sounded a theme repeated by subsequent generations of presidentialist scholars on war powers—that the Constitution says relatively little about foreign affairs and left much to be determined by later practice.[92] He argued that "[t]he Constitution left to the judgment and wisdom of the Executive and the Congress the task of working out the details of their relationships."[93] Constitutional powers over foreign affairs were thus presumed to be shared in a way that implied a cooperative spirit between the branches. Katzenbach also highlighted the relevance of a fundamental shift that had occurred after World War II in the global role of the U.S.: there had been "a revolutionary change in the political structure of the world—and of the relative importance of foreign affairs to the United States."[94]

Although it has been largely overlooked, Katzenbach's presentation demonstrated the consistency of the executive branch's position throughout the Cold War. In broad terms, this position had three elements. First, war powers were shared between the executive and legislative branches, with their meaning being determined largely by historical practice—practice that of course Katzenbach and other executive officials believed favored the expansive claims of the executive branch. Second, whatever the meaning of Congress's power to "declare war" under Article I Section 8, it was *not a check* on presidential power, limiting the significance of the superficially attractive notion that the war power was shared. Third, declarations of war were obsolete in the new international legal order given life in the U.N. Charter.

Katzenbach had a remarkable exchange with Senator Bourke Hickenlooper of Iowa on the issue of shared war powers.[95] Hickenlooper disputed the view that all powers in foreign affairs were shared, contending that some, like declarations of war, were reserved to Congress.[96] Katzenbach disagreed, but then said the very discussion they were having illustrated his point. In effect, Katzenbach was saying, "because we disagree, that demonstrates powers are shared."[97] By contrast, Hickenlooper thought the purpose of the hearings was to determine who was right about the power to control when the nation went to war.[98] Katzenbach then trumped him, pointing out there was no chance the Supreme Court would decide the issue.[99] Katzenbach drew the lesson that without a final authority to decide the constitutional question, this meant that it was for the executive and legislative branches to work out in practice. But his statement also well illustrated my claim that war powers are not within the legalized Constitution.

Thus the key post-1950 claim of presidents was that they had the power to take the nation to war in order to implement U.S. strategy in foreign policy. This claim is specific enough so that we can usefully compare it to the understandings concerning the constitutional plan for war that prevailed when the Constitution was written.[100] Having specific questions in view is critical because this enables us to determine with greater precision whether there is any relevant textual and historical evidence. For instance, if our concern is with the general allocation of foreign affairs or war powers, the evidence may be lacking or indeterminate. If we ask the more specific question whether the founding generation addressed themselves to the initiation of war, we will have a better chance of making sense of the available materials. This point is worth emphasizing. In considering the evidence from the adoption of the Constitution, I am not trying, as so many scholars have, to determine what the Constitution requires in any situation involving the use of military force. Again, the relevant issue is the constitutional plan for war.

Two questions become relevant: (1) Does the Constitution require authorization by Congress before the U.S. engages in war? and (2) Does the Constitution grant power to the president to initiate war independent of Congress? While these questions are obviously related, they are not mirror images. The framers of the Constitution might have created a system in which presidents had some power to initiate war without Congress, while requiring congressional authorization in most situations. It is worth looking at the historical evidence for answers to both.

Post-World War II presidents tended to deny (1) (although members of their administrations occasionally contended that this power was shared) and robustly affirmed (2) (while temporizing on occasion by talking in terms of hostilities or the use of armed force rather than war). However, no post-1945 president rejected Truman's assertion that he had the authority to intervene in Korea. As we have seen, Korea was regarded by subsequent presidents as a clear precedent in their favor.[101] The pattern of endorsing Truman's action shows clearly that post-1945 presidents both denied (1) and affirmed (2).

The Constitutional Plan for War

The question of what the Constitution requires with respect to war-initiation is such well-traveled ground that it may seem at first there is little new to say. Indeed, this is partly why scholars regard the war powers debate as a stalemate. One way to make progress with respect to a stalemate is to ensure the issues are carefully defined. So I am approaching the debate on a fairly narrow front in terms of the two questions just posed. In addition, I discussed the three episodes from the early republic in part to debunk the widely held view that the founding generation disagreed on war-initiation just as much as they disagreed on other constitutional matters having to do with foreign affairs. Rather, Hamilton, Madison, and Jefferson, an impressing group of far-reaching thinkers who were often at odds in the early republic, *agreed* that Congress had sole power to initiate war. It is reasonable to infer that this group reflected widely shared views on the meaning of the "declare war" clause. The evident purpose of the clause was to give Congress control over the decision to go to war. Further, the phrase "declare war" was not used in a technical, lawyerly sense. In particular, neither Hamilton nor Madison so much as hinted in their 1793 exchange that the clause had something to do with the nation's responsibilities under international law. Finally, some of the members of the founding generation were worried about possible negative consequences should the executive be given the power to initiate war.

The evidence we have from the period in which the Constitution was written and ratified is consistent with the convictions expressed in the exchange between Hamilton and Madison, indicating a settled judgment that persisted over time. Rather than a serious debate over where to locate the power to authorize war, there was impressive harmony and agreement.[102] No member of the founding generation presented a serious argument that the executive should have the power in the "declare war" clause properly identified by Madison—to decide when war should be commenced.

Another way to make progress with a stalemate over historical evidence is to bring to the surface hidden methodological assumptions. I suggest that when we evaluate a dispute over what history tells us, we should ask which perspective explains the evidence in the most coherent and fruitful way. Explanations for why the founding generation would have located the war power with Congress are much easier to come by than explanations for why the framers would have given the war power, a power they clearly saw as consequential, to a single person.

Yet a third way to make progress with a stalemate is to ensure all relevant evidence has been considered. Some commentators hold that the only discussion in the 1787 Philadelphia Convention relevant to war powers is the famous exchange on August 17, in which the proposal of the Committee of Detail to grant Congress the power to "make" war was changed to the "declare war" phrase in the ratified document.[103] This is true if our concern is with question (1) above. But post-1945 presidents have *affirmatively* claimed power *independent* of Congress based especially on the commander in chief clause. This means a far wider range of evidence is relevant, both from the Philadelphia Convention and ratification debates.

We can regard answers to the two questions as hypotheses to be tested against the available record.[104] We can begin with the debate on June 1 that concerned the nature of the "national Executive."[105] Charles Pinckney observed that while he favored "a vigorous Executive," he "was afraid the Executive powers of (the existing) Congress might extend to peace & war &c which would render the Executive a Monarchy, of the worst kind, to wit an elective one."[106] John Rutledge agreed, stating he was not for giving the Executive "the power of war and peace."[107] James Wilson followed along with an interesting observation, saying that the "Prerogatives of the British Monarch" were not "a proper guide in defining the Executive powers."[108] The delegates knew that the prerogatives of King George III included those of war and peace,[109] but Wilson clearly stated that the new American executive should not include those powers.[110] This was of course consistent with the position Madison later advanced in the Pacificus-Helvidius exchange.

This exchange early in the Philadelphia Convention suggests another question requiring explanation. When faced with the general issue of how to constitute the executive branch, why did the delegates focus immediately on the question of war and peace? We know this was considered a crucial power of government by the founding generation because it was addressed in five of the thirteen articles that comprised the Articles of Confederation.[111] The Articles created an assembly[112] with delegates called "Congress"[113] and gave it "the sole and exclusive right and power of determining on peace and war."[114]

There could also have been reasons of recent experience. Among other things, the Philadelphia Convention was a reunion of war veterans.[115] Everyone at the Convention had been touched by the Revolutionary War and its often-forgotten dark side.[116] The war was a drawn-out, costly, and brutal conflict which claimed more lives on a percentage basis than any other U.S. war except the Civil War.[117] It illustrated the tangible gains that could be won through force of arms, but also the tremendous risks and costs of a military conflict that could have easily resulted in defeat and dishonor.

War was thus known to the framers as one of the most momentous powers of government. While the framers were familiar with the operation of legislatures, their opinions about the role of the executive and judicial branches were tentative.[118] A proposal to create a new branch of government that might have something to do with war therefore excited the framers' immediate attention and comment. Given that the framers remained attached to the positions expressed in the June 1 debate, the hypothesis that question (2) can be given an affirmative answer is not supported by the evidence. As Michael Ramsey notes, "[a]t least eight delegates spoke against presidential war-initiation power."[119] There was no significant dissent.

This brings us to the debate of August 17, in which the framers voted to substitute "declare" for "make" when reviewing the draft of the Committee of Detail.[120] There is no evidence that this change either diminished the war-initiation role we would expect Congress to have on the basis of the June 1 discussion or the Committee's draft, that it shifted this power to the president, or that it resulted in a sharing of the power. When the clause granting power to Congress "To make war" came up for consideration, delegates began by debating which branch should be vested with this power.[121] This approach showed that they thought of war-making as a discrete power, something that should be allocated to a particular branch of government. James Madison and Elbridge Gerry made the substituted language motion seemingly out of a concern with military necessity, as the word "declare" would leave "to the Executive the power to repel sudden attacks."[122] There was an outburst of republican fervor by Gerry as he cautioned he "never expected to hear in a republic a motion [by Pierce Butler] to empower the Executive alone to declare war."[123] By this point, it was clear that the delegates were not referring to a declaration as a formality, but an authorizing act that no branch but Congress could make.[124] The debate over the Madison-Gerry motion closed with Oliver Ellsworth and George Mason stating that it should be more difficult to begin a war than to make peace, something which Mason felt argued against any involvement of the Executive with "the power of war."[125]

While this exchange was considered decisive evidence in favor of the congressionalist position early in the war powers debate, more recently scholars have become cautious.[126] One point that worries them is the lack of relationship between the various remarks and what the framers actually did. If the president was left with a "power" to repel sudden attacks, what was its textual basis?[127] During and after the ratification of the Constitution, the framers seemed certain what they had done: the power to commence war was vested in Congress alone.[128] But some scholars believe the August 17 debate never achieved this level of clarity.[129]

What these scholars have been overlooking is that the level of clarity they demand is unnecessary to resolve whether post-1945 presidential war powers claims are inconsistent with the original constitutional order.[130] During the ratification debates, no one disagreed with the position taken by James Wilson, a member of the Committee of Detail at the Philadelphia Convention, who claimed in the Pennsylvania ratifying convention that "[i]t will not be in the power of a single man, or a single body of men, to involve us in [war]; for the important power of declaring war is vested in the legislature at large."[131] We can agree with those scholars who have seen a vigorous executive as the outcome of the Philadelphia Convention, while also bearing in mind that there were limits to what Americans could tolerate.[132] Those skeptical of the proposed Constitution in the ratifying conventions were not fans of increased executive power.[133] It is reasonable to infer that the Constitution could not have been ratified had it been admitted that the president had the power to commence war, other than in cases of necessity.[134] As Casto concludes, "there is no record of any member of the founding generation even stating that the president may lawfully start a war."[135] There is thus no hypothesis consistent with the evidence from the framing and ratification periods that justifies the post-1945 power presidents have claimed.

While scholars often wish there had been more discussion in the Philadelphia Convention on the "declare war" clause, the evidence we have is reasonably good relative to the deliberation on the other enumerated powers in the Constitution.[136] After all, much of the deliberation at the Convention did not concern drafting particulars, strictly speaking, but rather settling the broad outlines and purposes of the government. Drafting was done by committees and the delegates did not come to grips with the significance of choosing this or that word for later lawyerly interpretation so much as they tried to ensure that the wording chosen would reflect their purposes. This is why a purposive approach is especially helpful in making sense of the evidence.[137]

These conclusions about the meaning of the "declare war" clause have been reached by scholars relatively recently and it is worth briefly exploring why this is so. We can gain some critical distance on the war powers debate by observing that the state of legal knowledge on presidential war powers itself has a history. Most legal scholars, even those expert and prominent in the 1960s, had not thought much about presidential war powers and understandably floundered somewhat in the Vietnam-era debate. The lack of case law was a serious problem. American constitutional law is firmly based on the common law tradition. To oversimplify a bit, this means there is no law without precedents and there are very few meaningful precedents in the area of war powers. This gave competent lawyers very little to work with.

When Senator Fulbright offered his "National Commitments Resolution" in 1967, a measure that was a precursor of the WPR, there were not many full-scale scholarly discussions of the constitutional power to wage war on which he could rely. A July 1970 compilation of documents by the Foreign Relations Committee included one law review article, one student note, two memos prepared by students at Yale and NYU, and two scholarly papers.[138] This was not an impressive collection.

The only recent comprehensive treatment of presidential power which senators could consult in the 1960s was Edward Corwin's treatise.[139] Corwin, for decades a prominent and respected constitutional expert at Princeton, had published the last (fourth) edition in 1957.[140] His discussion of war powers was uncharacteristically weak and he did not devote much attention to the meaning of the "declare war" clause.[141] Rather, Corwin discussed whether Congress or the president had taken the initiative in creating circumstances which led to war.[142] Perhaps believing like some at the time that President Roosevelt had cleverly manipulated the nation into a naval war against Germany in the months preceding the December 1941 attack on Pearl Harbor, Corwin thought that in modern times the practical initiative lay with the executive.[143] Corwin thus offered a political rather than a legal analysis and so it was not much help to anyone struggling with what the Constitution had to say about war powers.

Once legal scholars began investigating, the weight of the evidence in favor of the exclusive power of Congress to commence war began to tell.[144] By the 1991 Gulf War scholarship on war powers was fully developed and many leading constitutional and international law scholars participated in litigation to show that the executive branch had been overreaching.[145] Citing earlier sound work by Charles Lofgren and Taylor Reveley, Abraham Sofaer concluded that "[t]he power to 'declare' war could not tenably be read, after examining both the Convention and ratification processes, as limiting Congress's control to formal war-making. Congress was seen by all who commented on the issue as possessing exclusive control of the means of war."[146] But he did not inquire into what position the executive branch had taken during the post-1945 period and so assumed that this conclusion settled very little.[147] Here Sofaer was spectacularly wrong. In fact, his analysis of the founding era, like that of almost every other scholar, had strongly suggested that the Cold War executive branch position that the president had the power to initiate war was on the order of an amendment to the Constitution.[148] An enormous constitutional change had occurred, but Sofaer and others refused to credit it.

Yoo's Alternative Account of the Founding Period

John Yoo, famous for writing the "torture memo" in the Bush II administration, has presented a much different account of war powers that ratifies the broad claims made by post-1945 presidents.[149] Yoo is perhaps best known for the position that the chief purpose of the "declare war" clause was to signal a new state of relations under international law between the United States and another country.[150] As we shall see in subsequent chapters, this and other arguments were created by presidentialists after 1950 in order to help justify the change in the constitutional order required by the new circumstances of the Cold War. They had no prior role in the American constitutional tradition.

Yoo's main innovation is to rely for support chiefly on eighteenth-century evidence, rather than later practice.[151] Unfortunately, it is not easy to describe Yoo's historical methodology. In general, he is more interested in British-American colonial views on executive power than in the founding era of the 1780s. He simultaneously embraces historical context in describing pre–Revolutionary War views of executive power, while ignoring relevant evidence from the Philadelphia Convention and any evidence after the ratification of the Constitution.[152] Yoo carries out this project directly in the face of the contrary advice of James Madison and James Wilson, who encouraged us to be wary of British practices and the public law writers of the seventeenth and eighteenth centuries with respect to the specific topic of war powers. This has the effect of making Yoo's discussion selective and legalistic, rather than contextual in the manner of the historians he admires.[153]

In building his account, for example, Yoo draws on the magisterial work *The Creation of the American Republic* by Gordon Wood.[154] Wood's book was seminal for our understanding of the early republic and it had special significance for legal scholars. It provided a panoramic perspective on the evolution of political ideas in America from 1776 to the Philadelphia Convention. Wood showed the sheer density of American political thought and was able to transmit an uncommon sense of how fundamental ideas, including those concerning separation of powers, were altered within a short span of time. For Wood, this meant that when the Constitution was presented to the states, it "presented no simple choice between accepting or rejecting the principles of 1776. During the intervening years, in newspapers, pamphlets, town meetings, and legislative debates, the political assumptions of 1776 had been extended, molded, and perverted in ways that no one had clearly anticipated. Under the severest kinds of political and polemical pressures old words had assumed new meanings, and old institutions had taken on new significance."[155] The comments made by Wilson and Madison are excellent illustrations of how a dramatic change from the British model was possible with respect to ideas concerning legislative and executive power.

Yoo's account goes badly astray by ignoring Wood's insight into how American thinking changed from the pre-Revolutionary and Revolutionary period through the adoption of the Constitution. Yoo assumes that ideas about executive power remained static between the pre–Revolutionary War period and the Philadelphia Convention. He thus reads the evidence from the Confederation, framing, and ratification periods against the background of an assumed consensus among Americans that the executive power included the power to make war.[156] This lack of attention to the reality of changing ideas Wood so painstakingly established is quite ironic, given that Yoo has used Wood's work to criticize congressionalist scholars for ignoring the kind of contextual evidence historians favor.[157]

As noted, Yoo differs from many presidentialist scholars by resting his case almost solely on evidence of original meaning rather than subsequent practice. He argues that a declaration of war by Congress was required only in the case of a "total war,"[158] leaving the conduct of other sorts of wars to the executive branch.[159] This conclusion is supported by a historical account of how the founding generation "would have" understood the foreign affairs powers of government based on their experience as British subjects.[160] Yoo uses the British constitution to establish the baseline that members of the founding generation would have understood that "warmaking and treatymaking were widely understood to be executive powers."[161]

Yoo deals swiftly with the Confederation period by contending, somewhat surprisingly, that the Congress under the Articles "was the nation's executive branch."[162] He notes the Confederation Congress's unique role, as it exercised "a mixture of judicial, legislative, and executive functions."[163] In a deeply misleading move, Yoo treats the debates at the Philadelphia Convention as if they concerned allocating the preexisting functions of the Confederation government, rather than founding a new constitutional order.[164] This allows him to treat the June 1 and

August 17 debates in a highly unusual way.[165] To Yoo, the change from "make" in the draft of the Committee of Detail to "declare" "made clear that the president could not unilaterally take the nation into a total war, but also suggested that he might be able to engage the nation in hostilities short of that."[166] By "total war" Yoo presumably means a conflict on the scale of World War II. Everything else is apparently fair game for the executive. This startling conclusion well reflects Yoo's assumption that a preexisting consensus as to the nature of executive power guided all the deliberations at Philadelphia.[167]

Whereas Yoo makes much of his devotion to history, scholars familiar with the evidence will notice many fault lines in his account. To highlight these difficulties, I will employ two rough distinctions between direct and circumstantial evidence and legal and contextual arguments about history. Direct evidence can be found when a framer and ratifier such as James Wilson says that the president does not have the power to take the country into war. An example of circumstantial evidence is the observation that Framer X read famous Book A which contained various Opinions C. In this case we might infer that Framer X held Opinions C, although there is no direct evidence. In turn, by "legal" argument I mean an argument based on an assumption about the truth of a proposition of law. A "contextual" argument is historicist and allows for the possibility that the understanding of the law might change over time.[168]

With these distinctions in hand, it is evident that Yoo's entire argument is based on circumstantial evidence guided by strict adherence to a particular legal proposition, namely, that the eighteenth-century understanding of executive power included the power to initiate war. It is surprising to realize that Yoo has *no direct evidence* in support of his general position. It would be difficult for him to produce any evidence from the Revolutionary or Confederation periods with respect to the presidency created by the Constitution because the idea of creating a republican, unitary, national chief executive was not commonly accepted prior to the Philadelphia Convention.[169] This means that quite literally no one had an opinion on the powers of such an executive prior to 1787. However, the most serious problem with Yoo's argument is that he is unable to find a single person in the Convention or ratification debates who advocated the kind of presidential war-initiation power he favors.

This circumstantial approach leads to critical shortfalls in Yoo's argument. Yoo admits he cannot explain the important comments about the "declare war" clause made in the Convention and ratification debates by key framers such as George Mason and James Wilson.[170] Yoo also ignores all the post-ratification evidence that the founding generation, including founders who had participated in the Philadelphia Convention and ratification debates, were in agreement that only Congress could initiate war.[171] Yoo might be right to eschew the use of post-ratification evidence as a matter of legal theory.[172] But this ignores the historical relevance of such evidence. The point is not necessarily that post-ratification evidence is legally binding. It is rather that evidence from, for example, the Pacificus-Helvidius exchange is impossible to explain without assuming that the framers and ratifiers had the common sense view, still widely shared today, that the Constitution required wars to be authorized by Congress. This is the evidence Yoo cannot explain.

Yoo's argument rests on the assumed truth of a specific legal proposition—that prior to the framing of the Constitution there was a widespread consensus in America that a republican executive would have the power of the British monarch to initiate war. Yoo does not confront the overwhelming historical evidence that no such consensus existed.[173] Understandings on such matters as the proper scope of legislative and executive power and the general nature of separation of powers were hammered out in the Philadelphia Convention itself.[174] This helps explain the significance of remarks like Wilson's that the British experience could not guide the Convention debates.[175]

At the root of Yoo's difficulties is a failure to engage with the context of the Philadelphia Convention. He paints a picture of continuity that runs counter to the sense of many delegates that the Confederation had failed and a fresh start was required.[176] Just as important, the delegates could not be guided by their familiarity with the British constitution, as Yoo assumes, because they were haltingly working their way toward the creation of fundamentally new institutions—a truly national and republican legislature, chief executive, and judiciary.[177] Finally, Yoo cannot account for what many historians have noticed about the founding generation—"the pervasive fear of excessive executive power."[178] Yoo has no way to explain this evidence because his entire analysis is based on the assumption that what was true of the British constitution was true of the U.S. Constitution.[179]

In considering the work of Yoo and other presidentialist scholars, a historicist approach leads us in the right direction by asking for the best explanation of the evidence from the founding period and the early republic. There was no group in the founding generation and there were barely any framers who advocated anything like a position capable of underwriting the post–World War II claims of Cold War and later presidents. Their assertion of power implied a massive constitutional change outside of formal amendment and judicial doctrine. As later chapters will show, however, it was a change widely approved by Congress and the public.

The Significance of Authorized Wars

One of the most widely known "facts" concerning how the U.S. goes to war is that while the U.S. has fought five declared wars (War of 1812, Mexican War of 1846, Spanish-American War, World War I, World War II), there have been many instances of the use of military force by the president without congressional authorization. While the presidentialist argument from historical practice is considered in Chapter 2, what is important to establish here is the significance of declared—understood as authorized—wars in U.S. history.[180]

Because the "declare war" clause grants a substantive power rather than serving as a literal reference to documents with "Declaration of War" written across the top, Congress may authorize war through means other than formal declarations. By this standard, the list of wars fought under the aegis of the "declare war" clause is longer than the familiar five and, with the special exception of Korea, includes *all* of America's most consequential, successful, and appalling military conflicts.[181] These wars are summarized in the accompanying table.

As previous discussion has demonstrated, the Quasi-War with France and the conflict with the Barbary states were authorized by congressional legislation.[182] The resolutions approved by Congress with respect to military conflicts in the Eisenhower, Kennedy, and Johnson administrations are part of this history. So are the "AUMFs"—the Authorizations to Use Military Force employed to approve the 1991 Persian Gulf War, the War in Afghanistan against al Qaeda, and the 2003 War in Iraq. Other than Korea, which will be discussed in Chapter 2, there are no nonauthorized military conflicts in American history that are of the same level of magnitude judged by the relevant criteria of casualties and costs.

Authorized foreign wars of the United States, 1798–2003

War	Acts	Costs	Casualties
Naval war with France, 1798	Act of May 28, 1798, ch. 48, 1 Stat. 561 Act of July 9, 1798, ch. 68, 1 Stat. 578	N/A	N/A
War with Barbary States, 1802 and 1815	Act of February 6, 1802, ch. 4, 2 Stat. 129 Act of March 3, 1815, ch. 90, 3 Stat. 230	N/A	N/A
War with Great Britain, 1812	Act of June 18, 1812, ch. 102, 2 Stat. 755	$1.55 bill.	6,765
Mexican War, 1846	Act of May 13, 1846, ch. 16, 9 Stat. 9	$2.37 bill.	17,435
War with Spain, 1898	Act of April 25, 1898, ch. 189, 30 Stat. 364	$9.03 bill.	4,108
World War I, 1917 (Germany and Austria-Hungary)	Act of April 6, 1917, ch. 1, 40 Stat. 1 Act of December 7, 1917, ch. 1, 40 Stat. 429	$334 bill.	320,518
World War II, 1941 (Japan and Germany)	Act of Dec. 8, 1941, ch. 561, 55 Stat. 795 Act of Dec. 11, 1941, ch. 564, 55 Stat. 796 (Other declarations of war against Italy, Bulgaria, Hungary, and Romania)	$4.10 trill.	1,076,245

Korean War, 1950	(nonauthorized)	$341 bill.	139,858
Vietnam War, 1964	Gulf of Tonkin Resolution, P.L. 88-408, 78 Stat. 384, August 10, 1964	$738 bill.	211,523
Persian Gulf War, 1991	P.L. 102-1, 105 Stat. 3, January 14, 1991	$102 bill.	850
War in response to terrorist attacks of September 11, 2001 (Operation Enduring Freedom)	P.L. 107-40, 115 Stat. 224, September 18, 2001	$321 bill.	5,922
Iraq War, 2003 (Operation Iraqi Freedom)	P.L. 107-243, 116 Stat. 1498	$784 bill.	36,016

Sources: Stephen Daggett, "Costs of Major U.S. Wars," Congressional Research Service (June 29, 2010); Jennifer K. Elsea and Richard F. Grimmett, "Declarations of War and Authorizations for the Use of Military Force: Historical Background and Legal Implications," Congressional Research Service (Mar. 8, 2007); Anne Leland and Mari-Jana Oboroceanu, "American War and Military Operations Casualties: Lists and Statistics," Congressional Research Service (Feb. 26, 2010). For comprehensive lists of declared wars (5), declarations of war (11), and authorized wars (11), see Elsea and Grimmett.

Notes: Amounts are in 2011 dollars. Casualties include total deaths and wounds not mortal. The act citations for the 1798 Naval war with France and the wars with the Barbary states have been corrected from the original. Casualties for Operation Enduring Freedom were considerably higher as of November 2012: 2,150 deaths and 18,081 wounded in action, for a total of 20,231 casualties. See Defense Casualty Analysis System, www.dmdc.osd.mil/dcas/pages/about/xhtml.

Most legal scholars agree that such authorizations are the constitutional equivalents of declarations of war. In a comprehensive treatment of the September 2001 AUMF, Curtis Bradley and Jack Goldsmith persuasively contended that "almost no one argues today that Congress's authorization must take the form of a declaration of war."[183] They noted the relevance of historical practice—Congress has authorized wars by legislation throughout American history.[184] The enactment of the WPR gave additional legal support to this view by explicitly endorsing the use of congressional legislation to authorize war.[185] Of special relevance to Katzenbach's 1967 testimony highlighted earlier, they gave the further reason that "the international law role for declarations of war has largely disappeared."[186] Bradley and Goldsmith cited the very reason Katzenbach gave in 1967, the fact that the U.N. Charter had shifted the focus of international law away from "war" to "armed attack" or the "use of force."[187]

Many believe that declarations of war are a thing of the past. But while *literal* declarations of war may be outmoded, nothing at all has happened to the *substantive power of Congress to authorize war* or, if you like, the use of armed force. The reality that the Constitution has a rule, institutionalized in the pre–World War II constitutional order, with respect to how wars can begin has consequences. No one believes that rules in the Constitution can be changed by later practice. Nonetheless, some of the participants in the war powers debate have proceeded as if evidence of practice was decisive from a legal point of view.[188] Especially on the presidentialist side, participants tend to avoid the uncomfortable truth that the rule providing Congress the responsibility for authorizing war is supreme law and hence legally obligatory.[189] Subsequent practice could not count against or nullify the rule without placing the entire Constitution in question.[190]

On the other hand, it is hard to deny that beginning with Korea an amendment-level constitutional change did somehow occur. The theory of constitutional orders enables us to understand and explain what has happened. We would expect that a rule could not be changed by later practice if we inhabited the world I described at the beginning of this chapter—one in which war powers had been legalized. Because war powers are exercised in the sphere of the nonlegalized Constitution, they can be changed without going through the amendment process or the Supreme Court. Unfortunately, given that the supreme law of the Constitution and the institutions and expectations created with the original constitutional order are still with us, this evolution has created serious tensions within our system of government.

Prior to the Cold War, authorized war necessarily involving interbranch deliberation was an integral part of the nation's constitutional order. Far from being a "formality," there was an awareness of the constitutional rule as establishing a framework for decisionmaking that governed how the nation went to war. As I will show in Chapter 2, this awareness played a key role in the diplomatic calculations not only of President Roosevelt, but of other countries as well. Put simply, declarations (or authorizations) of war were primary components of national mobilization.[191] As FDR knew, the United States could not be properly readied to shoulder the staggering tasks involved in winning World War II unless a proper case was made in advance. Indeed, it was the thought that it had taken far too long to move the interbranch machinery in response to the Nazi threat that drove public officials and members of the foreign policy elite to found a new constitutional order stressing presidential initiative in foreign policy after 1945.

The ground-level reality is that the executive branch and a significant number of members of Congress came to believe that the presidency would have to be given the unilateral power to initiate war in commanding what came to be called the "national security state."[192] To be sure, there was criticism, especially after Truman's Korea decision, but the baseline of power in foreign affairs had been altered. As the discussion in subsequent chapters will show, contrary to some appearances, the executive branch has never relinquished that power. Given that the text was unhelpful to these constitutional entrepreneurs, the change to the pre–World War II constitutional order had to come through the manifestation of different policies and attitudes in both branches and political parties and by expanding the capacity of the executive to commit the armed forces to battle.

In this post-1945 or Cold War constitutional order, presidents were certain that they were chiefly or even solely responsible for advancing the foreign policy and defending the national security of the United States. Crucially, they viewed the use of force, including "war," as one instrument among others in the making of that foreign policy. Reflecting this understanding, post–World War II presidents have literally claimed that they could take the nation to war based on their Article II constitutional authority. When less inclined to be maximalist, however, they could be understood more reasonably as saying, "The President must lead in foreign affairs and the use of armed force always has to be one option." Nevertheless, presidents were implicitly rejecting the founding generation's view that war required a special measure of deliberation.

In evaluating presidential decisions for war under the post-1945 constitutional order, we must be mindful of the perils of formalism. In the context of war powers, "formalism" is an overemphasis on presidential compliance with the rule of law under the Constitution. One of the problems with the standard critique of presidential war powers is that congressionalists have been relatively disabled from offering suggestions about how to improve the constitutional situation. This is at least in part because of their insistence that the difficulty lies with the simple failure of presidents to comply with the Constitution's undoubted requirement that the issue of war must be taken to Congress. Yet this requirement is in service of a larger vision of separation of powers designed to encourage interbranch deliberation and, through such deliberation, a democratic exchange with the people with the creation of a cycle of accountability being the ultimate end in view.

The formalist critique of presidential war powers has proven too narrow. Our standards of evaluation must engage with the realities of presidential decisionmaking and thus move into the nuanced terrain of democratic judgment. This will allow the critique of presidential war powers to move in a more constructive direction. Thus I pay as much attention in the chapters that follow to whether presidential decisions were underwritten by adequate interbranch and democratic deliberation as compared to whether they were formally authorized. These more complex standards of evaluation will better enable us to formulate constructive suggestions to improve the constitutional order.

It is worth reflecting on what war means and the role it has played in our lifetimes. Since the beginning of the Cold War, there have been several periods in which Americans seriously thought that war might be obsolete. One of the crueler ironies of "postwar" or post–World War II history is that war is still with us. The U.S. keeps fighting them.

As shown in the table earlier in this chapter, from World War II until 2010 there have been at least 394,000 U.S. deaths and casualties in the major wars fought in Korea, Vietnam, the Persian Gulf, Afghanistan, and Iraq. Of these casualties, nearly 90 percent occurred in Korea and Vietnam. Casualties suffered in other conflicts have been small by comparison.[193] While the era of war by airpower and remote control has been announced and abandoned several times since 1945, the overwhelming majority of these casualties were incurred by the "boots on the ground"—the Army and the Marines. It is reasonable to infer that putting Americans on the ground in foreign locales is the only sure way to prevail in war. Americans never again fought for Europe after 1945, but they kept fighting and dying far from home in Asia and the Middle East. There is no reason to expect the next few decades to be different. This is the most important reason for understanding what these wars have done to our country and our Constitution.

2

Truman and the Post-1945 Constitutional Order

THE BEGINNING of the Cold War was a watershed for U.S. foreign policy. This is the period running roughly from Stalin's speech in February 1946, appearing to promise a conflict with capitalism, to President Truman's 1950 decision to intervene in Korea and massively expand the armed forces.[1] As summarized by historian George Herring, "the Truman administration in the short space of seven years carried out a veritable revolution in U.S. foreign policy. It altered the assumptions behind national security policies, launched a wide range of global programs and commitments, and built new institutions to manage the nation's burgeoning international activities."[2]

This period has been extensively studied by historians, but there has been an absence, especially in general accounts, of assessment of the constitutional significance of epochal events such as the Truman Doctrine, the formation of NATO, and the Korea decision.[3] At the same time, historians have shown that officials were aware that the nature of the constitutional order was changing.[4] According to Michael Hogan's insightful account, there was an unceasing debate, centered on fears of a coming "garrison state," over the effect the new global responsibilities of the United States would have on American government and society.[5] How would the coming "long war" affect the Constitution?

In this chapter, I will describe how political elites convinced themselves, the government, and the public that the pre–Pearl Harbor constitutional order was inadequate to the challenging circumstances that the U.S. faced in the Cold War. From the point of view of the executive branch, questions of war powers had to be subordinated to the larger objectives of that policy. Within a short span of time the U.S. moved from the pre–Pearl Harbor constitutional order in which Congress was understood to be the gatekeeper for war, amid generally robust interbranch deliberation, to the uneasy establishment of a new post-1945 constitutional order. That order rejected the idea that Congress had a check on presidential war power independent of its appropriations authority. When this rejection was combined with an expansion in the capabilities of the U.S. military as compared with the situation prior to Pearl Harbor, the consequence was that President Truman and his successors had the ability to initiate war on their own authority.

We will also consider how the inherent conflict between the post-1945 constitutional order and the original order embodied in the Constitution caused trouble almost from the outset. The decisionmaking failures in the wars fought after 1945 fell into recurrent patterns that were emblematic of a broader derangement in the system of governance. More precisely, they were predominantly failures by the executive branch that originated from the lack of interbranch deliberation built into the post-1945 constitutional order. The most prominent patterns were a failure to engage in realistic war planning, a closely related failure to decide on war aims, and a fatally mistaken assumption that the president, as chief officer of the executive branch, could carry the entire burden of war decisionmaking alone.

I also examine the historical origins of the war powers debate in the reaction to Truman's unilateral decision to intervene in Korea. In particular, I evaluate two arguments advanced by the Truman administration—the well-known argument from historical practice and the "U.N. theory," the idea that the ratification of the U.N. Charter had changed the legal playing field with respect to war. Finally, I urge that despite Truman's departures from the pre–Pearl Harbor constitutional order, we should take a balanced view of Truman's use of his constitutional powers. Despite his tendency to act unilaterally, the label "imperial presidency" does not help us understand Truman or his decisions.

Before Pearl Harbor

Believe it or not, it is easy to find important public officials, including presidents and justices of the Supreme Court, affirming the essential meaning the "declare war" clause had in the eighteenth century in every major period of American history.[6] This is one reason why I posit that there have been only two constitutional orders with respect to war and foreign affairs: the pre–Pearl Harbor order which showed an essential continuity with the original constitutional order of the early republic and the post-1945 order. Diplomatic historians may be understandably skeptical of this claim, given the level of U.S. military involvement abroad prior to World War II, especially in the empire-building period of the late nineteenth and early twentieth centuries.

Diplomatic historians have been steadily trying to educate us for some time that U.S. involvement with the world prior to Pearl Harbor is best conceptualized in terms of engagement rather than isolationism. They point, for example, to the frequent military adventures abroad, especially in Latin America and East Asia.[7] While I will have more to say about these episodes when dealing with the argument from historical practice later in this chapter, it is necessary to say now is that there is a significant difference between describing and contextualizing historical events and accounting for constitutional orders.

My theory of constitutional orders does not posit that each distinctive period of American history has had its own accompanying order. Such a notion would not take seriously the constant relevance and "sticky" nature of a text that, secessionists aside, has always been acknowledged to have the status of supreme law. We need to consider the possibility, hinted at by scholars of legal history, that this understanding has given the Constitution a certain relative autonomy from the ordinary wear and tear of the forces of history. Indeed, as I shall argue, part of the tension that helped *define* the Cold War period and its aftermath was between what were seen as the requirements of a sound foreign policy led by the president and the constitutional powers of Congress exemplified by the "declare war" clause. As we shall see, the Constitution was always an available text ready to hand—a legal document to be sure, but one which laypersons believed they could understand. Even in the crisis-filled years of the early Cold War, citizens, soldiers, and covert operatives wondered how the prevailing post-1945 order was compatible with the Constitution.

I labored the example of Alexander Hamilton's career in Chapter 1 partly to show that changing a reigning constitutional order is not simply a matter of articulating a new interpretation of the Constitution or even passing laws, as in the case of Hamilton's ill-fated "New Army."

Changing a republican and democratic constitutional order is rather a matter of state-making and state-building, of working with many people to move new state capacities and institutions into place. The example of Hamilton also suggests that making a new constitutional order is a self-conscious activity. Thus, reacting to a foreign threat by sending the troops in cannot create a new order by itself. The purpose and nature of the new order must be articulated and defended so the stakes are publicly known.[8]

So the actions of a single president or even a group of presidents cannot change a constitutional order. We look for change that persists over time along all three dimensions of a constitutional order: plausible interpretations of the text linked to attractive visions of public policy that can be implemented through changing the capacities of state institutions. I will be using the concept of a constitutional order to sift through the welter of events, especially in the years prior to Pearl Harbor and in the age of empire, to show that despite the many undoubted substantial developments in American diplomacy from the nineteenth century onward, no one acted with sufficient energy to create a new constitutional order for war powers.

Roosevelt's Prewar Diplomacy

The substantive constitutional requirement of congressional authorization before the United States went to war structured the twisting political path followed by President Roosevelt in the years prior to Pearl Harbor. In the pre–Pearl Harbor order, the requirement of congressional authorization fueled a robust process of deliberation among the president, Congress, and the public.[9] In conducting diplomacy with other countries FDR was well aware of the role Congress had as the decider of whether the nation went to war.[10] He was also painfully cognizant of America's lack of preparedness and the fact that Congress would eventually have to underwrite a massive military buildup.[11] As Hitler went from victory to victory in 1939 and 1940, the U.S. was weak, at least in terms of ground forces—its military ranked twentieth in the world in terms of numbers of troops and could field only five divisions against the 141 Germany sent against France and Great Britain.[12]

Congress's gatekeeping role over whether the U.S. went to war was widely accepted in the run-up to the Second World War. Far from being a formality, a declaration of war was an integral feature of the nation's diplomacy, a crucial substantive commitment that America's eventual allies sought with increasing urgency.[13] Yet by and large, the tremendous obstacles FDR faced in winning this commitment in the years prior to Pearl Harbor have been minimized by *both* sides in the war powers debate. Presidentialists and congressionalists alike have tended to accept a caricature of Roosevelt as a crafty leader manipulating the nation into war, which for those skeptical of presidential power has served as an early sign of the trend toward an "imperial presidency."[14] For presidentialists, FDR's maneuvers show both the necessity of vigorous presidential leadership in times of foreign crisis and the practical reality that war powers are shared.[15] Both sides have thus been led away from the evidence that declarations of war played a central role in the nation's diplomacy prior to the Cold War. Somewhat surprisingly, no one has investigated the political and cultural meaning that declarations of war had for FDR's contemporaries.

FDR knew that war was a Rubicon he could not cross alone.[16] For nearly three years, he diligently sought to line up the many moving parts of the pre–Pearl Harbor constitutional order so that the eventual conflict would have the full support of the people.[17] It was a long, hard road. Initial efforts to encourage rearmament in 1939 led nowhere. Under Secretary of State Sumner Welles spoke of a "nightmare of frustration" as the government seemed to have no means short of war to prepare for a challenge that threatened the very survival of the country.[18] Although public opinion began to change after Germany's September 1939 invasion of Poland, the simple fact was that it remained peacetime and FDR had no war powers.[19]

As Hitler's blitzkrieg finished off France in July 1940, French prime minister Paul Reynaud and British prime minister Winston Churchill begged Roosevelt to involve the U.S. in the struggle and issue a declaration of war against Germany.[20] FDR replied that "he could not commit the United States to military intervention in the war. 'Only the Congress,' Roosevelt concluded, 'can make such commitments.'"[21] Less than a year later in May 1941, Hitler was still on the march and Churchill renewed his request, which Roosevelt again declined.[22] According to historian David Reynolds, "FDR judged that the opposition in Congress was too substantial, and that the American public, whose whole-hearted commitment was essential to sustain any war effort, still had no real grasp of the issues at stake."[23] Presidential leadership could carry policy only so far against the forces of isolationism and American doubts about whether any war would be worthwhile.[24]

Roosevelt began what seemed to be a final push to win over Congress and the public to the commitment necessary for war in May 1941.[25] By this time, the Lend-Lease program of aid to Britain had been approved by Congress, although the public did not want to commit U.S. forces.[26] FDR's push involved major speeches and declarations such as the Atlantic Charter designed to advance a rationale for going to war.[27] More aid to Britain meant some degree of protection had to be given to the ships carrying supplies. At first rejecting the aggressive measure of providing naval escorts recommended by some of his advisors, FDR instead pursued a strategy of establishing a large defensive sphere that extended to occupying Greenland and Iceland in the mid-Atlantic.[28] FDR subsequently used incidents between American warships and German submarines to demonstrate to the public that the U.S. was already under attack.[29] Despite increasing efforts in this regard, the president was not in the driver's seat and had to wait upon events. He was encased in a constitutional order that made it impossible for him to simply command the nation to war.[30]

Given the constraints on the president, it is somewhat misleading to highlight FDR's uses of unilateral executive authority as setting precedents for the "imperial presidency."[31] FDR transferred largely obsolete destroyers to Britain in exchange for naval bases in 1940 by executive order and, as noted, dramatically extended the defensive sphere the U.S. was willing to patrol in 1941.[32] But these actions bear little resemblance to those of post-1945 presidents once we situate FDR within the reality of the pre–Pearl Harbor order. Our attention is more appropriately focused on the problematic nature of the order in which FDR had to work. The danger posed by executive overreaching was relatively slight, given the lack of state capacity to take meaningful overt or covert military action. Given this lack of capacity, pushing the envelope of executive authority before Pearl Harbor meant something quite different than it did just a few years later.

This ground-level reality was reflected in the sound advice FDR received from the Army's War Plans Division in 1941: "only land armies can finally win wars."[33] Roosevelt had hoped that providing supplies and possibly air and naval support to Great Britain would be enough to prevail against Germany.[34] His hope was in vain, yet it was likely influenced by the lack of public support for anything greater.[35] Measured by the enormous forces that would be required to defeat Germany and Japan, FDR had failed in his effort to mobilize the country. This should caution us that FDR's reputation among constitutional scholars as a master manipulator has been oversold. The uncertain path to war rather shows the constraining effect of a constitutional order in which the role of Congress as the decider was assumed.[36]

The long period of time necessary to build the consensus required by the pre–Pearl Harbor order to take action against the Nazi threat had significant implications for the post-1945 era. Lord Lothian, the shrewd British ambassador to the U.S., accurately advised his government in September 1940: "Yet owing to the size of the country and its constitution it is usually impossible to get important decisions taken without at least six months preparation."[37] Many prominent Americans began to wonder whether international crises could wait that long.[38] There is little doubt that the isolationist sentiment and congressional intransigence forming the background for Roosevelt's labors made a deep impression on the emerging foreign policy elite.[39]

Perhaps the nadir in executive-legislative relations was reached in July 1939 as FDR personally appealed to congressional leaders to lift the arms embargo in the Neutrality Act. When Secretary of State Cordell Hull backed the president by citing diplomatic reports, isolationist Senator William Borah of Idaho responded that he had sources of information superior to those of the State Department![40] Borah asserted blithely that he saw no likelihood of war in Europe, two months before Germany and the Soviet Union invaded Poland.[41] The kind of arrogance and irresponsibility demonstrated by senators like Borah in an era when "American isolation [became] the handmaiden of European appeasement"[42] went a long way toward discrediting Congress among the foreign policy establishment.[43] Those who would be later called the "wise men" disapproved of the effects of the Neutrality Acts and were drawing their own conclusions about the appropriate shape of the post-1945 constitutional order.[44] The members of this elite might well be regarded as the framers of contemporary presidentialism.

As the war ended, presidential wartime powers did as well and congressional leaders began efforts to restore the pre–Pearl Harbor order. They saw the increase in presidential power during the war as temporary and no longer wanted to defer to executive leadership.[45] But by 1946, there were conflicting policy currents. In response to Soviet threats, members of Congress and the public wanted a more aggressive foreign policy.[46] This implied a *permanent* increase in the military capacities of the national state and thus a different system of governance. As historian John Lewis Gaddis notes, confronting the Soviet Union put in question traditions that had guided U.S. diplomacy for generations: "nonentanglement in the political affairs of Europe, and fear of a large-scale peacetime military establishment."[47] Abandoning those traditions would necessitate building a new constitutional order.

Constructing a New Constitutional Order

The development of U.S. foreign policy during the beginning of the Cold War can be summarized very briefly in terms of three stages of policy action within an overall strategy.[48] Initially there was a stage of economic, social, and military aid exemplified by the Truman Doctrine, the assistance sent to Greece and Turkey, and the Marshall Plan.[49] Next came formal pledges of military alliance, exemplified by the NATO treaty.[50] Finally, there was the deployment of U.S. armed forces and the militarization of the Cold War, represented both by the military buildup after the June 1950 Korean intervention and Truman's closely related decision to send several divisions of troops to Europe.[51] The multi-pronged strategy can be described as one of stabilizing key areas of the globe, containment of the immediate threat of communist advance, and achievement of victory over the Soviet Union, though without a general war, through what historian Melvyn Leffler has termed a "preponderance of power."[52]

Stabilization and containment were intended to preserve U.S. national security by targeting those areas of the world nearest to the Soviet Union and opposing the extension of Soviet power into those areas.[53] As formulated by key State Department figures such as George Kennan, this strategy, at least originally, was not aimed at defeating the Soviet Union through purely military means, but rather producing a balance of power that would prevent countries, particularly in Europe and Asia, from going over to the Soviet side.[54] Maintaining the military advantages the U.S. possessed at the end of World War II was part of this balance, as was stabilizing border countries such as Germany and

Japan from within so to enable them to resist Soviet diplomatic and military pressure.[55]

In constructing a new constitutional order to support this strategy, Truman had several signal advantages over FDR. Isolationism as a political movement was dead.[56] Although senators with isolationist leanings remained, the careful maneuvering in which FDR engaged to satisfy a substantial bloc of isolationist voters was absent from Truman's political calculus. Further, despite post-1945 demobilization the U.S. still possessed the most capable armed forces in the world, especially with respect to air and naval power, in addition to atomic weapons.[57] Moreover, America reigned supreme as the world's only economic superpower.[58] As a consequence, the state and military capacity available to Truman at the beginning of the Cold War was vastly greater than that possessed by FDR in the years preceding Pearl Harbor. In turn, this meant that Truman's ability to act unilaterally as chief executive had been enhanced. What Soviet military doctrine called the "correlation of forces" was moving in favor of the presidency.

Interestingly, Kennan admitted that there was a tension between the strategy of containment and the institutional order of American constitutionalism. Gaddis comments that Kennan "never succeeded in reconciling in his own mind the need for precision and flexibility in diplomacy with a constitutional framework that seemed at best inhospitable to those qualities."[59] The tension would grow more severe once the strategy of containment was formalized in NSC-68, the general assessment of the threat posed by the Soviet Union requested by Truman in 1950.[60]

NSC-68 attempted to persuade the different parts of the executive branch that the struggle against Soviet power would be permanent, a "long war," requiring a substantial military buildup.[61] There were several significant elements to its argument. The global strategy of the U.S. was to confront Soviet power along the entire perimeter where nations under Kremlin and communist control met free states.[62] Therefore, in language later famous, "the assault on free institutions is world-wide now, and in the context of the present polarization of power a defeat of free institutions anywhere is a defeat everywhere."[63] If taken seriously by policymakers, this statement would mean that the U.S. could not lose a single nation to communism. Further, the position of the U.S. rested just as much on maintaining the credibility of its power and perceptions of that power as it did on the actual balance of power. Finally, NSC-68 endorsed the use of force where necessary to oppose the Soviet Union.[64] These points amounted to a rejection of Kennan's balance of power approach. Instead, the U.S. would seek global supremacy based on military power.[65]

Historians have observed that NSC-68 was crafted deliberately as a sort of white paper for a new constitutional order.[66] It invoked the preamble to the Constitution and its values, although there was no lawyerly discussion of specific clauses and powers.[67] It did not call for any alteration to the Constitution, nor did it assume that its strategy could be implemented only by the executive branch. Nonetheless, its argument had significant constitutional implications.

What sort of constitutional order did NSC-68 require? To do a thorough analysis of this question would have required its authors to examine the original constitutional order and how it had been maintained in the pre–Pearl Harbor order. They would have had to examine, for example, whether the founding generation had created a state with powers of deliberation and decision robust enough to support a military with a global war-fighting capacity similar to that enjoyed by the British empire in the eighteenth century. They would also have had to address whether the relationship the Constitution assumed between the executive and legislative branches took into consideration the requirements of a perpetual state of war.

Although such an analysis was never undertaken, it is likely that the authors of NSC-68 assumed a malleable or "living" Constitution that could adapt to changing circumstances, no matter how different they were from the conditions of the early republic. This was roughly the approach taken later in the war powers debate by presidentialists.[68] This view belied the reality that constitutional powers are implemented by institutions. Altering those powers formally through a constitutional amendment would alter those institutions. The theory of constitutional orders advanced in Chapter 1 alerts us that the *reverse* is also true—altering the capacities of government institutions effectively changes their constitutional power, at least outside the judicially supervised sphere of the legalized Constitution. The change contemplated by NSC-68, however, ran against the meaning of the text embodied in the original constitutional order and thus was inherently problematic, creating tensions that ran throughout the Cold War and after.

One source of tension was what the military buildup meant for presidential power. An expanded military would produce a situation that had no parallel in previous history—one in which the president had the ability to intervene anywhere in the world.[69] Further, an actual military confrontation with the Soviet Union or its communist proxies was possible. It was widely believed, both then and now, that war increases the power of the executive branch, and legitimately so. But what would then happen in a "long war" that involved a continuous cycle of such conflicts?

Those with doubts about whether such developments were compatible with American constitutional traditions would not have felt assuaged by the sort of militancy reflected in NSC-68 and taking hold in Washington after shocks such as the "loss" of China and the news that the Soviet Union possessed atomic weaponry.[70] According to Gaddis, the response of NSC-68 was "while in principle a democracy should choose its methods selectively, when confronted with an absolute threat to its survival *anything was fair game.* . . . The world crisis, as dangerous in its potential as anything confronted in World Wars I or II, rendered all interests vital, all means affordable, all methods justifiable."[71] This precept was confirmed in frightening terms in a 1954 report (known as the Doolittle report) on the CIA's covert capabilities:

> It is now clear that we are facing an implacable enemy whose avowed objective is world domination by whatever means and at whatever cost. There are no rules in such a game. Hitherto acceptable norms of human conduct do not apply. If the United States is to survive, long-standing American concepts of "fair play" must be reconsidered. We must develop effective espionage and counterespionage services and must learn to subvert, sabotage and destroy our enemies by more clever, more sophisticated and more effective methods than those used against us. It may become necessary that the American people be made acquainted with, understand and support this fundamentally repugnant philosophy.[72]

To be fair, we can reconstruct how the Truman administration and its allies in Congress would have responded to the charge that their strategy necessarily involved overthrowing the original constitutional order and, along with it, the values on which America was founded. Many Americans in and out of government were convinced that Congress, especially the Senate, was guilty of a long series of mistakes in foreign policy that had weakened the U.S. and opened the door to an unthinkable victory by Hitler's Germany and Japan.[73] They included the rejection of the Treaty of Versailles after World War I, thus guaranteeing no U.S. participation in the League of Nations, the spirit of isolationism that had prevailed in the following decades, the ill-advised Neutrality Acts which hamstrung FDR's response to the growing crisis in Europe, and the general lack of military preparedness for the storm that finally broke on the U.S. in the attack on Pearl Harbor.[74] Congress had been judged by many thoughtful Americans as feckless and irresponsible. Truman and Secretary of State Dean Acheson appeared to agree.[75] At the Cold War's outset, the theme of "no more Pearl Harbors" was hammered home time and again.[76]

While this makes for a persuasive critique of the pre–Pearl Harbor constitutional order with which FDR struggled, it does not deny that Truman was proposing to construct a new order involving an unprecedented increase in presidential power. As the fundamental strategy of the U.S. with respect to foreign affairs and national security, containment dictated the constitutional stance of the presidency with respect to war. This is a crucial point and an example of the reciprocal relationship between policy conditioned by state capacities and the authoritative text of the Constitution which it implements. In assessing the post-1945 position of the executive branch on whether the president could initiate war on his own authority, we should not look solely to understandably infrequent presidential pronouncements. Rather, we should take the requirements of the global strategy to which the U.S. was committed as our starting point. If that strategy involved the capacity to respond quickly to multiple foreign threats with overwhelming force, that meant the president *had* to possess the power to initiate military action, even war, as he saw fit.[77]

At the same time, it should not be thought that the new order had *no* basis in the Constitution. As we saw in Chapter 1, contemporary scholars have argued cogently that there was a constitutional basis for executive leadership in foreign affairs generally.[78] Helpful judicial precedents were available as well. Executive branch lawyers soon found their way to *United States v. Curtiss-Wright Export, Corp.*, in which the Supreme Court had, in the context of a case involving a congressional delegation of power to the president, given a ringing endorsement of presidential leadership in foreign affairs.[79] The Court made clear that it had a whole variety of presidential actions in mind, including the negotiation of treaties, in referring to "the very delicate, plenary and exclusive power of the President as the sole organ of the federal government in the field of international relations."[80] At the same time, it did not place the president beyond the checks and balances in the Constitution or even approach the issue of Congress's substantive power under the "declare war" clause.[81]

Rather than being supportive of presidentialism with respect to war powers specifically, the consistent later use of *Curtiss-Wright* by executive branch lawyers in fact exemplified the post-1945 belief that war powers could be subsumed under foreign affairs, thus well illustrating one of the main theses of this book. As we saw in Chapter 1, presidential defenders like Katzenbach argued that war powers were a variety of presidential power under foreign affairs. For them, the "declare war" clause applied only to epochal conflicts such as World War II.[82] Presidentialists maintained that surely the chief executive had the authority necessary to defend the national security of the United States. While no one was quite ready to add "even if the Constitution is to the contrary," that was implied of necessity.[83]

As discussed later in this chapter, other elements in post-1945 foreign policy, particularly the role of the United Nations, were subordinate to containment. Key theorists like Kennan never put much stock in the ability of the U.N. to serve as the fulcrum of U.S. foreign policy efforts.[84] The leaders of the executive branch gradually came to the same conclusion after 1945.[85] As the Joint Chiefs of Staff put it in early 1947, "faith in the ability of the United Nations as presently constituted to protect, now or hereafter, the security of the United States would mean only that the faithful have lost sight of the vital security interest of the United States and could quite possibly lead to results fatal to that strategy."[86]

Although there was widespread political support for the Truman administration's stance toward the Soviet Union, citizens and officials did worry about its constitutional implications. There were persistent concerns about the adverse domestic effect of greater involvement abroad.[87] In Hogan's rich and perceptive account, the concept of the "garrison state" was invoked repeatedly as a summary of these concerns.[88] He records "the dawning realization that national security needs could alter fundamentally the country's basic institutions, and not necessarily in a fashion compatible with its commitment to democratic principles and civilian rule."[89] These worries were salutary in that they promised a direct engagement with the issue of how the constitutional order should be changed. Closer inspection reveals difficulties both with the conceptualization of the issue and a failure to grapple with the most serious difficulty, the derangement of the structure the Constitution establishes for policymaking.

The debate over the garrison state was motivated primarily by economic and civil liberties concerns. It did not confront the reality that an adaptation of amendment-like proportions would be required to keep the Constitution relevant in fundamentally new circumstances. Fears of a garrison state were directed against the collective power of the federal government and the dangers it posed. Critics lamented increased federal regimentation of the economy, deficit spending, high taxes, and an imbalance between military and civilian power.[90] There were also concerns about a permanent increase in executive power, the first intimations of the critique of the "imperial presidency."[91]

This debate was more of a missed opportunity than a meaningful engagement with the constitutional challenges posed by the new global role assumed by the United States. The most important issue that had to be faced was how the executive and legislative branches of government should be reorganized to preserve constitutional values such as deliberation and accountability in radically new circumstances. Although the National Security Act of 1947 and subsequent follow-up measures readied the executive branch to a limited extent for its new global role, nothing of comparable significance happened with respect to Congress.[92] In making this point, I am not disputing Hogan or other historians who would see the debate that did occur as a source of insight into American values and political identity. But the debate missed the inevitability of the constitutional change that would follow the massive increases in the military and intelligence capacities of the state.

Despite the reality of executive dominance in shaping Cold War strategy, it would be a mistake to assume that Congress played no role in fashioning the Cold War constitutional order. The 1951 "Great Debate" in Congress over Truman's unilateral decision to deploy U.S. troops to Europe and the conflict over the Bricker Amendment in the Eisenhower administration were examples of Congress warning the executive branch about limits to its power while attempting to contribute to the formulation of foreign policy.[93] But the pressures to react and decide in foreign affairs relentlessly pushed the executive branch to the forefront once the Cold War got under way in 1946 and 1947.

Because Congress was not reorganized to play a vital part in the post-1945 constitutional order, the executive branch treated it as a junior partner. A recurrent pattern in the post-1945 order was the persistent overselling of foreign threats in order to win congressional approval of new policies.[94] In a famous episode, Truman was told by Senator Arthur Vandenberg that he would have to "scare hell" out of the American people in order to get the aid package to Greece and Turkey passed in 1947.[95] Vandenberg said this after then–Under Secretary of State Acheson had gone out of his way in a meeting with congressional leaders to portray the confrontation between the U.S. and the Soviet Union as a key moment in human history.[96] Following Acheson's suggestion, Truman and his advisers increasingly characterized the conflict as one of confronting communist ideology.[97]

The president's effort at getting Congress to move after his speech announcing the Truman Doctrine is often implicitly portrayed as a matter of dynamiting members of Congress out of their post-1945 demobilized complacency.[98] But it was at least as much a matter of overcoming staggered congressional terms, bicameralism, and the committee system—the ordinary constitutional roadblocks in the way of any president in a hurry. We might nod our heads in approval, thinking rightly that the purpose of such roadblocks is to encourage deliberation. But what this judicious response ignores is that whatever we might think of Truman's salesmanship, the administration had compelling reasons for thinking that Greece and Turkey, indeed all of Europe, required emergency help.[99] We might understandably respond that the constitutional system was not designed to work quite so fast! And with this response, we are on the threshold of appreciating the reality of the persistence of the pre–Pearl Harbor order and the dilemma created for Truman by how the Constitution was implemented in that order.

Parenthetically, I suggest it is difficult to place Truman's actions in proper perspective if we maintain the general skeptical attitude toward U.S. foreign policy in this period that has dominated the contemporary war powers debate. We should at least sympathetically engage (although not required to agree) with the perspective of Truman and his advisers and the realistic policy choices they faced.[100]

In winning support for justly celebrated measures such as the Marshall Plan, Truman and his advisers were in fact operating as latter-day framers, for they were on the road to an amendment-like constitutional change of historic proportions.[101] What finally convinced Congress to approve such measures was not so much the scare talk (although this did have important secondary effects) or careful consultation with and persuasion of members of Congress like Vandenberg, or members gradually convincing each other through a deliberative process, but the pressure of events.[102] Fear of war with the Soviet Union, inflamed by its takeover of Czechoslovakia, worked wonders for approval of the Marshall Plan.[103] The legislative process was forced into high gear.[104]

One reasonable conclusion is that Truman faced a constitutional system that was not so much slow and deliberative as inert.[105] The New Deal experience had convinced many that constitutional amendments were impractical as a way to alter the powers of government.[106] The option of signaling constitutional change through amendment was never open to Truman and there is no evidence that it was considered. But it is worth noting that if the option of amendment had existed, there were many reasons for thinking that the structure of government had to be rethought.

The inadequacies of the preexisting constitutional order, including the lack of a realistic amendment option, created the framework in which Truman and his advisers made their decisions. It is true that they already were believers in executive leadership in foreign policy, but Congress did relatively little to suggest it was up to the challenge.[107] The enormous effort required to move the largely static constitutional machinery left by the framers and their nineteenth- and twentieth-century successors was thus partly to blame for the overselling of the Cold War as a global ideological struggle. Among the consequences were the bitterly partisan fight over the "loss" of China, the increasing militarization of the government's effort, and the Red Scare of McCarthyism.[108]

The most important aspect of the post-1945 constitutional order, one with subtle, far-reaching, and long-lasting effects, was the gradual erasure of the difference between wartime and peacetime.[109] Because all foreign wars prior to 1950 had been authorized or approved by Congress through interbranch deliberation, the pre–Pearl Harbor constitutional order featured a sharp distinction between the powers of government in war and peace. As Hogan demonstrates, the beginning of the Cold War featured a massive effort to convince the President, Congress, and the public that this distinction no longer made sense.[110] This new "national security ideology" promoted the concept of "total war" in which all elements of government, society, and the economy would be mobilized to meet the Soviet threat.[111] As Hogan explains, "[i]n total war, the battle was not confined to the front lines but extended to the home front as well."[112] Modern atomic weaponry meant that tremendous destruction could come with little warning. In these new circumstances, "American leaders would no longer have the time to debate the issue of war or peace or to prepare at a slow pace."[113]

Hogan describes a series of budget battles in the latter part of the Truman administration that extended into the early years of the Eisenhower administration.[114] Interestingly, neither Truman nor Eisenhower personally endorsed the concept of total war.[115] Rather, they sought a middle ground between the relentless advocacy of greater military expenditures by the State and Defense Departments and those worried that excessive spending on arms would lead to an economic nightmare and the kind of oppressive government control identified with the "garrison state."[116]

Disagreements over foreign policy in the executive branch were mirrored in Congress. While some advocated restraining the military buildup, others vigorously endorsed the new national security ideology.[117] During a debate over universal military service, Representative Carl Vinson argued that "[w]e cannot have business as usual' . . . when the 'free world' was 'watching mighty America today and wondering if she has the determination to meet the challenge of the times."[118] Even opponents of greater defense spending such as Senate Republican Robert Taft conceded that there was "'a new status' that was neither 'all-out war' nor 'a state of peace' . . . [but rather] 'a special state of semiwar.'"[119] According to Hogan, Taft meant to denote "a period of prolonged struggle and constant preparedness in which the usual distinction between war and peace had disappeared."[120] During the debate to approve the NATO treaty, liberal stalwart Senator Hubert Humphrey argued that clear distinctions between war and peace, as well as declarations of war, were a thing of the past.[121] The U.S., claimed Humphrey, had entered a period of permanent or total war.[122] Liberals and Democrats such as Humphrey and Senator Lyndon Johnson were among the most ardent proponents of the new national security ideology.[123]

Despite the budgetary and administrative restraints imposed by Truman and Eisenhower, Senator Taft was ultimately correct. The history of the American state had entered a new phase. The state was now responsible for maintaining a permanent war-fighting capacity and a global military and intelligence establishment. This development was driven by a new ideology that had few precedents in prior historical experience. As Hogan concludes:

> Many American policy makers, particularly in the State and Defense departments, found the principal threat in Soviet aggression or Communist expansion. To their way of thinking, which was guided by the new ideology of national security, the United States had entered an era of semiwar against a totalitarian enemy who was hostile to any government not under its control. And because liberty was indivisible, at least to these officials, the United States had no choice but to contain communism everywhere through a global system of collective security, ambitious foreign aid programs, and a large military establishment. Containment also required a new vigilance against internal subversion, the permanent mobilization of essential resources, and a new spirit of discipline and sacrifice as war and rearmament necessarily took precedence over social investment, lower taxes, and a balanced budget.[124]

Three further points should be highlighted concerning the post-1945 or Cold War constitutional order. First, the new constitutional order, sometimes subsequently called the "national security state," was as much a product of the failure of the pre–Pearl Harbor order as it was the result of programmatic lobbying by those who favored a militarized version of containment. As precedent-shattering as the new order was, its adoption was bound up with well-founded judgments about the inadequacies of the pre–Pearl Harbor order. Second, the expanded power of the presidency had little to do with any desire on the part of Truman or Eisenhower to arrogate power in a personal sense. Rather, it was a logical consequence of a fundamentally new approach to foreign policy. One led to the other, which further implied that if the Constitution had been harmed, the damage could not be undone without undermining the global role of the United States. Third, the effort to found the post-1945 constitutional order demonstrates the validity of the theory presented in Chapter 1 that there is a reciprocal relationship between the perceived meaning of the Constitution and the structure of the state.

It is difficult not to have sympathy for those who judged the pre–Pearl Harbor order deficient. Despite FDR's enormous efforts over a three-year period, all Americans were willing to do by fall 1941 is contribute material aid and perhaps air and naval support to Britain.[125] As we have seen, the situation actually required U.S. ground forces.[126] Failure to make this commitment could have led to years of Nazi domination in Europe, with incalculable consequences for its subject peoples as well as for U.S. national security.[127] The obduracy of the U.S. political system showed the dangers of isolationism and congressional blunders in the making of foreign policy. The disaster of Pearl Harbor convinced many that a more substantial military and intelligence establishment was required. Yet all of these critical policy issues were inextricably connected to a constitutional order that gave Congress considerable influence over foreign policy without subjecting its members to any reasonable accountability. There was no ready solution for this problem without changing the Constitution.[128]

Hence the felt postwar need for constitutional change. In some fashion, the government had to be reenergized and reorganized so that the challenge posed by Germany and Japan could never happen again. Congress was plausibly the problem, not the solution, as it showed little inclination to implement the kind of organization and leadership implied by the new global role of the U.S. If there were constitutional doubts, those would have to be set aside or dealt with using a lot of scary talk about an overwhelming ideological threat.

Despite the activism of the Truman administration after 1946, the story of the beginning of the Cold War is not well described in terms of a bid for power by an ambitious imperial president. There is little doubt that Truman and Acheson thought the president should be at the forefront of U.S. foreign policy. But there was also no doubt that they could not rule alone in order to restore the postwar world. The Constitution required them to work with Congress; although in a paradoxical way, their efforts to move an often inert Congress created pathologies, such as an overly ideological stance, that were to haunt U.S. foreign policy for decades. The principal difficulty with using the concept of the "imperial presidency" to understand the Cold War is that it ignores the independent role of events and public opinion in supporting the rationale for presidential leadership.

When Truman seized the opportunity provided by the invasion of South Korea to create a new constitutional power—the president's power to initiate a foreign war—it illustrated with startling clarity the reciprocal relationships between the different elements of a constitutional order. The Constitution gave gatekeeping authority over war to

Congress in the "declare war" clause. As we have seen, every principal player in the drama that led to Pearl Harbor acknowledged this authority. Truman's decision was a departure from the Constitution and the American constitutional tradition. Members of Congress and commentators have puzzled for decades over how Truman was able to create a novel power that later presidents would claim as a "precedent."[129] It is easier to find the answer once we focus on the reciprocal relationship between the text and policy considerations conditioned by the institutions responsible for implementing them.

The Korea Decision: Creating the Presidential Power to Initiate War

Under the leadership of Kim Il Sung, North Korea invaded South Korea on June 25, 1950 (June 24 in the U.S.).[130] This followed a tense and conflictual period after the end of World War II in which Korea had been divided by the occupying forces of the U.S. in the south and the Soviet Union in the north. South Korea was under the temporary supervision of a U.N. Commission.[131] In less than a week Truman made a series of momentous decisions, although he had time for deliberation and the input of his major advisers, especially Secretary of State Acheson.[132] The decisions involved a set of escalating responses to what was seen as aggression by North Korea backed by the Soviet Union, eventually resulting in Truman's June 30 commitment of U.S. ground forces stationed in Japan.[133] The responses were accompanied from the beginning by the support of the U.N. Security Council, made easier by the happenstance that the Soviet Union was boycotting its meetings.[134]

Previous scholarship on the constitutional propriety of Truman's decision, particularly by historians, has sometimes fallen into confusion, principally arising from the role of the U.N. and the argument, made subsequently by the administration, that Truman acted under its aegis.[135] Given the U.N.'s responsibility for South Korea, Truman certainly acted in part to preserve its credible role in world affairs.[136] Others have seen the sequence of events as important because Truman committed U.S. military forces to action prior to the request by the Security Council for member states to come to the aid of South Korea.[137] Too much, however, can be made of the role of the U.N. in Truman's decision given the strong likelihood that he would have acted in accordance with the general U.S.

strategy to oppose the Soviet Union regardless of what the U.N. decided. As for the legal issues surrounding action by the U.N., they are complex and therefore are discussed separately in the next section.

Commentators have also divided over the significance of Truman's limited consultation with congressional leaders.[138] Truman spoke to various members of Congress during and after the crucial period of decision. With respect to the constitutional requirement of obtaining authorization from Congress, some members such as Senator Tom Connally told Truman what he wanted to hear—that he had the authority as president to intervene.[139] Other members of the opposition Republican Party such as Senator Robert Taft and Minority Leader Kenneth Wherry sounded the constitutional alert.[140] Taft and Wherry, however, were perceived by many, including Truman and Acheson, as among the most partisan members of Congress.[141] Their objections were probably discounted on this ground.[142] In the end, Truman made a report to Congress in late July but did not ask for congressional authorization.

If Truman's decision had occurred within the sphere of the legalized Constitution, we would be in the imaginary world described at the beginning of Chapter 1. Truman and his advisers would have had to reckon with how different policy options fit within the channels cut by Supreme Court precedent. Of course, Truman had no such worry. As we shall see, given that Truman was not operating in the sphere of the legalized Constitution, he could, so to speak, create his own constitutional reality. His decision to intervene would be claimed and regarded as a "precedent," almost from the moment it occurred, despite its arguable incompatibility with the text of the Constitution.[143]

Although Truman was not limited by prior judicial decisions, he was also not empowered by the judiciary. Instead, his new power was enabled by the institutional capacities the executive branch had been given as a consequence of victory in World War II. Thus, Truman's situation differed in crucial respects from that of FDR in the years leading to Pearl Harbor. Having conquered Japan and employed it as a base for troops, military supplies, and the Seventh Fleet, the U.S. had the ability to intervene quickly (although without the immediate ability to prevail) in Korea.[144] These two factors—the existence of new state capacities and the absence of legalization—were crucial to what followed.

Without any judicial doctrine to frame and highlight the relevant constitutional issues, Truman and his advisers were left to grapple with a Cold War emergency in a novel context.[145] At a conceptual level, they found it difficult to regard the Korean intervention as a "war," even after the military situation clarified in late July.[146] By June 1950, they had been anticipating the possibility of World War III with the Soviet Union for more than four years.[147] That war was expected to involve a direct confrontation with Soviet forces and require the use of every resource in the U.S. arsenal, including nuclear weapons.[148] The sudden appearance of what would later be called "limited war" caught the Truman administration (and everyone else) genuinely off guard.[149] Nonetheless, U.S. grand strategy meant that "the commitment of US ground forces, readily available in occupied Japan, was virtually automatic," once it had been made clear that the survival of South Korea was at stake and the Soviet Union was not attacking elsewhere.[150] Relative to the sort of all-out war that he expected to fight against the Soviet Union and in light of his commitment to the U.N., Truman was sincere in accepting a reporter's nonetheless misguided description of Korea as a "police action."[151]

Unfortunately for Truman, this characterization did not successfully address the constitutional issue of whether the U.S. was engaging in a war without congressional authorization accompanied by meaningful interbranch deliberation. Even in the sphere of the nonlegalized Constitution, the document is still supreme law. It is an available text providing a normative frame of reference against which shifting political events can be evaluated.[152] Outsiders to the executive branch, including members of Congress, understandably saw the major troop movements, subsequent casualties, and open-ended commitment to South Korea in a different light.[153] As discussed in Chapter 1, the Constitution established "war" as a meaningful category of constitutional power and government action. Once the scale of the conflict became evident, no one in the Truman administration denied the U.S. was fighting a war in Korea.[154]

Constitutional scholars have not fully taken into consideration the substantial evidence that Truman's sudden departure from the status quo was deliberate—that he wanted to lay down a marker and establish a "precedent" for the exercise of presidential war powers in the new circumstances of the Cold War.[155] Not asking for a congressional resolution was ultimately Truman's decision.[156] Biographer Alonzo Hamby writes that the decision "was fully consistent with all of Truman's instincts and reflected the broad view of executive power he had developed from the time Andrew Jackson had been his boyhood hero."[157] Truman was implementing the strategy of containment by creating a new power for himself and for future presidents with respect to the use of military force. Truman was certainly relying on his constitutional status as commander in chief, as illustrated by the argument in the State Department memorandum, which I discuss below, that Acheson had prepared to justify the decision.[158] But Truman could not have been successful were it not for the new institutional capacities the executive branch had acquired in World War II. At stake, therefore, was whether he would be successful in creating a new constitutional power.

Congressionalist analyses go astray in condemning Truman's action as a pure usurpation of Congress's power without taking into consideration that he was not operating in the sphere of the legalized Constitution. To be sure, by the standards of conventional legal argument the Korean War was probably unconstitutional because it was not authorized by Congress.[159] But because the war powers of the legislative and executive branches had never been legalized by the judiciary, Truman was able to order U.S. military forces to intervene without producing a permission slip from the legislative branch.

Truman's action was consistent with the post-1945 constitutional order and had consequences that illustrated the inherent conflict between that order and the original constitutional design. Consider what happened after the dust had settled from Truman's initial June decisions. Everyone agrees that he enjoyed unanimous support at first.[160] But subsequent events showed that the missing congressional authorization was not a mere formality. In the pre–Pearl Harbor constitutional order, declarations of war and other authorizations were part of a system that encouraged interbranch deliberation before the decision for war was made. The deviation from an order maintained since the early republic sent shock waves through the constitutional system, illustrating the reciprocal relationships between the elements of the constitutional order.

It first became apparent that in the absence of an authorization based on deliberation, Congress had a *constitutional* excuse it could use to avoid responsibility for the war. The Korean War thus became "Truman's war."[161] Congress assumed the role of bystander or junior partner rather than responsible participant. Because the cycle of accountability never started, Congress was cut off from the political experience that would have flowed from acknowledging shared responsibility with

Truman for the progress of the war. Moreover, because there was no legislative process to encourage deliberation, there was a notable lack of war planning or discussion of war aims in the executive branch.[162] This left the government unprepared for what followed.

For there were *two* presidential decisions for war in Korea. The June 1950 decision to respond to the North Korean invasion by restoring the status quo was the first, as Truman ordered General MacArthur not to go north of the 38th parallel.[163] As weeks and then months went by, Truman's advisers realized that the tremendous buildup of forces in the Korean theater would create the possibility of fighting a different war. This led to a second decision for war in September to cross the parallel in an effort to unite Korea.[164] It was this decision that led to a counter-intervention by China, a military disaster of the first order that transformed the nature of the war.[165] Amid dark days in late 1950, Truman and his advisers believed there was no point in responding with a general war against China and possibly the Soviet Union.[166] By early 1951, they had in effect renewed their initial commitment to restore the status quo on the Korean peninsula, a decision for a "limited war" bitterly contested by General MacArthur. However by this time, the lack of any cycle of accountability or substantial congressional support based on proper deliberation had taken its toll. Because these decisions for war were solely those of the executive branch, the Truman administration had lost credibility amid the changing fortunes of war. The rationale for a limited war was not explained fully by the administration until the congressional hearings that were held in the aftermath of Truman's dismissal of MacArthur for insubordination in April 1951.[167] By then, the public had stopped listening and Truman was on his way to a diminished presidency.[168]

These observations are not offered as a critique of Truman's decisions per se. What the Korea decision demonstrated was the critical role constitutional orders play in implementing the Constitution. Truman was able to alter the pre–Pearl Harbor constitutional order and change the power of the presidency by leveraging the new capacities of the executive branch, acting decisively as the first mover, and, as discussed in the next section, articulating an easy-to-understand rationale that borrowed from the forms of legal argument without quite being tied to them. At the same time, the new post-1945 constitutional order was in considerable tension with the text of the Constitution. Granting the president broad discretion in foreign policy and the resources to match did not change the limitations on the presidential office in the Constitution or somehow increase the president's ability to make fully informed-decisions in the absence of interbranch deliberation.

The sequence of events after the June 1950 decision demonstrates the relevance of the original constitutional order. That most members of Congress and the public *agreed* with Truman, both about the initial intervention and the decision to cross the 38th parallel, did not alter the structure of accountability that flowed from the Constitution. The deeply troubled aftermath of the Korea decision showed the persistent and inimitable tidal influence of the original constitutional order.

The need to support an internationalist foreign policy and greater military preparedness did little to justify undermining not simply the text of the Constitution, but the underlying institutional architecture that implemented it. One of the cruelest ironies of the "Cold War" was that the major wars fought under its aegis provided an overwhelming practical demonstration that the founding generation was correct—there were dramatic differences between states of war and states of peace. The onset of the Korean War meant that thousands of citizens who had served their country in World War II were suddenly recalled to active service.[169] By the end of the war, the number of Koreans killed, wounded, or missing totaled three million, a tenth of the population.[170] Five million had been made refugees.[171] On the U.S. side, of the two million men who served, 36,574 died in battle or from other causes.[172]

Although the Korean War exacted a terrible toll, balancing the scales is not easy. The decision to intervene was expressive of the post-1945 order and had very broad public support. In this sense, the post-1945 order had a democratic foundation. With the advantage of decades of hindsight, we can also agree with those scholars who have argued that the war was justified on balance as a matter of policy. It was instrumental in creating the democratic and prosperous Republic of Korea, a state and society that are surely better off than they would have been under the rule of Kim Il Sung.[173] If these were the only consequences of the war, commemorated today in the Korean War Veterans Memorial in Washington, we could say the efforts of the U.S. and U.N. armed forces on Korea's behalf had been repaid in full.

Yet the constitutional damage was real. Truman set the precedent he wanted and it was a very bad one. He created a new constitutional power that future presidents would wield poorly. And Truman did not use his new power wisely. While domestic political pressure played a role, it was his decision to risk intervention by China. That was one of the worst mistakes of the entire Cold War, yet in the end it was put down solely to Truman's account. For by removing Congress from the process, he created a negative spiral of irresponsibility rather than a cycle of accountability. Congress and the American people were off the political hook. They were spectators at the presidential show rather than participants. The stage was set for future policy disasters.

The Power to Initiate War: Continuity or Change?

As mentioned earlier, Secretary of State Acheson had his department publish a legal memorandum justifying Truman's Korea decision.[174] This 1950 State Department memo is the most important official source of the broad view of presidential war powers based on an appeal to historical practice.[175] It also featured what I will call the "U.N. theory," the idea that the U.N. Charter provided an independent legal basis for Truman's decision. These arguments, especially the argument from practice, have had a long life in the executive branch.

The thrust of the memo was that prior instances of presidents ordering the military to use force "to protect specific American lives and property" and "in the broad interests of American foreign policy" provided support for the Korea decision.[176] So the State Department did not see Truman as committing the nation to war, but rather advancing the foreign policy of the United States through the selective use of armed force. In addition, these prior instances were framed within the adoption of the U.N. Charter, which the memo described as "a landmark in the development of American foreign policy" and the creation of a new international legal order.[177] The memo pursued the argument that Truman's action was justified under the Charter in order to ensure the continued existence of the United Nations.[178] This was followed by a list of eighty-five occasions in which the president had used U.S. armed forces without authorization from Congress for a variety of purposes related to foreign affairs and the protection of American citizens.[179]

Assessing the memo is a complex task because there are two versions of both arguments, which we can refer to as the "legal" and the "historical." The "legal" argument from practice and the creation of the

U.N. involves using certain legal materials and showing how they are supportive of presidential power within a common law framework. The "historical" versions are arguments about the political and cultural meanings of certain past events. To make any progress with the arguments from practice and the U.N. theory, we must carefully distinguish these two different methods of argument.

On the legal side, the argument from practice has long been one of the most disreputable arguments ever made within separation of powers jurisprudence.[180] Both in 1950 and later, proponents assembled long lists of interventions, but never developed criteria that would explain why certain incidents counted and others did not. This raised the credible suspicion that a double standard was being employed—when presidents ordered the use of force without authorization from Congress, the incident would make the list, but when Congress prevented such action, affirmatively indicated its disapproval, or failed to acquiesce, the incident was not counted.[181] A "triple" standard also arguably existed with respect to not counting incidents when presidents *agreed* that Congress had the exclusive power to decide for war.[182]

These difficulties with the arguments made by presidentialists created a confusing terrain for the war powers debate that began in the wake of Vietnam. Congressionalists criticized the "lists of wars" offered by presidentialists on the ground that no one believed the U.S. has gone to war 85, 125, or 153 times in its history.[183] If the point of such lists was to provide pre-1950 analogues to Korea in the common law style, most would agree that the number of presidentially initiated wars was relatively small. On the other hand, many presidentialists probably were not making an argument from analogy. Their favored arena was the making of U.S. foreign policy, with military action being one tool among others.[184] They contended that each presidentially authorized military action had been taken in the course of pursuing the nation's foreign policy objectives, in which presidents had exercised leadership while also sharing authority with Congress from the early republic onward.[185] So we can understand them as making a "historical" argument from practice, rather than a strictly legal one.

Here as well, however, trouble loomed because presidentialists were typically not concerned with all of American history, just the parts that were favorable to their case. There were three enormous historical roadblocks in the way of acknowledging a consistent presidential practice capable of justifying Korea—World War I, World War II, and the debate over ratification of the U.N. Charter. Neither presidentialists nor later historians of U.S. military involvements abroad were much interested in the political and cultural meaning of declarations of war. But as the earlier discussion of FDR's prewar diplomacy showed, the reality that Congress was the gatekeeper of the decision for war was widely accepted.

Historical investigation shows that prior to the State Department's work on the U.N. Charter during World War II, no official claimed that past interventions provided the basis for a broad presidential war power. The history of both world wars poses severe difficulties for presidentialists, no matter how they base their argument. Woodrow Wilson and Franklin Roosevelt did not make policy as if they already had the constitutional power, acquired through prior practice, to involve the U.S. in war. As we have already seen, FDR's statements and actions were to the contrary. These world wars, among the most significant conflicts in the history of the U.S., cast considerable doubt on whether prior uses of the commander in chief power created legal precedents or an accepted historical practice in favor of a unilateral presidential power to initiate war.[186] In fact, it turns out that the very idea of a "practice" of unilateral presidential military interventions was a tradition invented for the Cold War.

An important test of the argument from practice, whether made on legal or historical grounds, occurred when President Wilson and Congress grappled with the questions raised by the Treaty of Versailles ending World War I. During his personal participation in the Paris Peace Conference, Wilson drafted Article X of the proposed treaty as part of his effort to establish the League of Nations.[187] The article "guaranteed the political independence and territorial integrity of League members against external aggression, and it required members to take action, even to the extent of using military force, against violators of this guarantee."[188] During the conference, the French delegation proposed that the League have an independent enforcement arm, an international military force with the ability to intervene anywhere in the world.[189] Wilson objected that assigning U.S. troops to such a force was incompatible with the Constitution, specifically, the control Congress had over whether the U.S. engaged in war.[190]

Once he returned home, Wilson had to defend the treaty and Article X became a chief focus in the fight to get the treaty ratified by the Senate. One argument used by treaty opponents was that Article X undermined Congress's authority to decide when the U.S. went to war. Wilson responded that "the president would have to seek legislative authority in order to furnish 'the necessary means of action,' and he scoffed at the notion that Congress's constitutional power to declare war might be impaired in this process."[191] When the treaty was presented to the Senate, Republican Henry Cabot Lodge, Chair of the Foreign Relations Committee, ensured a reservation was attached to Article X which stated Congress "has the sole power to declare war or authorize the employment of military and naval forces of the United States."[192] At least in principle, Wilson did not disagree with this point. He thought it was important to say that Article X left Congress's "war-making power unimpaired."[193] However, the treaty was defeated in the Senate partly because of the controversy over Article X and the worry that the role of Congress in authorizing war would be usurped.[194]

Because of the fight over the treaty, prominent leaders felt they had to take a position on the meaning of the Constitution. Charles Evans Hughes, the Republican nominee for president in 1916 and a former (and future) Supreme Court justice, held that Congress had "exclusive authority to declare war."[195] James Cox, the presidential candidate of Wilson's Democratic Party in 1920, asserted "Congress and Congress alone has the right to declare war."[196]

I do not mean to suggest that no one believed that the president had some authority either to defend the territory of the U.S. (in the manner of repelling sudden attacks) or to protect American lives or property abroad without explicit authority from Congress. As we shall see in the case of the Latin American interventions of the early twentieth century, the opposite was the case. But there were many dogs that did not bark in the treaty debate. If there were preexisting precedents, analogous to the status of well-settled judicial precedents, for the president to commit significant U.S. forces to military interventions abroad without authorization by Congress, no one noticed. Article X could have been defended by Wilson on the ground that it contemplated purely defensive actions against international aggression and that the president already had such authority founded on legal precedent or historical practice. Both Wilson and Lodge, his chief congressional opponent, made no sign that they were even aware of this possibility.

What the treaty debate showed was that interventions prior to World War I did not have the status of legal precedents. We should distinguish between the significance attributed to such episodes after 1950 and what presidents and congressional leaders thought at the time. Presidents such as Wilson did not in fact claim such episodes as precedent for the kind of unilateral authority asserted by presidents after 1950. As a somewhat more conservative alternative, such interventions could have been regarded as part of a practice of unilateral presidential actions commanding troops to solve problems in foreign affairs. If so, however, the practice did not add up to what the State Department claimed in 1950—the authority to send large forces to other countries to meet the challenge of foreign aggression. If such had been the case, Wilson would have had a far more secure basis for arguing that the treaty was not a departure from the text of the Constitution or its unwritten traditions.

As we have seen, President Roosevelt's statements prior to World War II showed no sign that he believed he had the authority based on prior practice to simply order U.S. armed forces to war. The deliberation over the U.N. Charter is also instructive in this regard. The reason the State Department began to assemble lists of past presidential foreign interventions in the first place was to justify U.S. participation in the sort of international military force originally proposed to Wilson by the French. Once the Charter was ratified by the Senate, the idea was that the president would be solely responsible for deciding when to use U.S. forces—but for *peacekeeping* missions only.[197] Although the State Department's internal deliberations led it away from a true international police force, Secretary of State Hull still worried about the sort of objections that had proved effective against the League of Nations and sought ways to reassure the senators involved in the process that the congressional power to declare war remained unimpaired.[198]

These internal arguments were publicized as World War II ended by James Grafton Rogers, a former assistant secretary of state in the Hoover administration and distinguished member of the Colorado bar. He published a substantial pamphlet addressing the question of whether the U.S. could constitutionally participate in an international police force to provide collective security.[199] Rogers assumed the United Nations would be formed, with an enforcement arm designed to keep the peace (not to fight wars).[200] He sounded some key themes that would be elaborated later by both the executive branch and scholars defending a broad view of presidential war power.[201]

Rogers maintained that the text of the Constitution was unhelpful in discovering what powers the executive and legislative branches had with respect to foreign affairs.[202] His fundamental appeal was to historical practice.[203] Experience showed that declaring war was a relatively unimportant step in a world in which the president had to lead in foreign affairs.[204] He assembled a list of 149 historical instances in which the U.S. had used armed force abroad (although the list included some declared wars).[205] Of these, he claimed at least 100 occurred solely on the basis of executive order without authorization from Congress.[206]

When the Senate debated ratification of the Charter, concern over Congress's role in war making did not slacken. According to Jane Stromseth's comprehensive analysis, the congressional debate showed a distinct concern for the "preservation of Congress's exclusive authority to declare war."[207] While Congress recognized that U.S. troops might be used under agreements to be made later for limited "police actions," this in no way was viewed as the practical end of Congress's power to decide when the nation would engage in a major military conflict.[208] Further, it was assumed that any troops provided to an international force would be subject to approval by Congress.[209]

This record is inconsistent with the notion that there was a well-understood set of precedents or a general practice prior to 1950 supporting the unilateral commitment by the president of troops to fight in an overseas conflict.[210] If there had been such an understanding, it would have posed a considerable problem for advocates of the Charter, as opponents kept insisting that it had the practical effect of delegating Congress's war power to the president.[211] As Stromseth shows, both the legislative and executive branches assumed that Congress's sole authority to initiate war was alive and well.[212] This should not be surprising, given that the U.S. had just been victorious in the greatest military conflict in world history, a conflict authorized by Congress from the beginning.

During the Vietnam-era debates, the State Department repeated its 1950 claim that "practice and precedent have confirmed the constitutional authority [of the President] to engage United States forces in hostilities without a declaration of war."[213] This contention makes little sense when placed within the context of U.S. diplomatic history during both world wars. The record of the agonizing political and diplomatic maneuvering by President Wilson prior to involvement in World War I and President Roosevelt prior to World War II is inexplicable under the assumption that they already had, as a consequence of past precedent or practice, the power to commit U.S. forces to aid our European allies.[214] The political terrain would have been entirely different had members of Congress acknowledged this authority and deferred to presidential leadership. In other words, it would have been similar to the circumstances prevailing *after* the beginning of the Cold War and Korea, not before.

The record presidents themselves compiled in both world wars should show the danger of assuming that past incidents of presidential use of force automatically count as "precedents" or amount to well-understood historical practice. But some scholars point to President Theodore Roosevelt's vigorous assertion of presidential leadership in foreign affairs and the accumulated weight of presidential interventions in Latin America and East Asia during the age of empire in the nineteenth and early twentieth centuries.[215] During the initial phase of the war powers debate, for example, the respected constitutional scholar Henry Monaghan thought that the interventions in Latin America, which ran from roughly 1900 to 1920, were of a different order compared to minor altercations with pirates.[216] There is indeed something impressive about the list of U.S. military interventions which started with the Spanish-American and Philippine War (promoted and authorized by Congress at every stage) and continued through the turn of the century with the Boxer Rebellion in China and involvement in the Dominican Republic, Cuba, Panama, Honduras, Nicaragua, Haiti, and Mexico.[217] In the case of the Boxer Rebellion, President McKinley sent a substantial force of 6,300 troops as part of an eight-nation intervention into the interior of China to rescue besieged foreign legations in Beijing.[218]

These interventions were taken as part of a new mode of American involvement with the world, commonly referred to as imperialism and in service of frankly racist ideas of white supremacy expressed in the notion of the "white man's burden."[219] The point could be made that no one looks back on this era with pride, but the more relevant issue here is that these interventions were inextricably bound up with the pursuit of specific U.S. foreign policies consistent with these ideals. The intervention in China was a classic example of the kind of imperial adventure by the great powers that was incompatible with the anticolonial stance taken by FDR during World War II and also later repudiated with the adoption of the U.N. Charter.[220] The interventions in Latin America were underwritten by the "Roosevelt Corollary" to the Monroe Doctrine announced in 1904 by Secretary of State Elihu Root.[221] Under the corollary, the U.S. could intervene in Latin America to forestall European efforts to force Latin governments to pay bad debts.[222] These interventions resulted in years of poor relations between the U.S. and Latin America. The corollary was eventually repudiated by President Hoover's administration and later in the "Good Neighbor" policy adopted by President Roosevelt.[223] Under FDR, the occupations of countries in Latin America were terminated and the U.S. disavowed the right of military intervention.[224]

On the legal side, it would be bizarre for any president today to regard the interventions in China and Latin America as anything but negative precedents to be avoided. If we take the arguments based on the U.N. Charter seriously, there is no room in the legal order it created for treating other countries as imperial colonies.[225] If, however, we turn from arguments based on precedent and analogy and rely on historical understandings, matters do not improve. We could not take on the historical orientation of presidents such as McKinley to support military interventions without also taking on the racist orientation which was essential to their justification. Of course, no president today would do this. Furthermore, we would face the unavoidable roadblock of the repudiation of such policies by FDR. It would appear difficult to base a *contemporary* argument for presidential intervention on obsolete foreign policies that later presidents officially repudiated.

Finally, officials and commentators of the time did not treat interventions abroad as evidence that the president had the unilateral power to start a war. They justified the interventions on other grounds. Former president William Howard Taft, in his famous lectures collected in *Our Chief Magistrate and His Powers,* stated that many of the interventions, particularly in Latin America, did not count as acts of war, having more of a "police" character because they were undertaken to protect American lives and property.[226] The issue that concerned Taft and other commentators was that, as a practical matter, the president might have the initiative in involving the United States in war with Congress having no option but to go along.[227] Although their concerns in this respect were probably overstated, this was the context of Edward Corwin's discussion of the war power referred to in Chapter 1. But none of these arguments involved the assertion that the president had the power under Article II to start a war *regardless* of what Congress might say. This was the claim made by Truman and his successors.

During the debates that led to the 1973 War Powers Resolution, Senator John Stennis, a conservative Democrat and chair of the Armed Services Committee, spoke for many of those who had lived through World War II and the postwar period in describing what might be termed the cultural meaning of the "declare war" clause:

> The fact of the matter is that the decision to make war is too big a decision for one mind to make and too awesome a responsibility for one man to bear. There must be a collective judgment given and a collective responsibility shared. That is exactly the tone, the letter, and the spirit of the Constitution of the United States.[228]

It is hard to avoid the conclusion that the very idea of an officially endorsed list of legal "precedents" in favor of a unilateral presidential power to initiate war was an artifact of the Cold War itself.[229] The arguments made by the State Department in 1950 were novel and not anticipated by anything in the prior record of executive or legislative action. There is little doubt that past presidents sometimes involved the U.S. in military actions unauthorized by Congress. But their actions were justified in terms of rescuing citizens and protecting property, dealing with the exigencies of the moment and avoiding a greater conflict, rather than against the background of a well-settled understanding that they and their executive successors had the authority to involve the U.S. in a *war* without the consent of Congress. Such a precedent or historical practice did not exist prior to 1950.[230]

The U.N. Theory

In Under Secretary of State Katzenbach's 1967 testimony discussed in Chapter 1, he revived the claim of the 1950 State Department memo that the U.N. Charter had made a fundamental difference to how wars were fought. In Katzenbach's telling, prior to the adoption of the U.N. Charter, declarations of war were used to announce military adventures of aggression and conquest.[231] Presumably this was the meaning such acts had when the Constitution was adopted.[232] With the acceptance of the Charter came the abolition of war as a matter of international law and so declarations of war became obsolete.[233] Katzenbach implied strongly that the "declare war" clause was therefore outdated.[234] But the assembled senators, many of whom, like Senator Stennis, had served in Congress in the late 1940s, had never heard of the idea that acceptance of the Charter implied the irrelevance of declarations of war.[235] Senator Fulbright responded that regardless of developments in international law, the "declare war" clause still had a critical domestic significance.[236] The senatorial reaction suggested the U.N. theory had never made it beyond the confines of the State Department.

A review of presidential decisions regarding major wars after 1945 shows no indication that the U.N. theory was generally accepted by the executive branch.[237] It would have been difficult for the executive branch to adhere to this theory consistently because many of the major conflicts of the period, including Vietnam, were fought outside the U.N. system.[238] But the U.N. theory was revived after the end of the Cold War by some academics enthusiastic about the potential of the Charter in new circumstances.[239]

In fact, the Cold War showed why the potential of the Charter will always be around the corner. As noted earlier, consider that the role of the U.N. in the early Cold War was subordinate to the overall strategy of containment, that is, subordinate to U.S. interests. During the Truman administration, the U.S. maintained its support for the U.N. but did not base its foreign policy on the U.N. Charter's system of collective security.[240] Acheson, the acknowledged leader of U.S. foreign policy during this period, attached little importance to the U.N.[241] He favored traditional great power alliances and appreciated that the U.N. only had relevance to the extent that the great powers cooperated.[242] Basic decisions that structured the Cold War such as the announcement of the Truman Doctrine, aid to Greece and Turkey, and the Marshall Plan were made without consulting the U.N. or proceeding through the institutions created by the Charter.[243] This was not so much because the Soviet Union kept exercising its veto in the Security Council as it was that the basic principles of Soviet and U.S. foreign policy, at least in terms of national security and defense policy, were inconsistent with the idea of collective security at the foundation of the Charter.[244]

Put simply, no president was ever willing to give up the sovereignty required to make the U.N. system work. Carried to its logical conclusion, the U.N. theory means that a decision for the use of armed force by the president is legitimate under international law and the Constitution if it is endorsed by the Security Council. Advocates of international law as well as members of Congress were properly impressed, for example, in 1990 after President George H. W. Bush won the approval of the Security Council for military action against Iraq for invading Kuwait.[245] While this diplomatic success played a role in persuading members of Congress to approve a resolution authorizing the Gulf War, it did not imply the executive branch's agreement that this was the only legitimate way to go to war. To the contrary, as we saw in Chapter 1, the Bush administration believed from the beginning that the president had the authority to order the use of military force under the Constitution, no matter what Congress or the U.N. did.[246] Moreover, acceptance of the U.N. theory would mean that any subsequent war *lacking* Security Council approval would be not only contrary to international law, but an unconstitutional abuse of power as well. Understandably, no one in the executive branch has ever advocated such a theory. By proceeding with the 2003 Iraq War without the approval of the Security Council, President George W. Bush showed that the government does not adhere to the U.N. theory.[247]

Beyond this, it should be pointed out that the U.N. theory made the argument of the 1950 memo inconsistent. There was an inherent tension between relying on the Charter and the argument from the list of eighty-five past "precedents" of presidential military action. Truman's lawyers never made clear how they could *simultaneously* base a power to intervene on the U.N. Charter and the requirements of international law and also on incidents occurring *prior* to the ratification of the Charter that were in considerable tension with those same requirements.[248]

Finally, we should pause to notice the effect of the U.N. theory on the argument John Yoo and other presidentialist scholars have made, described in Chapter 1, that the chief purpose of the "declare war" clause was to signal U.S. intentions under international law. Katzenbach's argument that the Charter had, as a matter of international law, abolished war and substituted the justified use of armed force did have merit. But the combination of these positions had an amazing effect that Katzenbach only hinted at in his 1967 testimony—that the "declare war" clause was a nullity, an obsolete provision of the Constitution. This position was properly rejected by Congress in the Vietnam-era debates and the executive branch never raised it again.

This discussion completes the consideration of the standard war powers debate begun in Chapter 1. There is no version of the arguments from precedent or historical practice that can underwrite the claim of post-1945 presidents that they have the authority to initiate a foreign military conflict. Because Truman's claim was truly new and unprecedented in constitutional history, the Korea decision was a constitutional change outside the accepted legal means of amendment and judicial interpretation. This demonstrates that the 1950 thesis advanced in Chapter 1 is correct. At the same time, we should remind ourselves that Truman's actions in Korea were genuinely in service of U.S. foreign policy objectives. The expansion of presidential power that resulted is best understood as a byproduct of these objectives rather than in terms of the advancement of the "imperial presidency." To develop this point, we need to explore the context of Truman's presidency a bit further.

Truman and the "Imperial Presidency"

Although the Korea decision was a key moment in the formation of the post-1945 constitutional order, it would be deeply misleading to understand the Truman administration as an "imperial presidency." Truman believed in a strong presidency on principle, but the idea that he was master of Washington, let alone the executive branch, after he won election in his own right in 1948 would have struck many contemporary observers as a cruel joke. To imagine Truman as imperial, we would have to ignore the unremitting assaults on the administration by members of Congress, overlook the significance of McCarthyism, and fail to consider a rising tide of congressional activism on foreign affairs that extended well into the Eisenhower administration.[249]

The story of opposition to the Truman administration's foreign policies after 1948 is familiar to historians, but apart from some singular episodes, such as the "Great Debate" in Congress over sending U.S. troops to Europe in 1950–1951, it has not figured prominently in the literature on presidential power. The intensity of the period is difficult to recapture and comprehend today. Charges of treason, incompetence, and conspiracy, often directed at high executive branch officials, flowed unceasingly from irresponsible members of Congress.[250] Robert Beisner, Acheson's most recent biographer, states accurately that the administration's opponents "unleashed the most vicious campaign of abuse and slander against political leaders in American history."[251] Partly due to frustration at their failure to defeat Truman in 1948, Republicans took every opportunity to excoriate the administration on issues involving nuclear weapons, communist influence in government, failure to prevail in Korea, the "loss" of China, and the necessity of placing "Asia first" over Europe.[252]

Truman became more vulnerable to the partisan critique after the crises of China's intervention in the Korean War and the dismissal of General MacArthur. From 1951 onward, Truman was an unpopular president leading the nation in a deeply unpopular war, which had a destabilizing influence on domestic politics the longer it continued.[253] As we have seen, Republicans agreed with Truman on the wisdom of the Korean intervention and the later decision to completely defeat the North Koreans and unify the peninsula. But the original constitutional order and its mandate of interbranch deliberation turned out to be relevant nonetheless. Not for the last time, the post-1945 order's promise of granting great discretion to presidents with respect to the use of armed force turned out to be contrary to the president's long-term interests. It mattered politically that Truman had not locked Republicans into approval of his Korea policy by having them go on record in a war authorization. Republicans were free to criticize the Korea commitment from all angles and use the war and MacArthur's dismissal to put the administration on the defensive.[254] As with the later presidencies of Lyndon Johnson and George W. Bush, Truman lost much of his practical authority to govern because of a foreign war.

Congressional investigations and aggressive criticism had serious effects on the ability of the executive branch to carry out American diplomacy.[255] The State Department's expertise in China and Asia was gutted by brutally unfair charges directed at foreign service officers who had served in China during World War II. As a consequence, the Department's civil servants became cautious and unhelpful.[256] They could not serve as an appropriate balance to the militarization of the Cold War being pushed by other parts of the government. With respect to the future war in Vietnam, it cannot have helped that the State Department purges encouraged "a hard-line, Manichaean view of East Asia that bore little relation to what was happening there."[257]

We could use the term "imperial Congress" to describe these episodes, but it should be apparent that adding the word "imperial" does little to promote an understanding of what was at issue in the relationship between the branches. Both branches and parties were under serious stress as they worked through the implications of the post-1945 constitutional order in an atmosphere of constant crisis. We should keep this context in mind when considering the last famous "imperial" episode of the Truman administration, *Youngstown Sheet & Tube Co. v. Sawyer,* otherwise known as the *Steel Seizure* case.[258] In the legal community, *Steel Seizure* is famous both for the fact that Truman lost a major case in which presidential power was at issue and Justice Robert Jackson's concurrence, which provided the inestimable benefit of guidance in a murky area of the law.[259] Harold Koh, former dean of the Yale Law School and legal adviser to the Department of State in the Obama administration, has claimed that Jackson's concurrence was the foundation of a "National Security Constitution" whose influence persists today.[260] Whatever the validity of Koh's claim, we will see the relevance of Jackson's concurrence throughout this book.

No one thinks Truman and the Justice Department handled the case particularly well.[261] It began with a labor dispute in the steel industry that threatened a lengthy and costly strike as the Korean War was mired in stalemate in 1952, a presidential election year.[262] Truman refused to use statutory authority available to him for dealing with the strike and went to the extreme of seizing the steel mills by invoking his constitutional powers under Article II. In defending Truman's action, the DOJ advanced maximalist interpretations of executive authority that struck everyone as implausible.[263] In light of the troubles that beset Truman from every side in 1952, his action today looks less like a dictatorial bolt from the blue and more a dubious opportunity for a lame duck president at a low ebb to reassert a measure of control over national policy.[264]

Pursuing this line further, we can achieve insight into the post-1945 constitutional order if we attempt to see the seizure from Truman's perspective. Understanding Truman means appreciating the circumstances in which presidents made decisions in the Cold War era.

So imagine you are the president. You are responsible for the successful prosecution of a war occurring thousands of miles from Washington and involving seven U.S. and eleven international divisions against a foreign enemy.[265] Congress has provided you with the funds and economic authority necessary to prosecute the war, but little other help.[266] Your most senior and respected defense advisors inform you that a lengthy strike in the steel industry poses a substantial risk of interfering with the war effort. As an example, U.S. forces are expending one million artillery shells a month beating off persistent enemy attacks.[267] If a strike occurs and your advisors are correct, you know Congress and the public will blame you for the harm to the war effort, even if the war is unpopular.

What would you do? To be sure, Truman could have used existing labor laws to address the situation, but those laws would not have prevented the strike forever.[268] Then again, he could have done nothing, waiting for the strike to occur and taking his chances with Congress once the military supply situation clarified. Truman chose preemptive action, which is why the seizure struck observers as extreme. Once the Supreme Court ruled his action unconstitutional, the strike occurred and histories do not record any harm to the war effort.[269]

Unfortunately, presidents cannot predict any better than anyone else what will happen in the future. What they did know in the Cold War era was that they were responsible for defending the national security of the United States.[270] Secretary of Defense Robert Lovett, one of the most respected "wise men" of the post-1945 era, advised Truman that even a short strike posed a serious risk of harming the war effort. Other important advisers including Acheson said the same.[271] As president, Truman experienced what might be termed the anxiety of responsibility, in which he had to respond to a perceived crisis where the risks were hard to gauge.[272] This was a recurrent situation in the new militarized circumstances of the Cold War. Truman's response to the Supreme Court decision (much like his reaction to the North Korean invasion) was that the president "must always act in a national emergency."[273]

It is worth speculating that Truman might have been influenced by the similarity of the steel crisis to the 1946 railroad strike.[274] Six years prior almost to the month, Truman was faced with an unprecedented nationwide strike by two railroad unions which could have paralyzed the entire economy. When he threatened to put into effect an executive order seizing the railroads, the strike was postponed for a few days.[275] Negotiations broke down and once the strike occurred, the effect on the country was similar to the grounding of all planes after the 9/11 terrorist attacks. Passengers were stranded everywhere. Panic buying broke out and grain shipments to a postwar Europe in severe distress were held up.[276] After receiving evidence of a national emergency, Truman told his

Cabinet that he had decided on the drastic step of drafting railroad workers into the Army. Attorney General Tom Clark objected, but Truman was not interested in hearing about the Constitution.[277] Truman announced that he would call out the Army to break the strike.[278] At the eleventh hour in the middle of an address to Congress proposing legislation to draft the workers, Truman was told the strike was over. By this time, many thoughtful observers had concluded that drafting the workers was unconstitutional and dictatorial. But Congress, the press, and the public showered praise on Truman for his boldness in meeting the crisis.[279]

While commentators have argued that the steel seizure situation was not a genuine emergency, the same could not be said of the railroad strike.[280] Truman might have assumed that taking bold steps under the aegis of his constitutional powers was what the public wanted (although he contemplated legislation to assist him in both cases).[281] This turned out to be spectacularly wrong.[282] The Supreme Court's negative verdict in *Steel Seizure* was arguably the final price Truman paid for not seeking congressional authorization for the Korean War.[283] The government repeatedly emphasized that the case involved the national security of the country in wartime, but the justices were openly skeptical.[284]

Truman faced more than the usual number of difficult crises and decisions during his presidency. As his reaction to *Steel Seizure* showed, Truman resisted understanding that there were constitutional limits on executive power.[285] Did this make him a dangerous, "imperial" president or was he simply unlucky to be president in turbulent times? The 1946 railroad strike should remind us that there can be emergency situations even in peacetime. Truman believed in a strong presidency and had a tendency to act more decisively than wisely, but he showed no obsession with power.

The real problem with the post-1945 constitutional order lay elsewhere. *Steel Seizure* functioned more as a rebuke to an unpopular president who had overreached than a decisive check that forced the executive branch to reassess what the Cold War was doing to the Constitution. Surprisingly, until the detainee cases that followed 9/11, Justice Jackson's remarkable concurrence was not thought by executive branch attorneys even to be relevant to presidential decisionmaking concerning war.[286] Despite the national security considerations that pervaded the government's argument in 1952, the executive branch as well as some distinguished scholars refused to see *Steel Seizure* as a case which concerned presidential power in foreign affairs.[287] This is perhaps one reason why the decision had such little impact on the executive branch.

Although it is not necessary to review *Steel Seizure* in detail, it will be helpful to make some observations about Jackson's concurrence. This opinion remains fascinating for his effort to integrate a diverse set of personal experiences relating to the exercise of presidential power into a guiding framework for analysis.[288] Jackson's reasoning was based on an especially deep understanding of the Constitution's purposes, which made his opinion reminiscent of the best commentaries on the Constitution in the early republic.

After observing that the Constitution "contemplates that practice will integrate the dispersed powers into a workable government,"[289] Jackson described his famous categories of presidential authority. In category 1, when the president acts "pursuant to an express or implied authorization of Congress, his authority is at its maximum."[290] In category 2, Congress is silent and the president "can only rely upon his own independent powers, but there is a zone of twilight in which he and Congress may have concurrent authority, or in which its distribution is uncertain."[291] In category 3, the president is acting against the express or implied will of Congress and thus "his power is at its lowest ebb, for then he can rely only upon his own constitutional powers minus any constitutional powers of Congress over the matter."[292]

Jackson matched each category with a standard to determine the constitutionality of presidential action. In category 1, the president's power "would be supported by the strongest of presumptions and the widest latitude of judicial interpretation," and thus would likely be upheld.[293] In category 2, Jackson could not articulate a doctrinally satisfying standard, saying that in the zone of twilight, "any actual test of power is likely to depend on the imperatives of events and contemporary imponderables."[294] In category 3, where the president acts against Congress, Jackson thought that a "[p]residential claim at once so conclusive and preclusive must be scrutinized with caution, for what is at stake is the equilibrium established by our constitutional system."[295] Jackson thus strongly implied that placement in category 3 would usually result in the president's action being held unconstitutional. Truman's seizure of the steel mills fell into this category.[296]

When Jackson examined the Article II powers cited to justify Truman's decision, he either rejected or expressed considerable skepticism with respect to the arguments presidentialists have made to justify broad executive powers.[297] He rejected the idea that the clause that vests executive power in the president "is a grant in bulk of all conceivable executive power."[298] In discussing the reach of the president's role as commander in chief, he appeared to suggest that the constitutional status of the Korean War was in doubt.[299] He described the war as an instance of the president "having, on his own responsibility, sent American troops abroad."[300] Jackson would not accept that a president could use the role of commander in chief to initiate a war. In terms that echoed the plain statements of Hamilton, Madison, and Jefferson reviewed in Chapter 1, Jackson reaffirmed that only Congress can declare war, which means that the president cannot on his own authority commit "the Nation's armed forces to some foreign venture."[301]

At the same time, Jackson suggested that the judiciary should defer to the president's judgment when he appropriately exercised his role as commander in chief, "at least when turned against the outside world for the security of our society."[302] The impact of this acknowledgment was diminished somewhat by the implicit conditions that the role of commander in chief could not be used to initiate a war or as a source of emergency powers.[303] While Jackson implied that the role of commander in chief involved something beyond the power to command, he left unclear the scope of the power in circumstances short of war.

In a passage that usually does not appear in legal casebooks, Justice Jackson highlighted the importance of constitutional change outside the formal amendment process. Invoking the ability of the president to command the public's attention in the media and the president's political power as head of his party, Jackson summarized:

> [I]t is relevant to note the gap that exists between the President's paper powers and his real powers. The Constitution does not disclose the measure of the actual controls wielded by the modern presidential office. That instrument must be understood as an Eighteenth-Century sketch of a government hoped for, not as a blueprint of the Government that is. Vast accretions of federal power, eroded from that reserved by the States, have magnified the scope of presidential activity. Subtle shifts take place in the centers of real power that do not show on the face of the Constitution.[304]

Jackson's opinion thus helped suggest the research agenda I am pursuing in this book. How should we understand the expansion in presidential power? The critique of the "imperial presidency" appeared to be inspired by arguments that came straight from the eighteenth century. Presidents try to expand their power because that is what men of ambition seek to do. As Jackson implied, however, presidents have had plenty of assistance from Congress and the public in providing the institutions and capacities necessary for them to exercise their power to command the military on a global basis. This meant that the expansion in presidential power after World War II had a democratic foundation and could not be easily characterized as an abuse of power. As we shall see in the next chapter, when congressional "Old Guard" Republicans carried over their objections to the new power of the presidency from Truman to Eisenhower, they found themselves unable to maintain their political position in the post-1945 constitutional order.

The Post-1945 Constitutional Order and Its Discontents

As the next four chapters concern what happened to the post-1945 constitutional order after the Truman administration, it will be helpful to summarize and highlight its key elements. Recall the building blocks of a constitutional order described in Chapter 1. An order consists of reciprocal relationships between the text of the Constitution and the political and policy objectives of state officials, elites, and the public, all influenced by the structure and capacity for action of state institutions. To simplify somewhat, the post-1945 constitutional order is an interpretation of the Constitution put forward by government officials and elites that advocates increased presidential power in foreign affairs accompanied by an enormous expansion in the capacity of government institutions to take action on a global basis.

From the perspective of the foreign policy elites or "presidentialists" who created it, the post-1945 order is based on a sound critique of the situation that had prevailed prior to Pearl Harbor. The pre–Pearl Harbor order had placed the nation in peril, especially from the aggression of Hitler's Germany. Returning to that order after 1945 would, if anything, place the nation in even worse circumstances, given the greater threat posed by communism. It follows that the critique of presidential war power developed in the wake of the Vietnam War, including the concept of the "imperial presidency," necessarily involves a naïve return to isolationism or even appeasement. For supporters of the post-1945 order, the

Constitution has to be understood in light of the only possible foreign policy that would preserve the national security of the United States in a profoundly threatening world.[305]

Because it is still with us today, the most familiar element of the post-1945 constitutional order is presidential supremacy in foreign affairs. This element has a number of riders. One is that in setting defense or national security strategy, Congress is effectively a junior partner, subordinate to the president. Another is that the use of military force, including covert war, is simply one tool among others in advancing U.S. diplomacy and certainly does not have a "need permission of Congress before using" sticker attached.

A second element of the post-1945 constitutional order is the erasure of a clear distinction between wartime and peacetime. As subsequent chapters will show, throughout the Cold War there were government officials who believed it to be a "real" war and acted accordingly. The consequences of this belief ran in many directions. One theme explored in subsequent chapters documents the acceptability of using the morally repugnant tactics of communist states against them. This permitted departures from long-standing American values.

A third element is the concept that the president has the power to take the nation to war on his own authority. Especially from a point of view outside the executive branch and its reality distortion field, this idea is indeed something new. To the amazement of some, Truman's Korea decision was considered a "precedent" for future presidential action. Partly because of the criticism of that decision after the Korean War became unpopular, presidents after Truman have decided it is better to get the political protection of congressional resolutions when possible approving their actions. But aside from the special case of Eisenhower, reviewed in the next chapter, presidents have never conceded that such resolutions are legally required and the power that Truman claimed for the presidency in 1950 has never been relinquished.

Such are the essential elements of the post-1945 constitutional order. What are its discontents? The interbranch synthesis advanced in Chapter 1 holds that the Constitution granted a measure of authority over foreign affairs to the president while giving Congress gatekeeping authority over the decision for war. This check on the president's power promoted interbranch deliberation by creating the practical reality that the president had to run the risk that a proposal for war could be rejected, thus compromising not only his foreign policy but also his political position. Crucially, it was therefore implicit in the original constitutional order that presidents should be placed in a position where they are forced to make the best possible case that war is necessary.

It was this element of the original constitutional design that presidents, starting with Truman, rejected time and again. Under the influence of the post-1945 constitutional order, presidents have been unwilling to accept that the "declare war" clause was created as a check on their general power to set the nation's course in foreign affairs. This has resulted in an unstable situation in which the post-1945 order has been in conflict with the original constitutional order. The stunning fact is that no major war after 1945 was approved through a collaborative (or, for that matter, conflictual) process of interbranch deliberation. The cycle of accountability never began, as the executive branch took the entire burden of deciding for war on itself.

The consequence of this expansion of executive power to wage both overt and covert wars has not so much been restrictions on civil liberties (although those certainly occurred) than the gradual derangement of the nation's foreign policy, accompanied by a series of constitutional crises. Concentrating the complexities, tensions, and emotions inherent to decisions for war inside the executive branch has affected diplomacy as well as civil-military relations, while minimizing the policy, argumentative, and political quality control checks connected with the legislative process. An executive-led process also has tended to increase the secrecy of decisionmaking, further reducing the quality of interbranch deliberation.

In this chapter we began to explore the recurrent patterns of executive failures in decisionmaking that were the ultimate consequence of the post-1945 constitutional order. Truman and his advisers had trouble settling on ultimate war aims and, partly because of this vacillation, had difficulty explaining their policy to the public. In subsequent chapters, we will explore additional examples of these failures of deliberation, including a lack of realistic war planning and adherence to the mistaken assumption that the president could carry the entire burden of war decisionmaking alone. In one way or another, all of Truman's successors have been touched by these deliberative failures.

Those who grew up in the aftermath of Vietnam and Watergate should find the post-1945 constitutional order familiar. It might trigger a flashback to Arthur Schlesinger's classic critique *The Imperial Presidency* or perhaps contemporary disputes over the WPR. But familiarity does not necessarily promote historical understanding, at least not when anyone who grew up in the 1970s and after was already far removed from the superheated crisis atmosphere that enveloped the government at the beginning of the Cold War. Although it is always appropriate to critically examine the actions of presidents, we should not be alienated from them. This is why I have stressed understanding Truman and the difficult decisions he made on their own terms.

3

War and the National Security State

Creativity and flexible adaptation to circumstances characterized the Truman administration's policy responses to the challenges of the post–World War II world until the enormous setback of Chinese intervention in the Korean War. Yet from the standpoint of building government institutions to undergird what came to be known as the "national security state," the administration's achievements were halting and uncertain. Once we highlight the inescapable relevance of the Constitution, it becomes apparent that nothing approaching a charter was adopted for the national security state. Fundamental constitutional questions were not resolved or even identified. These questions were especially pressing with respect to the clandestine operations which in 1947 became the responsibility of the CIA.

It was not until former general Dwight Eisenhower won the presidency and finished a review of American foreign policy that the complexity of war powers issues faced by post–World War II presidents became fully apparent. Eisenhower's presidency also well illustrates why we should analyze war powers in terms of the fundamentals of foreign policy rather than occasional presidential statements. It became clear during Eisenhower's presidency that there were three different dimensions to military action: conventional, nuclear, and covert. While the different dimensions were related, each posed separate issues of how presidential war powers should be exercised.

The implications of the different dimensions of military action and the risks of covert operations became more apparent to policymakers after the interventions directed at Fidel Castro's Cuba in the Eisenhower and Kennedy administrations ended in multiple policy disasters. Fueled by popular sentiment and party competition, a momentum toward military conflict built up by the end of the Eisenhower administration as the U.S. hurtled toward an improbable but deadly war over the issue of communism and Soviet influence in Cuba. The Bay of Pigs invasion and the events which led to the October 1962 Cuban missile crisis showed the post-1945 constitutional order at its worst. Fortunately, Presidents Eisenhower and Kennedy both realized that a toxic brew of domestic considerations was making the Cold War unstable, inviting an ultimate nightmare of world devastation. This hard-won insight, however, did not contribute to a relieving of the strains that were rendering the Cold War constitutional order increasingly fragile.

The National Security Act and Covert War

If the National Security Act of 1947 had established a permanent template for the national security state, it could serve as a clear point of departure.[1] Unfortunately, while the power of this state could appear awesome, it was actually an unwieldy set of institutions born in uncertainty.[2] Although the act represented a start at reconfiguring the executive branch for the new global role of the United States, it was at best a halfway house and could not serve as a charter that meaningfully addressed constitutional concerns. In spite of its all-encompassing title, the main effect of the act was to call a temporary truce in the unceasing struggle over how to configure a unified defense establishment in the circumstances prevailing after World War II.[3]

In allying itself with Great Britain during World War II, the United States had encountered a better organized political-military system.[4] The U.S. had a War Department (concerned with the Army) and a Navy Department, but no centralized ministry of defense. Britain also possessed a unified command structure of service chiefs that had no counterpart in the U.S.[5] The command structure of the U.S. armed forces mirrored the fragmented and uncoordinated nature of the American state. President Roosevelt created the Joint Chiefs of Staff (JCS) as a wartime expedient which the National Security Act made a permanent institution.

Interservice rivalries were a problem throughout the war but became especially pressing as the services demobilized after 1945. The

Army, arguably the neglected service prior to World War II, pressed for a unified defense structure while the Navy resisted.[6] The National Security Act was a halfway house in the sense that it created a "National Military Establishment" rather than a Department of Defense and did not assign sufficient authority to the secretary to control the military.[7] These difficulties would not be addressed nor the Department of Defense properly created until the act was amended in 1949.[8]

The creation of the National Security Council and the CIA were more permanent consequences of the 1947 National Security Act.[9] However, Truman saw the NSC as a congressional imposition on his constitutional powers and did not employ it as an instrument of policy until after the beginning of the Korean War.[10] As for the CIA, everyone recognized that it was something completely new, a civilian intelligence agency that would function in both peace and war.[11] It was widely understood as a necessary response to the surprise attack on Pearl Harbor.[12] Unfortunately members of Congress and policymakers did little to clarify what exactly the CIA would do to fix the problem with intelligence.[13] Perhaps they were assuming that the Japanese attack could have been predicted amid the welter of conflicting intelligence, although subsequent analyses judged this unlikely.[14] After all, the various elements of the military did not give up their own intelligence operations, believing they were still responsible for anticipating a surprise attack.[15] Thus, the military had reasons to be skeptical of the CIA's function and gave the agency trouble from the beginning.[16]

The CIA was established as an agency responsive solely to the president and without a detailed charter.[17] This meant it could function abroad as an all-purpose arm of the executive to carry out tasks that the State or Defense Departments were reluctant to take on.[18] Most post-1945 presidents relied at one time or another on this useful capacity.[19] When the CIA director had the confidence of the president, the Agency had the capability to cut through bureaucratic resistance and accomplish tasks in a flexible way.[20] A hidden consequence was that the CIA had little ability to resist questionable presidential orders.[21] Perhaps understandably in the context of the time, no one considered what would happen if the CIA lost the president's confidence.

The constitutional issues created by the CIA went much deeper than the question of accountability. These issues have been overshadowed by the nagging questions left by the ambiguous terms of the National

Security Act. Although the Truman administration and members of Congress intended to create a civilian capability for espionage and clandestine operations, this was not spelled out clearly in the 1947 act.[22] This led to charges later that covert action was not authorized, although for obvious reasons it was never likely that Congress would explicitly sanction such operations.[23]

The CIA's birth was staged awkwardly because the merger of the War and Navy Departments dominated the process. To facilitate the merger, the Truman administration downplayed other aspects of the act, including the creation of the CIA.[24] A detailed draft statute organizing the CIA was set aside in favor of a strategy that would provide the Agency with the authority it needed in two steps.[25] The National Security Act would create the CIA and then be followed by legislation enabling it to conduct covert operations.[26] Congress did not approve the follow-on legislation, the CIA Act, until 1949.[27] In the meantime, in June 1948 the NSC had approved Directive 10/2 which ordered the CIA to conduct "espionage and counter-espionage operations abroad."[28]

The CIA Act confirmed that Congress had authorized the Agency to engage in covert operations in the National Security Act.[29] It essentially relieved the Agency from having to account for how it spent government money.[30] Thus freed from the most basic type of oversight, it appeared the CIA could do anything, at least overseas.[31] But different types of covert action posed distinctly different types of legal problems.[32] Engaging in espionage against foreign governments or spreading propaganda outside the U.S. posed few issues. But covert action also included paramilitary operations that involved the capacity to wage war against foreign states.[33] These sorts of operations posed obvious constitutional issues that went unaddressed.[34]

The CIA was sometimes defended against later legalistic critics by the argument that as an agency engaged in espionage and clandestine activity, it necessarily had to operate outside the law.[35] This sort of response illustrated the constitutional ambiguity of the Cold War period. Was it wartime or not? As John Ranelagh points out in his perceptive history of the CIA, the Agency had quasi-military responsibilities without the accountability of the military services. "In war a President enjoys enormous legal freedoms; in peace the position is quite different. What would be the position if the CIA killed someone? In war the question would not be asked. In peace it certainly would be."[36] Ranelagh speculated that by comparison, the position of the Secret Intelligence Service (MI6) in the United Kingdom was different. Operating under the theoretically unlimited sovereignty of the Crown and Parliament, its authority could not be questioned.[37] By contrast, in the U.S. popular sovereignty prevailed and authority was given to government by the supreme law of the Constitution. Thus there could be no government agency or official outside the Constitution. What this meant for the CIA was that in order to be beyond the law of the Constitution, it had to operate not only beyond U.S. shores but also without U.S. citizens or funds. Although this was impossible, no one thought the matter through.

Such conundrums went unaddressed for years because, especially in the Agency's first decade after the passage of the CIA Act, there was a constant sense of war and crisis.[38] As discussed in Chapter 2, the line between wartime and peacetime had been effectively erased. The CIA perceived itself as on the front lines of the Cold War and the Agency was dominated by its covert operations arm.[39] In addition, the CIA was required to operate in such a way so as to maintain "plausible deniability."[40] If this had been realistic, secrecy would have provided a welcome cloak over whatever the Agency did.

In 1953 Robert Joyce, a member of the State Department's Policy Planning Staff, looked back at the crisis-filled years of 1949 and 1950.[41] Events such as the Soviet Union's acquisition of atomic weapons and the Korean War made the American people feel "a sense of urgency to prepare for the possibility of additional Communist attacks against the free world which might lead to an all-out military conflict, including an attack against the United States."[42] Joyce referred to a belief in 1950, widespread in the wake of NSC-68, that there was a critical period for U.S.-Soviet conflict approaching in 1954–1955 for which the government had to be ready.[43] This was part of the background against which the early CIA operated.

In addition, there was a notable lack of accountability. It was difficult to evaluate the legal meaning of a possible conflict between the Constitution or a statute and a covert operation because the Agency did not have a charter and operated under the broad authority of the president in foreign affairs. A conflict over funding or a political battle with Congress could not occur because Congress exercised no meaningful oversight.[44] Congressional relations were in the hands of a few key committee chairmen in the Senate, who enjoyed being part of a select few in the know and discouraged the inquiries of other senators.[45] There was thus no opportunity for a cycle of accountability to develop.

Consider the jarring consequences when the institutional order that had protected the CIA began to erode at the end of 1974. The Agency was pummeled with questions about its covert operations.[46] Ranelagh characterized the response of CIA officials: "In one way or another their answers were always the same: *Don't you understand? We're fighting the cold war.* The trouble was that Americans no longer understood or wanted to understand."[47] Laurence Silberman, the acting attorney general in 1975, told CIA Director William Colby that a 1973 compilation of the Agency's "skeletons" should have been reported to the DOJ, presumably for assessment of whether anyone should be prosecuted![48] But in the 1950s, with the CIA operating in tandem with the president, this would have been unthinkable. The atmosphere in the 1970s could not have been more different from the picture Joyce described in 1953. As I will describe in Chapter 5, the nature of the Cold War and constitutional authority it provided had changed.

As we will see in later chapters, what happened to the CIA in the investigations of the mid-1970s illustrated the jerry-built structure of the Cold War constitutional order. It also illuminated an important feature of that order that historians perhaps have not noticed sufficiently. The sense of emergency that helped erase the difference between war and peace could not be sustained indefinitely. The kind of high morale and extraordinary efforts that were critically necessary to mount covert operations eventually wore the Agency down.[49] The early Cold War was thus a distinct period in which the perception of emergency and crisis dominated. Further, there was no escaping the legal supremacy of the Constitution. After the crises of the early Cold War receded, the tidal force of the original constitutional order reasserted itself and the post-1945 constitutional order became unstable.

Eisenhower's Way of War

In the war powers debate former general Eisenhower is seen as a president who, unlike other postwar presidents, was committed to the proposition that Congress had an essential role mandated by the Constitution in deciding whether the nation went to war.[50] There is a reasonable amount of evidence supporting this claim, although from a political point of view Eisenhower had little choice.[51] A key segment of the Republican Party, particularly the "Old Guard" in the Senate, had staked out a strong position in opposition to excessive presidential power during the Truman administration.[52] Eisenhower has often been described as supremely self-confident in matters of foreign affairs, defense policy, and national security.[53] But he had to expend enormous energy, especially in his first term, to reassure Congress that the separation of powers would be respected in foreign affairs.[54] By contrast, in his second term Eisenhower became increasingly concerned that the tensions inherent to the Cold War would circumscribe or possibly overwhelm the autonomy of the president.[55]

Eisenhower's record is in fact more complex than allowed in the standard war powers debate. As I argued in Chapter 1, we should approach war powers issues in the context of foreign affairs and national security policy. Once we do this, it becomes apparent that there were three separate dimensions of warfare in which presidential power was exercised during the Eisenhower administration and after: conventional, nuclear, and covert. The increased importance of nuclear and covert warfare was specifically highlighted by the Eisenhower administration in its "New Look" defense policy.[56] One purpose of the "New Look" was to ratchet downward the enormous increases in defense spending that had occurred during the Korean War buildup by emphasizing forms of defense that were less costly than conventional forces.[57] Eisenhower's beliefs about congressional involvement tended to vary depending on the form of war he was considering.

In terms of conventional warfare, Eisenhower's endorsement of a role for Congress was real enough. As the administration considered what to do about French soldiers trapped at Dienbienphu in 1954, Eisenhower insisted that Congress must be involved. At a press conference, he stated there would be "no involvement of America in war unless it is a result of the constitutional process that is placed upon Congress to declare it."[58] Similarly, in a telephone conversation with Secretary of State Dulles, the president insisted that it would be "'completely unconstitutional and indefensible' to use American forces to assist the French without congressional approval."[59] In several foreign affairs crises, including Dienbienphu and the China-Formosa (Taiwan) war scare of 1955 (involving the islands of Quemoy and Matsu), Eisenhower made it a point to consult with members of Congress before making a decision.[60]

In the 1956 Suez crisis, Eisenhower insisted several times that the nation could not go to war without the consent of Congress.[61]

In invoking the constitutional role of Congress, Eisenhower was mindful that Truman's unilateral decision to intervene in Korea was widely viewed as a negative precedent. It was associated with what was seen as a failed war and had attracted substantial criticism.[62] Eisenhower and Dulles drew the lesson that Congress should be on record as supporting any future military action with an authorization resolution. In the Dienbienphu crisis a resolution was prepared, but never introduced. This set a pattern for resolutions approved by Congress in the 1955 Formosa crisis and for the Middle East in 1957.[63]

Some historians have regarded the Formosa Resolution as a dramatic enhancement of executive power, a sort of advance declaration of war.[64] By contrast, constitutional scholars have not seen the resolution as a significant departure.[65] Given the authorization of war understanding of the "declare war" clause advanced in Chapter 1, legal commentators have the sounder position. The idea of approving military action in advance may have seemed novel. From a constitutional perspective, however, what mattered was that Congress had a reasonable opportunity to assess the nation's war aims and, if necessary, reject the president's policy. As long as adequate interbranch deliberation took place, there was nothing unusual in terms of the legal authority granted by the Formosa Resolution. It is worth emphasizing here, however, that each post–World War II congressional resolution must be assessed separately for its deliberative adequacy.[66]

Nonetheless, by themselves such resolutions could not address the breach in the pre–Pearl Harbor constitutional order opened up by Truman's Korea decision and the circumstances of the Cold War. In practical terms, they proved to be ways for presidents to get Congress on board rather than truly deliberate and build a cycle of accountability.[67] The proposed Dienbienphu resolution, for example, was more of a political necessity rather than something Eisenhower wanted out of devotion to constitutional principle.[68] His party barely controlled Congress and he needed Democratic support to pass any resolution.[69] In some respects, Eisenhower did not deviate that much from Truman's legacy. During the Formosa and Suez crises, he acknowledged believing that he had the authority to respond unilaterally if he thought it was in the nation's interest.[70] More important, it was questionable whether either Truman's unilateralism or Eisenhower's instinctive respect for Congress's role could serve as stable "precedents" when the exercise of presidential power in foreign affairs was deeply contested between the parties and within Congress itself.

In response to the Truman administration's presidentialist and arguably Eurocentric foreign policy, Republicans in Congress articulated a contrasting vision of America's place in the world. In Julian Zelizer's useful account, their alternative was "conservative internationalism."[71] This rested on anticommunism, putting "Asia first," rolling back Soviet power rather than containing it, and a notable preference for the use of airpower rather than ground forces.[72] After twenty years of rule by activist Democratic presidents, there was a strong strain of anti-executive sentiment in the Republican Party, exemplified by such measures as the Bricker Amendment which occupied Eisenhower's attention during the winter of 1953–1954.[73] The Bricker Amendment's essential thrust was to restrict the president's power to negotiate treaties and thus conduct foreign affairs effectively. This controversy most likely emphasized to Eisenhower that strong feelings had developed in Congress that presidents had abused their power.[74] This probably encouraged Eisenhower to emphasize that Congress had a legitimate role to play in foreign affairs in his subsequent statements about the Dienbienphu crisis.[75]

If Eisenhower's personal views had been the only variable, perhaps a stable consensus could have formed around a proper balance between the branches with respect to presidential war power. But views on the scope of presidential power had become an element in party competition for leadership in national security policy. As described in Chapter 2, the Truman administration had been savaged by Republicans suspicious of communist influence in government who made skepticism toward executive power part of their critique. Democrats in Congress eventually pushed back, partly to defend the Truman administration's record, but also to advance a critique of how Eisenhower fought the Cold War.[76] Congressional liberals championed a strong presidency, arguing that the conservative emphasis on the congressional role in foreign policy was a prescription for weakness in the struggle against the Soviet Union.[77] Thus in the 1960 presidential election, Senator John F. Kennedy ran as a Cold War hawk against the failures of the Eisenhower administration to protect the U.S. from threats such as the supposed "missile gap" with the Soviet Union and Castro's Cuba.[78]

Given these political variables, Eisenhower could not consistently maintain a chastened conception of presidential leadership compared to Truman. His "New Look" in national security policy emphasized brandishing nuclear weapons overtly and using military action covertly.[79] In these areas Eisenhower made unilateral decisions concerning matters related to war without consulting Congress. He planned to use nuclear weapons against China if the Korean War was not settled.[80] It appears he would have used nuclear weapons against China if the crisis over Formosa had turned into a shooting war.[81] He violated Soviet airspace with the new U-2 spy planes.[82] Moreover, as historian Fredrik Logevall concludes, Eisenhower exhibited an "aggressive approach to crises in the Third World, including in Vietnam."[83] He authorized covert actions all over the Middle East, including against the regime of Mohammed Mossadegh in Iran, and a paramilitary action against the elected government of Jacobo Arbenz in Guatemala.[84] While it is unlikely that Congress would have objected to any of these actions had they known, the point is that the cycle of accountability never began. Like other Cold War presidents, Eisenhower did not acknowledge a role for Congress in nuclear and covert warfare.

Given the strength and relevance of Eisenhower's apparent convictions concerning Congress's role in conventional warfare, however, it is worth asking why they did not have more of an impact in later debates over war powers. The answer seems to be that especially after the demise of the Republican "Old Guard" in the mid-1950s, there was no group in Congress who wanted to learn from them. When Democrats won the next round of party competition in 1960, ideas later associated with the "imperial presidency" were in the ascendancy. Democrats adopted Eisenhower's practice of asking for resolutions in advance of military action and ignored his views, applicable at least to conventional warfare, that important constitutional principles were involved. Ironically, the renewed emphasis in the Democratic Party on a strong president acting unilaterally to protect the national security of the United States was ultimately a response to the intensity with which Republicans had prosecuted the idea of Democratic weakness against the communist threat.[85]

Eisenhower left two other ambiguous legacies. As Castro's Cuba appeared to incline to an open alliance with the Soviet Union, Eisenhower ordered planning for what would become the Bay of Pigs operation.[86] He also gave a prescient warning about the influence of the "military-industrial complex" in his famous farewell address.[87] With respect to the latter, it is noteworthy that Eisenhower joined together a commitment to preserve a sphere of autonomy in presidential decisionmaking in national security to the policy of a balanced budget. From Eisenhower's point of view, abandoning a balanced budget would ultimately shift the balance of power within the government toward the Pentagon and those who wanted a militarization of the Cold War.[88] Although Truman had not been able to maintain a balanced budget after the start of the Korean War, Truman and Eisenhower were the last Cold War presidents who made balanced budgets a primary objective.[89] The restraints on the military that were implicit in this policy were loosened considerably after 1960.[90]

By authorizing the military training of Cuban exiles and possibly the assassination of Castro, Eisenhower set in motion a plan for Castro's overthrow that was approaching a *fait accompli* as Kennedy was inaugurated in January 1961.[91] As his term wound to a close, one of Eisenhower's key aides, General Andrew Goodpaster remembered Eisenhower expressing a worry that once the exiles had been trained, "then the pressures for their commitment and for their intervention must be expected to increase."[92] Although Goodpaster recalled Eisenhower concluding with the resolution that he would not be pressured by these circumstances, this exchange well expressed the lack of accountability which characterized the entire operation.[93] The obsession with controlling Cuba led to a cascading series of executive blunders resulting in the most dangerous foreign policy crisis of the entire Cold War.

Will Cuba Destroy the World?

It is difficult to review U.S. policy toward Cuba during the Eisenhower and Kennedy administrations without surmising that something was seriously amiss with American government in the Cold War.[94] There were clear signs of the derangement of policy that flowed from an unstable constitutional order. Because Cuba, indeed all of Latin America, was far from a central arena of the Cold War when Castro's forces deposed dictator Fulgencio Batista in January 1959, it is hard to explain subsequent U.S. policy toward Cuba as a response to a strategic challenge. This was arguably a period in which the domestic politics of the Cold

War overwhelmed the broader strategic picture and all but dictated a harsh response to the Cuban revolution.[95]

In straightforward terms, the Bay of Pigs was a U.S.-sponsored invasion of Cuba disguised as a covert infiltration which the CIA hoped would result in a popular uprising against Castro. The term "disguised" must be used advisedly, for it was only officials in the executive branch who were fooled. The operational plan for the Bay of Pigs was something of a moving target, given confusion about its objectives and the changing situation in Cuba, where Castro was growing stronger as the months went by.[96] In Guatemala where the CIA had sponsored the overthrow of Arbenz, the Eisenhower administration had the assistance of the country's military, but no such help was available in Cuba.[97]

The CIA's plan at first contemplated the covert infiltration of a few hundred guerrillas and later an invasion of 1,500 men trained by U.S. personnel that involved declaring a new government amid local support. Castro was aware of the CIA's role in Arbenz's overthrow and devoted considerable effort to building up his army and importing weapons.[98] The operation grew as planners realized they were in a race with Castro that would probably end in his favor when he acquired a substantial air force.[99] Two key elements of the enlarged plan seemed to have been lost in the transition between administrations. Any lodgment of troops would require significant and continuing support from the air in the form of supplies and offensive strikes in which the U.S. role would not be deniable.[100] In addition, even with air support, the CIA's small brigade could not be sustained unless there was a general uprising against Castro.[101]

As President Kennedy reviewed the plans Eisenhower had set into motion, he sensed trouble and that it would be difficult to conceal the role of the U.S.[102] The State Department bolstered his conviction by maintaining that given its diplomatic commitments, the U.S. could not afford to be an aggressor nation.[103] Although the president was under near-constant pressure to move forward, he took a consistent line that the operation had to be as low-key as possible.[104] The CIA hurriedly redrafted its plan and moved its location from the Cuban city of Trinidad to the Bay of Pigs. As the operation finally went forward, Kennedy still worried about the operation being too visible and canceled the air strikes that were necessary to ensure at least minimal success.[105] The Cuban brigade, which included a few American citizens, was cut to pieces and surrendered.[106]

Even historians have had a difficult time evaluating the Bay of Pigs in context. Howard Jones described the operation as the "first United States-sponsored regime change that relied on a combination of military force and assassination"[107] and strongly condemned it as contrary to American values.[108] While I am certainly sympathetic to such a critique, the issue throughout the Cold War involved defining true American values during a situation of constant emergency in which the line drawn in the Constitution between wartime and peacetime had been deliberately obscured. Recall that the 1954 Doolittle report on the CIA's covert operations quoted in Chapter 2 called for the frank use of methods characteristic of the Soviet Union and other totalitarian states, presumably including assassination.[109] It is important to keep in mind that using the methods of the enemy against him remained a valid conviction for many Americans, especially conservatives, throughout the Cold War and into the 1975 investigations of the CIA's plans to assassinate foreign leaders.[110]

The constitutional difficulties posed by the Bay of Pigs were legion. Our attention might first be drawn to the notion of the president having a foreign mercenary army at his disposal, although there was little risk that the brigade of Cuban exiles could be used anywhere except in Cuba. In fact, as the size of the operation grew, it became apparent that such large incursions were beyond the ability of the CIA to manage consistent with its goal of preserving deniability.[111] Eisenhower determined that small guerrilla infiltrations would not work but refused to acknowledge that the attack required a fairly large military operation, either conducted by U.S. troops or with U.S. forces providing such extensive assistance that their role could not be concealed. Eisenhower and Kennedy resolutely avoided the reality that the only way to depose Castro securely was to go to war in the open. Going to war covertly and without the checks and balances provided by the cycle of accountability meant that the flaws in the executive branch policymaking process were magnified enormously. It is noteworthy that although Kennedy had very limited contact with members of Congress, the senators who spoke out advised against the operation.[112]

Another serious problem with covert war was that it was difficult to turn the foreign army off. This was politely referred to as the "disposal" problem in the run-up to the Bay of Pigs.[113] If the operation did not go forward, what would happen to the Cuban brigade? They had been training in Guatemala, but the local regime wanted them out.[114] There was no place for them to go except the United States, where they would presumably reveal the existence of the effort to depose Castro and could even agitate to complete the operation.[115] To compound the policy problem with politics, their complaints could have been used by the administration's opponents to make Kennedy look weak on communism.

The disposal problem was related to the even more dangerous specter of the president being *forced* to go to war if the operation failed. There is strong evidence that top-level officials in the CIA and JCS thought this was the way the Bay of Pigs would play out.[116] As recounted by historian Lawrence Freedman, "[t]he best explanation for the failure to challenge the president's insistence on noninvolvement of U.S. forces is that the CIA did not actually take it very seriously. When the moment of truth arrived, Kennedy, like Eisenhower, would authorize overt action to prevent the ignominy of failure."[117] This would have created an ultimate constitutional nightmare—the decision to go to war being removed from Congress *and* the President by overenthusiastic officials in the CIA and the military. The later general charge calling the CIA a "rogue elephant" was misplaced because there was plenty of evidence that the Agency was consistently responsive to the presidents it served.[118] But there was an element of truth because of the huge momentum that had built up behind the operation.[119] This fact alone strongly suggested the executive branch could not handle the strains of decision inherent to war without the help of Congress.

These problems were related to deeper infirmities in the constitutional order. By creating the CIA to solve foreign policy problems covertly, an unforeseen capacity had been created to take military action, as well as covert *domestic* action, without appropriate checks.[120] The failure of the Bay of Pigs operation illustrated that the purpose of such accountability was not simply to provide legality or legitimacy. The constitutional plan was to ensure better policy through the participation of both branches. The Bay of Pigs suggested strongly that the executive branch was incapable of formulating and pursuing a sound policy for war without the meaningful participation of Congress. In addition, the rationales used to justify bypassing the Constitution had a corrosive effect on politics in general, something to which I turn in the next section.

The tragic outcome of the Bay of Pigs did not dim the Kennedy administration's enthusiasm for overthrowing Castro, although an interagency committee quickly scotched the idea of invading Cuba outright.[121] The CIA continued its covert war against Cuba with Operation Mongoose, essentially a program of infiltration and sabotage overseen by Attorney General Robert Kennedy.[122] No longer in Guatemala, the CIA ran the operation from Miami in a vast effort involving thousands of Cuban agents.[123] The effort to blur the line between war and peace turned up again in this operation, as the attorney general motivated the CIA and the Pentagon by telling them "[w]e are in a combat situation with Cuba."[124]

In an especially revealing episode, CIA agents began asking their general counsel to explain the legal foundation for launching a covert war against Cuba from U.S. territory.[125] Thus even in the midst of a secret war, it occurred to CIA personnel that the Constitution might be relevant. Nevertheless, in the course of the operations, agents sometimes ran afoul of the law and the CIA had to run interference with local law enforcement agencies. The foreseeable consequence was that the agents developed the impression that they were above the law. This made them susceptible to recruitment for illegal operations inside the U.S., including the 1972 Watergate burglary discussed in the next chapter.[126]

Yet the covert war against Cuba should not be regarded as an example of the "imperial presidency," if that means a president using the power of his office to pursue a foreign policy lacking public support. As Gaddis Smith and Robert Weisbrot have shown, public concern over Cuba had been raised to a fever pitch in the aftermath of Castro's revolution.[127] As Weisbrot describes, "[t]he public mood was alarmist, even apocalyptic, for a nation officially at peace, and no public figure could expect to contravene that mood and still retain credibility."[128] The public constantly importuned the political branches to be more aggressive against Castro.[129] Influential Democrats such as Senator Mike Mansfield affirmed that the president had the authority to intervene in Cuba without congressional approval.[130] The tendency was to see Cuba not as a sovereign nation but as an instrument of Soviet foreign policy planted on the doorstep of the United States.[131] To be sure, the public drew some distinctions and did not favor an invasion just prior to the October 1962 missile crisis, fearing it would start a general war.[132]

Although the reasons Soviet leader Nikita Khrushchev sent an extensive arsenal of nuclear weapons to Cuba have been contested, the most recent reviews of the evidence give a prominent role to his fears that the U.S. would mount another intervention like the Bay of Pigs or even a full-scale invasion.[133] The missile crisis was thus in part a consequence of the aggressive stance the executive branch had taken against Cuba with the support of the public since the Bay of Pigs.

The stakes in the missile crisis were of course very high. At the time, the U.S. had 7,000 strategic nuclear weapons to the Soviet Union's roughly 500.[134] If a nuclear war had resulted, it could have killed 500 million people and "rendered much of the northern hemisphere uninhabitable."[135] Critics of the imperial presidency would justifiably count this as the ultimate terrible consequence of presidential power run riot. Yet it should be noted that President Kennedy thought plausibly that if he had not ordered a firm military response to the Soviet move, he would have been committing political suicide.[136] One sign of his sound judgment was that during the only consultation with Congress during the crisis, its members were more bellicose than Kennedy![137] It is also relevant, however, that the members consulted softened after they heard Kennedy's speech to the nation on October 22 announcing his response and were generally supportive of his decision to blockade or "quarantine" Cuba.[138] This showed an evolution in thinking that was at least somewhat parallel to what had occurred inside the executive branch in the deliberations of the famous "ExComm" of the NSC.[139] It illustrated the beneficial effect of deliberation on policy, as first reactions to Khrushchev's move in the executive branch had been similarly pugnacious. For its part, the public thought Kennedy had hit on the right mix of firmness and restraint.[140]

The missile crisis is generally regarded as a turning point in the Cold War, after which both sides made efforts to reduce tensions and avoid direct conflict, especially with respect to nuclear weapons.[141] While there is a great deal of truth in this, the consequences of the crisis did not cause anyone to question presidential leadership in foreign policy. As Kennedy juggled crises in Berlin, Cuba, Laos, and Vietnam during his time in the White House, the post-1945 constitutional order was intact. But the strains of conducting an indefinite war against the backdrop of a Constitution not designed for such a conflict were showing.

The Strains of War and the Public Sphere

By the time President Kennedy was assassinated in November 1963, the United States could be said to have been in a war with the Soviet Union and the communist bloc for at least thirteen years, ever since the outbreak of the Korean War and the enormous military buildup it provoked. Counting from the announcement of the Truman Doctrine in 1947, it had been sixteen years of continuous "cold" war. America's leaders saw no end in sight. In his farewell address in January 1961, President Eisenhower referred to "the conflict now engulfing the world" between the U.S. and its allies and the "hostile ideology" of communism.[142] He observed that "[u]nhappily, the danger it poses promises to be of indefinite duration."[143]

Eisenhower's address showed clearly that some Americans had come to the understanding that a permanently large military posed new complex challenges for government and society. The strains of incessant war on the fabric of state institutions were less evident to Americans as the Kennedy administration took office, in part because they were occurring in the realm of secret deliberations and covert operations. Here otherwise sober-minded government officials were considering extreme measures such as assassinating foreign leaders.

As with the Bay of Pigs, historians have had a difficult time contextualizing the covert plots of the early Cold War era. There were multiple CIA assassination plots against Castro, for example, one of which included members of organized crime.[144] Christian Herter, John Foster Dulles's successor as Eisenhower's secretary of state and an impeccable member of the foreign policy establishment, proposed staging an attack on the U.S. base at Guantanamo in order to provide a *casus belli* for going to war against Cuba.[145] The concept of a war begun on a false pretext continued to circulate in the Pentagon during the Kennedy administration, resulting in "Operation Northwoods."[146] This bizarre plan involved simulating terrorist attacks by Castro's Cuba on the United States itself as a prelude to an invasion.[147] In order to be credible, such operations would have run the serious risk of killing U.S. citizens.

I suggest it is easier to understand the context of these early Cold War plots if we accept that presidents and executive branch officials in that era genuinely believed that it was wartime.[148] The early Cold War was a world in which President Eisenhower, in the midst of the 1956 Suez crisis, could complain privately about the British failure to "bump off"[149] Abdel Nasser, the leader of Egypt. As we saw in Chapter 2, fundamental policy papers such as NSC-68 and the Doolittle report maintained that the existence of the United States as a free country was at stake and accepted the government would at least temporarily have to adopt the same tactics as totalitarian states. In this light, executive branch officials were feeling the strain of being responsible for the preservation of U.S. national security. In fact, they were aware of being *solely* responsible as Congress was not participating in the cycle of accountability. What would happen if they failed? Who would be blamed? It was worries like these generated by a long war that led officials to advance proposals that would appear highly questionable only roughly a decade later.

Although government officials believed it was wartime, this perspective was not always shared with the public, nor were the strains of war readily apparent. During the secret executive branch inquiry which followed the Bay of Pigs, former director of the CIA Walter Bedell Smith remarked that the United States was indeed in a state of war but "the American people do not feel that they are at war at the present time, and consequently they are not willing to make the sacrifices necessary to wage war."[150] What Smith's remark implied was that those sacrifices would have to be made inside the government, without the knowledge of the public. The CIA was certainly familiar with this idea. The attitude of the CIA in the early Cold War was that it was a real war which made acceptable "the idea of killing people and manipulating people in the national interest."[151]

At the same time, CIA officials believed they were acting within the Constitution because they were operating under presidential authority.[152] William Harvey, the head of the CIA's foreign intelligence staff, was ordered by Richard Bissell, director of the covert operations arm, to develop the assassination effort against Castro.[153] Harvey believed such a program was justified, given the existence of an "imminent and mortal threat to the United States [so that such action] falls within the province of the President's power to defend the Republic under the Constitution itself."[154] This shows the officials who were following such questionable orders did not see themselves as having *carte blanche* to do as they saw fit. They understood themselves to be subject to the rule of law, but the rule of law as it applied during wartime.

As I noted earlier, the sense of emergency and wartime which helped define the CIA's mission in the early Cold War could not be sustained indefinitely.[155] Even in "long wars," morale is essential and the kind of high morale that normally prevails in emergency situations eventually waned. The Truman and Eisenhower administrations devoted much attention to convincing the public that the danger of communism was real and immediate.[156] Once the sense of emergency dwindled and the nature of the nuclear threat changed after the missile crisis, a crucial element propping up the post-1945 constitutional order was suddenly missing. The jerry-built structure of that order was coming undone.

Civil-military relations at the highest levels were another unsettled element of the post-1945 constitutional order that was beginning to cause serious trouble toward the end of the Eisenhower administration.[157] For his part, Eisenhower felt that interservice rivalries and insubordination toward civilian authority were completely out of hand.[158] The historical record is replete with evidence that the JCS system created by the 1947 National Security Act had never functioned to provide presidents with effective and timely military advice.[159] Each military service believed that it alone was crucial to the nation's security and resisted planning and operating in a truly joint fashion. In addition, both the tasks given to the military and expectations for results had been driven sky-high in the early Cold War. At one point during the Korean War, defense spending totaled 70 percent of the total federal budget and was still half of the budget when Eisenhower left office.[160] The military absorbed the message of fundamental policy statements such as NSC-68 and believed itself responsible for national security and the execution of the strategy against communism all over the world. When Eisenhower cut the defense budget in favor of the "New Look," a significant gap opened up between civil and military perspectives.[161] This was especially true of the Army, the service branch least favored by the new emphasis on nuclear weapons.[162]

The Kennedy administration was wary of the new power the military had acquired in the early Cold War and the close relations it had developed with Congress.[163] Even after the failure of the Bay of Pigs, the JCS kept after President Kennedy with proposals to invade Cuba and finish off Castro.[164] The JCS were thus distraught when the missile crisis ended without a decisive invasion.[165] As Lawrence Freedman recounts, when they complained that the resolution of the crisis was actually a defeat for the U.S., "Kennedy was shocked. He commented that the 'first advice' he would give his successor was 'to watch the generals' and not to think that 'just because they were military men their opinions on military matters were worth a damn.'"[166] The truly deplorable state of relations between the JCS and the civilians who ran the DOD and the White House did not improve in the Johnson administration, with adverse consequences for U.S. policy in Vietnam.

The failure of the JCS to function effectively in the Eisenhower and Kennedy administrations is a striking clue to how haphazardly the post-1945 constitutional order had been constructed. On a standard view of how the constitutional system works, the JCS effort to link with friendly members of Congress was unexceptionable. The military was using the dispersed nature of authority in the constitutional system to advance their agenda. From the point of view of Eisenhower and Kennedy, however, the JCS approach was contrary to the president's authority as commander in chief and antithetical to civilian control of the military. Eisenhower, no stranger to the way the military worked, thought it amounted to insubordination.[167]

This sharp disagreement as to the military's proper role showed clearly the consequences of constructing the post-1945 constitutional order without addressing fundamental questions. With these new capacities in hand, how was the military supposed to interact with the preexisting institutions created by the Constitution? The post-1945 order involved an enormous expansion in the size of the military without addressing the difference that this would make in its relationship to the executive and legislative branches. As we have seen, new capacities mean new constitutional powers and roles. An expanded military could be given new missions such as defending U.S. interests on a global basis. But new capacities and missions also changed the place of the military in the constitutional order. Because there was no serious attempt to anticipate and deliberate about what this meant for the existing institutional structure, the post-1945 order was further unbalanced.

Eventually, the strains of the long war began showing in the fragile foundations of the national security state in public opinion. Because much of the covert and nuclear dimensions of the Cold War military effort were out of sight, an enormous debt of absent public deliberation was building up in the public sphere. The public had little idea of what the CIA and the other intelligence agencies were doing and so a cycle of accountability could not begin.[168]

The public sphere was also poisoned by the narrowing of alternatives in national security policy that had occurred since the Truman administration. The entire political landscape had been skewed to the right by the impact of McCarthyism.[169] A powerful anticommunist consensus dominated public policy. Every public official wanted to show toughness with the Russians and no one wanted to be seen as an appeaser.[170] Every foreign policy crisis invited a comparison with the capitulation to Hitler at Munich, which meant that compromise was out of the question.[171] All sorts of inaccurate information influenced public debate. Americans, for example, thought they were lagging behind the Soviets in the nuclear arms race when in fact they enjoyed overwhelming superiority.[172] Once the sense of continual emergency ebbed away, it would become apparent that there was a substantial price to be paid in terms of public confidence and trust in government.

Few people asked what would happen if the premises of the long war and the post-1945 constitutional order came into question. What if the perception of constant foreign policy crisis ebbed away? What if the American people could not maintain the morale appropriate to an age of threat and emergency? What if they rejected the idea that the Cold War was in fact "wartime," justifying departures from time-honored American values and traditions? Without any formal changes to the Constitution or judicial doctrine to validate Cold War claims of authority, suddenly the presidency and the intelligence agencies would look like threatening equivalents to the kind of dictatorial rule which prevailed among our enemies. Indeed, they would look "unconstitutional." This was a formula for a constitutional crisis.

4

Vietnam and Watergate

The Post-1945 Constitutional Order in Crisis

A persistent attention to the lessons of history characterized the men who fought the Cold War. The lesson of Munich was that appeasement led only to greater aggression. Pearl Harbor showed the need for military preparedness and advance warning based on reliable intelligence. The "loss" of China meant that no country could be conceded to the communist side without serious political consequences at home. Amid these many lessons, it is noteworthy that the path to war taken by President Roosevelt described in Chapter 2 was not more influential during the crucial 1963 to 1965 period in which Presidents Kennedy and Johnson made the decisions which resulted in the Vietnam War or, as historians might prefer, the Second Indochina War.[1] Johnson in particular knew the value of the strong support FDR eventually summoned from the American people after years of debate.[2] As historian David Kaiser has usefully suggested, Johnson and his advisers appeared to believe that demonstrating firmness toward Hitler at Munich would have deterred him and averted World War II.[3] If, however, there was no way to deter Hitler, the only alternative was to take the difficult political path of mobilizing the nation and convincing the public that Germany and Japan had to be defeated decisively on the battlefield. This was the path FDR took but Johnson rejected with respect to Vietnam.[4]

The consequences of Johnson's decision were immense and are still reverberating today as we grapple with what remains of the post-1945 constitutional order. That order encouraged the Vietnam War by making it possible to treat the decision for full-scale war as simply another policy matter within the global strategy of containment. FDR confronted a resilient barrier between war and peace maintained by the pre–Pearl Harbor constitutional order. The post-1945 order had evaded this barrier amid the constant sense of emergency produced by the threat of communism. As Kennedy, Johnson, and Nixon saw it, under the post-1945 order presidents were solely responsible for leading the nation with respect to foreign affairs and national security. The role of Congress was to support the president.[5]

As we have seen, in the post-1945 constitutional order presidents had unquestioned authority with respect to the use of nuclear weapons and covert military action, two of the three dimensions of warfare. The only point of ambiguity lay in a full commitment of air, naval, and ground forces. Although Truman was viewed as a failed and unpopular president, his commitment of forces to Korea remained available as a "precedent." This point was not resolved during Eisenhower's presidency because the U.S. never engaged in such a war. During the Cuban missile crisis, Kennedy assumed he had the unilateral power to respond to the Soviet challenge, even if it required invading Cuba. In truth, however, focusing too closely on these episodes and scattered statements on war powers by presidents such as Eisenhower would miss a larger reality. The premises of the Cold War, generally supported by the public, required presidents to have the ability to respond if necessary with the full panoply of military force to the challenge of communist expansion. President Johnson was simply the latest heir to this legacy.

Thus Johnson had little reason to believe he was pushing the envelope of the post-1945 constitutional order in a way that would send it into a deep crisis. Given the terms of that order, Johnson wanted Congress's support, but did not see Congress or the American people as a check on his freedom of action, nor as contributors to formulating a sound foreign policy, nor, crucially, as sources of authority. The deliberation necessary before the nation went to war in Vietnam was done inside the executive branch rather than among the branches and the people. This resulted in catastrophe, both at home and abroad.

When the war did not go as expected, the presidency became a cockpit of tension and frustration. The strains of war led Johnson and Nixon to a fixated concern with internal security. They turned the capacities of the intelligence agencies built up during the post-1945 period to use against foreign powers inward against American citizens. This was one of the key causes of Watergate, the political scandal and constitutional crisis that brought down Nixon's presidency.

The appalling aftermath of the Vietnam War and the crash of Nixon's presidency displayed the jerry-built and provisional character of the post-1945 constitutional order. The qualitative difference that war makes to government reasserted itself with a vengeance and showed that the kind of deliberation permitted by the post-1945 order was shockingly inadequate. The premises of the Cold War order would never again be sufficient by themselves to drive the nation to engage in a conventional war. A further consequence was the crippling legacy of lost trust in government. Although not the only causes, Vietnam and Watergate nonetheless were significant contributors to a declining trust in government in the 1960s and 1970s that has never been restored to the level prevailing before the war.

The Limited Relevance of the Tonkin Gulf Resolution

Whether the August 1964 Tonkin Gulf Resolution was sufficient to underwrite the legality of the Vietnam War has been a flashpoint for discussion throughout the modern war powers debate. Yet the dispute over the resolution sheds more light on the nature of the Cold War constitutional order than in determining whether the war was fought according to the Constitution in a narrow legal sense. Because war powers are not part of the legalized Constitution, there is no authoritative *legal* answer to the question of whether the war was constitutional. Focusing on the resolution and the dubious circumstances of its enactment yields little insight into the most significant constitutional questions raised by the ten-year war America fought in Southeast Asia. Our attention should be directed rather to how the Johnson administration's legal arguments illuminated the assumed constitutional basis of the exercise of presidential power during the Cold War. At bottom, Johnson wanted Congress's political support, but like other post–World War II presidents, never conceded that congressional approval was constitutionally required.[6] This distinction has confused subsequent discussion among historians and legal scholars alike.

As Johnson and his advisers deliberated in early 1964 about the worsening situation in South Vietnam, officials realized that a congressional resolution would be politically helpful in underwriting more aggressive action to assist South Vietnam, and a draft was prepared.[7] Although the administration decided not to immediately submit the resolution to Congress, it remained part of executive branch deliberations because LBJ saw Truman's failure to obtain a congressional resolution of support for the Korean War as a costly political mistake.[8]

Johnson may have been planning to move a resolution of support through Congress after the 1964 presidential election in which he faced Republican Senator Barry Goldwater.[9] His plans suddenly kicked into high gear in August after the North Vietnamese attacked a U.S. destroyer in the Tonkin Gulf. After a rushed investigation confirmed that two separate attacks had occurred (although it now seems clear there was only one), the administration moved the broadly worded Tonkin Gulf Resolution through Congress, obtaining nearly unanimous support.[10] Although great attention has been paid to the circumstances in which the resolution was passed, it is important to grasp that it was not the sole or even primary legal justification for the war from the administration's perspective. The purpose of the resolution was to put Congress on the record politically in supporting the administration's response to the Tonkin Gulf attacks and its general policy of resisting communist aggression in Vietnam.[11]

In Chapter 1, I described briefly the 1967 testimony of Under Secretary of State Katzenbach, who presented a comprehensive statement justifying the legality of the war and, by extension, presidential power in the Cold War generally.[12] Senator J. William Fulbright, chair of the Foreign Relations Committee, had called the hearing to consider his "National Commitments Resolution," a measure that was a precursor of the War Powers Resolution.[13] An important target of the hearings was the Tonkin Gulf Resolution, which by 1967 had been attacked repeatedly by senators who regretted their votes. Katzenbach had been attorney general before moving to State, serving in the Department of Justice (DOJ) throughout the Kennedy administration as head of the elite Office of Legal Counsel (OLC) and then as deputy attorney general.[14] He was thus familiar with constitutional and international law and had formally advised President Johnson as attorney general on the legality of the Vietnam War two years earlier.

In his testimony, Katzenbach connected changes in post–World War II foreign affairs to the founding of the U.N. rather than the early history of the Cold War, especially the conflict with the Soviet Union.

His presentation was very much an international lawyer's view of postwar history. In this telling, prior to the adoption of the U.N. Charter, declarations of war were used to announce military adventures of aggression and conquest. This was presumably the meaning such acts had when the Constitution was adopted. But with the acceptance of the Charter came the abolition of war as a matter of international law and the obsolescence of declarations of war.[15] Katzenbach implied strongly that the "declare war" clause was therefore outdated.[16] When asked about the Vietnam War and the role of the Tonkin Gulf Resolution, Katzenbach made the remark, very controversial at the time, that the resolution was the "functional equivalent of the constitutional obligation expressed in the provision of the Constitution with respect to declaring war."[17]

Katzenbach's statement to the committee was broadly consistent with the formal advice he tendered to President Johnson in June 1965.[18] As Johnson was considering whether to take control or "Americanize" the war, Katzenbach was asked to analyze whether further congressional approval, beyond that already given in the Tonkin Gulf Resolution, was required in light of a planned substantial increase in the number of troops in Vietnam and a change in their mission.[19] In his memorandum, Katzenbach made a number of general claims. He held that presidential war power was based on the authority the president had as commander in chief and as sole organ of the U.S. in foreign relations.[20] This "authority has generally been broadly interpreted, and the armed forces have been used without legislative authority on scores of occasions including those involving 'acts of war.'"[21] Katzenbach read the "declare war" clause as relating to a World War II–style conflict. Congress has the power through this clause "to confer substantially unlimited authority to use the armed forces to conquer and, if necessary, subdue a foreign nation."[22] Absent an intent to wage "all-out war," the president could not be restrained by Congress in ordering troops into combat.[23] Katzenbach cited Korea as a key precedent in this regard. Given that, in Katzenbach's view, President Truman's action was accepted as legal, this showed the president had broad authority.[24] Finally, he analyzed the legal danger of asking for congressional permission. Once authorization was obtained, there were Supreme Court cases that suggested the president would be limited to the terms specified, even if his authority in the absence of such an authorization would be greater.[25]

Katzenbach did not maintain that the president's authority to wage the Vietnam War was essentially based on or limited to the Tonkin Gulf Resolution. President Johnson made it clear in a statement while Katzenbach was testifying that he did not need the resolution to carry on the war, a reiteration of a position he had first taken publicly in 1965.[26] This has been overlooked because it is well known that Johnson cited the resolution to members of Congress any number of times as the legal justification for the war.[27] Nevertheless, Johnson had told congressional leaders in a meeting prior to the adoption of the resolution in 1964 that he did not view formal congressional approval to be essential.[28] Thus, President Johnson's bottom-line position, like that of other Cold War presidents, was that he had the constitutional authority to intervene in Vietnam even without a resolution.[29]

The analysis provided by the State Department's legal adviser throughout the war agreed with Katzenbach. Some talking points the legal adviser prepared for the use of Secretary of State Dean Rusk in the hearings on the Tonkin Gulf Resolution are especially noteworthy. The adviser "made it clear that in the view of the executive branch, as was subsequently maintained, the President did not need congressional approval or authorization to use U.S. forces in Vietnam, even against North Vietnam, and that the resolution, therefore, was a political rather than a legal or constitutional instrument."[30] This position was based on historical practice.[31] A few months later the legal adviser submitted a memorandum on the specific issue of whether a literal declaration of war was necessary. In it, he commented on the effect of a declaration in light of international law: "A declaration . . . would place the U.S. 'in a most embarrassing position of being the first nation to declare war since the formulation of the [U.N.] Charter. We would be opening ourselves to universal condemnation.'"[32] Later in 1965, the legal adviser made it clear that the State Department regarded Korea as a precedent for action in Vietnam.[33] Finally, a lengthy memorandum by the legal adviser justifying the legality of the war under international and domestic law was made public in 1966.[34] The memorandum reiterated that the president's Article II authority was sufficient to prosecute the war.[35]

The framework in which the administration approached the constitutionality of the war was generally shared by members of Congress. Consistent with understandings developed at the beginning of the Cold War, members of Congress accepted that the president should take the lead in matters of foreign affairs, even when such matters involved committing troops to combat.[36] Katzenbach was probably correct to stress in a later interview that the actual circumstances of the incidents in the Tonkin Gulf mattered little to Democratic members of Congress.[37] Their objective was to support the president of their party in defending American interests, particularly in an election year.[38]

Historians have often termed Vietnam an "undeclared" war.[39] If they mean that the war never received its deliberative due, they are correct. For legal scholars, the issue is more complex. Later analysis endorsed Katzenbach's specific contention that wars may be constitutionally authorized through resolutions. Declarations of war are not literally required.[40] As discussed in Chapter 1, the appropriate focus from a constitutional point of view is whether a war was authorized after interbranch deliberation, not whether Congress enacted a document with "Declaration of War" written across the top.[41] Most constitutional scholars agree that the recent "Authorizations to Use Military Force" (AUMFs), employed both for the wars in Afghanistan and Iraq, are the legal and constitutional equivalents of declarations of war.[42]

The respected constitutional scholar John Hart Ely went further and argued that the resolution was completely effective to authorize the war, both in terms of its language and the deliberation that occurred in August 1964.[43] This is doubtful. Historians have persuasively shown that both publicly and privately, most senators expressed deep reservations and the resolution was far from a blank check.[44] But the most serious problem with Ely's argument is that Johnson's crucial decision to Americanize the war lay in the future. It was this decision, made largely in secret in early 1965 before anyone guessed what was going on, as we shall see, that most deserved full and intensive scrutiny by Congress. But this is exactly what did not happen in 1964 or later. If there was any original sin that gave essential life to the notion of the "imperial presidency," this was it. LBJ decided for a major conventional war on his own.

For his part, LBJ never saw the 1964 resolution as a legal instrument. He gave consideration several times to asking for *another* resolution of support from Congress, something that is hard to explain if the resolution fully authorized the war in a legal sense.[45] Although some senators later took back their votes on the resolution, saying they had been misled by the administration, it is likely that LBJ could have obtained successive resolutions of support or authorization from Congress every year if necessary. We tend to forget that once the war began in earnest in 1965, ardent opponents of the war were always a minority in Congress, having significant influence only in the Senate, and that Johnson's party firmly controlled both houses of Congress throughout his term.[46] Loyal Democrats were not about to humiliate their president with a negative vote on the war.[47] Johnson tended to steer clear of Congress because of a fear of divisive debates and nonunanimous support rather than out of a concern that Congress would actually terminate the war.[48] And at least in the Johnson administration, congressional opponents of the war had no real diplomatic or military alternatives to offer.[49] At the same time, it has to be kept in mind that all of the deliberation in Congress occurred amid a vacuum of information on the war's prospects, information that the executive branch systematically withheld.

Inquiries into the legal status of the Tonkin Gulf Resolution are helpful only up to a point. These inquiries are based ultimately on the premise that presidential authority with respect to war and foreign affairs could be circumscribed. But that is the premise the post-1945 constitutional order rejected. Presidents have treated such resolutions as political statements of support and have never acknowledged that they were legally required. We would do better to focus on how the resolution illustrated the nature of presidential decisionmaking within this order.

As we saw in Chapter 3, there were three dimensions in which presidential military action could be undertaken in the Cold War: nuclear, conventional, and covert. Early decisionmaking on the war illustrated the interaction among these different dimensions. Although the next section will describe executive decisionmaking to initiate the war, presidential approval of covert military actions was certainly relevant in the run-up to the Tonkin Gulf Resolution. In early 1964, President Johnson approved OPLAN 34A involving assistance to South Vietnamese guerrillas making raids into North Vietnam. In addition, the Navy engaged in patrols off the coast of North Vietnam, testing its military capabilities through electronic espionage.[50] Thus, leaders in North Vietnam were aware they were being challenged militarily by the United States in support of its ally and client state in South Vietnam.[51]

None of this was disclosed to Congress in August 1964. To be sure, the administration's actions against North Vietnam were limited, especially relative to the covert actions approved in the Eisenhower and Kennedy administrations in the Middle East and Cuba. There was, however, a disturbing similarity between the covert actions against North Vietnam and the Bay of Pigs. Each involved the possibility of leveraging foreseeable enemy responses to covert action into a conventional war. To the extent that this was a valuable lesson in the interaction of the different dimensions of warfare, it was a lesson denied to Congress. Once again, the cycle of accountability was frustrated.

Deciding for War without Congress

In the war powers debate there has always been a tendency to assume that major wars could start small and develop incrementally, despite the fact that both world wars and Korea provided no supporting evidence. No doubt proponents of restrictions on presidential war power had Vietnam in mind.[52] This reflects an outdated understanding of how the Johnson administration decided to go to war in 1964–1965. As Campbell Craig and Fredrik Logevall remark, the "release of massive amounts of archival documentation, however, renders this interpretation (the incremental or 'quagmire' thesis) untenable."[53] We may draw the inference and lesson that big wars do not begin without big presidential decisions.

Although debate continues among historians about when and how Johnson made his decisions on Vietnam, on balance the evidence strongly suggests that starting immediately after the 1964 presidential election, his administration began a process that would lead inexorably to the public announcement of the Americanization of the war in July 1965.[54] Craig and Logevall continue: "Johnson and his top aides, it is now clear, understood very well that their actions in early and mid-1965 represented more than an incremental step; it was a move to major war, and one that would be difficult to win."[55] Victory was defined as forcing the North Vietnamese government to accept U.S. terms for ceasing its aggression. The administration began an air war and then a ground war in early 1965 out of public sight in order to accomplish this objective.[56]

Johnson's ultimate responsibility for the war and thus the necessity to study closely executive branch decisionmaking at this crucial stage has been obscured somewhat by disputes over the context in which those decisions were made. Some scholars and commentators continue to believe that LBJ and his administration made their decisions in a permissive context in which the public and elites favored military intervention.[57] There is a substantial amount of evidence, however, that the context of decisionmaking was just as permissive in the opposite direction—there was no groundswell of support for a large-scale commitment of ground forces prior to July 1965.[58] The thesis that the decision for war was strongly determined by context ignores LBJ's own considerable ability, at the height of his popularity and in the wake of an overwhelming victory in the 1964 election, to change the context.

To be sure, the Johnson administration believed from the beginning that a relatively minor amount of force would be required and saw themselves as fighting a "limited war."[59] It was limited in the sense that they did not wish to repeat the Korean experience of intervention by China and they certainly did not want to provoke a general war that might lead to the use of nuclear weapons. Nonetheless, try as they might to treat the war as simply another policy within the structure of U.S. foreign affairs, Johnson and his advisers were soon overwhelmed by its demands.[60] Moreover, both Johnson and Nixon found themselves grappling with the ambiguities created by a Cold War constitutional order that was at odds with the text of the Constitution itself.

Despite the assurances of proponents of the post-1945 order reviewed in Chapter 2 that the U.S. was in a completely new state of affairs called "semiwar," both administrations confronted the reality that there was still a practical and constitutional dividing line between war and peace. The attainment of military objectives against a determined enemy meant the use of significant deadly force backed by substantial funding. But the task of providing for a major war went far beyond providing the required resources. As we saw in Chapter 1, war is qualitatively different from any other policy pursued by government, a reality recognized in the Constitution. War requires the sacrifice of citizens to objectives that must transcend ordinary political goals. The president must take an active role as commander in chief in guiding the overall war effort. This requires deliberation over war aims and the formulation of a strategy to specify how those aims will be achieved.

The tensions between the post-1945 constitutional order and the Constitution itself were intensified by the uncompromising way the Johnson and Nixon administrations interpreted the position of the presidency in that order. Johnson and Nixon both held strong views about presidential supremacy in foreign policy.[61] As described accurately in Arthur Schlesinger's history of the rise of the "imperial presidency," both presidents saw themselves as supreme in foreign affairs and Congress in a distinctly secondary role.[62] In practical terms, this meant that when LBJ assumed the presidency in November 1963, the nation embarked on roughly a ten-year experiment conducted by two presidential administrations who rejected key baseline assumptions of the original Constitution. If the public consensus behind the Cold War order had endured, this might have mediated the conflict. However, under the pressure of the failure in Vietnam, that order began to seem less compelling, at least to members of the Democratic Party.

Given the lack of interbranch deliberation, Vietnam's reputation as a one-branch war was accurate. Congress acquiesced to the war as a junior partner.[63] Johnson did meet with congressional leaders on a fairly regular basis, aided by their assumption that their role was to give advice in private rather than to spark public debate.[64] Consultation occurred mostly on the Senate side, given the traditional belief that the upper house had a special role in foreign affairs. In any case, the House was always more supportive of the war than the Senate. If there was to be public debate, the Senate appeared to be the only forum.

Given at least some level of congressional involvement, what more could Congress have contributed? Vietnam is an excellent test case for anyone who believes that interbranch deliberation and public debate matter little to sound policy or that interagency review in the executive branch can substitute for a robust exchange of views between the separate branches. Then and now, some doubt whether Congress has an effective role to play in the making of foreign policy. It is important to see that this belief is part and parcel of the Cold War constitutional order and illustrates the reach of that order into the twenty-first century. It is that order which assumed that wars were simply another instrument in the conduct of foreign policy by the president. The proper question from the perspective of the original Constitution is how Congress can contribute to the supremely important decision to go to war. Vietnam demonstrated clearly how war is qualitatively different from any other policy pursued by government and could be carried on effectively within the American constitutional tradition only by the executive and legislative branches working in tandem.

It is not news that the Kennedy and Johnson administrations concealed key aspects of their Vietnam policy from Congress and the American people. This is part of the conventional wisdom about what was wrong with the Vietnam War.[65] What is not as much appreciated were the further consequences of the notable lack of meaningful interbranch deliberation. The consequence deserving the most discussion, despite its underappreciation in the extensive literature on the war, was the truncated and inadequate policymaking within the executive branch that resulted from concealment. If the Kennedy and Johnson administrations had gone to Congress from the beginning this process would have provided a strong incentive for the different actors within the executive branch to settle on a unified justification for the already deep U.S. involvement in Vietnam by 1961. Later on, it would have encouraged the executive branch to articulate a justification for the war and a strategy to succeed. It is important to understand that we do not have to assume anything about the quality of interrogation in hearings or investigation by Congress or the usefulness of subsequent feedback from the press and the public to appreciate that the prospect of public testimony of itself would have compelled the executive branch to reconcile its policy accounts.

The effect of the close hold the executive branch kept over policy in Southeast Asia could be seen throughout the Kennedy administration. Making policy on a one-branch basis meant that President Kennedy and Secretary of Defense Robert McNamara were dependent on a narrow stream of information from Vietnam.[66] When push came to shove as the South Vietnamese government of Ngo Dinh Diem tottered in August 1963, executive branch officials were deeply divided and unwilling to acknowledge that no good policy was available.[67] As historian Lawrence Freedman comments, "Getting the optimum outcome—an independent and free South Vietnam—depended on the quality of the South Vietnamese military and political effort. The basic question was what should be done if that effort failed. The administration found this too awkward to confront directly at this time. They still assumed that the war could be won."[68]

We do not know what would have occurred had the Kennedy administration been forced to resolve these policy conflicts in order to present a united front in regular public hearings on Vietnam. But nothing was pushing the administration to identify the available policy choices with greater precision. At a minimum, public and regular interaction with Congress would have provided incentives in this direction. Kennedy seemed to sense how problematic the post-1945 constitutional order had become as he was being urged by his advisers to make a greater military commitment to Vietnam in late 1961. Kennedy "questioned the wisdom of involvement in Vietnam since the basis thereof is not completely clear. By comparison he noted that Korea was a case of clear aggression which was opposed by the United States and other members of the U.N. The conflict in Vietnam is more obscure and less flagrant."[69]

For all practical purposes, Congress and the public had initially unanimously endorsed Truman's Korean intervention.[70] But this was not necessarily an endorsement of the logic of the post-1945 order. As Kennedy intuited, it was rather that North Korea, backed by the major communist powers, had been seen to violate the clear dividing line between war and peace. The logic of the Cold War arguably compelled Kennedy's advisers to urge him to hold the line in Southeast Asia.[71] But there was no similar obvious crossing of the line by North Vietnam that would trigger public support for a stand against communism similar to Truman's. This suggested the post-1945 order was not stable in that it could not generate the public support for the kind of military action implied by the premises of that order.

Historians disagree about where Kennedy left policy on Vietnam when he was assassinated in November 1963.[72] But it is reasonably clear that LBJ rapidly established a framework for Vietnam policy that emphasized military over political options.[73] As noted above, historians have recently shown that the Johnson administration made policy decisions amounting to a decision for war much earlier than was appreciated in the histories of the war that were published in the 1970s and 1980s.[74] A course for war in Vietnam had arguably been set in the executive branch even prior to the 1964 presidential election.[75] But the principal studies and policy decisions were undertaken in the weeks and months that followed the election.[76] The decision for war was firmly in place in the executive branch by early 1965 and Johnson's famous July 1965 announcement that he would substantially augment General Westmoreland's force in Vietnam and thus Americanize the war was a follow-on to earlier decisions, rather than a fundamental turning point.[77]

Johnson went to great lengths to conceal these crucial decisions both from Congress and the public.[78] In February 1965 meetings with congressional leaders, he hinted at a change of approach in Vietnam, but said it would not involve escalating the war.[79] Throughout the first half of 1965, Johnson worked assiduously not to excite public interest in what was happening.[80] Even at the late July 1965 press conference announcing the troop increase, he downplayed the significance of the change in policy.[81] Johnson's avoidance of the political and legislative process was all the more ironic given the remarkable experience he had acquired over many years as a leader in Congress.[82] Given Johnson's deep knowledge of the legislative process, he could have used Congress if he had wished to generate policy alternatives for the administration and the country.[83]

The failure to use Congress meant that what happened inside the executive branch would determine whether the nation went to war. The deliberation that took place during 1963 through 1965 demonstrated the enormous difficulties with a one-branch decision process. It further illustrated the derangement of policy that followed from the post-1945 constitutional order, as historians have shown conclusively that critical questions about how to fight the war were not asked and important alternatives to war were not explored.[84] Key aides such as McGeorge Bundy, Johnson's national security adviser, did not marshal the bureaucratic resources available in the different departments to answer basic questions such as how much force would be necessary to compel North Vietnam to cease its aggression and begin negotiations.[85] The State Department did not assess the soundness of the long-held assumption that all of Southeast Asia would be in jeopardy if Vietnam were unified under communist rule.[86] Nor did the department seriously explore diplomatic alternatives to escalation such as neutralization of the conflict.[87] For his part, LBJ did not encourage any exploration of the alternatives to escalation. Like the legislative leader he once was, Johnson wheeled from one adviser to the next, satisfying each that his voice had been heard, while strenuously avoiding a truly collective process of decision-making.[88] As historian Fredrik Logevall comments, "Almost everyone outside the administration could agree that escalation was legitimately one of the options before Lyndon Johnson; they would have been flabbergasted, however, had they known that it was the only one under serious consideration."[89]

Avoiding Congress was all the more questionable because throughout the 1964–1965 decisions for war, the soundest and most expert policy advice was coming from that body. Senate Majority Leader Mike Mansfield, Frank Church, and Senator-turned-Vice President Hubert Humphrey, all Democrats, were outstanding examples. Having traveled in Asia and taught Asian history as a college professor, Mansfield arguably had greater expertise than any of Kennedy or Johnson's top advisers.[90] Although officials such as McNamara were aware of the lack of knowledge with respect to East Asia in the government, they did nothing to widen their circle of information.[91] By contrast, Mansfield traveled to Vietnam and actively sought sources of information that the Kennedy administration ignored.[92] Historians have credited Mansfield with writing some of the most incisive memoranda on Vietnam as he tried to convince the Eisenhower, Kennedy, and Johnson administrations to pull back from a full commitment.[93] Unfortunately Mansfield's advice was always private because, like many members of Congress at the time, he accepted the premises of the post-1945 order and thus saw the role of Congress as secondary to presidential leadership in foreign affairs.[94]

Senators Church and Humphrey gave prescient speeches in 1964 warning against a greater commitment to Vietnam.[95] Shortly after becoming vice president, Humphrey gave LBJ an insightful memorandum on why it was necessary to have a full public debate. He wrote, "American wars have to be politically understandable by the American public. There has to be a cogent, convincing case if we are to enjoy sustained public support. In World Wars I and II we had this. In Korea we were moving under United Nations auspices to South Korea against dramatic, across-the-border, conventional aggression."[96] Much like President Kennedy's 1961 analysis, Humphrey had properly identified the difference between Vietnam and these earlier conflicts.

Whereas in the 1949 debate over NATO Humphrey had maintained that declarations of war were obsolete, he now properly pointed to the importance of using an open debate to unite the public behind the war, while also reminding LBJ that public support could not be taken for granted.[97] Humphrey also warned, in effect, that the war could split the Democratic Party.[98] LBJ's response was to exclude Humphrey from decisionmaking on Vietnam.[99] Biographer Robert Dallek remarks that LBJ was displeased with Humphrey's memo because he feared what could happen from a full commitment to war.[100] The point of the Constitution, however, was to make this sort of shirking impossible by establishing a clear dividing line between war and peace. This is what President Johnson was consciously avoiding with the aid of the post-1945 constitutional order.

In many respects, the questions that were avoided by the executive branch in 1964 and 1965 were asked seriously only after the January 1968 Tet offensive shocked the government and the American people.[101] Clark Clifford, the new secretary of defense and a former aide to Truman, asked the JCS how long the war would take if they received a substantial proposed troop increase. They had no adequate response.[102] By then, the list of executive decisions that the Johnson administration had not disclosed was quite long:

- That covert actions were under way in 1964 prior to the Tonkin Gulf incident.
- That key decisions to escalate the war were made in early 1965.
- That substantial forces would be required in addition to those President Johnson announced in July 1965.
- That the U.S. was in a war by fall 1965 in which success might take years and thousands of American lives.
- That the war would cost billions of dollars, requiring a tax increase at a minimum.[103]

There was a very real sense, then, in which Congress and the public did not have constitutional responsibility for the war, although they did support it politically once it was under way.[104] As we have been exploring, one consequence of the choice not to decide for war through Congress and a public debate was that everything then depended on the flawed policymaking process inside the executive branch. Logevall and other historians have highlighted the role of domestic politics and even careerist considerations in making the decision for war.[105] One reason for the commitment to war was that to recommend withdrawal or negotiations would have meant a loss of personal credibility for Johnson's key advisers—McNamara, Rusk, and Bundy. They had too much invested in the idea that Vietnam was crucial to U.S. national security. Not for the last time did careerism affect the national security policymaking process.[106]

The Vietnam experience was another example that showed the executive branch could not handle the decision for war on its own.

Having avoided the need under the Constitution for an engagement with Congress and the public through the bypass provided by the post-1945 constitutional order, LBJ and his administration suffered the consequences. As we will see in the next section, this meant that the intense pressures attendant to running a major war descended almost immediately on the executive branch and the White House in particular.

What requires some further discussion is how the lack of credibility that resulted from the failures of disclosure flowed from the initial choice to avoid Congress and a public debate.[107] Deciding for war through Congress would have meant that the members of Congress could not have shirked their responsibility for war later. This would have created a stronger home front for Johnson to rely on, a well of trust he could have drawn on as the war went badly.[108] Conversely, if the result of the debate had been to avoid a massive military intervention and try instead for a negotiated political solution (as President Kennedy had accomplished earlier in Laos), trust in government would have still been maintained and the U.S. would have avoided an enormous tragedy.[109] Instead, Vietnam made a key contribution to the loss of trust that disabled American government in the ensuing decades.

As Robert Putnam described in *Bowling Alone,* his well-regarded study of civic engagement and social capital, "Americans in the mid-1960s were strikingly confident in the benevolence and responsiveness of their political institutions."[110] In contemporary times, however, this situation has been reversed. "In the 1990s roughly three in four Americans *didn't* trust the government to do what is right most of the time."[111] Although political scientists have charted ups and downs with respect to trust in government, trust has never returned to the level that existed before the Johnson administration took the nation to war.[112] Using evidence from the National Election Studies (NES), Gary Orren showed that trust in government was above 70 percent in the late 1950s and early 1960s.[113] He commented, "Trust fell by a full 15 percentage points from 1964 to 1968, years of intense racial turbulence and turmoil over Vietnam during Lyndon Johnson's administration, and then another 8 percent in the first two years of Richard Nixon's presidency."[114]

A number of scholars cite Vietnam as the explanation for the initial decline in trust shown in the 1966 NES. Margaret Levi and Laura Stoker remark that "the decline in trust from the 1960s to the 1970s was fueled by citizens' reactions to the war in Vietnam, Watergate, and civil rights initiatives."[115] Joseph Nye agrees that Vietnam and Watergate explain how the decline began, but not why it is still going on.[116] Of course, these are general observations. As we will see, significant elements of Watergate were directly related to Vietnam and thus part of the same historical process.

Another important consequence of bypassing Congress and the public that deserves mention was the missed opportunity for learning about the Cold War. Because the public was disengaged from the beginning of the war, some vital connections were never made and the public learning that did take place was limited. An open debate in early 1965 would have forced to the surface themes that were only dimly apparent even after Senator Fulbright held hearings challenging the Johnson administration in early 1966. In particular, it would have been apparent that the Cold War could be fought in different ways, some of them political and diplomatic rather than military. It would have been evident that some experts in foreign policy thought Europe was a more vital arena of confrontation with the Soviet Union compared to Asia and would have reminded the public that some military leaders had always viewed land wars in Asia with skepticism. The public could thus have more easily perceived the link between Vietnam and the Cold War. If the war had gone forward after all, this might have spurred a more general inquiry later into the viability of a diplomatic strategy based on militarization.

The Strains of War and Internal Security

War imposes unique psychological stress on the inhabitant of the Oval Office. The risks attendant to war and the personal responsibility that any president would feel for the men and women under his command tend to occupy the mind and crowd out everything else. Because LBJ and his top advisers made the decision for war alone, the stress was all the greater. Consider that *less than six months* after the muted July 1965 announcement of escalation, LBJ and his administration were under extraordinary strain.[117] Even in the fall of 1965, the administration could sense that the public was not strongly behind the war.[118] While this may have troubled them, it would not matter if their expectations of quickly forcing North Vietnam to negotiate had worked as planned.[119] When this did not occur by the end of the year, the administration plunged into a series of recriminations and a fruitless debate about halting the bombing.[120]

Somewhat unexpectedly, the decision for war had narrowed the range of options available to the president. Once LBJ chose bombing to force North Vietnam to negotiate, bombing *had* to work. This had the further effect of making administration policy hostage to the responses of the governments in both South and North Vietnam. LBJ could sense that now he must prevail or his presidency would be forever discredited.[121] A war fever took hold in the executive branch, creating a vicious circle which undermined effective policymaking as officials saw that the president wanted only good news and interpreted developments in their most favorable light.[122] It did not help that, being human, they were susceptible to the same distortions in viewpoint that afflicted the president. They knew as well that their personal credibility was on the line.[123]

Aides below the top level could occasionally rise above the executive branch swamp and perceive that something was seriously wrong with government decisionmaking.[124] In May 1967 John McNaughton, one of McNamara's chief assistants, took note of public opposition to the war and commented: "A feeling is widely and strongly held, . . . that 'the Establishment' is out of its mind. . . . Related to this feeling is the increased polarization that is taking place in the United States with seeds of the worst split in our people in more than a century."[125] By then McNamara had serious doubts about the progress of the war but could not convince LBJ to change course.[126]

Under the strains of war the administration's attitude toward critics took a hard set. By early 1966, LBJ thought that Senate critics such as Fulbright were actually under communist influence.[127] The ideological and McCarthyite downside of the Cold War had returned with a vengeance. FBI Director J. Edgar Hoover encouraged LBJ in his belief that critics of the war were subversives and operated from the worst motives.[128] All of the major intelligence agencies—the FBI, CIA, NSA, as well as the Army—developed covert domestic intelligence programs aimed at monitoring and disrupting opposition to the war.[129] Presidents Johnson and Nixon both believed that the antiwar movement was inspired by communist agents. When careful investigation by the intelligence agencies showed this to be false, they in effect ordered the agencies to prove the relationship.[130]

It has long been appreciated by historians of the Vietnam War that there was a meaningful link between the domestic intelligence operations used to counter the war's critics and Watergate.[131] More relevant here is how the strains of war affected Nixon.[132] With well over 500,000 U.S. troops in Vietnam when he took office and combat action continuing at a high tempo, Nixon rejected the option of a quick withdrawal in favor of a strategy that had several elements in pursuit of his overall goal of "peace with honor"—a negotiated settlement in which the North Vietnamese would somehow be persuaded to withdraw their forces and guarantee the viability of the South Vietnamese government. Roughly, Nixon's policy with respect to Vietnam was to satisfy domestic pressure for an end to the war by withdrawing American forces, but slowly enough to preserve meaningful military options. To compensate for the withdrawal, the U.S. would build up South Vietnam's ability to resist, a process of "Vietnamization" begun under Johnson. More ambitiously, Nixon wanted to reframe the war against a new global strategy of détente with the Soviet Union and opening relations with China. He felt sure that these leading communist states could bring pressure to bear on North Vietnam.[133]

Sooner than Nixon anticipated, his Vietnam strategy involved him in new military responses as North Vietnam continued to exert significant pressure, especially by using its sanctuaries in Cambodia, which was nonetheless a neutral country. At the same time, the reaction of the antiwar movement and the public generally was always a concern.[134] So when Nixon decided to bomb Cambodia early in his first year in office, he determined it would have to be conducted secretly, difficult to do with a major military operation.[135] When news of the operation leaked, Nixon was upset and ordered FBI Director Hoover to wiretap the phones of administration aides and journalists.[136]

Major antiwar protests were scheduled for fall 1969. At roughly the same moment, Nixon was considering "Duck Hook," a major strike to force North Vietnam to settle the war on U.S. terms.[137] Nixon knew that this expansion would require unusual "mental resolve" and a "go-for-broke public relations campaign, in which he would have to expend most or all of his political capital to survive 'the heat.'"[138] Duck Hook was dropped, but the idea of the decisive intervention remained. At the same time, Nixon appreciated by the end of 1969 that the war was now his responsibility in full. Taking control of the war amid hostile domestic opposition would mean going on the offensive both abroad and at home.[139] In April 1970, Nixon planned to order U.S. troops to invade border regions in Cambodia to eliminate the North Vietnamese sanctuaries. Characteristic of all of Nixon's Vietnam strategy, this deliberation occurred in secret. Nixon shared his plans with very few people other than Henry Kissinger, his national security adviser. Considering this operation occasioned intense stress, as he knew it would be perceived as expanding the war.[140]

Nixon could not foresee how much crisis management the Cambodian invasion would impose on the administration. Universities all over the country shut down in protest and several of Kissinger's aides resigned.[141] Under considerable pressure, Nixon began to act erratically.[142] In the period leading up to the invasion, he seemed hyperactive to his subordinates, indulging in an "aggressive mania" to steel himself for ordering a major military operation without congressional or public support.[143] The invasion of Cambodia was perceived, not without cause, as a major expansion of the war by members of Congress and the antiwar movement. As discussed more fully in the next chapter, the unprecedented backlash and public protest resulting from the Cambodian invasion was the turning point in giving significant credibility and impetus to efforts already under way to curb the war-making power of the executive branch.[144]

It was at this moment, amid the superheated atmosphere produced by the Cambodian invasion, that Nixon summoned the chiefs of the major intelligence agencies to chastise them for not cooperating more effectively against the nation's *domestic* enemies.[145] It would have been appropriate for Nixon to raise this issue with respect to foreign enemies, as the lack of cooperation between Hoover's FBI and the CIA had been causing trouble for many years.[146] But like Johnson, Nixon was convinced that the antiwar movement was inspired and led by agents of international communism. Not only was this false, but it also illustrated the Nixon administration's isolation from reasonable voices within the antiwar movement available for a meaningful dialogue.[147] Nixon, however, had worked himself into such a mania that he saw antiwar protesters on campus as terrorists threatening the state itself.[148] As summarized by historian Jeffrey Kimball, "The Vietnam War heightened Nixon's sense of world crisis, contributed to his emotional tension, compounded his personality disorders, and influenced his stratagems and tactics for dealing with home-front and foreign issues."[149]

The solution to the lack of cooperation among the intelligence agencies was later known as the Huston plan after the White House aide who wrote it at Nixon's direction.[150] The plan called for the centralizing of domestic intelligence activities in the White House and involved aggressive, illegal measures such as break-ins to combat domestic protest.[151] When FBI Director Hoover objected, fearing disclosure of illegal activities, the plan was formally abandoned. Informally, however, these options continued to percolate at the White House.[152] If the intelligence agencies would not take suitable action, the White House itself would go operational and conduct illegal break-ins and wiretaps in pursuit of information that would discredit its political enemies. This was one origin of what came to be known as Watergate.[153]

Watergate as a Cold War Constitutional Crisis

"Watergate" is often taken to refer to the scandal and constitutional crisis which followed the June 1972 burglary of the Democratic National Committee headquarters at the Watergate complex in Washington by persons associated with President Nixon's reelection committee and the subsequent cover-up, led by Nixon himself, of White House involvement in the burglary.[154] Watergate is perceived this way by many despite the clear connections between the earlier actions described above of the Nixon administration with respect to Vietnam and the Watergate burglary. So to understand the perspective I advance here, which might be called in brief "Watergate as foreign policy," requires making some distinctions. Nixon's misdeeds ran in many directions besides those connected with Vietnam or even the Watergate burglary itself.[155] To see Watergate afresh and understand how it makes sense as a crisis of the Cold War constitutional order requires some rearranging of standard understandings.

We should initially highlight some general features of Nixon's presidency. Always intending to be a foreign affairs president, Nixon wanted to achieve reelection in 1972 and be remembered in history as someone who brought peace to the United States and the world.[156] At the same time, Nixon retained beliefs with respect to foreign policy that he had formed as a senator and then as vice president in the Eisenhower administration. He accepted the verities of the Cold War and saw the conflict between the United States and communist countries as central.[157] Like many political leaders in the early Cold War, Nixon was intrigued by the potential of covert action and, in the Eisenhower administration, he advocated its use to promote regime change.[158] At the same time, he perceived strategic opportunities arising from the relatively new conflict between the Soviet Union and China. Nixon saw Vietnam in this context. It was a war he had to settle, but on a global basis with terms favorable to the U.S.[159]

Crucial to Nixon's conception of his presidency was his desire to carry out this far-reaching strategy entirely in secret in order to announce it at the right moment to secure reelection and establish his place as one of the greatest presidents, while confounding his political opponents.[160] This meant that during his administration an enormous amount of unaccountable diplomatic and military activity occurred off the bureaucratic books. This did not bother Nixon, as he entered office with grievances against a number of government agencies centrally important to foreign policy, such as the State Department and the CIA, which he felt had mistreated him as vice president.[161] He therefore resolved to be his own secretary of state, and he and Kissinger centralized control of foreign affairs and national security policy in the White House. The State and Defense Departments, as well as the CIA, were often cut out of both formulating and implementing policy.[162] The White House and especially the national security staff thus went "operational" in foreign affairs from the beginning of Nixon's presidency.

This operational setup assisted Nixon in making swift, decisive moves to advance U.S. interests. With respect to intelligence, John Ranelagh makes the valuable point that although the CIA had become something of a status quo agency by the late 1960s, Nixon did not want to be a status quo president. He wanted aggressive action to create a more favorable balance of power.[163] Kimball has persuasively argued that Nixon's "madman theory" of exercising power in unpredictable ways was related to the Eisenhower administration's "massive retaliation" policy.[164] While Nixon saw himself as an American Charles de Gaulle, a world leader in the grand European manner, his chief diplomat Kissinger thought the primary objective of the government was order.[165] Neither Nixon nor Kissinger believed in democratic governance of foreign affairs in the sense of building support for their policy in Congress and the Senate.[166]

Any breach in the wall of secrecy around the White House or Nixon and Kissinger's diplomatic efforts was therefore a mortal threat. It was all the worse if the breach could be traced to someone who was part of the antiwar movement, a movement which to them was inspired by communists and led by revolutionary terrorists.[167] Thus the administration had a severe reaction in June 1971 to Daniel Ellsberg's leaking of the Pentagon Papers to major newspapers including the *New York Times.* The Pentagon Papers were a secret Department of Defense history of the Vietnam War ordered by Robert McNamara during the Johnson administration. Nixon directed his aides to destroy Ellsberg's credibility and, by extension, the credibility of the antiwar movement in the eyes of the public.[168] Unbelievably, Nixon and his aides planned to dig up information on both Ellsberg and the Johnson administration by committing illegal break-ins.

Nixon's remarks on the Pentagon Papers and Ellsberg, recorded by his taping system in the White House, leave an indelible and disturbing impression. Nixon believed the young lawyers on his team did not have the proper attitude:

> These kids don't understand. They have no understanding of politics. They have no understanding of public relations. John Mitchell is that way. John is always worried about is it technically correct? Do you think, for Christ sakes, that the *New York Times* is worried about all the legal niceties. Those sons of bitches are killing me. I mean, thank God, I leaked to the press [during the Hiss controversy]. This is what we've got to get—I want you to shake these (unintelligible) up around here. Now you do it. Shake them up. Get them off their Goddamn dead asses and say now that isn't what you should be talking about. We're up against an enemy, a conspiracy. They're using any means. *We are going to use any means.* Is that clear?[169]

Nixon went on to refer to a scheme to burglarize the Brookings Institution, a Washington think tank, to retrieve classified documents on Vietnam he believed might be in their possession. He continued, "Did they get the Brookings Institute raided last night? No. Get it done. I want it done. I want the Brookings Institute's safe *cleaned out* and have it cleaned out in a way that it makes somebody else [responsible?]."[170]

The Special Investigative Unit (otherwise known as the Plumbers), a team set up in the White House to combat leaks, was available to conduct the projected break-ins.[171] One was carried out in September 1971, a burglary of the office of Ellsberg's psychiatrist in Los Angeles.[172] Once this happened, Nixon and his men were ensnared in a criminal conspiracy. Everyone involved in the operation knew something which could be of mortal danger to Nixon and his top aides in the White House. When the burglary at the Watergate complex was discovered in June 1972, Nixon had to lead a cover-up of the operation in part to ensure that the links between the Ellsberg and Watergate burglaries would not be discovered.[173]

These operations were carried out in the main by E. Howard Hunt, who had recently retired from the CIA.[174] Hunt had participated in various CIA operations, including the Bay of Pigs. Nixon and his aides believed that Hunt could be relied on to carry out the kind of operations originally anticipated in the Huston plan.[175] When Hunt needed men to help him, he turned to Cubans who had been trained by the CIA to commit acts of sabotage against Castro.[176] Many of these same people were involved in the 1972 break-in at the Watergate complex along with James McCord, a former chief of security at the CIA.[177]

After the Watergate burglars were arrested, the leading idea among Nixon's men was to quash the FBI investigation by claiming that Watergate was a CIA operation having to do with the Bay of Pigs.[178] Nixon was later convicted in the opinion of Congress and the public by the disclosure of a June 23, 1972, tape in which Nixon directed his chief of staff H. R. Haldeman to order the CIA to carry out this plan.[179] CIA Director Richard Helms and his deputy Vernon Walters were confident that Watergate had nothing to do with the Bay of Pigs and resisted White House overtures to assist with the cover-up.[180]

There was an important sense, however, in which Watergate *did* relate to the Bay of Pigs. The break-ins were carefully planned, requiring training, discipline, and knowledge of specialized equipment.[181] The men carrying them out could not be ordinary criminals. That would leave the administration too vulnerable to involvement with unpredictable characters. As we saw in Chapter 3, the Eisenhower and Kennedy administrations invested significant resources in training a covert army of operatives against Castro. These operatives came to the U.S. after the failure of the Bay of Pigs. In this respect, the efforts of two presidential administrations against Castro became braided together with Nixon's efforts to destroy domestic opposition to his war policies in a very dangerous way. It is likely that the break-ins could not have occurred as they did had these operatives, accustomed to living above the law, not been available to the administration.[182] The Cuban operatives were hard line anticommunists who perhaps believed they were acting to protect the United States against the communist-inspired antiwar movement.[183]

Nonetheless, once they were caught the imperatives of a criminal conspiracy took over. This put the president of the United States in the unbelievable position of being vulnerable to blackmail by the Watergate burglars.[184] The country was fortunate that Hunt and his fellow conspirators simply wanted President Nixon to give them money to pay their defense and expenses. Suppose they had wanted changes in government policy? This dire possibility was a logical consequence of presidential involvement in a conspiracy to break the law.

If Watergate had simply been a matter of the June 1972 burglary, which Nixon did not order, and the subsequent rather improvised cover-up, it might be appropriate to view it as a kind of external hindrance to the policy initiatives of the administration.[185] But Watergate was inextricably connected with the foreign policy of the Nixon administration and thus with the Cold War itself. As we saw in Chapter 2, the maintenance of the Cold War or any conventional war required an enormous effort on the part of the government to overcome the inertia of the original Constitution and maintain morale on the domestic front. Given the rising concern with the communist challenge from 1947 through 1950, Truman had the public behind him when he went to war in Korea, despite the lack of congressional authorization. Nixon's task was far more difficult and, indeed, suggested the waning of the Cold War. He knew the Vietnam War was unpopular and that the end would at least have to be in sight by the time he ran for reelection.[186] He decided to combat the antiwar movement with all the means available to him, including the intelligence capabilities built since the 1950s. This pushed the entire political system into a constitutional crisis.

Watergate has been regarded as a paradigm case of a constitutional crisis, not simply in the heat of the moment but in the sober reflection of history.[187] So it was, although a few knowledgeable and historically minded scholars have surprisingly claimed that it was not.[188] The problem with these accounts may be an overemphasis on the fact that the crisis ended in Nixon's prospective impeachment and resignation, procedures allowed by the Constitution, rather than with riots and troops in the streets. Although we can be thankful that Nixon did not attempt to retain his office by force, the inescapable *constitutional* aspect of Watergate was how all of the circumstances I have highlighted flowed from Nixon's abuse of his office, an office whose powers had been greatly altered by the post-1945 constitutional order. But Nixon's extreme abuse of his powers was not the only reason defining Watergate as a constitutional crisis. The consequences of Watergate also mattered, chiefly that Nixon was rendered ineffective as president.

By the time of Nixon's inauguration for a second term in January 1973, the Watergate cover-up was in deep difficulty. The blackmail demands of the burglars were escalating and various parties in the White House saw themselves under threat.[189] In fact, Nixon would be effective as president for only three more months. At the beginning of the pivotal month of April 1973, Nixon's popularity and standing with the public were still intact.[190] But he had conceded to his chief of staff Haldeman that governance would become impossible if the pressure increased.[191] By the end of the month, a mounting series of disclosures had forced him to dismiss Haldeman and John Ehrlichman, his two most essential aides.[192]

After the dismissal of Haldeman and Ehrlichman, Nixon sank into a depression and sometimes could not function as president.[193] During the October 1973 Arab-Israeli war, Nixon was incapacitated by the sudden crisis which followed from his dismissal of special prosecutor Archibald Cox and was unable to make crucial foreign policy decisions.[194] After another special prosecutor, Leon Jaworski, was appointed, Nixon's remaining time in office until August 1974 was consumed with Watergate.[195] He could not take meaningful action, for example, in addressing the serious energy crisis in the winter of 1973, which was the consequence of the war in the Middle East.

Watergate was also a constitutional crisis because in some sense Nixon willed it to be. Arguably like other conservatives during the 1970s, he sensed the high degree of entrenchment liberals had achieved in institutions both inside and outside government.[196] It is likely he was weary of struggling with a persisting Democratic Congress and the interest groups which supported the Democratic Party. After the 1972 election in particular, he was psychologically in a mood for revenge on the many people and groups who in his belief had wronged him.[197] As he recounted in his memoirs, "In this second term I had thrown down a gauntlet to Congress, the bureaucracy, the media, and the Washington establishment and challenged them to engage in epic battle."[198] Another self-willed moment of crisis occurred when Nixon fired special prosecutor Cox and earned the whirlwind of an impeachment inquiry. The relevant point is that Nixon deliberately generated crises as a way of coping with the unwelcome reality that there were effective limits on his ability to reorder the policy universe. He certainly had no scruples about challenging any checks and balances the original Constitution put in his way. This was the most fundamental reason why "Watergate as foreign policy"—Nixon's way of managing the burdens of the Cold War—was a constitutional crisis.

Ending the War without Congress

Often overlooked in the growing rush of Watergate-related events in early 1973 was that Nixon had won what may have been the most meaningless overwhelming election victory in American political history. As Nixon himself sensed, his victory was ashes.[199] The election did not produce a Republican majority in Congress nor any strong endorsement of Nixon's policies. The Congress that would take office in January 1973 would be more eager than its predecessor to quickly terminate the Vietnam War. Nixon and Kissinger knew that they had lost any room to maneuver in their four-year-old negotiations with North Vietnam. If the war had persisted, Congress would have certainly cut off the funds necessary to support the fragile Thieu government in South Vietnam.[200]

Some Americans had an impression of the Nixon years as a "time of illusion."[201] If we add the revelations that came in 1975 about CIA activities such as assassinations, this quality had existed to an extent from the Truman administration onward, as there was much Americans did not know about how the United States fought the Cold War. But the label was especially apt with respect to Nixon, who had concealed vast amounts of what would otherwise be the nation's public diplomacy with the Soviet Union and China, as well as the negotiations to end the war.[202] Nixon's Vietnam secrets were at least as damaging as Johnson's because they influenced the lessons that Americans drew from the

Vietnam experience. By 1973, the list of Nixon's failures to disclose was quite long:[203]

- That preservation of Thieu's Saigon regime was his primary goal.
- That his initial strategy was to win the war through military means.
- That Cambodia had undergone a bombing campaign since 1969.
- That Cambodia was invaded in 1970 without prior consultation involving Congress.
- That significant reconstruction aid to Vietnam would be required after the war ended.
- That he had given Thieu guarantees of continued military protection.
- That a "decent interval" was all he expected before South Vietnam collapsed.

There is substantial reason to believe that Nixon did not gain much by prolonging the war an additional four years. U.S. forces suffered an additional 20,000 combat deaths during Nixon's term in office. For this sacrifice Nixon obtained a concession from North Vietnam, which he could not have obtained in 1969, that Thieu's regime would survive the immediate transition to a completely "Vietnamized" war.[204] Was this concession worth the cost? Because the cycle of accountability never began, Congress and the public never had a chance to decide.

Despite being aware of constraints on his freedom of action in Vietnam, Nixon had always contemplated the need for selective military escalations of the war as long as significant American forces remained.[205] As suggested earlier, his most important initiatives came with respect to Cambodia. These were attended by Nixon's customary secrecy. Not only was Congress not consulted on the 1969 bombing or prior to the 1970 invasion, but large swaths of the government did not know what was going on. The 1969 bombing was kept secret within the military itself. Prior to the 1970 invasion, the State and Defense Departments were both cut out of planning, as was the JCS.[206]

Cambodia was a problem because North Vietnam had used its territory to base supplies and troops. What could Congress have contributed to deliberation over possible military action? Nixon knew very well that any action against Cambodia would be perceived as an escalation of the war and would be opposed by Congress.[207] If Congress had been given the chance to deliberate about the 1970 invasion, there was much for them to consider. They might have discovered the ongoing secret bombing which would of course have undermined support for an invasion. They might also have raised questions about whether bombing and invasion would destabilize the Cambodian government, one eventual consequence of Nixon's secret actions.[208] Congressional deliberation might well have saved the U.S. and Cambodia from a tragic episode. It would have also saved Nixon from a political disaster, as the invasion seriously damaged confidence in Congress concerning his overall Vietnam policy.[209] Consulting with Congress would have put the nation's foreign policy on a much sounder basis.

The task of justifying the constitutionality of the invasion of Cambodia fell to William H. Rehnquist, then in charge of the OLC and later chief justice of the United States.[210] His opinion was a reasonably thorough review of the state of war powers arguments at the time, although much of it was not directly relevant to the question of whether Nixon could expand the war by attacking a previously neutral country. Of the different presidentialist themes described in Chapter 1, Rehnquist associated himself with the view that the Constitution did not specify "a detailed allocation of authority between the two branches" with respect to war powers.[211] Rather much remained to be specified through later practice, which gave "rise to a number of precedents and usages."[212] Thus Rehnquist relied on subsequent practice, endorsing the commonly held view that Truman's intervention in Korea was a precedent.[213] Interestingly, Rehnquist specifically rejected relying on the U.N. Charter to justify U.S. military action, stating the accepted legal view that a treaty could not override the Constitution.[214] He then abruptly concluded that the Cambodian invasion, which he characterized as an "incursion" and a "tactical" decision on the part of the president, was not so far outside past practice as to require congressional authorization.[215]

To be sure, the Cambodian invasion was not a permanent expansion of the war, as Nixon shortly withdrew American forces, albeit under tremendous political pressure. Nevertheless, Rehnquist avoided a burden that was rightfully his. What Rehnquist characterized as an "incursion" was controversial within the White House, especially Kissinger's NSC staff, precisely because it was an invasion of another country.[216] War powers issues should not be resolved by resort to semantic games.

Rehnquist's assessment of the Cambodian invasion, unlike his general discussion of war powers, was not forthright.

Like other executive branch justifications for broad presidential war powers, the most vulnerable aspect of Rehnquist's general analysis was that it rendered the "declare war" clause virtually meaningless. Rehnquist attempted to avoid this result in the same manner as Katzenbach's 1965 opinion for LBJ and John Yoo's later analysis for President George W. Bush. Rehnquist stated that if the "divided war power" in the Constitution was to have meaning, the president must go to Congress for authorization "for the conduct of hostilities which reach a certain scale."[217] In other words, for world wars or "total wars," congressional authorization was still required. Here we must keep in mind that, according to Rehnquist, such wars did not include Korea or Vietnam, certainly two of the most significant military conflicts in American history. In this respect, Rehnquist's memo again illustrated the lack of credibility inherent to broad presidentialist arguments in support of the post-1945 constitutional order.

Nixon finished America's involvement in the war in early 1973 by insistently promoting a deceptive narrative of his own place in history.[218] In Kimball's perceptive analysis, Nixon viewed himself as a courageous leader who saw a difficult task through despite facing constant attack. It was *Congress* that had prolonged the war by offering resolutions against it and advancing plans for unilateral withdrawal that would have been a disgraceful surrender. By contrast, Nixon had achieved his goal of peace with honor and had preserved American credibility on the world stage.[219] The effect of this rewriting of history, however, was that Nixon did not highlight the real implications of the peace agreement with North Vietnam and "left many Americans unprepared for Thieu's defeat in April 1975."[220] Especially odd was the fact that the "peace" agreement "left North Vietnamese troops in South Vietnam . . . with both sides fully aware that a civil war in new guise would ensue for the future of Vietnam."[221]

American air and naval power sufficed to break up the last big North Vietnamese offensive in early 1972. Nixon was hoping that despite obvious congressional opposition, similar military force could be brought to bear at least until the end of his term in 1976.[222] That way, he would not be the first American president to "lose a war."[223] From Nixon and

Kissinger's perspective, Watergate intervened to spoil this scenario. One could reply that much of Watergate related to how Nixon fought the war at home, but it is more relevant to note that there was growing evidence by early 1973 that Nixon and Kissinger's entire diplomatic string had run out. The country and Congress were understandably weary of a false-front diplomacy that was not based on democratic decisionmaking. As William Bundy concludes, "The key factor was the Congress and the people were rebelling at last against inadequate participation and consultation, most of all because of their sense that the President had never really leveled with them."[224] At the same time, as we shall see in the next chapter, one of Nixon's most troubling legacies was his contribution to a sense in the Republican Party that they had little responsibility for what had happened in Vietnam.

After misleading Congress on an epic scale for more than a decade, there were still those in the executive branch who, like Kissinger, wanted to pin the blame for Vietnam on Congress as South Vietnam began to collapse in March 1975.[225] It was difficult for President Gerald Ford to believe that Congress would not support another appropriation to give South Vietnam the supplies they needed to maintain their territorial integrity. Feelings ran high in the executive branch at the time. At one point, Ford remarked to Kissinger that if Congress denied aid, "then the efforts of five Presidents, 55,000 dead, and five Congressional efforts are in vain."[226]

Ford came close to blaming Congress for the entire war in a speech requesting aid, saying that Congress deserved responsibility for failing to support South Vietnam since the signing of the peace agreement.[227] With no one in the executive branch, past or present, willing to take the slightest responsibility for what had happened in Southeast Asia, certainly one of the most appalling failures of leadership in American history, the U.S. commitment ended in recriminations and amnesia.[228] Congress as usual spoke in many voices and could not respond effectively to Ford's intransigence on the question of responsibility.

It is ironic that although Nixon saw himself as an American version of Charles de Gaulle and Kissinger advocated a European *realpolitik* balance of power approach, they did not have the courage that de Gaulle showed in Algeria in 1962—pulling out of a foreign commitment gone bad. Algeria had over one million French citizens and obviously posed much greater domestic risks than Vietnam. The U.S. had no such close connections to Vietnam, yet presidents up to and including Ford proved to be bitter enders to the last. That none of them ever acknowledged their responsibility to the American people remains one of the greatest stains on the historical reputation of the American presidency.

5

The Constitutional Order in the Post-Vietnam Era

During the 1973 Senate Watergate hearings, President Nixon's former chief of staff H. R. Haldeman praised Nixon for his many accomplishments in foreign policy—including ending the Cold War![1] Nixon's opening to China and his pursuit of détente with the Soviet Union certainly represented a new stage in relations with both countries. But the view that the Cold War was over, quite common during the early 1970s, seemed anachronistic by the end of the decade and certainly as Ronald Reagan took the oath of office in 1981.

Although the Cold War did not end with Richard Nixon, the period I have referred to as the early Cold War was over even before he took office. The high tensions and constant foreign policy crises that characterized the Truman, Eisenhower, and Kennedy administrations had declined markedly. As Nixon withdrew troops from Vietnam and negotiated arms control agreements with the Soviet Union, the Cold War ceased to serve as an organizing concept for more and more Americans. Arguably, this new period should have been marked by a major review of foreign affairs and national security policy.[2] Yet aside from the largely behind the scenes diplomatic maneuverings of Nixon and Kissinger, such a review never took place.

In a widely noted address at Tulane University in April 1975, President Gerald Ford declared that the Vietnam War was "finished."[3] But what lessons would be drawn from the Vietnam experience? Every post-Vietnam president and government officials across the political spectrum were keenly aware that the public wanted "no more Vietnams."[4] As a practical matter, this meant that the U.S. was not interested in fighting a large-scale conventional war for an indefinite period. Time would show that this did not mean an abandonment of military force as an instrument of policy. Rather, attention eventually moved to the other two ways of making war in the post-1945 period: building up and brandishing the nuclear arsenal and covert paramilitary action.

Without a series of external crises such as Berlin and Cuba that challenged ordinary Americans to focus on foreign policy, the post-Vietnam period was one in which the Cold War was fought and the viability of the post-1945 constitutional order was determined in terms of domestic party political conflicts. The parties diverged on the use of force in foreign affairs and the constitutional role of the president. Democrats, bitterly divided over Vietnam and increasingly a party based in Congress, could not agree on a strategy in foreign affairs other than a no-use policy with respect to military force. They also tended to accept the critique of the "imperial presidency."[5] They were the chief sponsors of the War Powers Resolution (WPR) and struggled to implement it in a meaningful way across several administrations.[6]

While cautious about employing conventional military force on a large scale, Republican presidents remained willing to consider other forms of military action to combat what they saw as the ongoing conflict with the Soviet Union and communism, especially in Central America. Republicans generally rejected the critique of the imperial presidency and reaffirmed the fundamental principle of the post-1945 order that the president must lead in foreign affairs. When Ronald Reagan, the president who best embodied the spirit of a newly aggressive Republican Party, was challenged by the Iran-contra affair, Republicans were driven to articulate this commitment to a strong presidency in an extreme form. They contended that in foreign affairs, presidents had an independent constitutional authority that was beyond the control of Congress. This set the stage for the administrations of President George H. W. Bush and his son President George W. Bush. They pushed the boundaries of presidential power to the furthest extent yet seen. This steadfast Republican commitment to a strong presidency influenced the making of foreign policy during the Clinton and Obama administrations as well and ensured that the post-1945 constitutional order would persist.

Taking Stock of the Cold War

If the Cold War began with the articulation of the Truman Doctrine in 1947, it reached the quarter century mark in 1972 as Nixon went to China and the Soviet Union for summit meetings. If it started in earnest with the period of heightened danger in 1949 and 1950 as the Soviet Union acquired the atomic bomb and the Korean War began, then the twenty-fifth anniversary occurred as the U.S. transited from Nixon to Ford and began to grapple with the aftermath of the Vietnam war. However one might calculate, more than an anniversary was at stake. A full-scale reassessment of American foreign policy was long overdue. Such assessments had been done in the Truman administration in terms of George Kennan's advocacy of the strategy of containment and the later development of strategic doctrine in NSC-68.[7] President Eisenhower had ordered the unique "Project Solarium," in which government experts (including Kennan) were summoned to articulate three alternative strategies detailing how the U.S. should continue the Cold War.[8]

Such comprehensive policy reviews grew scarcer after Eisenhower. One of the remarkable features of both the Johnson and Ford administrations was that the former vice presidents who were now presidents decided to keep their predecessors' principal advisers.[9] The natural effect of LBJ's decision to retain advisers like McNamara and Rusk and Ford's retention of Kissinger was a disinclination to engage in any fundamental questioning of the policies of the prior administrations they had served. Meanwhile, by the mid-1970s much had changed since the early Cold War. There was no longer a unified "communist bloc" as China and the Soviet Union were seriously at odds. The situation in Europe had changed as well. Moreover, the inevitable recasting of American policy in Southeast Asia meant that the overall shape of American strategy would be different. Yet critically, there was no policy review in the aftermath of Vietnam to determine future Cold War strategy.

A fundamental strategic reassessment would have been useful for many reasons. Consider some additional contrasts with the early Cold War. Truman and Eisenhower may have been the only Cold War presidents who cared about balanced budgets in service of striking a balance more generally between military requirements and fiscal objectives.[10] Kennedy and Johnson seemed less concerned about the effects of defense spending and deficits on the economy.[11] Yet everyone agreed in the aftermath of Vietnam that the war had detrimental economic effects such as inflation. What was the proper balance between military spending and the government deficits it helped to create? This was the sort of question that could be answered only after an updated assessment of America's strategic position relative to the Soviet Union.

That several principal objectives of the Cold War had been achieved by the 1970s, if not earlier, offered further compelling reasons for a policy review. The Truman administration was centrally concerned with stabilizing the situation in Europe and Japan, assisted by initiatives such as the Marshall Plan. While the status of Germany and Berlin remained troublesome through the Kennedy administration, both Europe and Japan were clearly on the right path economically and Europe as a whole was able to contribute to NATO's military efforts even in the 1950s. Preventing Soviet predominance on the Eurasian continent, one of the central objectives of the Truman and Eisenhower administrations, had been achieved.[12] This meant that in a conventional war, the U.S. would be backed by the industrial strength of Europe and Japan combined. In addition, unlooked for by the U.S., European leaders such as Willy Brandt had emerged to pursue meaningful diplomatic initiatives with the Soviet Union, such as *Ostpolitik* and the 1975 Helsinki accords. This created a European zone of détente apart from whatever U.S. efforts yielded during the Nixon administration.[13]

There were still other new circumstances that should have sparked a meaningful review of U.S. strategic options. The Soviet Union had achieved a rough strategic parity with the United States in terms of nuclear weapons, although it relied much more heavily on land-based ICBMs. Nixon and Kissinger appeared to accept the new reality of nuclear "sufficiency" rather than "superiority," but it remained unclear whether this would sell politically.[14] The future status of détente was unknown as Ford took office in August 1974, although he pledged that it would continue.

Some of the concepts that underlay the commitment to Vietnam were also in need of reassessment. Historians agree that one of the reasons the U.S. felt it had to support South Vietnam with troops was to preserve the credibility of American commitments elsewhere.[15] U.S. policymakers had not perceived Vietnam to be a central theatre of the Cold War. Nonetheless, the U.S. commitment to South Vietnam, articulated first in the Eisenhower administration, in effect stood for American commitments around the world. Now that South Vietnam had fallen, presumably America's credibility was in serious question worldwide. Yet this proved not to be the case in any meaningful sense. Kissinger went to some lengths to reassure Ford on that score, saying that America's alliances were secure.[16] Kissinger, however, remained firmly wedded to the doctrine of credibility as were many members of the foreign policy establishment. Given that America's credibility had not been damaged to any discernible degree by the earlier "losses" of China and Cuba, views such as these were in need of some rethinking.[17]

Finally, the bipartisan public support policymakers could count on in the early Cold War was gone in the wake of Vietnam.[18] The foreign policy establishment itself was in turmoil.[19] It is often said that the Cold War "consensus" had disappeared, but this is unhelpful if it is taken to mean that a majority of the public had rejected the Cold War as a way to understand world affairs. We should take shorter steps to understand the complexities of the 1970s. It was never very plausible to think that the high morale and extreme tensions characteristic of the early 1950s and continuing through the Cuban missile crisis could be maintained indefinitely. Even inside the government, things were different. As I suggested in Chapter 4, the CIA was more of a status quo agency by the mid-1960s, increasingly doubted by Washington insiders long before the 1975 intelligence investigations. Although there was less desire for foreign policy confrontations, it seems likely that a majority of Americans continued to be concerned about the Soviet Union and wanted the U.S. to have military superiority. At the same time, in the wake of Vietnam and détente, a significant segment of the public had decamped from the Cold War. More Americans were questioning Cold War verities while not willing to abandon them altogether.[20] As one historian suggests:

> By the mid-1970s, therefore, it was not clear exactly who or what the United States was fighting or how serious was the threat. . . . In the late 1970s, the Cold War was out of focus: there was no consensus on what it was about, or how important it was in US priorities, or how to gauge who was winning it.[21]

The increasing criticism of Nixon and Kissinger's policy of détente with the Soviet Union on the right showed that not everyone was willing to let go of the Cold War as it stood during the Eisenhower and Kennedy administrations.[22] Without another widely agreed upon external threat such as an invasion by the Soviet Union or one of its clients into a zone protected by a U.S. alliance, disputes over the Cold War were played out in the theatre of domestic politics amid growing partisanship and a perception of American decline.[23] Instead of reassessing its foreign policy according to the nature of external threats and opportunities, the U.S. entered a period in which foreign policy was strongly influenced by partisanship and domestic political struggles.[24] During the 1970s presidents sensed that domestic issues were ascendant in American politics.[25] Arguably this remained the case until September 11, 2001.

This highlights the misperceptions that can result from treating the spheres of "domestic" and "foreign" policy separately. Historians have become uncomfortable with analyses that do not treat them in relationship. Campbell Craig and Fredrik Logevall, for example, have called for more attention to what they call the "'intermestic' (international-domestic, whereby the two are dynamically intertwined) dimension of policy."[26] The relevance here lies in the amount of public support presidents need for using the military in service of American foreign policy. Although I've contended that previous presidents usually had public support for their actions, we also saw in previous chapters how presidential actions were responsive to and constrained by domestic political concerns. But while the foreign policy crises highlighted in the previous chapters always had a domestic shadow, presidents after Vietnam were not wrong to believe that domestic issues had a new prominence.

With the passage of measures such as the War Powers Resolution in 1973 (discussed later in this chapter), it was widely understood that Congress and the president were increasingly in conflict over foreign policy. Within Congress, it was harder to see that, although the WPR had bipartisan support (it was adopted over Nixon's veto), a bifurcation was taking place between the parties over the role of the president.[27] Many Democrats were convinced of the dangers of the "imperial presidency," but could not settle on a reasonable role for Congress.[28] Republicans, still in possession of the presidency after Nixon resigned, reacted strongly against this Democratic consensus. As Julian Zelizer has insightfully shown, the 1970s was the key period in which conservatives wholeheartedly embraced a strong presidency.[29] From the beginning of his accidental presidency President Ford believed that Congress had intruded on the constitutional role of the executive branch.[30] His chief of staff (and future secretary of defense and vice president) Dick Cheney strongly agreed with this position.[31]

The emerging differences between the parties over presidential power in foreign affairs and the nature of the Cold War itself were especially evident during the "Year of Intelligence"—the 1975 House and Senate investigations of the CIA, NSA, and FBI.[32] As I described briefly in Chapter 3, these investigations also illustrated the difference between the early Cold War and the post-Vietnam era. They demonstrated serious divisions among members of Congress about the Cold War. There was deep confusion, indeed denial, concerning actions the executive branch had taken in the early Cold War (particularly in the Kennedy administration), questions about the purpose of intelligence agencies, especially with respect to covert action, and uncertainty about the nature of the Cold War itself.[33]

An exchange during the Senate's public hearings on the NSA's Shamrock program showed the continuing ambiguities plaguing the post-1945 constitutional order. Shamrock involved a secret 1947 agreement between the NSA and communications companies allowing the agency to access all international telegrams from Americans without their knowledge.[34] Throughout the intelligence investigations, conservatives such as Barry Goldwater and John Tower strongly endorsed the legitimacy of the national security state and tended to defend the intelligence agencies.[35] But what could justify Shamrock?

> *Goldwater.* I guess a lot of us are guilty of operations like this because many of us censored letters during World War II, reading those letters. So I think I would have to join the guilty as you would have to, also.
>
> *Church.* I think that we should recognize the distinction between war and peace. It poses the question whether this country in peacetime wants to live always under the customs of war. This was a peacetime operation.
>
> *Mathias.* The law provided—in fact, the law compelled us to read those letters to make the appropriate changes that were required, and it is the law that I think is important here. I think that the law does not extend to the activities of the NSA. The law must be made to extend to the NSA.
>
> *Tower.* I think that we cannot draw this in strict terms of war and peace, in terms of whether or not the United States is actually at war. We are in effect in a war of sorts. That is a war of the preservation of the climate in this world where national integrity will be respected.[36]

Democrat Frank Church, who chaired the Senate investigation, had provided great insight early on with respect to the Vietnam War and was highly regarded in the Senate. But he had difficulty comprehending the close links between the CIA's plots against America's enemies and the philosophy by which the government fought the Cold War.[37] Like many Democrats, Church could not understand how President Kennedy could have authorized secret sabotage plots against Castro's Cuba. This led him to make the famous and misleading charge that the CIA had acted in the early Cold War as a "rogue elephant," pursuing operations on its own authority.[38] Those who were familiar with how the Eisenhower and Kennedy administrations operated knew that such orders could come only from the "higher authority"—the president—in circumstances that preserved his ability to deny knowledge.[39] Certainly the plots against Castro were logical continuations of the kind of sabotage operations begun in the Bay of Pigs, an operation sanctioned by Presidents Eisenhower and Kennedy as we saw in Chapter 3.

The confrontation between Church and Tower was especially instructive. Was there a war? From Church's point of view, no doubt influenced by the aftermath of Vietnam, much of the Cold War was in fact "peacetime" and could not justify covert operations that intruded on civil liberties. Republicans like Tower in effect took the position that the circumstances of the early Cold War still prevailed. This justified the use of wartime measures, as well as employing the tactics of the enemy. The 1954 Doolittle report, discussed in Chapter 2, still expressed their guiding philosophy.[40] Recall that this report held that in the contest with communism, there were "no rules" and "[h]itherto acceptable norms of human conduct do not apply."[41]

The parties were also increasingly diverging over the constitutional power of the president. While Democrats read Arthur Schlesinger's *The Imperial Presidency* with approval, Republicans perused *The Fettered Presidency* and complained of congressional excess.[42] No doubt from the perspective of Church and other Democrats, the point of view expressed in the Doolittle report was an excuse for throwing the Constitution out the window. While Republicans agreed that the Constitution applied at home, they still believed that in operating abroad against the enemies of the United States, the CIA had to use all means available. Although President Ford issued a famous order prohibiting the CIA from engaging in assassinations, Ford and congressional Republicans defeated efforts to follow up the intelligence investigations with a comprehensive charter.[43] The investigation of the intelligence agencies itself became a partisan issue. Republicans, including future president George H. W. Bush, promoted a narrative in which the investigations had weakened national security.[44] Given this atmosphere, there was no bipartisan consensus on whether the presidency had posed a danger to the constitutional system in the Cold War.

The 1980 election of Ronald Reagan gave further impetus to the growing belief among conservatives that the presidency must be strengthened. As Julian Zelizer notes, "Reagan championed the authority of the president to take charge against threats facing America."[45] Young attorneys in the DOJ promoted the idea of the "unitary executive," the theory that the president must have sole control over the entire executive branch, including independent regulatory agencies.[46] As reviewed below, this aggressive definition of presidential power was influential throughout the 1980s and was further articulated in the minority report of Congress's Iran-contra Committee.[47]

It is fair to say that Democrats had trouble coming to grips with the mixed legacy of the Kennedy administration. They wanted to remember the martyred JFK as a hero-president. The fact that Democrats like Church denied strenuously that the Kennedys were mixed up in dubious covert operations showed the enormous gap that had opened up between the circumstances prevailing in the early Cold War and the much different atmosphere after Vietnam. We should recall that Americans strongly endorsed aggressive action against Cuba when JFK took office. But by the 1970s, many liberals had gotten off the Cold War bus and were engaged in a fundamental questioning of the nation's course in foreign affairs. It is important to keep in mind for purposes of understanding the future of the post-1945 constitutional order that Republicans did not follow them.

As a final comment on the status of the Cold War in the aftermath of Vietnam, it is relevant to note that this bifurcation between the parties has been concealed somewhat by the way historians have approached the Cold War. Historians ordinarily like to periodize and argue about which periodizations are most illuminating in making sense of the past. But histories of the Cold War are largely devoid of periodization. There is no consensus on the existence of what I have termed the "early Cold War," for example, and it is not typically divided into, say, "early," "middle or détente," or "late" periods.[48] In standard histories of the Cold War, this produces the odd effect that the struggle between the U.S. and the

Soviet Union is presented as identical in form regardless of whether we are talking about the 1950s or the 1970s.[49] Yet the two decades were very different along multiple dimensions and we must take those differences into account.

Nuclear Weapons and the Reagan Presidency

To this point, I have not addressed the role of nuclear weapons in the post-1945 constitutional order, except for some brief mentions in Chapter 3. I am concerned with how presidents made decisions for war and coped with their responsibilities under the post-1945 constitutional order and, fortunately, nuclear weapons were never used. But in the aftermath of Vietnam, highly abstract questions of nuclear strategy were suddenly thrust into the political arena as elements in the Republican Party refused to accept Nixon and Kissinger's apparent endorsement of nuclear sufficiency and new weapons such as the MX missile came closer to deployment. With the prospect of a conventional war off the table, attention was moving back to the other two arenas for presidential military decision—nuclear war and covert action. The rhetoric and policy moves of the Reagan administration arguably came close to starting an actual nuclear war during a period of high tensions in 1983. More generally, the nuclear weapons debate in the Carter and Reagan administrations showed how the Cold War was being fought out mainly in terms of the demands of domestic politics rather than as a response to a genuine external threat.

The U.S. arsenal of strategic nuclear weapons (not counting those available in Europe) had stabilized during the Johnson and Nixon administrations around the "triad" of 1,054 land-based ICBMs (almost all of the "Minuteman" variety), nuclear bombs deliverable by long-range aircraft such as B-52s, and missiles launched from Polaris submarines (SLBMs). The triad took years to develop and was based on decisions made as far back as the Eisenhower administration. Secretary of Defense McNamara commissioned studies that showed very little would be accomplished in a nuclear war by further increasing the number of warheads or vehicles to deliver them.[50] Nonetheless, during the Nixon administration the U.S. proceeded to use new MIRV technology to increase the number of warheads on each Minuteman ICBM from one to three. Meanwhile, the Soviets continued the buildup they had resolved on in the wake of the

Cuban missile crisis.[51] The U.S. watched in alarm as the Soviets introduced multiple new ICBMs, including the SS-18, capable of carrying many more warheads than the Minuteman. The Soviets also added two new missile carrying submarines and the "Backfire" bomber.[52]

Once the Soviets possessed a significant arsenal of strategic nuclear weapons, both sides sought to preserve a "second strike" capability that would assure the survival of sufficient nuclear forces after a surprise first strike by the enemy. The U.S. triad was well adapted to this goal. A first strike that destroyed nearly all land-based ICBMs was a highly uncertain proposition. But with the addition of bombers on alert and undetectable missile submarines, the U.S. deterrent was safe. There was thus a stable "balance of terror" in which each side could deliver "assured destruction" on the other, thus negating the likelihood that either side would be tempted to resort to nuclear weapons in a crisis.[53]

Or so most observers assumed until Republicans opposed to détente and Democrats unhappy with the antidefense posture of their party began an all-fronts campaign in the late 1970s to convince the American public that the nuclear deterrent was threatened.[54] As promoted by Reagan in the 1980 presidential campaign, a "window of vulnerability" had opened in which the Soviets might use their new ballistic missiles with multiple MIRVs to take out U.S. land-based missiles and degrade the other two legs of the triad in a single massive "counterforce" strike.[55] This vulnerability would exist until the U.S. had deployed the new MX missile, which could carry more warheads than the Minuteman. To be survivable, the MX would have to be deployed in such a way as to confuse the Soviets and deter them from attacking in the first place. For if the MX were deployed in existing Minuteman silos, its multiple warheads would be a tempting target. By the time Reagan took office, the Carter administration had decided to solve this problem through a gigantic "multiple protective shelter" system that would cost $33 billion and involve building thousands of miles of roads over large portions of Utah and Nevada, much to the dismay of their Republican representatives in Congress.[56]

The way this scenario was sold to the public and Congress is worthy of comment. There was something distinctly odd about the strategic nuclear debate that began in the mid to late 1970s.[57] The U.S. nuclear triad took years to plan and build. It was based on worst-case assumptions about Soviet capabilities that gave officials in multiple administrations high confidence in the U.S. ability to respond to a nuclear attack.[58] Those promoting the idea of a window of vulnerability, chiefly the "Committee on the Present Danger," were in effect arguing that a fatal flaw in U.S. war planning had somehow been missed. They were suggesting this, moreover, without access to the kind of classified information needed to make sound judgments about highly complex matters of nuclear war-fighting. There was more than a whiff of careerism and bitterness over what conservatives saw as the abandonment of South Vietnam behind the vitriol and exaggerated claims the committee and its acolytes unleashed on the Carter administration and the foreign policy establishment. This suggested strongly that domestic political considerations were dominating what should have been a debate about the global balance between the U.S. and Soviet Union.[59]

It had been understood inside the executive branch for some time that there was an essential stability or stalemate in the strategic nuclear balance of forces.[60] Eisenhower left the presidency realizing that as long as the Soviet Union had some nuclear capability, a nuclear war could never be fought.[61] In 1963 President Kennedy received a briefing from the NSC in which he was told that neither side could escape horrific consequences once a nuclear war was initiated. If the Soviet Union launched a preemptive attack in 1964, the NSC estimated U.S. fatalities at 93 million, rising to 134 million in 1968. If the U.S. went first, U.S. casualties would still be 63 million in 1964 and 108 million in 1968. The general giving the briefing told Kennedy that reestablishing strategic superiority was impossible.[62] The Soviets reached similar conclusions by at least the 1970s.[63]

Reagan essentially rejected the idea of "assured destruction" on moral grounds without being able to do anything about the reality of the stalemate in the balance of forces. He appeared to reject the possibility of arms control, thus igniting a powerful "nuclear freeze" movement.[64] Caspar Weinberger, Reagan's secretary of defense, proceeded to reject the Carter administration's MX basing mode solution without having a reasonable alternative.[65] The policy chaos that resulted from Weinberger's inability to address the basing mode issue led Congress in turn to reject the MX until a solution could be found. In truth, there was no solution and the entire problem was papered over by a presidential commission. The "window of vulnerability," if it ever had existed, was never used by the Soviets to pressure the U.S. in the manner suggested by the Committee on the Present Danger. The policy problem vaporized in a way that suggested that the entire episode had more to do with domestic politics, especially the politics of what defense policy the right wing of the Republican Party was willing to accept, than with any real strategic threat.[66]

Meanwhile, Reagan's lack of interest in arms control and negotiations and his strident rhetoric had led to a period of tension with the Soviet Union that was similar to the early Cold War.[67] Reagan was construed by many as making a bid for strategic superiority. The Soviets themselves became convinced the Reagan administration was willing to launch a preemptive nuclear attack.[68] They began a global intelligence effort (called RYAN) designed to alert them to any indication that such an attack might be in preparation.[69] According to historian Beth Fischer, "[b]y the fall of 1983, superpower relations were more hostile than at any period since the Cuban missile crisis."[70] Soviet suspicions appeared to be confirmed when in November 1983 NATO launched a large-scale military exercise called Able Archer that the Soviets understood as a prelude to full-scale war.[71]

Reagan eventually came to the personal realization that the Soviets were genuinely concerned the enormous military might of the United States might actually be used against them.[72] In other words, after several years of experience as president, Reagan reproduced an essential strategic insight of the Eisenhower and Kennedy administrations that had guided U.S. foreign policy until the advent of his presidency.[73] Although this episode illustrates the enormous influence presidents have had over the strategic posture of the United States, fortunately no significant harm came from Reagan's astonishing ignorance of the history of the Cold War.[74] As we shall see, the same cannot be said for the results of the "covert" war the Reagan administration waged in Central America.

The War Powers Resolution

We owe the WPR to Richard Nixon. Although congressional Democrats were unhappy with President Johnson's Vietnam policy, it is unlikely they would have undertaken a comprehensive effort to restrain presidential war powers had LBJ remained in office or had Vice President Humphrey been elected in 1968. Nixon's 1970 invasion of Cambodia energized efforts to restrain the executive branch.[75] As we saw in

Chapter 4, Cambodia was a political disaster for Nixon and he could never again muster strong support from Congress for his Vietnam policy. It was also a surprise, which brought home the lack of consultation that characterized Nixon's presidency.[76] The publication of the Pentagon Papers in 1971 also did not help, as it reminded members of Congress that they had been misled about the conduct of the war by the Johnson administration.[77]

The post-1945 constitutional order gave a great deal of discretion to the executive branch with respect to the use of military force. This suggested that the president would have to be actively involved in any effort to redress the balance between the branches. But Nixon avoided engaging in a substantive way with war powers reform. He consistently opposed the mandatory restrictions developed by the Senate in favor of weaker measures advanced in the House. Nixon's aides, including Kissinger, monitored war powers legislation closely from 1970 onward.[78] They worked behind the scenes with Representative Clement Zablocki, an influential Democratic member of the House Committee on Foreign Affairs. Zablocki's initial resolutions encouraging consultation with Congress but nothing more were the preferred alternative of the White House.[79]

It was Nixon's bad luck that he vetoed the WPR in October 1973 just as the Watergate drama of the "Saturday Night Massacre"—Nixon's firing of special prosecutor Archibald Cox—roiled the political waters. Some observers have attributed Congress's successful override of Nixon's veto to Watergate.[80] But there was a broad bipartisan coalition behind rebalancing war powers long before Watergate occupied the nation's attention in 1973. Particularly important was the 1971 endorsement of Senator John Stennis, a conservative Democrat from Mississippi.[81] Stennis was revered in the Senate, an unimpeachable stalwart of national security who chaired the Armed Services Committee (and later had an aircraft carrier named after him). Like many in the Senate, Stennis had nonetheless come to believe that Congress's role in decisions for war had been violated too many times.[82]

This sort of principled stand was common enough at the time. Yet it left obscure the relationship of the WPR to the post-1945 constitutional order. As constitutional scholar Keith Whittington has observed, during the debates over the WPR members of Congress avoided challenging the Cold War and thus the essential roots of the post-1945 order.[83] This was symptomatic of a deeper difficulty. Pitching the arguments favoring the WPR in the relatively abstract terms of separation of powers avoided the unpleasant reality that the entire debate was the result of a breakdown in relations between the branches on foreign affairs, a relative lack of trust that lasted, as we shall see, well into the Reagan presidency. It also avoided the even more unpleasant reality that both parties were complicit in the policy disaster of Vietnam. This explained the lack of mention in the WPR; though obviously about Vietnam, how it related to (or would have prevented) the war was never discussed. Members of Congress spoke of their prerogatives and the lamentable acquiescence to the executive branch in the past.[84] There was not much attention to how the WPR would make a concrete difference in the future. This meant that members failed to grapple with the influential rationales presidents were employing to justify the use of military force.

What then was the WPR supposed to do? The two provisions regarded as crucial by its sponsors involved mandatory consultation with Congress and the automatic termination of the commitment of military force after sixty days.[85] The consultation provision commanded the president "in every possible instance" to "consult with Congress before introducing United States Armed Forces into hostilities."[86] But the legislative committees made no examination of executive decisionmaking on Vietnam and interbranch interaction through history to enable future presidents and Congresses to understand their expectations. The sponsors produced no "test suite" for the WPR, showing through a series of historical examples how it would have worked in the past. This perhaps accounted for the absence of a practical way to implement the consultation requirement. Presidents reasonably wondered whom they were supposed to consult. While members of Congress clearly expected a different situation to prevail in executive-legislative relations after the WPR was passed, they provided no guidance on this question nor whether the consultation necessarily involved "advice and *consent*" or was simply informational. Even after complaining subsequently about a lack of consultation, members of Congress were nonetheless unable to agree what sort of consultation would satisfy the law.

The most famous provision of the WPR was the sixty-day clock. The idea was that unless there was a declaration of war, the president would file a report to Congress under Section 4(a)(1) when armed forces were introduced into hostilities. If Congress took no action, the president was required to terminate the use of the armed forces after sixty days under Section 5(b). So a *lack* of action by Congress would force the president to cancel a military operation that he had presumably already found to be in the interests of U.S. foreign policy. The clock was an attempt to outmaneuver the president on the ground that if Congress had to terminate a military involvement through positive action, the president could always wield his veto.[87] While this point was well taken, the preemptive nature of the clock was more an expression of the lack of dialogue between the branches that characterized the whole war powers debate rather than a sound way to approach the problem. In any case, the clock was unacceptable to Nixon, who did signal to Congress a number of times while the WPR was being considered that he found it unconstitutional.[88]

Although the stark command of Section 5(b) has always discomfited presidentialists, there is little doubt that this provision was constitutional given the purpose behind the "declare war" clause discussed in Chapter 1. Acknowledging the later controversies over the constitutionality of the WPR reviewed below, however, a brief commentary is appropriate here. Nixon no doubt believed that once he had ordered troops into hostilities, it would be an unconstitutional infringement of the commander in chief power for Congress to terminate the action, especially without a separate vote.[89] The problem here is that Congress has its own set of constitutional powers with respect to the use of military force, including the substantive "declare war" power (the power to start a war or other hostilities) and the necessary and proper clause (specifically invoked by Congress in the WPR).[90]

The confrontation of legislative and executive powers over war would create a conflict that could be resolved in terms of Justice Jackson's three zones of presidential power set forth in the *Steel Seizure* case (reviewed in Chapter 2).[91] The president would be in zone three, at his lowest ebb of power, in opposing the WPR supported by the mighty array of military powers given to Congress in Article I. Because the WPR did allow the president the leeway to introduce military forces into hostilities anywhere in the world for sixty days, it is unlikely that it would be unconstitutional for Congress to mandate their withdrawal. After all, the armed forces can remain if the president simply exerts himself to convince Congress that they are necessary. This does not unduly burden the presidency and thus violate general principles of separation of powers, given the stakes involved in any military action and the poor track record accumulated by the Kennedy, Johnson, and Nixon administrations with respect to the Vietnam War.[92]

For my purposes, the most interesting aspect of the continuing controversy over the constitutionality of the WPR was how it well illustrated the ambiguous status of the post-1945 constitutional order.[93] War powers are not part of the legalized Constitution and so a garden-variety doctrinal justification of the sort just offered cannot be fully satisfactory. Indeed, no president would be satisfied with such arguments. We can thus better understand the ground of the continuing presidential objections to the WPR if we proceed within the framework set out in Chapter 1. This means interpreting provisions of the Constitution such as the commander in chief clause in light of the new post-1945 responsibilities of the presidency in foreign affairs.

Here the evaluation of the WPR by Nixon's attorney general, Elliot Richardson, is relevant. On the policy side, Richardson objected that "[t]he bill tries to regulate by law the unpredictable." Richardson believed declarations of war were inappropriate in a variety of situations in which the United States might become involved, including insurgencies and circumstances involving "terror groups."[94] Richardson treated the "declare war" clause in a literal manner, in effect asserting that it applied only when Congress enacted documents labeled "Declarations of War" rather than creating a substantive power to commence war.[95] He continued:

> From the constitutional point of view, we do not believe that Congress has the authority to define the President's war powers by legislation enacted pursuant to the Necessary and Proper Clause. That clause relates to the authority of the Federal Government as such, but cannot form the basis of legislation limiting the power of the three branches *inter se.* Otherwise Congress could through the exercise of its legislative authority completely destroy the fundamental principle of the separation of powers underlying the Constitution. . . .
>
> Implementation of the war power provisions of the Constitution by legislation purportedly enacted under the Necessary and Proper Clause is also contrary to the spirit and purpose of our basic document. As Chief Justice Marshall said in *McCulloch* v. *Maryland,* 4 Wheat. 316, 415 (1819), the Constitution was 'intended to endure for ages to come, and consequently to be adopted [sic] to the various *crises* in human affairs.' Hence, it was not to have 'the properties of a legal code.' The bill, however, would

> confine in a narrow statutory straitjacket, enacted without knowledge of future crises, the President's ability to meet the unpredictable situations which may confront the United States.[96]

Nixon's position that the WPR was unconstitutional thus becomes more plausible if we take seriously Richardson's implicit claim that the use of military force, including "war," is simply one element of a sound national security policy. It follows that the president must have a granular control over the nation's armed forces that the WPR made more difficult. If we assume that the Constitution gave the president primary responsibility for foreign affairs, then measures like the WPR which interfere with that responsibility *must* be unconstitutional.

This point of view was reflected in Nixon's veto message.[97] Apparently drafted by the State Department, it has always struck congressionalists as half-hearted, given that it did not come to grips with the Article I sources of Congress's power over war.[98] It did demonstrate the consistency of the executive branch's position with respect to war powers in the post–World War II period. Like Katzenbach's testimony described in Chapter 4, Nixon emphasized that the Constitution did not "draw a precise and detailed line of demarcation between the foreign policy powers of the two branches."[99] Nixon asserted that the WPR would take away "authorities which the President has properly exercised under the Constitution for almost 200 years," but did not specify whether he was referring to Article II or later historical practice.[100] Members of Congress responded by noting that Nixon seemed to be running together his power over foreign affairs with the war power.[101] This showed very well the true ground of the conflict between the branches.

From a presidential point of view, placing a clock on the exercise of the foreign affairs power is anathema. What is in question is not starting a "war," but rather protecting the national security of the United States. The term of a foreign affairs crisis that may involve the use of military force is usually unknown. Stating a term in advance may cause allies to doubt our commitment and enemies our resolve.[102] Stipulating that the president can go to Congress during the sixty days for authorization is no help. Presidents should not have to concede that they need congressional permission to exercise what are, after all, their own constitutional powers. Most important, this would make the exercise of the foreign affairs power conditional on the president's general standing with Congress. This might indeed be viewed as the real purpose of the WPR, although it introduces more than a whiff of Westminster-style parliamentary government into American constitutionalism. More concretely, this means placing policies which may be crucial to national security at risk to quotidian politics.[103]

The conflict between Congress and the president over the status of the WPR has been a source of confusion ever since it was enacted. In fact, the WPR has often been proclaimed a dead letter by politicians and pundits.[104] The most prominent reason was voiced by influential senator Sam Nunn during the run-up to the 1991 Gulf War. He noted that the sixty-day clock had never been started by any president (aside from an after-the-fact action by President Ford) and would likely never be started. Presidents have filed reports with Congress, but have avoided filing under the particular section that starts the clock. Although Congress could presumably start the clock in separate legislation, this would be subject to a veto.[105] Despite Nunn's cogent reasoning, there is little doubt that the WPR expressed the changed political relationship between the branches in the post-Vietnam era.

Implementing the WPR: Politics, Policy, and the Constitution

To see how the WPR has been relevant to the subsequent exercise of presidential power in foreign affairs requires a rough-and-ready distinction of three different levels of interbranch interaction—political, policy, and constitutional. Politics refers to the balance of power between the parties and how both branches always have electoral considerations in mind. Policy refers to what course of action best serves the interests of the United States. The constitutional realm is what the Constitution permits or denies as a matter of law.

As an initial observation with respect to the politics of the WPR, it is worth keeping in mind that very few members of Congress expended any energy opposing it. Public support was overwhelming at 80 percent.[106] Gerald Ford was the first president to make meaningful decisions under the statute. While Ford had his doubts about the wisdom of the WPR, he had to maneuver carefully to show compliance given the broad political support for the legislation and the tense relations between the branches on matters of foreign policy.[107] In the midst of the evident collapse of South Vietnam in early 1975, Ford wanted Congress to approve substantial funds for military support and to evacuate both Americans and the South Vietnamese who had assisted the war effort. He therefore affirmed that he would comply with the WPR (although this cost him nothing because he likely did not need it) and sought specific authority from Congress to evacuate South Vietnamese.[108] As discussed in Chapter 4, Ford and Kissinger attempted at the same time to pin the blame for Vietnam on Congress. For its part, Congress was intensely suspicious of giving the executive branch further leeway and failed to approve Ford's reasonable request in time. Ford thus had to evacuate Vietnam on his own authority.[109] In the aftermath of the war, trust between the branches was low and obviously no one behaved very well.

Through the end of the 1970s and well into President Reagan's first term, Congress was full of sponsors and supporters of the WPR. Mostly Democrats, they were vigilant, one might even say hypervigilant, that the executive branch acknowledge it even in the most obscure military operations.[110] Despite only intermittent success in implementation, the WPR was clearly the central focus of war powers negotiations between the branches. When the Justice Department's Office of Legal Counsel (OLC) finally issued an opinion in the Carter administration, it found the WPR, including the sixty-day clock, to be constitutional.[111] Once President Reagan took office, senators used nomination hearings to ensure that executive branch officials supported the statute.[112] At the same time, as noted earlier, members of Congress were consistently dissatisfied with the executive branch's record on consultation. Sometimes members were notified only after military operations were under way.[113] This did not indicate executive branch noncompliance, however, given the statute's essential vagueness and unworkability on this point. As many commentators have suggested, Congress should have designated a relatively small permanent group of congressional leaders with whom the president could consult.[114]

Despite the early record of general compliance, the impression grew that the WPR's constitutionality was in question. This was partly because both Presidents Ford and Carter, in addition to President George H. W. Bush, spoke out against the WPR after they left office and supported an unsuccessful repeal effort launched by the Republican-controlled House of Representatives in 1995.[115] This impression was also created by the first real war powers conflict in the Reagan administration. During a period when Reagan lacked a secretary of state (due to the dismissal of

Alexander Haig) in 1982, he ill-advisedly agreed to place a detachment of marines in Lebanon as part of an international peacekeeping force.[116] The marines left quickly, but shortly thereafter resumed their role as putative peacekeepers. Eventually their mission changed and they became targets for warring factions in that divided country. Once this occurred, Congress insisted that the WPR be applied and Reagan agreed to sign legislation to this effect. In his signing statement, however, he appeared to suggest that the statute might infringe his powers as commander in chief.[117] The administration also tussled with Congress over the applicability of the WPR to the October 1983 invasion of Grenada. The administration responded to its difficulties with Congress in 1984 by aggressively pushing back against the idea that Congress had a role in the implementation, as opposed to the formulation, of foreign policy.[118]

Ignoring the Carter OLC opinion that the WPR was constitutional, the Reagan and Bush I administrations took the line that every president since Nixon had challenged the constitutionality of the law while in office, the sixty-day clock in particular.[119] While the record was far more complex than indicated by this simple statement, it was so widely reported in the press that the notion was difficult to debunk.[120] This illustrated the growing split over war powers between the parties, especially between Republican presidents and Democrats in Congress. Democrats continued to keep faith with the WPR while Republicans, as just noted, eventually sponsored a symbolic effort at repeal.[121]

Another episode that cast doubt on the effectiveness of the WPR was a consequence of the long-running Iran-Iraq war in the 1980s. Iran in particular began attacking oil shipping in the Persian Gulf and the Reagan administration initiated a military operation in 1987 to protect Kuwaiti oil tankers. Several rounds of hostilities followed with Iran. Despite the clear relevance of the WPR, the Senate was unable to agree that it was applicable. By the end of the 1980s, the view that the WPR was unconstitutional as well as ineffective was far more common in Congress.[122]

While the pessimism of members of Congress over the future of the WPR was perhaps overstated, difficult questions had to be faced as the Clinton administration began. As the WPR's doubters noted, there was no clear instance in which a military conflict had followed the pattern laid out in the WPR. No president had ever triggered the sixty-day clock or withdrawn troops because the clock was about to run out. At the same time, the historical clock was not turned back. Congress, especially when led by Democrats, had often shown itself to be an aggressive watchdog, involving itself in multiple military operations in a way that was unthinkable prior to the WPR. Although Congress could not overturn the post-1945 order with a single law, William Bundy, who had served in the Kennedy and Johnson administrations and was thus in a position to make comparisons, concluded that the WPR made a difference: "The passage of the War Powers Act was not a lasting solution to a perennial problem, but it was a significant change in the balance. No legislation can anticipate all contingencies, but the burdens of proof, consultation, and approval for a President ordering American military forces into action were undoubtedly made greater than they had been for Richard Nixon, Lyndon Johnson, or John F. Kennedy."[123]

The Gulf War and the Persistence of the Cold War Order

The story of war powers in the post-Vietnam era is much larger than the fate of the WPR. In many ways, the WPR was an effect of the changed relationship of the branches rather than a cause. And the rather arcane debate over the extent to which presidents actually disputed the constitutionality of the WPR is unhelpful. We would be going down the wrong path, therefore, if we were to confine a discussion of war powers in this era to a blow-by-blow description of each instance in which the WPR was applied or not. Concentrating on individual military actions would miss the forest for the trees.[124]

The forest was constituted in part by the overwhelming political consensus that there should be "no more Vietnams"—the so-called "Vietnam syndrome." A tribute to the massive and cascading consequences of Johnson's fateful 1964–1965 decisions, that syndrome was never overcome and is still with us, as the bitter debates over the 2003 Iraq War showed all too clearly. In practical terms, no more Vietnams meant that the U.S. would never again fight a major conventional war, at least outside of Europe, for reasons related to the Cold War doctrines of containment and credibility. In hindsight, it is clear that the only way forward to a significant use of military force would be a situation in which the Cold War was not in play, either because it had ended (which all Americans eventually perceived during the Bush I if not the Reagan administration) or in the event of a direct attack on the United States.

"No more Vietnams" was actually implemented, at least within DOD, in terms of the Weinberger-Powell doctrine.[125] This called for the U.S. to intervene militarily only when it could bring to bear overwhelming force backed by the solid support of the American people. Democrats in Congress concerned about war powers appeared to overlook this apparent acceptance by the executive branch of the separation of powers principles behind the WPR. Whatever the cogency of the doctrine as a matter of geopolitical strategy, its influence demonstrated the powerful political constraints both branches were operating under in the post-Vietnam era.[126]

Another part of the forest was the 1991 Gulf War, a major war by any standard and certainly the most significant military conflict between Vietnam and 9/11.[127] It would not be fully accurate to call it the first war of the post–Cold War era. The Cold War had a long half-life and there were a number of interesting continuities between it and the Gulf War. One of the reasons for the heavy U.S. involvement in the Middle East during the previous two decades was its Cold War status as a sphere of both diplomatic and military influence. The executive branch worked for years to keep the Soviet Union out of the Middle East, an effort that was the source of bitter Soviet complaints during the era of détente.[128] When the Soviet Union invaded Afghanistan in 1979, President Carter announced a doctrine stating any outside effort to gain control of the Persian Gulf region would be met by U.S. military force.[129] As the examples of involvement in Lebanon and the reflagging of Kuwaiti tankers discussed earlier show, the U.S. remained deeply involved in the region throughout the Reagan administration.

It is sometimes overlooked that the Bush I administration was even more focused on aggressively defending presidential prerogatives than the Reagan administration.[130] President George H. W. Bush found the post-Vietnam assertiveness of Congress to be onerous.[131] How onerous became clear in the run-up to the Gulf War. As discussed in Chapter 1, Bush believed and was advised that he did not need the consent of Congress to go to war in the Gulf.[132] Contrary to what most legal scholars believe, there is little doubt Bush would have gone to war either without Congress or even against its contrary judgment. Although I review the constitutional issues as seen by administration lawyers below, what should be highlighted first and foremost is how the post-1945 constitutional order retained its influence even in a post–Cold War environment. Bush's initial unilateral decisions made it very difficult to conduct an adequate round of interbranch deliberation. At the same time, the lack of a cycle of accountability rebounded on the administration in terms of severely limiting the extent to which the war could advance the goals of U.S. foreign policy.

Controlled by the dictator Saddam Hussein, Iraq invaded Kuwait with little warning on August 2, 1990, and occupied that country along with its valuable supplies of oil. The invasion also potentially threatened the oil resources of Saudi Arabia, a lightly populated country with an inexperienced military. Like post-1945 presidents before him who had to deal with sudden crises, President Bush had to make a series of decisions about how the U.S. would respond to an event that had implications not simply for the geopolitical order in the Middle East, but for the post–Cold War international order. After discussion within the administration, Bush ordered the launching of Operation Desert Shield in less than a week. It consisted of a multinational force, including U.S. troops, to protect Saudi Arabia while the U.N. Security Council imposed economic sanctions on Iraq.[133]

While this rapid decisionmaking conveyed a sense of purpose and resistance to Iraq's blatant violation of international norms, it obscured the costs of making strategic decisions based solely on executive authority. Serious diplomacy was required before American troops were allowed to enter the closed state of Saudi Arabia, despite the obvious threat posed by Iraqi forces. Consider the pledges Bush and National Security Adviser Brent Scowcroft had to make to the Saudi leadership. When the Saudis indicated doubts about American resolve, Bush promised U.S. troops would remain until the threat had ended. Bush also promised not to disclose the fact of U.S. troop deployment until they were actually in country. Nothing about these promises was disclosed to Congress.[134]

Because Desert Shield was meant to simply defend Saudi Arabia, no doubt Bush and his advisers thought these promises did little harm. But the operation posed the risk that the substantial military deployment would lead to a commitment to war without adequate interbranch and public deliberation. Time for deliberation was plentiful, despite the air of emergency. Despite great technological advances in air warfare since World War II, it was still the case that the only sure way to drive Iraq out of Kuwait was through a substantial commitment of U.S. ground forces. Bush was told by his military advisers that a buildup to provide an adequate defensive force would require a minimum of seventeen weeks.[135] Although congressional elections were approaching, there was plenty of time for Bush to ask for congressional ratification of his decision to defend Saudi Arabia with American troops.

Bush never considered this option seriously, electing not to start the cycle of accountability during the crucial months of the military buildup in August and September. From his point of view, seeking a congressional vote of support would ignite a debate over presidential war powers in general, something he claimed (somewhat self-servingly) that no one wanted.[136] Of course, the main danger of inviting such a debate was that a rejection of his position would constitute a precedent and so restrict not only his own power but potentially that of future presidents as well. Like other post-1945 presidents, Bush was unwilling to run the risk that his proposal for war would be rejected by Congress. He thus never had to cope with making the case for war under the threat of the political damage he would suffer if his proposal was rejected.

Avoiding a decisive interbranch debate at which his course in foreign policy would be at stake sent Bush down the wrong path. It accentuated his tendency not to rely on public justifications, but to rather have Congress and the public infer policy justifications from his actions.[137] At the same time, what Bush did say showed the Gulf War's essential continuity with the post-1945 order. Analogies to World War II were ever present as Bush likened Hussein to Hitler. Like other members of the post-1945 foreign policy elite, Bush believed the failure to stand up to Hitler was a lesson that had to be relearned every time the U.S. was challenged.[138]

Moreover, like other presidents during the Cold War who took on the sole burden of decision, Bush could not avoid the stress inherent in considering a commitment to battle. He began to personalize the conflict, obsessing somewhat over reports of Iraqi atrocities in Kuwait.[139] This distracted him from formulating a persuasive public justification for ordering American troops into combat. This was all the more important a task as it became clear that for practical reasons the administration could not wait months or years for sanctions to work.[140]

Administration insiders were aware of a drift toward war during October.[141] Bush held two meetings with his key advisers which focused on the necessity of military action to remove Iraq from Kuwait. In order to guarantee success, Bush ordered the dispatch of substantial additional

U.S. forces to the Gulf.[142] It was a crucial moment of decision, yet one that was based on virtually no debate inside the administration and for which Congress and the public were completely unprepared.[143] This showed not only how the lack of interbranch deliberation was not made up for by interagency deliberation, but also how the lack of interbranch deliberation actually undermined appropriate decisionmaking inside the executive branch.

As a result, when the decision to expand the deployment was revealed after the congressional elections, the administration paid an immediate political price and lost control of the public debate. Different parts of the executive branch offered varied rationales for going to war.[144] As Secretary of State James Baker admitted later, the administration did a "lousy job" of explaining the dangers that flowed from Iraq's aggression.[145] The administration went into damage control mode to mollify Congress with diplomatic efforts designed to show that war was a last resort. The approval of military action by the U.N. Security Council, an action which surprised and impressed members of Congress, was a key to this effort.[146]

The administration eventually recovered from this blunder and, as discussed in Chapter 1, went on to obtain a congressional resolution of support in January 1991. But irreversible damage had been done to the administration's conduct of foreign policy. There was no avoiding the question of war aims. Without the discipline imposed by a timely request for congressional support, one which the executive branch would abide by no matter the outcome, there was no unified approach in the government with respect to the purpose of the war. What was the war supposed to accomplish beyond removing Iraq from Kuwait? This question was never answered in a meaningful way because the executive and legislative branches never deliberated jointly on a unified set of war aims.[147]

In consequence the war had no clear purpose within the larger structure of U.S. foreign policy. Analysts noted that the policy effects of the war seemed to dissipate quickly. This was because no one in the executive branch had been forced to make a compelling case that the war would promote important foreign policy objectives. Was it in fact the dawn of a "new world order," as Bush originally projected? Because the president was never willing to risk the political defeat of his military project, such broad notions had no democratic hold on the public and Congress and thus left no policy legacy.[148]

In addition, presidentialists might take note that Bush's stubborn refusal to go to Congress at an early stage was arguably contrary to his political interests. It hurt his chances for reelection as he could not find any lasting meaning in the war on which he could base an appeal to the electorate. Having rejected the path of meaningful public debate on a crucial matter of foreign policy, Bush had to run on the relatively unfavorable terrain of the economy.

In the midst of the uproar over the announcement of new troop deployments, Secretary of Defense Cheney laid down a marker concerning presidential power at a Senate hearing. Using the same argument from historical practice first made by Truman's State Department, Cheney made it clear that he believed the president could order the country to war on his own constitutional authority and that all Congress could expect was consultation.[149] No one in the administration disagreed with Cheney. As discussed in Chapter 1, the position of Bush and his advisers was essentially the same as that taken by Cold War presidents.[150] The members of the foreign policy establishment serving in Bush's administration thought it was clear that congressional authorization was not constitutionally required. The only topic of discussion was whether it would be a good idea to ask Congress for its *political* support (as opposed to constitutional authorization) through a resolution. Secretary Baker favored this approach, which was eventually adopted by Bush and Scowcroft.[151]

During the run-up to the war, administration lawyers told Bush in plain terms that he had the authority to order U.S. forces to engage in war. White House Counsel C. Boyden Gray wrote the most comprehensive memo and made a number of interesting observations. Gray made use of the popular distinction between offensive and defensive war discussed in Chapter 1. At bottom, Gray believed that congressional authorization was required only when the U.S. intended to wage aggressive (offensive) war. As a general matter, he reasoned that because the U.S. does not engage in aggressive war (a questionable historical assumption), "the Executive branch has generally held that the President can order U.S. forces into combat without a declaration of war."[152] Gray concluded by telling Bush, "In the event that the United States undertakes any sort of military response to Iraq's invasion of Kuwait, you will have three options: (1) proceed on your inherent authority as Commander-in-Chief without seeking congressional authorization, (2) seek a joint resolution of Congress approving your action, or (3) request a declaration of war. We believe it is legally sufficient to proceed with no formal congressional authorization at all." Gray also noted that counsel in the executive branch believed the WPR's sixty-day clock to be unconstitutional.[153]

Although Bush certainly wanted Congress's political support and thought his Gulf policy might be hurt without it, the president was firm in his conviction that he had the constitutional power under Article II to go to war.[154] By contrast, congressional Democrats defended the WPR and stated flatly that Bush had to obtain congressional authorization to avoid an unconstitutional abuse of power.[155] It is apparent that Bush would have exercised that authority even if Congress had *rejected* a resolution of support. Bush concluded in his memoirs: "In truth, even had Congress not passed the resolutions I would have acted and ordered our troops into combat. I know it would have caused an outcry, but it was the right thing to do. I was comfortable in my own mind that I had the constitutional authority. It had to be done."[156]

The uniformity of opinion in the executive branch showed the deep influence the post-1945 constitutional order retained among political elites, at least in the Republican Party. Secretary of State Baker illustrated this consensus when he later wrote, "The Constitution is unassailable on this point: the authority to conduct foreign policy, particularly when it involves the prerogatives of the commander in chief, is preeminent in the executive. There was absolutely no doubt in my mind that the President didn't legally have to have congressional approval for ordering troops into combat."[157] Notice Baker's conflation between the president's broad power over foreign policy and his ability to initiate a war. While the former role is questioned by very few scholars, there is a consensus, discussed in Chapter 1, that congressional authorization for war is constitutionally obligatory. But Baker's certainty that the president had this power showed very well the fundamental premise of the post-1945 order—power over foreign affairs means power over war.

I have argued that beyond removing Saddam Hussein from Kuwait, the Gulf War meant little in terms of long-term foreign policy objectives. We would be remiss, however, if we failed to notice some diffuse implications of the war. The military campaign showed that very few civilians in either party had kept adequate track of the new and improved capabilities of the all-volunteer force, particularly in terms of ground and air warfare. Before the war began, even knowledgeable politicians like Senator Nunn believed casualties would be high.[158] Because most Democrats opposed the war, they looked weak and out of touch concerning military affairs. But it must be said that most public officials, including President Bush, were quite surprised by the dominance displayed by the American military.[159] The gap between the military performance of the United States and a secondary power like Iraq equipped with inferior weaponry by the Soviet Union turned out to be very wide.[160] This had a further implication. Saddam Hussein was now a recognized adversary of the United States whose military had been defeated decisively in a way that did not spark memories of Vietnam. This would prove to be quite suggestive to Bush's son George W. Bush and members of the foreign policy elite looking for a way to change the status quo in the Middle East.[161]

Covert War and the Iran-Contra Affair

It is sometimes forgotten that the denouement of the Iran-contra affair occurred in December 1992 as President Bush pardoned Caspar Weinberger and other Reagan administration officials who had been targeted by the investigation of independent counsel Lawrence Walsh. Although the officials pardoned had not been tried or, in some cases, indicted, Bush gave Walsh no opportunity to justify his conduct. While the length of Walsh's investigation and his reindictment of Weinberger just prior to the 1992 presidential election raised legitimate issues, Bush's action was highly questionable and well expressed his evident contempt for Walsh's investigation.[162]

Nonetheless, it is true I am rewinding the clock somewhat to end this chapter with the Iran-contra affair, an episode that dominated the last part of 1986 and 1987 in the Reagan administration.[163] This is partly because it is useful to consider the WPR and the Gulf War together. But my principal reason for dealing with this topic last is that it enables a more unified treatment of the subject of covert war in the post-Vietnam era. This arena of warfare, in which the Reagan administration made its greatest effort, showed the instability of the post-1945 order and led to a constitutional crisis. At the same time, the crisis impelled Republicans to assert their commitment to presidential leadership in foreign policy in a new and extreme form—the doctrine of the "exclusive" presidency.

Ronald Reagan accepted the political reality of "no more Vietnams"—that the public wanted no conventional military interventions that risked significant casualties. Like Eisenhower after Korea, Reagan looked to the alternative of covert action against the nation's enemies, particularly in Central America and Afghanistan. In Nicaragua, Anastasio Somoza, a U.S.-supported dictator, had been overthrown and a new government established by the leftist Sandinistas. In El Salvador, the government was struggling to cope with a guerrilla insurgency. In the wake of the Soviet Union's invasion of Afghanistan, the Carter and Reagan administrations both implemented a strategy of encouraging and supplying counterrevolutionary movements to wear the Soviets down.[164]

Going beyond generalities in assessing Reagan's policies and understanding the Iran-contra affair requires an appreciation of how his administration operated. This is made more difficult by the seemingly universal consensus that Reagan was a passive president, especially with respect to policy. Multiple sources attest to Reagan's lack of interest in policy details, implementation, or how government worked in general. Further, there is strong agreement that Reagan tended to postpone making decisions until his foreign policy advisers agreed among themselves, something they achieved only on rare occasions.[165] These observations lead toward the assumption that the policy actually developed in the Reagan administration was made at the behest of his immediate advisers or their subordinates.

As time has passed, a more complex picture has emerged. True to his reputation as the "Great Communicator," Reagan took an active interest throughout his presidency in how his policies were explained and justified to the public. Reagan was often his own best speechwriter, personally making changes that demonstrated his comprehension of the purposes of administration policies.[166] The realization that Reagan could take an active role when he wished has called attention to those moments when he laid down a clear strategic direction.[167] His policies toward Nicaragua and Central America as well as the initiative to Iran aimed at obtaining the release of U.S. hostages held in Lebanon both offered moments when Reagan established a clear line for policy, even when his advisers openly disputed him. Once Reagan had expressed a view or made a decision, he tended to defend it tenaciously, a quality on conspicuous display after the Iran-contra affair became public.[168]

It is therefore appropriate to begin where we usually do in understanding a presidential administration—with the values and perspective of the president himself. With respect to the Cold War, Reagan was akin to an iceberg that had broken off the mainland of foreign policy around 1960 and had, with the exception of his antipathy to détente, skipped intervening developments. He retained the commitment, common in the Eisenhower and Kennedy administrations, that U.S. superiority over the Soviets must be maintained at all costs.[169] William Casey, the new director of the CIA and one of Reagan's principal advisers (despite the CIA's ordinary role as a policy implementer), also had 1950s-era views about the Cold War, including the position, common among conservatives as we have seen, that it was a real war justifying the use of the enemy's tactics.[170] Casey also refused to accept the implications of the 1970s-era reforms that directed the CIA to keep Congress informed of its covert operations in a timely fashion. To Casey, as to many officials in the Reagan administration, Congress (despite Republican control of the Senate from 1980 to 1986) was a nuisance.[171]

For Central America, this meant that the spirit of the early Cold War had returned with a vengeance. In many respects, the Reagan administration's aggressive policy toward Nicaragua resembled what American policy toward Cuba circa 1960 would have looked like had Cuba been located on the mainland rather than in the Caribbean. Nicaragua's land border with Honduras allowed the CIA to quickly establish a covert paramilitary force (the democratic resistance or "contras") made up largely of former members of the Somoza military. Although the contras grew much larger than the force defeated at the Bay of Pigs, they were similarly never likely to provoke a counterrevolutionary uprising against a government that was broadly popular.[172]

The strategic situation south of the U.S. border was little different from the state of affairs prevailing at the end of the Cuban missile crisis in 1962. Cuba remained the most active communist state in the region and had the ability to project power abroad to cause the U.S. trouble in Africa. The U.S. was the overwhelmingly dominant power in the hemisphere and could easily crush Nicaragua (or Cuba for that matter) by conventional military means if the president so desired. At the outset of the Reagan administration, Secretary of State Haig strenuously advocated an intervention into either Cuba or El Salvador as a way of rolling back communism and showing that the "Vietnam syndrome" was over.

But Reagan's political advisers were aghast at Haig's overt plan of attack and Reagan himself never showed much interest in ordering U.S. forces to invade Central America (although he did invade the island nation of Grenada).[173] Because Nicaragua had little ability to project power beyond its borders, the issue for the Reagan administration seemed to be showing that communism as an ideology could be defeated, in part to appease the right wing of the Republican Party.[174]

With full-scale conventional war off the table, the administration turned to covert war against Nicaragua as the least bad option at the end of 1981. Within two years, this became a wide-ranging, partly overt campaign to intimidate the Nicaraguan government and cause its overthrow, without quite admitting either. Action was not only covert in terms of raids by the contras but also conventional in the form of large-scale military exercises in Honduras and off the Nicaraguan coast designed to raise the specter of invasion. CIA operatives, including U.S. military personnel and foreign mercenaries, dropped bombs and, in one famous incident in early 1984, mined Nicaragua's harbors to destroy international shipping and oil supplies. Unlike the actions against communist states in the early Cold War, however, all of this was done against prevailing sentiment in Congress and the strong headwinds of public opinion.[175]

Before going further we need to take note of an additional feature of Reagan's presidency—his largely overlooked antinomian tendencies. For example, Reagan did not understand Watergate to have involved criminal actions and thought Nixon was unfairly run out of office by his political enemies.[176] While Reagan always paid attention when his advisers told him directly that a proposed course of action would violate the law, when he was left to his own counsel he did not appear to have a high regard for what legal scholars call the autonomy of the law. He tended to formulate policy based on moral opinions without regard to relevant legal distinctions and restrictions.[177] This was particularly true in foreign affairs, where a president always has a greater scope for discretionary action. When Congress enacted restrictions on the funding of the contras, Reagan and advisers such as Casey sought to evade them. When advised of possible illegalities in the course of selling arms to Iran to win the release of American hostages, Reagan thought the moral imperative of winning their release trumped the law.[178]

Reagan's antinomian perspective and his firm adherence to the policy of supporting the contras created the potential for an epic constitutional clash after Congress began enacting restrictions on appropriations. Known as the Boland amendments, the legislation first prohibited the administration from using funds to overthrow the Nicaraguan government and then cut off funding of the contras entirely. Reagan began defending his policy in Central America more openly in 1983, although many in Congress continued to oppose supporting the contras.[179] Certainly a constitutionally appropriate way of settling the dispute was by highlighting the issue in the 1984 presidential election. However, Reagan ran a campaign lacking in specifics and suggested the possibility of settling the dispute with Nicaragua through negotiations. Reagan thus chose not to submit his aggressive policy to a democratic test. Having won an overwhelming reelection victory, Reagan immediately returned to the path of overthrowing the Nicaraguan government.[180]

By this time it was apparent that the contras had serious difficulties. As noted, they never demonstrated any ability to win a conventional military conflict. Nor were they able to foment an insurgency against the Sandinista government. On their occasional forays into Nicaragua, they committed numerous atrocities, including murder of noncombatants, torture, and rape.[181] Yet the Reagan administration resolved to keep them going until Congress could be convinced to change its mind. Once the most restrictive of the Boland amendments took effect, Reagan wanted the contras to be kept together "body and soul" with funding obtained from other governments or private sources, despite warnings that this might be an impeachable offense. The task was given to NSC Adviser Robert McFarlane and Lt. Col. Oliver North of the NSC staff.[182] Not for the last time, a part of the White House went operational.

The basis of the Reagan administration's commitment to the contras in Cold War anticommunist ideology helps explain the peculiar politics of what became known as the "Iran-contra affair." This designation puts the emphasis on the administration's ill-fated initiative in which arms were traded for hostages held in Lebanon starting in mid-1985, during Reagan's second term. To highlight the place of this affair in the post-1945 constitutional order, however, I have emphasized the "contra" or covert war side. We must keep in mind that while the Iran initiative was rejected across the political board after disclosure in November 1986 and eventually repudiated by Reagan in March 1987, the contras were never abandoned by Reagan and the Republicans. Congress was still debating aid to the contras well into 1988,

Reagan's last year in office.[183] To oversimplify somewhat, to Democrats Iran-contra was about selling weapons to Iran behind the back of Congress in violation of the law. To Republicans it was about anticommunism and the contras. This helps explain why Reagan always defended North as "a national hero" for keeping the contras alive. It also explains the dogged defense of Reagan by congressional Republicans, especially those like Dick Cheney who was serving in the House of Representatives at the time. This defense was expressed through the extraordinary and extreme doctrine, reviewed below, that they adopted to advance presidential supremacy in foreign affairs.[184]

Reagan made his concern about American hostages held in Lebanon evident to members of his administration. He took an active role in a meeting in early July 1985, expressing frustration about the lack of actionable intelligence.[185] Despite a clear policy against dealing with states like Iran that sponsored terrorism, Reagan agreed to pursue an initiative in which arms, principally antitank missiles, would be traded for the Iranian-influenced release of the hostages. For its part, Iran needed the missiles to even the odds in its ongoing war with Iraq. Reagan clothed this ill-advised scheme in the guise of a diplomatic initiative toward "moderates" in Iran. Despite the objections of Secretary of State Shultz and Secretary of Defense Weinberger, the initiative went forward in earnest after two high-level meetings in December 1985 and January 1986. At the December meeting Weinberger warned about legal difficulties, but Reagan trumped legality with the moral imperative to win the release of the hostages.[186] At the January meeting in which Reagan made the final decision to proceed, Attorney General Edwin Meese attended and argued that if laws stood in the way, they could be bypassed based on the president's inherent authority to conduct foreign policy and as commander in chief.[187]

Once the arms for hostages deals were revealed, Reagan and some of his advisers tried mightily for a time to keep them going in the face of intense adverse political reaction. But the president's public defense of the policy undermined his position, as it contained many inaccuracies sponsored by advisers trying to protect themselves. What is noteworthy is the president's firm and consistent defense through November 1986 of what to him was a crucial foreign policy initiative.[188] This explained the drastic impact on the administration when Reagan realized that the public did not accept his version of events. The president went into a kind of withdrawal, and he and the White House ceased to function effectively for several months.[189]

Reagan's bold decisions and stalwart leadership with respect to both the contras and the Iran arms initiative were largely obscured in the firestorm that resulted from the sudden disclosure by Attorney General Meese that the NSC staff led by NSC Adviser John Poindexter and North had arranged for proceeds from the Iran arms transfers to be sent to the contras. This created the issue, fascinating to Washington insiders, of whether the president knew of the illegal diversion of funds. This framing of the affair truncated the inquiry into the more important issue of how to assess what Reagan had indisputably decided in both initiatives versus what the law required. Drilling down to the truth was made more difficult by North and Poindexter's Olympic-level destruction of evidence in November, unimpeded by any preservation order from the president or attorney general. It was also made more problematic by the sudden illness and death of CIA Director Casey.[190]

Washington was consumed with the issue of the diversion of funds to the contras and the larger possibility that Reagan might be impeached by an opposition Congress. But the mix of "Iran" and "contra" was highly combustible. While no one defended selling arms to Iran, the contras had become a litmus test for the Republican right and were deeply intertwined with anticommunist commitments at the core of the Cold War.[191] Iran-contra aside, Reagan was the most popular and successful Republican president since Eisenhower. He had a stature on the right similar to President Kennedy's standing among Democrats—a hero-president beyond reproach. It was therefore unthinkable for Republicans to allow Reagan's name and legacy to be tarnished by Iran-contra. They embarked on a no-holds-barred effort to dynamite the congressional hearings that were supposed to establish the facts and cleanse the constitutional waters.[192]

Congressional Republicans were aided by the popularity that North, a decorated Marine and Vietnam veteran, acquired during the hearings by playing on anticommunist themes. Ultimately, this was an expression of the frustration of Reagan's supporters at experiencing months of setback in what to them was a transformative administration. Somewhat unnoticed, North also introduced a new and fundamental theme—that the world is permanently dangerous—which would aid conservatives in the rapidly approaching transition to a post–Cold War world.[193] Whereas the Reagan administration saw North as an excellent foil to its congressional critics, there were still divisions in the ranks of Republicans and in the administration itself over what had happened. Secretary Shultz in effect adopted the position that Iran-contra did resemble Watergate in some respects.[194] He disagreed with North's testimony and thought North had perpetrated "a rogue operation and an immense constitutional threat."[195] This put him on the outs with his own administration and increased the pressure on conservative Republicans to demonstrate that Iran-contra was not a scandal or a crisis.[196]

The Arrival of the Exclusive Presidency

During the Bush II presidency, the Minority Report of the joint congressional committees investigating the Iran-contra affair had a brief moment of fame when Vice President Cheney (who signed the report as a member of the House of Representatives) recommended it as reading material supporting broad claims of presidential power in foreign affairs.[197] Commentators have tended to run the theory of the Minority Report together with claims of a "unitary" presidency made earlier in the Reagan administration with respect to presidential control over administrative agencies.[198] While the issues posed by presidential leadership in foreign affairs and administrative law may be related, it is analytically clearer to separate them, as the Reaganite claims for the presidency in foreign affairs were relatively unique across the corpus of constitutional law while also being broadly consistent with the post-1945 constitutional order.

In response to the Iran-contra affair and the threat to Reagan's status as a hero-president, conservative Republicans were driven to make claims of presidential supremacy in foreign affairs. More technically, they argued that presidential power was "exclusive" or "preclusive" of control by the other branches of government.[199] In plain terms, they claimed that the president could ignore laws passed by Congress when he believed them to be unconstitutional infringements of his power to conduct foreign affairs.[200] Although this argument has the flavor of "the president is above the law" and appears to be directly contrary to the president's Article II Section 3 duty to "faithfully execute the laws," scholars know that the details can be technical and complex.[201] Nevertheless, the basic thrust of this claim is surely one of the most extreme and dangerous in all of constitutional law. The very fact that it was seriously advanced by knowledgeable lawyers is evidence of the intense polarization between the branches that characterized Reagan's second term—indeed, a constitutional crisis.

Executive branch claims made prior to the Reagan administration had been directed mainly at congressional interference with military deployments and did not include the claim that the president could ignore the law across broad areas of foreign affairs.[202] But we should observe how the lengthy argument over the WPR had potentially laid the ground for broader claims. Not coincidentally as discussed earlier, these claims were pressed most vigorously during the Reagan administration. The argument that the WPR was unconstitutional could easily slide into the much different claim that presidents were ignoring it (rather than evading its spirit although adhering to its terms) because they had determined for themselves that it was unconstitutional. This latter claim was pressed by the Minority Report against statutes like the Boland amendments that interfered with Reagan's covert war against Nicaragua.

The Minority Report stated that in the case of a conflict between a congressional statute and "core presidential foreign policy functions," the statute should be regarded as unconstitutional.[203] This had the form of an argument to a court and could be read as saying the president should comply with the law until the courts had so ruled. However, the general thrust of the Minority Report was that the president had a freedom of action in foreign affairs with which Congress could not interfere. The Minority Report was far from a detailed treatment of the question. In particular, it did not address how to distinguish interference with "core functions" in specific cases from regulations of presidential discretion based firmly on Congress's enumerated powers. The report had to concede that "Congress does have some legislative power in the [foreign policy] field."[204] This meant that Justice Jackson's authoritative concurrence in the *Steel Seizure* case was relevant and the Minority Report had no idea what to do with Jackson's insistence that when the president acts against the will of Congress, "his power is at its lowest ebb."[205] The arguments made in the Minority Report should have produced a win for Truman in the *Steel Seizure* case, discussed in Chapter 2. The report made no attempt to explain why this did not happen.

The thesis of the Minority Report was taken up by the DOJ in a memorandum filed in November 1988 as independent counsel Lawrence

Walsh was preparing for the trial of Oliver North.[206] The narrow purpose of the memorandum was to rebuke Walsh for arguing that government officials could be accused of a conspiracy to violate a congressional policy unconnected to any specific legal requirement.[207] However, the DOJ went on to argue that the president had certain areas of "exclusive" power in foreign affairs: "there is a sphere of presidential activity that could not constitutionally be limited by any congressional enactment."[208] Without citing or discussing the *Steel Seizure* case, the brief relied on the vesting clause of Article II as a source of the president's "plenary authority" over foreign affairs.[209] In addition, the brief employed the *Curtiss-Wright* case to support the president's "far-reaching discretion to act on his own authority in managing the external relations of the country."[210] Although *Curtiss-Wright,* unlike the *Steel Seizure* case, did not deal with a congressional restriction on executive discretion with respect to a matter of national security, the brief asserted that *Curtiss-Wright* stood for the principle that "Congress may not enact legislation infringing the President's inherent Article II authority in [foreign affairs]."[211]

The memorandum was written to lay down a general marker that the independent counsel had gone too far in the North prosecution. As such, the DOJ did not identify any laws that it considered as having placed unconstitutional restrictions on the president's ability to conduct foreign affairs. But the implications of the DOJ's position were clear enough. The DOJ was suggesting that the Boland amendments were unconstitutional if they were interpreted as prohibiting the president from influencing other countries to support the overthrow of a "totalitarian government."[212]

The most basic flaw in these arguments and the reason why they were so dangerous had to do with checks and balances. One might read these analyses and never surmise that the president had the ability to veto or otherwise object to "unconstitutional" legislation when it was passed. The circumstances surrounding the Boland amendments exhibited this flaw, as Reagan did not veto or even object.[213] He could hardly do otherwise, as the administration was rarely willing to defend openly its goal of overthrowing the Nicaraguan government, which never had any significant support from Congress or the public. The danger came from the possibility that after the legislation was passed, whether over the president's veto or not, the president would in effect exercise an absolute veto by ignoring the law, something he was denied by the

Constitution itself. Of course, a president might pursue the matter in the courts, but it was never clear in these presidentialist analyses whether he was limited to that remedy. Rather, the analyses both stated and implied that the president had a residual power to violate the law. The routine exercise of such a power would be more than sufficient to bring the entire constitutional system to a crashing halt.

Unfortunately, the Majority Report of the Iran-contra committee did not make these matters clear. The Majority Report was long on facts, but short on constitutional analysis. We should examine briefly one influential attempt to provide the missing elements in the Majority Report's analysis. In response to the Iran-contra affair and in particular Congress's failure to analyze what had gone wrong, Yale Law School professor (later dean and afterward legal adviser to the State Department in the Obama administration) Harold Koh offered a well-researched portrait of the "National Security Constitution."[214] He defined this constitutional tradition in foreign affairs around the principle of "balanced institutional participation"[215] and built a case that it was a combination of fundamental precedents and framework statutes that had evolved in the twentieth century to both empower and restrain the executive.[216] For Koh, these arrangements were exemplified by Justice Jackson's concurring opinion in the *Steel Seizure* case which promoted a vision of the executive and legislative branches sharing powers.[217] As he saw it, this tradition had been violated by the Reagan administration's wrongdoing during Iran-contra.[218] He urged the adoption of a national security charter to redress the problems pointed up by the scandal and more vigorous oversight of the executive by both Congress and the judiciary.[219]

Although Koh's suggestions for reform were valuable and still worth considering, he did not penetrate to the heart of the problem in his analysis of presidential power during the post-1945 period. Although Koh acknowledged the existence of a counter-tradition celebrating executive power, his analysis depended ultimately on the assumption of a consensus behind the judicious tradition of the "National Security Constitution."[220] By the time Koh published his book in 1990, Democrats perhaps were willing to accept his insights. Republicans were not.[221] As just described, they saw the events leading to the Iran-contra affair in terms of unwarranted *congressional* interference in foreign policy, the proper domain of the executive branch.[222]

The problem with Koh's analysis was insufficient attention to the relationship of the Constitution to historical change in the early Cold War. Koh did not attempt a detailed explanation of why and how presidents had increased their power in foreign affairs after World War II. Koh recognized the importance of the National Security Act of 1947, but left out the historical context presented in Chapter 2 of the struggle to stabilize Europe, contain the Soviet threat, and rebuild U.S. military power—circumstances that led officials in all three branches of government to believe that an unprecedented increase in presidential power was necessary literally to save the world.[223] If there was a "National Security Constitution" during the Cold War, it was based on the kind of presidential unilateralism that Koh deplored.

Koh's work, along with Arthur Schlesinger's earlier critique of the "imperial presidency," accurately reflected a widespread sense in the wake of Vietnam, Watergate, and now Iran-contra that something was amiss with presidential power in the constitutional system. But this judgment was not generally shared by conservatives and Republicans. They saw the world differently. The Reagan administration had carried forward the commitments made in the Truman, Eisenhower, and Kennedy administrations to fight the Cold War by whatever means available. Koh thus failed to appreciate that Iran-contra was not an isolated case of an administration gone awry, but was based on an approach to national security firmly rooted in the post-1945 constitutional order. Especially in light of the Bush II presidency, we cannot make progress understanding the course of presidential power in the post-1945 period without acknowledging the existence of a competing perspective to the imperial presidency, one associated with a distinctive set of ideas about foreign policy and emphasizing the need for swift decisionmaking and military strength in a dangerous world.[224]

Unlike Koh, I do not assume that American constitutionalism is a continuous fabric formed from unbroken traditions or successive settlements. Rather, as exemplified by the tensions between the original Constitution and the post-1945 constitutional order, it has serious discontinuities that have made it more difficult than Koh believed to reach a consensus about presidential power in foreign affairs. In fact, there has been no "National Security Constitution" in the sense of a well-settled judgment concerning the proper scope of presidential power in the post-Vietnam or post–Cold War periods. The disagreements between the parties have been long-lasting and profound and the conflicting claims of liberals and conservatives were well illustrated by the Iran-contra affair itself and the controversies, discussed in the next chapter, that attended the Bush II administration.

What remained of Central America? During the post-Vietnam era, it is not too much to say that a scythe of death was moving through the region. According to historian Walter LaFeber, the 1979–1991 period was "the bloodiest, most violent, and most destructive era in Central America's post-1820 history."[225] The contra war alone left 40,000 dead and made refugees of many more. Right-wing death squads in league with the government in El Salvador as well as attacks by leftist guerrillas killed 75,000.[226] By some counts, the complete toll was *10 percent* of the entire population of Central America.[227] Historians have made clear that this bloodletting originated from developments that began in the 1960s, long before the Reagan administration.[228] Nonetheless, President Reagan not only did little to alleviate the suffering of the people of Central America, but also increased their burden with a policy of aggressive war conducted by mercenaries who used brutal tactics.[229] Moral judgments in the face of such a monumental toll are sometimes too easily made. But as Reagan emphasized the role of moral principles in evaluating political action, his policies are appropriately judged on such a basis.

6

The 9/11 Wars and the Presidency

JUDGING by the number of critical works produced by constitutional scholars alone, George W. Bush was one of the most controversial presidents in American history.[1] Yet it has not been easy to discern whether each of the contentious legal issues raised during the Bush administration's "war on terror"—military commissions, detainee treatment including renditions and harsh interrogation techniques, government surveillance—resonated with the public in the same way that they fascinated journalists, human rights lawyers, and legal scholars. Throughout the Bush administration, it was not clear whether the public understood the details of the various disputes or whether they agreed with the major premises of the administration's critics.[2]

Nevertheless, by any reasonable standard Bush left office a deeply unpopular president who had lost the confidence of the American people. Aside from his inadequate response to Hurricane Katrina in 2005, the principal reason for Bush's failure was that he was still presiding over an unpopular war in Iraq, a war many Americans had come to believe was not only unnecessary but actually contrary to the goals of the war against al Qaeda and the Taliban that Congress authorized after the ruthless and terrifying attacks of September 11, 2001. But the Iraq War was not just unpopular; it was widely regarded as a policy disaster.[3] This makes it important to determine how it was related to the post-1945 constitutional order.

That order was instituted by President Truman and advisers such as Acheson along with supporters in Congress, and there are obvious parallels to be drawn not only between Bush and Truman but also between

Obama and Eisenhower. As for Bush and Truman, both presidents were perceived in their own time as failures and their last years in office were quite unhappy. Ironically, Truman is now admired for being a stalwart of the struggle against the Soviet Union. Although time will reveal whether Bush is gradually accepted as a foresighted leader of what may yet be a decades-long global struggle similar to the Cold War, there are many differences, not only between the Truman and Bush administrations, but also between the early Cold War and the war against al Qaeda. One clear difference is the extent to which the beginning of the Cold War depended on the cooperation of Congress. As recounted in Chapter 2, winning approval of aid to Greece and Turkey, the Marshall Plan, and the NATO Treaty was not easy but Truman and Acheson worked assiduously to win Congress over. By contrast, much of the early effort against al Qaeda and, most controversially, the run-up to the Iraq War was notable for the lack of interbranch deliberation.[4] With respect to Obama and Eisenhower, as we will discuss in the next chapter, both presidents were expected to terminate major wars begun by their predecessor. Yet both also sought to continue the military struggle of a "long war," although using covert rather than conventional means.

The crucible for understanding the Bush II and Obama administrations from a constitutional perspective is thus the same as the central topic of this book—the relationship of presidential power in foreign affairs to decisions for war. As we should remind ourselves, war is a unique kind of policy. While the contentious rule of law issues mentioned above are all significant, one theme I develop in this chapter and the next is that ultimately they are secondary to the far more pressing questions posed by failures of democratic deliberation. The Bush II administration was only the latest in a long line of post-1945 administrations that encountered severe difficulties in making decisions for war.

Because President Clinton did not make a decision for a major war, it is tempting to skip over his administration. But this would result in an incomplete analysis. Each administration from the time of Bush I has taken place in a post–Cold War environment unfamiliar to American policymakers.[5] At a minimum, we need to trace what this new environment for foreign policy meant for the post-1945 constitutional order. Further, substantial military operations did occur in the Clinton administration. Peacekeeping missions were maintained in Somalia and undertaken in Haiti and Bosnia. As a follow-on to the 1991 Gulf War, there were airstrikes against Iraq. Clinton also ordered an extensive air campaign against Serbia in 1999 to protect rebels in Kosovo and struck at al Qaeda in Afghanistan after it bombed U.S. embassies in Kenya and Tanzania in 1998.

The split between the parties that developed in the 1970s on matters of war powers and the War Powers Resolution (WPR) continued after the end of the Cold War. The Clinton and Obama administrations advanced a sounder interpretation of the "declare war" clause relative to their Republican predecessors and did not contest the constitutionality of the WPR. On the other hand, with the possible exception of President Obama (explored in the next chapter), these Democratic administrations never abandoned the idea that presidents order military actions on the basis of their Article II authority as commander in chief, rather than on the basis of authority provided by Congress. All of these post–Cold War presidents, including Obama, continued the Cold War tradition of regarding Congress as a junior partner whose consent was not required to take the nation to war.

The End of the Cold War and the Persistence of the Post-1945 Constitutional Order

As discussed in the previous chapter, in the 1970s the United States missed a chance to rethink its foreign policy in the aftermath of Vietnam. Although political conditions were not very favorable, the implosion of Nixon's presidency and the hostility of the right toward détente also obscured the reality that the early Cold War had ended. Moreover, unless its allies in Europe and the Far East were challenged in some fundamental way, the U.S. was not prepared to fight a conventional war. But the Soviet Union and China showed no interest in posing such a challenge. While President Reagan dramatically increased the defense budget, he was uninterested in actually using conventional military force in any significant way.

As the Cold War era began to close at the end of the Reagan administration, there were multiple missed chances for institutional reorganization in the Reagan, Bush I, and Clinton administrations. Policymaking elites found it difficult to imagine a post–Cold War future for foreign policy and there was no successor to containment as a master national security strategy. Instead, the U.S. resolved to continue its status as the only global superpower.[6]

Nonetheless, there were signs of new threats to national security. The CIA sensed that terrorism might pose a challenge for the future and terrorist groups were at least of concern to presidents from Nixon onward.[7] The Reagan administration repeatedly emphasized the danger of state-sponsored terrorism and struck at Libya's leader Muammar al-Qaddafi with a bombing raid in 1986 after especially deadly attacks on U.S. citizens overseas. There was clearly a new threat from then ill-defined groups of Islamic terrorists in the 1990s, beginning with the February 1993 bombing of the World Trade Center.

In a largely overlooked irony, the Cold War ended much as it began with Americans debating whether actions by the U.S. had determined the fate of another very large communist country. In 1949, it was "Who lost China?" After the fall of the Berlin Wall in 1989, the debate was not only "Did the U.S. win the Cold War?," but also "Did President Reagan win the Cold War?" Conservative "triumphalists" claimed that he had.[8]

As described in Chapter 2, it difficult to recapture today the superheated atmosphere of the beginning of the Cold War in which figures like Truman and Acheson, now universally regarded as pillars of the struggle against the Soviet Union, were denounced by Republicans as betrayers of their country. Acheson never comprehended the fuss made over the defeat of Jiang Jieshi (Chiang Kai-shek) by Mao Zedong.[9] The U.S. had supported Jiang for years, pumping billions in money and supplies into China during World War II and after in an ultimately futile attempt to keep China out of communist hands. Although Mao's victory came as a shock to unprepared Americans, it was an event that had little to do with any American failure to help and more to do with Jiang's inability to lead and inspire his troops and followers. The fall of China to the communists had more to do with decisions in China than in Washington.

The tangle of causality surrounding the fall of any major regime makes it difficult to separate the threads of U.S. responsibility for the collapse of the Soviet Union and its empire from the influence of the Soviet leadership, its economy, and its people. We can make some progress by remembering the basics of U.S.-Soviet interaction during the Cold War. Trailing the U.S. badly in nuclear weapons during the Cuban missile crisis, Soviet leaders vowed that they would never again be caught in a position of weakness.[10] To the Soviet Union, détente in the 1970s was about American recognition that the Soviets had attained superpower status and were fit to be an equal partner with the U.S.

on the world stage. Once past the tensions of the early Cold War and (to the Soviets) the distraction of Vietnam, the way was clear for progress on arms control.[11] On the U.S. side, if the tensions had continued and the Sino-Soviet split not occurred, Nixon would not have been able to launch détente in the first place. Nixon's confidence in taking a less aggressive stance toward the Soviet Union showed that the nature of the Cold War had changed.

Thus the fact that détente was interrupted by a renewed spirit of confrontation on the part of the U.S., especially after the Soviets invaded Afghanistan in 1979, tended to obscure the reality that the instability of the early Cold War had not returned. The aggressive spirit that Khrushchev had brought to the communist cause in the early 1960s was missing from the sclerotic Kremlin leadership provided by Leonid Brezhnev.[12] As discussed in Chapter 5, despite what the Reagan administration may have thought, there was no realistic way the Soviets could challenge the U.S. in Central America. The lack of interest on the part of the Reagan administration in negotiating arms control agreements tended to obscure the deeper reality that, past nuclear weapons, there was nothing much to negotiate about. Issues left over from the end of World War II that had sparked tensions in Europe for years were settled in the 1975 Helsinki accords. Unlike Khrushchev's constant threats during the Kennedy administration concerning Berlin, for example, there were no areas of the globe in the 1980s where the Soviets could press the U.S. sufficiently so as to force engagement and negotiations.

Following the invasion of Afghanistan, President Carter threw everything in the diplomatic arsenal at the Russians and instituted a military buildup.[13] But at least as far as the U.S. was concerned, this did little to alter the general strategic situation. As noted, there was no interest in fighting another conventional war. Covert paramilitary war was also not viewed with enthusiasm, as the saga of the contra war against Nicaragua showed. Reagan's efforts to frighten the Soviets also frightened everyone else and posed an unacceptable risk of a nuclear war. After the 1983 war scare, Reagan dropped his hard line stance and actively sought to negotiate, although introducing the new element of the Strategic Defense Initiative (SDI).[14]

As argued in the previous chapter, comparing the early Cold War period to détente shows that the nature of the struggle had changed irrevocably in the 1970s. On the U.S. side, domestic politics rather than pressing foreign policy challenges were driving strategic interactions with the Soviet Union. In many respects, the war the U.S. now had to win was over itself and the strong inclination, which existed in many different quarters at the end of the 1980s, to believe nothing would ever change in U.S.-Soviet relations.[15] Consider that it was likely the U.S. could not make progress in strategic arms control during Reagan's second term, not so much because the new Soviet leader Mikhail Gorbachev was unwilling to listen or because of any intransigence on Reagan's part, but rather because there were such serious divisions in the government that the U.S. *could not make any proposals,* nor respond effectively to Gorbachev's own meaningful efforts. This happened in part because Reagan took little interest in matters of governance and so never tried to motivate his advisers to work out their differences. But it was also because the accumulated weight of Cold War decisionmaking and institutions set in their ways made it unlikely that even an Eisenhower could have propelled the government to respond meaningfully to Gorbachev.[16]

Gorbachev thus found he was on his own, without much support from the U.S. in his effort to transform the Soviet Union.[17] Recent scholarship shows that the most significant causes of the collapse of the Soviet Union were domestic rather than external, as one might expect.[18] With respect to the possibility of contributing to the Soviet collapse or responding effectively once it was under way, the U.S. was largely paralyzed by its own domestic conflicts over foreign policy and a lack of vision in the Bush I administration.[19] It is hard to escape the impression that in the aftermath of Vietnam, the U.S. was no longer able to initiate an "offensive" capable of dismantling the Soviet Union.[20] But Campbell Craig and Fredrik Logevall have offered a nuanced analysis that points to a limited role played by Reagan and Bush in the events that led to the end of the Cold War. They suggest that Reagan and Bush were prudent in not treating Gorbachev as a standard Soviet enemy (although they did not offer him much help) and that Reagan's fear of nuclear war and advocacy of SDI played a role in Gorbachev's decisionmaking on arms control.[21]

With the government having difficulty responding in a meaningful way to the end of the Cold War, it was unlikely that there would be a major rethinking of the role of the presidency in the constitutional order. That order was no longer precisely "post-1945" because invoking that era implicitly referenced the Cold War. Yet it was unmistakably the case that the essentials of the post-1945 order remained amid the events of the 1980s and 1990s. Republicans had reaffirmed their commitment to presidential leadership, if not supremacy, in foreign affairs as recently as the 1987 Iran-contra affair. They saw no reason to change. Democrats in Congress could have insisted on a rethinking of the "imperial presidency," but they made no move to do so and, in any case, were out of power after the 1994 congressional elections. There was also no sign that any post–Cold War president had foresworn military action as one arrow among others in the nation's national security quiver.

What surely changed and had to change was the idea of permanent wartime. But we should observe that the capacity of institutions to manage a constant state of war remained. To be sure, the notion of "semi-war," to use Senator Taft's interesting neologism discussed in Chapter 2, was no longer heard. To some observers, the nation appeared to be drifting into an uneasy sleep in foreign affairs.[22] Again, however, for at least some on the Republican side, perceptions were different. As I suggested in Chapter 5 and develop further below, the idea of permanent war was replaced for conservatives by the perception of a world that was continually threatening, as if the globe was concerned to pump out a succession of dangers to U.S. national security.[23]

As far as the power of the president to take military action to advance the nation's diplomatic objectives, this did not change at all. As discussed below, Clinton was ready to command a forcible intervention into Haiti and ordered air strikes on Bosnia. While his purpose was to promote peaceful democratic change, he did not go to Congress for permission. Most elements of the post-1945 order therefore remained intact after the end of the Cold War. Julian Zelizer argues persuasively that the reason so little changed during the 1990s was that the Clinton administration closely adhered to Reagan's stance on national security, which Zelizer calls "conservative internationalism."[24] Its elements included "a willingness to use military force and threats of force, war without substantial sacrifice from the citizenry, a reliance on technology over ground troops, [and] skepticism toward international alliances."[25] There were thus many continuities between the Cold War and post–Cold War eras.

In Chapter 5, we noted that the parties split on the issue of war powers during the Reagan administration. While Democrats continued supporting the WPR, albeit doubting its effectiveness, Republicans held that the sixty-day clock was unconstitutional and attempted to repeal the WPR in 1995. Because the Office of Legal Counsel (OLC) in the Justice Department finally weighed in with respect to war powers in the Clinton administration, it is both necessary and useful to examine the evolution of thinking among executive branch lawyers.

War Powers after the Cold War

In the Clinton administration OLC attempted to smooth the troubled waters of the war powers controversies of the 1980s by at least partially adopting a perspective previously associated with congressional Democrats.[26] In a 1994 opinion concerning the deployment of U.S. troops to Haiti, OLC offered the view that the purpose of the WPR "was to prevent the United States from being engaged, without express congressional authorization, in major, prolonged conflicts such as the wars in Vietnam and Korea, rather than to prohibit the President from using or threatening to use troops to achieve important diplomatic objectives where the risk of sustained military conflict was negligible."[27] Troops were deployed to Haiti peacefully to promote a democratic transition, although only because the intransigent military leadership of that country realized at the last moment that Clinton was willing to order a forcible intervention on his own authority.[28] Interestingly, OLC went on to argue that the Haiti deployment was "not a 'war' within the meaning of the Declaration of War Clause."[29] OLC followed up on this approach in another opinion concerning deployment of troops to Bosnia in 1995. It argued that the deployment was not a war because it had a limited purpose, which was largely in the nature of peacekeeping without much prospect of "extensive or sustained hostilities."[30]

These opinions were significant because OLC had recognized that the Constitution created "war" as a meaningful category of government action. OLC argued this meant that when the president deployed troops in circumstances not involving "war," the requirement of congressional authorization contained in the "declare war" clause did not apply. On the other hand, OLC had apparently conceded that congressional authorization *was* legally obligatory if the president proposed to conduct another war along the lines of Korea or Vietnam. If this analysis seems familiar, this is because it is consistent with the interpretation of the clause I developed in Chapter 1. We should, however, also note also that the OLC analysis remained consistent with the general perspective taken by the executive branch in the post-1945 era—that military action was one option among others in the conduct of diplomacy.

These opinions thus suggested a continuum. At one end was "war" or deployments that may lead to war which must be authorized by Congress. Limited deployments promoting democratic transitions, peacekeeping, or for humanitarian purposes do not constitute "war" and are thus not subject to the "declare war" clause. These Clinton OLC opinions could be read as a strategic retreat from the broad presidentialist arguments described in Chapter 1. Recall that one argument made by the executive branch since at least Vietnam was that whatever the meaning of the "declare war" clause, it was not a limit on presidential power. By contrast, the Clinton OLC opinions appeared to acknowledge that there were circumstances (real "wars") in which the clause would operate as a limit. As we shall see, while this was a step forward in executive branch legal analysis, it occurred only within Democratic administrations.

The Obama administration cited these Clinton OLC opinions with approval in concluding that President Obama could order air strikes on his own and in conjunction with NATO on Libya in 2011 in support of rebels seeking to overthrow the country's leader, Muammar al-Qaddafi (the Libya intervention is discussed in greater detail in Chapter 7). The key determination, once again, was whether the U.S. was engaged in a "'war' in the constitutional sense"; OLC thought not.[31] So the Libya operation did not require congressional approval. Quoting the Haiti opinion, the Obama administration's OLC concluded: "[T]he historical practice of presidential military action without congressional approval precludes any suggestion that Congress's authority to declare war covers every military engagement, however limited, that the President initiates. In our view, determining whether a particular planned engagement constitutes a 'war' for constitutional purposes instead requires a fact-specific assessment of the 'anticipated nature, scope, and duration' of the planned military operations."[32]

The Clinton OLC opinions contained some analysis that was less sound. The Bosnia opinion adopted the point of view, common to presidentialist arguments since Korea, that because the "scope and limits of that power [in the "declare war" clause] are not well defined by constitutional text, case law, or statute . . . the relationship of Congress's power to declare war and the President's authority as Commander in

Chief and Chief Executive has been clarified by 200 years of practice."[33] The opinion referenced with approval the memoranda by the State Department justifying the Korea and Vietnam wars on the grounds of long-standing historical "precedent."[34] These are the arguments based on historical practice critiqued in Chapter 2. OLC and the State Department have never acknowledged the serious conceptual and historical problems with these arguments.[35]

During the conflict with the Republican-controlled Congress over Clinton's efforts to prevent Serb attacks on Kosovo in 1999, Assistant Secretary of State Barbara Larkin provided a succinct summary of the power of the president in the post-1945 (and post–Cold War) constitutional order: "As a matter of law, there is no need for a declaration of war. Every use of U.S. Armed Forces since World War II has been undertaken pursuant to the President's constitutional authority—in some cases with congressional authorization, but never by declaration of war."[36] Larkin well expressed one of my basic theses—that after 1945 presidents always based military action on their Article II authority, rather than congressional consent. Consistent with past administrations, she contended that presidential authority was based on the powers to conduct foreign relations and as commander in chief.[37]

Although I discuss the record of the Bush II administration in detail below, it is helpful to conclude this discussion by describing briefly the public position of that administration on war powers to show the consistency of the executive branch since Truman. In contrast to the mild softening implied in the approach of the Clinton and Obama administrations, the Bush II administration deliberately emphasized the unilateral and exclusive power of the president. John Yoo, serving as deputy assistant attorney general of the OLC, testified in 2002 that "[t]his administration follows the course of administrations before us, both Democratic and Republican, in the view that the President's power to engage U.S. armed forces in military hostilities is not limited by the War Powers Resolution."[38] Yoo argued that presidential power to initiate war flowed from the Constitution itself. He stated that the vesting and commander in chief clauses of Article II "give the President the constitutional authority to introduce U.S. armed forces into hostilities when appropriate, with or without specific congressional authorization."[39] Like earlier representatives of the executive branch in the Cold War, Yoo explained that although there was nothing constitutionally obligatory about asking for

Congress's permission before engaging in war, it was surely in the interest of both branches to work together.[40]

In saying that no president had ever acknowledged the WPR as a limit on his authority, Yoo ignored the complex history recounted in Chapter 5. In fact, it was not until Reagan's 1983 intervention in Lebanon that the executive branch began to officially resist the WPR. It is also worth noting that during the later Libya controversy, the Obama administration made clear that it did not contest the constitutionality of the sixty-day clock.[41] But in the end there was little difference between the position of the Bush II administration and that taken by Under Secretary of State Katzenbach in the Johnson administration described in Chapters 1 and 4. Post-1950, the executive branch has never conceded that the president lacks the authority to commit the nation's military forces to action. Thus a key element of the post-1945 constitutional order remains in place.

After 9/11: The Role of History and Memory

Historical analogies came thick and fast after 9/11. Analogies to Pearl Harbor were obvious and appropriate.[42] Osama bin Laden and Saddam Hussein were likened to Hitler. There were general analogies to World War II and the effort necessary to sustain a long-term global war.[43] The analogies to the Civil War were harder to follow. But what these analogies had in common was the need for strong presidential leadership in wartime. Abraham Lincoln and Franklin Roosevelt are always ranked among our greatest presidents and this is surely due in part to their inspirational leadership through the travails of war.[44]

At the same time, there was a distinct sense after 9/11 that analogies to the past were of limited use. The idea that we were in a new age was widely promoted. Perhaps we had entered a new period in American history dominated by the threat of irrational terrorism and mass destruction. The executive branch clearly believed that there were more al Qaeda cells in the United States, waiting to strike.[45] Government officials ratcheted up threat levels accordingly. The anthrax scare that closely followed 9/11 certainly did not promote cautious decisionmaking, as it appeared to confirm the reality of a continuing terrorist threat.

Somewhat ironically, both the analogies and sense of disanalogy pointed to the need for increased presidential power. If a foreign war was called for, the president would naturally take the lead. But if the threat was not simply overseas, but was near to hand in the homeland, this called for a single coordinated response. After 9/11, members of Congress and government employees of all stripes might well have realized that they had been targets. They were saved only by the heroism of the passengers on United flight 93, a plane aimed by the terrorist plotters at some major target such as the White House or the Capitol.[46] These thoughts, along with the knowledge that Congress as a collective body could not take the lead, might have inspired substantial deference to the executive branch after 9/11, at least within the Beltway.

Historical analogies have a special importance in the realm of the nonlegalized Constitution. In the absence of extensive judicial doctrine on war powers, arguments as to presidential power could be made and unmade based on what people knew, or thought they knew, about the past. As we have seen, the argument from practice, popular with presidentialists since 1950, is an argument from history. But it is also a kind of deliberately constructed tradition. Such arguments were never based on systematic and deeply contextual accounts of the past. Thus presidential claims to authority can be based on the surprisingly fragile grounds of what we remember or choose to forget.

So it was with the use of historical analogies after 9/11. President Bush, for example, remembered Truman as a stalwart defender of freedom. The rest of the enormous and freighted legacy left by the Cold War was distinctly missing from the post-9/11 public debate. This is why I have gone to some trouble to recreate the world of the Cold War as it was experienced by the executive branch. As we have seen in our discussion of the post-1945 constitutional order, the context of the Cold War is in many ways still our context.

The general silence on the Cold War after 9/11 was all the more remarkable, indeed disturbing, given that this was our nation's only prior example of a long war, not to mention that the sense of permanent wartime came back so quickly. As far as the historical analogies that were invoked, such as the Civil War and World War II, it is hard to say what role they played in public debate. President Bush turned to Lincoln's example of leadership in a dark hour of emergency, but did not consider that Lincoln later submitted his decisions to Congress for validation.[47] Similarly, we heard about FDR's use of military commissions to try Nazi saboteurs, but not much about the removal of Japanese-Americans from the West Coast. To be sure, President Bush to his credit kept the Japanese-American internment in mind in encouraging Americans not to discriminate against Muslims.[48]

The most straightforward explanation for avoiding the Cold War after 9/11 was that Americansdeeply disagreedabout what it meant beyond victory in the struggle with the Soviet Union. Beyond this "first world" conflict lay not only Vietnam, but also other third world conflicts over which Americans continue to disagree. Further, there were substantial foreign policy problems left over from the Cold War that embodied either unresolved conflicts (North Korea) or derived at least in part from American policy misjudgments (Iran). Looming above all of these nagging conflicts was the issue of presidential leadership in the Cold War. For faithful Democrats and Republicans, the Cold War evoked memories of the inspirational leadership provided by hero-presidents such as Kennedy and Reagan. But it could also mean the deep harm wrought by the unilateral and undemocratic decisionmaking of Johnson and Nixon. If presidents were conceded to be in charge of foreign affairs and national security, this did not mean that they had always performed in a way that reflected well on them or their country.

Not talking about the Cold War helped clear the decks for another round of aggressive presidential leadership under the mantle of the post-1945 constitutional order. This gave conservatives a golden opportunity to revive the presidentialist agenda pioneered in the Reagan and Bush I administrations and advocated by Republican members of Congress in the Iran-contra affair. Unfortunately, the instability and accompanying policy dysfunction inherent to the post-1945 constitutional order had not gone away. Among other points, that order was based on the assumption that the executive branch was able to make decisions for war without the meaningful participation of Congress. When George W. Bush attempted to faithfully implement his father's presidentialist agenda in a long war, it led to constitutional disorders not seen since Watergate and a disastrous war in Iraq which shook the credibility of the American government.

In the remainder of this section I highlight several key aspects of how history and memory interacted with the post-1945 constitutional order before and after 9/11. I discuss first the freighted question of responsibility for avoiding the terrorist attacks, how this related to the assumption of the post-1945 order that the president is responsible for national security, and, in turn, how this affected the Bush administration's response. I then examine how forgetting the legacy of questionable presidential actions during war created the conditions under which torture and abuse of terrorist detainees could take place.[49]

Responsibility for 9/11

After 9/11, officials in the Clinton and Bush administrations were understandably defensive concerning their own responsibility for not avoiding the attacks. Some Americans clearly continue to believe that a proper accounting never took place and wonder how it could be that no one resigned or was fired.[50] One relatively overlooked answer is that the attacks occurred only seven months after a presidential transition. In the last few decades the politicized, even juvenile, politics of presidential transitions has deeply wounded the United States in the conduct of foreign affairs. It arguably contributed directly to the success of the 9/11 attacks. The fact that the discontinuity of a transition is the natural outcome of a presidential election has obscured the reality that foreign policy does not always benefit from a fresh start and certainly not from a clean slate.[51]

In his comprehensive history of U.S.-Soviet relations, Raymond Garthoff argues in effect that the decisive break in presidential transitions came with the shift from Carter to Reagan.[52] While in a sense this is not surprising, given the perception of Carter's presidency as failed, the sense of Republicans that a fresh start was required in national security policy ignored the extent to which Carter and Reagan pursued the same policy of a military buildup without contemplating negotiations. Reagan's dismissal of Carter's legacy in toto empowered advisers such as Secretary of Defense Weinberger to reject specific Carter policies that were at least defensible solutions to widely understood national security problems. For example, as recounted in Chapter 5, Weinberger for years unnecessarily chased the rabbit of an alternative basing mode for the MX missile, thoroughly undermining his credibility with Congress, not to mention the nation's defense policy.

As the Obama administration soon learned, unless other countries (and terrorist groups!) cooperate, no new administration can write on a clean slate.[53] There is no obvious reason for countries and groups to change their goals simply because the U.S. has had a presidential election. Further, there is the issue of relative judgment and experience. Regardless of what partisans may think, the policy IQ of the incoming administration is always lower than the outgoing administration, especially with respect to ongoing issues which have received adequate study.

There were substantial bumps in the policy road experienced in each transition after Reagan. The Bush I administration put Soviet policy in a deep freeze while it did a lengthy review, something that arguably undermined Gorbachev's position and Russia's democratic transition.[54] Clinton so believed in the primacy of domestic issues that he suspended the regular foreign policy process for a time.[55] While Clinton could not ignore the challenges of foreign policy forever, there is little doubt some damage was done. Eventually, he began focusing on foreign affairs, including issues such as terrorism, and proposed legislation to Congress. The effectiveness of Clinton's policies with respect to domestic and foreign terrorism is still being debated, but it is relatively clear that he received little help from Congress in adjusting the nation to the nature of the threat.[56]

It is well known that the government effort against al Qaeda got lost in the transition from Clinton to Bush. It is still disconcerting to recall that there was no military strike in response to the attack on the USS *Cole* in Yemen, a serious blow against the U.S. by al Qaeda. Unfortunately, the attack occurred in fall 2000, as the country was distracted by the presidential election. The Clinton administration was on its way out and did little. The Bush II administration apparently adopted the attitude that it was not their responsibility to respond to something that occurred in the prior administration![57] Responding properly to the *Cole* attack would have at least focused the Bush administration's attention on al Qaeda and Osama bin Laden.

President Clinton and the members of his foreign policy team did warn the incoming Bush administration about the threat posed by al Qaeda and Bin Laden. But all of the members of the Bush foreign policy team—Secretary of State Colin Powell, National Security Adviser Condoleezza Rice, Secretary of Defense Donald Rumsfeld, Vice President Dick Cheney—were carrying heavy historical baggage from their past government service. They were not impressed with Clinton and tended to unthinkingly dismiss the relatively new issues that had occupied his administration.[58] The threat of terrorism in particular did not impress them and, after all, to this point all of al Qaeda's attacks had occurred overseas. Policy developed slowly on terrorism in the Bush administration in spite of the CIA's clarion call in July 2001 that the government should go to a war footing against Bin Laden.[59]

This points to another of the interwoven problems of history, memory, and politics left over from the Cold War. The role of the CIA prior to the 9/11 attacks was one aspect of government responsibility that few officials wanted to review candidly. According to many accounts, the Agency was in a terrible state by the mid-1990s in the wake of post–Cold War budget cutbacks and general demoralization.[60] Both Congress and the president were responsible for this state of affairs. Focused on domestic policy, Clinton initially spurned his daily briefing from the CIA. Without a close relationship to the president, which was the Agency's original *raison d'etre,* there was little for the Agency to do and directors came and went until Clinton appointed George Tenet in 1997.[61] This was extremely short-sighted because in many ways the Agency and the rest of the intelligence community function like an insurance policy against foreign policy disasters.

Clearly a civilian intelligence agency had a key role to play in developing a strategy against international terrorism. But the question of the future role of the CIA after the Cold War carried deep political freight. Democrats remembered the 1970s intelligence investigations as at least putting the CIA on a constitutionally sound path. Otherwise, they seemed not to know what to do with the Agency, especially with respect to covert operations. By contrast, Republicans had for years promoted the idea that the investigations had weakened the Agency and the effort against the Soviet Union. In particular, the Bushes, father and son, remembered the CIA investigations as pernicious.[62] To them, the CIA had to be protected against Congress to the extent the Agency was carrying on difficult and dangerous tasks.

At the same time, Bush II administration hard liners had their own issues with the CIA. Because of disputes running back to the 1970s, they believed that the Agency had underestimated the Soviet threat and so would be likely to underestimate the threat of states that supported terrorism, such as Iraq.[63] There are multiple ironies here, some of them tragic. Whereas the Bush administration obviously did not pay adequate attention to the Agency's warnings in the summer of 2001, it would later bypass the Agency's substantial doubts about whether Saddam

Hussein had stocks of chemical and biological weapons and whether he was continuing an earlier quest for nuclear weapons. One theme that thus tied together the late Cold War and post–Cold War periods was the lack of focus on the proper role of the CIA. The Agency never got the attention it deserved from the president or Congress.

Imperial Presidency or Failure to Protect?

When the full record of the Bush administration's response to 9/11 began to emerge in 2004, including the scandal at Abu Ghraib prison in Iraq and the "torture memo," some suggested its response was motivated by existential panic.[64] While there is no doubt a sense of emergency played a role in shaping the administration's response, we should consider the possibility that the post-1945 constitutional order was providing a far more lasting motive—fear of accountability from a failure to protect the country.[65] Regardless of how the Bush administration's actions prior to 9/11 are assessed, everyone in the executive branch was acutely aware that they would be blamed for another attack.[66] This well illustrates the logic of the post-1945 constitutional order, in which presidents since Truman have been handed what seemed to them sole responsibility for protecting the country from danger. Thus, administration officials could have reasonably believed there was a national consensus that all measures necessary must be taken.[67]

Illustrating this sense of responsibility, after 9/11 President Bush put an unsustainable burden on top administration officials. He told Attorney General John Ashcroft directly, "Don't ever let this happen again," an impossible and dangerous order that Ashcroft and his subordinates nonetheless attempted to implement.[68] Jack Goldsmith, the head of OLC during 2003–2004, remarked that "[t]he Commander in Chief's order had an enormous impact on the Attorney General . . . the President's personal mission to check Islamist terrorism at any cost trickled down and pervaded the administration."[69]

Seeing the Bush administration as driven by accountability concerns complicates the common narrative that the Bush administration mounted an aggressive attempt to restore the "imperial presidency."[70] This assumes an understanding of presidential motivation unchanged since the eighteenth century. When the opportunity arises, ambitious presidents always seek to amass and retain power.[71] This ignores the point that presidents generally want power *for* a purpose, as a means to accomplish a policy end presumed desirable by a majority. The post-1945 order provided the compelling purposes of leading the country in foreign affairs and defending national security.

After 9/11 it was reasonable to suppose that the American public wanted to be protected against future attacks. The Bush administration responded by doing everything it could think of to protect the country. By saying this, I am not suggesting a rationale or excuse for the controversial policy choices that followed. I am rather arguing that the circumstances that drove the administration forward were themselves rooted in the assumptions of the post-1945 constitutional order. Although Bush administration officials went too far, they were on pathways traveled earlier by presidents such as Truman, Johnson, and Nixon, who were widely condemned during their terms, as well as by presidents such as Eisenhower, Kennedy, and Reagan, who were widely praised.[72]

Lawyers and the Legacy of Internment

As we saw in Chapter 3, in the early Cold War the CIA functioned as an all-purpose clandestine agency abroad, willing to do what diplomats and the military would not.[73] After 9/11, the Agency in a sense still had that mandate and capability. It was natural for the White House to turn to the CIA in seeking information from detainees in foreign countries in order to prevent another terrorist attack. As an institution designed to be maximally responsive to the president, it was equally natural for the Agency to volunteer. Yet the legacy of the 1970s remained. Prior to the intelligence investigations, what mattered was the backing of the president. After the 1970s, there was more law to worry about. Before it could assist with interrogations, the CIA had to have a guarantee either that there would be no prosecutions of Agency personnel or a blanket assurance that their specific interrogation program would not violate the law, especially the Convention against Torture and the allied federal law making torture a crime. When the DOJ refused to guarantee that there would be no prosecutions, this set in motion the process that led to OLC's production of the August 2002 "torture memo."[74]

It has been appreciated for some time that the torture memo provided a number of independent rationales designed to assure the Agency that it could engage in harsh interrogation techniques that could easily amount to torture in practice without fear of prosecution. When the DOJ's Office of Professional Responsibility finished its inquiry into how such advice could have been provided, it concluded that all of the rationales provided by OLC head Jay Bybee, as well as his deputy, John Yoo, were badly flawed. Indeed, it found that Bybee and Yoo had engaged in professional misconduct.[75] In its final review, the DOJ in the person of Associate Deputy Attorney General David Margolis declined to endorse this conclusion.[76] I will discuss in the next section how the torture memo related to the decisions for war made by President Bush and, ultimately, how it relates to the post-1945 constitutional order, but my concern here is the relationship of the memo to the legacy of past misconduct by lawyers in time of war.

What should draw our attention is one of the most common excuses for Bybee and Yoo's rationalization of torture. Margolis stressed that 9/11 was unique: "The terrorist attacks of September 11, 2001, engaged the United States in an unprecedented conflict involving a non-sovereign enemy."[77] He quoted Jack Goldsmith, head of OLC after Bybee, who suggested that "great caution [should be exercised] when assessing the professional responsibility of executive branch lawyers who act in time of national security crisis."[78] Although Goldsmith was quite critical of the arguments in the torture memo and decided to formally withdraw it, he was clearly sympathetic, as was Margolis, to the fact that the OLC attorneys were working under great stress.

There is some tension between the common claims that 9/11 was unprecedented in American history and the equally common claims that it was sufficiently like the Civil War or World War II to allow meaningful analogies. As I have already observed, both claims arguably supported increased executive authority. But proceeding as if 9/11 were unique by invoking a literal description of the events of that day allowed Margolis (as well as Bybee and Yoo) to approach the issue of torture in a normative vacuum, with a corresponding loss of legal, historical, and moral perspective.

It is especially odd that these knowledgeable government attorneys never mentioned Pearl Harbor as a possible parallel to 9/11. This obvious analogy occurred to many people in the immediate aftermath of the attacks, including President Bush and Secretary of Defense Rumsfeld.[79] But the months after Pearl Harbor were a famous low point in the DOJ's history, as Attorney General Francis Biddle deferred to Secretary of War Henry Stimson and the War Department's plan to remove approximately 110,000 Japanese-Americans from the West Coast.[80] These American citizens became "unpersons" for the duration, losing their freedom and property in a process contaminated with blatant racism. Stimson at least had the character and presence of mind to write in his diary that "a tremendous hole in our constitutional system" had to be created in order to permit the internment.[81]

To their credit, a number of prominent executive branch officials realized fairly quickly that President Roosevelt's order implementing the War Department's internment plan was a terrible mistake and had to be corrected.[82] But the fact remained that thousands of Japanese-Americans had to live in internment camps for years, while many of their sons and brothers volunteered for the army and fought and died for their country in Europe. The Supreme Court upheld the internment under the Constitution in the *Hirabayashi* and *Korematsu* cases, essentially deferring, like Biddle, to the judgment of the military.[83]

The Supreme Court's weak response to what amounted to suspending the Constitution on the basis of race immediately drew criticism from the legal community. In the leading commentary on the internment cases, Eugene Rostow, who later worked under Acheson in the State Department and defended presidential war power against the WPR, condemned the Supreme Court decisions as a disaster even before the war was over.[84] Rostow did not pull any punches in contending that "the internment of the West Coast Japanese is the worst blow our liberties have sustained in many years."[85] He argued that the principal danger of the decisions was that they "upheld an act of military power without a factual record."[86] Rostow pointed out that the cases had not meaningfully applied any standard of review. This meant that the military was allowed to do what it wanted with the Japanese-Americans without anyone asking for supporting evidence and a clear rationale.[87] As a counterpoint to *Hirabayashi* and *Korematsu,* Rostow held out the famous Civil War case of *Ex parte Milligan* as "a monument in the democratic tradition, and [it] should be the animating force of this branch of our law."[88] *Milligan* stood for the proposition that as long as there was nothing standing in the way of the ordinary provision of due process through civilian adjudication, the military did not have jurisdiction.[89]

The legal situation was actually far worse than Rostow imagined. Later investigation showed that the judicial process, including the briefs submitted to the Supreme Court, had been poisoned by false representations. Ambitious and unscrupulous attorneys in the War

Department, led by Colonel Karl Bendetsen, had fabricated the threat of sabotage and engaged in dubious tactics in an atmosphere colored by unreasoning panic over the possible invasion of the West Coast and racist sentiments toward Japanese-Americans.[90] DOJ attorneys who resisted were undercut by Biddle's refusal to stand up to Stimson and the War Department attorneys. The whole episode made a hash of any sort of reasonable interagency process, with a proper factual record and an appreciation of constitutional values getting lost in the rush.[91] When a factual review was conducted in the middle of the litigation, the FBI and FCC, the agencies most knowledgeable on the subject of saboteurs and secret communication, reported no evidence that Japanese-Americans were disloyal.[92]

That the appalling consequences of the internment were in part the responsibility of attorneys who failed in their professional obligation to uphold the Constitution and slow the rush to judgment has been well known and appreciated in the American legal community for decades.[93] Yet the legacy and lessons of this episode made no impression on any of the supposedly "expert" attorneys involved in the torture episode after 9/11. Not even in the various reviews of the torture memo did it occur to the DOJ that something similar to the internment episode had occurred again. Despite his professional qualifications, Yoo was all too similar to Bendetsen—inexperienced in government service, and lacking in judgment and respect for the American constitutional tradition.[94]

The excuse of a national crisis used by Margolis was suspect in the light of this history. Bybee and Yoo were not in fact performing their tasks in the immediate aftermath of 9/11, but more than eight months later. By that time, many alarms and predictions of further terrorist attacks had come and gone. Reasonable persons, not to mention lawyers, would have taken this into consideration in reacting to any crisis pressure emanating from the White House. More to the point, experienced attorneys with a knowledge of the aftermath of Pearl Harbor would have anticipated in advance that extreme and misleading claims are often made, however sincerely, in time of war.

Margolis also failed to appreciate that invoking an atmosphere of crisis cut a number of different ways, not all of them favorable to the OLC attorneys. The preferred meaning seemed to be that government attorneys were justified after 9/11 in construing executive power broadly and legislative power to restrict the executive narrowly. Yet crisis also means trauma and there is little doubt that the 9/11 attacks traumatized official Washington, as well as the DOJ itself. Such trauma could well have affected the ability of attorneys to evaluate the unusual arguments Yoo brought to the table from academia, arguments, analyzed in Chapter 1, that had made Yoo a distinct outlier in the ongoing debate over war powers. Margolis surely did not mean that the crisis had impaired the ability of OLC attorneys to carry out their duties, steady the ship of government, and resist dubious claims, but the record suggests otherwise.

There is an additional parallel between the Japanese-American internment and the torture controversy. As we shall see in the next section, the most devastating criticisms of the torture memo came from inside the government. The role that DOJ attorneys played in 1942 as they tried without success to slow the rush to internment was played in 2002 by lawyers at the State Department.[95] As the full record of the torture controversy has been slowly revealed, it has become apparent that Yoo's memos could never have survived any fair-minded interagency process. If they had had the chance, more experienced government attorneys would have torn them to shreds.[96]

As a final historical point, we should note some connections between the Cold War and the torture controversy. Anyone who grew up in the Cold War reading novels like George Orwell's *1984* and Arthur Koestler's *Darkness at Noon*, often required texts in high school and college, would have come away with the impression that torture was something that characterized totalitarian states, not democracies.[97] Presumably one of the points of emphasizing such books at that time was to highlight the differences between the oppressive ideology promoted by communist states and the liberal philosophy of freedom and democracy. Torture faded in and out as a concern in the Cold War, most often associated with repressive anticommunist regimes in Latin America.[98] We can sharpen this impression by recalling that a steady underlying controversy throughout the Cold War was whether the U.S. should use the tactics of the enemy. This controversy certainly resurfaced after 9/11.[99] When Saddam Hussein used torture against the citizens of Kuwait after invading the country in 1990, President George H. W. Bush was sickened and repelled. His son, however, believed that after 9/11, lawyers had given a green light to methods that were harsh, but fell short of torture.[100] Unfortunately, we are never likely to know the full story.

Because no general and impartial government inquiry armed with subpoena power was ever conducted, either by President Bush or President Obama, a full and public accounting never took place.[101]

9/11 and the Post-1945 Constitutional Order

Well into President Bush's second term, political scientist Michael Nelson observed with some wonderment that an exclusive focus on the president's political influence, his power to persuade, could not account for the power Bush wielded in office:

> Bush is wildly unpopular. His public-approval rating has been troughed at 30 percent longer than any other modern president's. In Congress, Bush's post-election efforts to enact landmark legislation concerning Social Security and immigration have failed utterly. By Neustadt's standard, the president's inability to persuade almost anybody to support almost anything should have rendered him nearly powerless. And yet Bush remains one of the most powerful presidents, well, ever.[102]

Although he was very unpopular by the end of his second term, Bush had the aura of a powerful president, at least in foreign affairs, because of the persistence of the post-1945 constitutional order. As we have seen, nothing replaced that order after the end of the Cold War. But Bush arguably set a new standard for the exercise of executive power, even in wartime. Indeed, foreign affairs scholars have argued that Bush's agenda made him a "revolutionary" president.[103]

The mix of prior conservative conviction about the need for a strong presidency, especially with respect to foreign affairs and national security, combined with the massive shock of 9/11 produced the kind of opportunity rare in American history. President Bush and Vice President Cheney seized this opportunity with both hands.[104] It is well known that both men took their oaths of office in January 2001 with the intention of permanently increasing the power of the presidency.[105] As recounted by Goldsmith, "[t]he President and the Vice President always made clear that a central administration priority was to maintain and expand the President's formal legal powers."[106] As we have seen, this was perfectly consistent with the line Republicans, Cheney in particular, had taken since President Ford's administration and especially since the Iran-contra affair.

In turn, the Bush presidency provided quite a shock for constitutional commentators. Legal commentator Stuart Taylor listed the following examples of "almost unlimited, unilateral wartime powers:" (1) detention of "enemy combatants" anywhere for indefinite periods without due process; (2) torturing those detained in violation of law; (3) trying detainees before military tribunals with no judicial review; (4) secretly defying the Foreign Intelligence Surveillance Act (FISA) for more than five years; (5) claiming the power to invade Iraq without the need for congressional authorization.[107] In his comprehensive book on Bush's "imperial presidency" journalist Charlie Savage cited the Bush administration's pattern of secrecy and its belief in inherent and exclusive presidential power to wage war, as well as its use of secret wiretapping not in compliance with FISA, military commissions, detention at Guantanamo, policies of rendition, torture in interrogation, and signing statements to contradict the provisions of federal law.[108] Frederick A. O. Schwarz Jr. and Aziz Z. Huq provided a more lawyerly analysis.[109] They criticized the Bush administration for pursuing a "monarchical executive theory"[110] and cited many of the same examples as the legal journalists previously cited: the use of torture in interrogation, extraordinary rendition, detention of enemy combatants, and National Security Agency (NSA) wiretapping.[111] The respected constitutional scholar Louis Fisher criticized the Bush administration for threatening the nation's civil liberties and devoted particular attention to abuses of presidential power such as military tribunals and detention without trial, torture and detainee treatment, the state secrets privilege, NSA surveillance, and extraordinary rendition.[112]

In a thorough review of the Bush presidency, James Pfiffner specified the Bush administration's departures from the status quo:

> President Bush has undermined the constitutional balance among the branches in four policy areas:
>
> - by denying the writ of habeas corpus to people deemed to be "enemy combatants";
> - by suspending the Geneva Conventions and allowing and encouraging harsh interrogation methods that amounted to torture;
> - by ordering surveillance of Americans without obtaining a warrant as required by law; and
> - by issuing signing statements that declare that the president has the option not to enforce parts of laws that he believes interfere with his executive authority.[113]

These examples of genuine concern among both liberal and conservative scholars about the Bush administration's expansion of presidential power could be multiplied many times. In general, they suggest that the problem of Bush's presidency was a turn to unilateralism, combined with signal departures from the status quo that threatened civil liberties. While these issues were undeniably important and received much discussion during Bush's presidency, these accounts were afflicted by the same problems that limited the persuasiveness of earlier narratives of the "imperial presidency."

The crucial difficulty is that these accounts lacked a historical framework to explain how the Bush administration could have taken the constitutional system so far so fast. Without discussing how the presidency acquired power in foreign affairs during the Cold War, they lacked a context for understanding Bush's exercise of power. The omissions from these lists were striking—there was no reckoning with the fact that the Bush administration believed for good reason that it was at war with al Qaeda and that the United States was in a period of permanent wartime similar to the Cold War. Commentators also rarely discussed how assiduously Congress had supported Bush, thus lending him the full measure of constitutional power suggested by Justice Jackson in the *Steel Seizure* case.[114] In general, these critiques emphasized formal rule of law considerations so heavily that they missed the greater relevance and importance of failures of democratic deliberation. Or so I will argue.

In understanding the Bush II administration, we should direct our attention first to setting the president's decisions for war within the context of the post-1945 constitutional order. It is that order which structures presidential action in foreign affairs. Second, we should be aware how the lack of interbranch deliberation inherent to that order can lead to the derangement of policy. That is the pattern I have analyzed throughout this book.[115] The primary danger after 9/11 was not so much from a general failure to comply with the rule of law, the multiple genuine threats to civil liberties or from the expansion of presidential power, but rather that the lack of interbranch deliberation would undermine the war effort and lead to a policy disaster and, possibly, a constitutional crisis. To support this claim, this section concentrates on how Bush used the post-1945 order to organize the war on terror in the executive branch, with specific reference to interrogation policy. The next section reviews the decisions for war with respect to Afghanistan and Iraq.

The theory of constitutional orders highlights the latent power contained within roles created by the text. History suggested that after an attack such as Pearl Harbor, vast power to shape the nation's response would flow to President Bush as commander in chief. The single most important constitutional action in the aftermath of the disorienting events of 9/11 was Bush's assertion that the United States was at war.[116] President Bush immediately categorized the attacks as a military operation, akin to an invasion by a foreign state.[117] The President told his advisers, "we're at war," just hours after the attacks occurred and made a global war on terror the official policy of the executive branch.[118]

To Bush, framing the conflict with al Qaeda as a war was clearly warranted and he had little patience for contrary views. In his memoir, he recounts this exchange:

> Members of Congress were united in their determination to protect the country. Senator Tom Daschle, the Democratic majority leader, issued one cautionary note. He said I should be careful about the word *war* because it had such powerful implications. I listened to his concerns, but I disagreed. If four coordinated attacks by a terrorist network that had pledged to kill as many Americans as possible was not an act of war, then what was it? A breach of diplomatic protocol?[119]

Bush's response to Daschle was dismissive, even sarcastic, but it illustrated Bush's sense that it was clear the nation had to go to a war footing against the threat of terrorism. It also well illustrated Bush's insensitivity to the kind of separation of powers and civil liberties concerns that are typically raised by wartime.[120] What we need to appreciate is that Bush's framing decision sent a powerful signal to the public, Congress, and the bureaucracy that the permanent wartime and lack of restraints on government that had characterized the pre-1970s Cold War had returned.

It is worth noting that the potent framing effects of Bush's statements that the nation was at war pose a serious difficulty for theories legitimizing informal constitutional change through complex processes of public deliberation or constitutional constructions.[121] Change after 9/11 was fostered primarily by an executive clique, not by an aroused citizenry deliberating over their options.[122] Indeed, Bush's definition of reality so thoroughly disabled the public sphere that the press and the public were still having trouble escaping the 9/11 frame as the Iraq War began in 2003.[123] Because of the Bush administration's efforts, many Americans came to believe that the reason the U.S. went to war with Iraq had something to do with Saddam Hussein's involvement in the

9/11 attacks.[124] This suggests that a theory not dependent on specifying a particular normative path for legitimate change and more attuned to the disruptive potential of the exercise of power based on the text of the Constitution is more useful in understanding the presidency after 9/11.

By immediately describing 9/11 as a war, the president harmed the quality of the subsequent deliberation by short-circuiting meaningful debate over the nature of the attacks and the appropriate response. But his constitutional claim was arguably more significant. While the president participated in the process that led to congressional adoption of the September 2001 Authorization to Use Military Force (AUMF), he claimed independent authority to prosecute the war based on his Article II powers.[125] In subsequent messages to Congress, the president ignored the AUMF and relied on his power under Article II, stating that he had ordered military action "pursuant to my constitutional authority to conduct U.S. foreign relations and as Commander in Chief and Chief Executive."[126] This meant that the president was not bound even by the broad terms of the AUMF.[127] In his memoir, Bush was clear that he was fighting the 9/11 War under the authority provided by Article II of the Constitution and the AUMF.[128] Each provided independent authority and thus each was sufficient to prosecute the war. The administration took the same position with respect to the Iraq War.[129] This consistent resort to the president's Article II powers lined up with the pattern we have observed in the post-1945 constitutional order. It also necessarily diminished the role of interbranch deliberation.

At the same time he was invoking his Article II authority, the president was treating the war as a precedent-shattering world struggle against evil.[130] In a major speech to the nation on November 8, 2001, less than two months after 9/11 and amidst the anthrax attack scare, the president described an existential struggle between the United States and terrorist groups worldwide.[131] Finally, in his January 2002 State of the Union address, the president included states supporting terrorism—the "axis of evil" comprising Iran, Iraq, and North Korea—in the nest of enemies the U.S. faced.[132]

Taken cumulatively, these statements described a presidency at the zenith of constitutional power—a commander in chief responding to a surprise attack with the backing of Congress.[133] As Bush and his administration perhaps intended, this put the war on terror on a legal and normative plane with World War II and suggested President Bush could exercise the same authority possessed by President Roosevelt.[134] Executive branch attorneys lost no time suggesting that because Roosevelt had used military commissions to try Nazi saboteurs as "unlawful combatants," Bush could do the same with respect to captured terrorists.[135]

The Difference a Vice President Makes

The role of Vice President Cheney and the Office of the Vice President (OVP) was one of the most unique features of the Bush administration.[136] Under Cheney, OVP went operational and enabled Bush to implement his policies in a far more effective manner. It became evident later that the cost was the undermining of the interagency process throughout the government. Cheney has been described as "[t]he most powerful vice president in American history."[137] The positions advocated by Cheney and his lawyer, David Addington, were often decisive in the administration's councils.[138] As discussed in Chapter 5, Cheney had strong views about restoring presidential power prior to becoming vice president.[139] His service in the Ford administration evidently left a strong impression. He believed that the presidency had sunk into a trough of weakness in the wake of mid-1970s congressional reform efforts and had never recovered.[140]

Cheney's unusual role in the Bush administration flowed in part from his political status.[141] Cheney was more staffer than politician, having begun his career in the Ford White House as it tried to regain ground for the presidency after Watergate. He had never run for national office in his own right and thus never had his political views tested by a national constituency. He had no ambitions for the presidency, which meant as a practical matter he was accountable only to Bush.[142] This meant that with Bush's obvious permission and encouragement, he could function as a policy overlord, his influence flowing both from his position as constitutional officer and uber-staffer.[143] In fact, Cheney seemed to loathe the standard forms of political accountability. After the 2006 elections in which Republicans lost control of Congress because of the Iraq War, Cheney referred to the election results as if they were a lone poll of public opinion.[144]

Cheney's assignment of power from Bush enabled the OVP to go operational in the manner of a cabinet department.[145] We have seen how under the stress of the responsibility imposed by the post-1945 order, a number of presidents made ultimately dangerous innovations in the institutional architecture of the executive branch. In this respect, operations in the Bush II administration had a noteworthy resemblance to Watergate in the Nixon administration and the Iran-contra scandal in the Reagan administration.[146] These episodes all involved part of the White House going operational to make policy directly. As discussed in previous chapters, Nixon used the "Special Investigative Unit" (the Plumbers) to investigate intelligence leaks outside the FBI and CIA.[147] The Iran-contra scandal resulted when the National Security Council under Admiral Poindexter and Lt. Col. Oliver North assumed responsibility for saving American hostages.[148] Although conducting operations from the White House provides the president with greater secrecy and flexibility, it leads inevitably to grave constitutional difficulties.

Giving OVP operational responsibility had far-reaching implications for how the executive branch functioned during the Bush presidency. It meant OVP could intervene with respect to any policy without being subject to normal statutory and interagency checks.[149] The power OVP wielded intimidated even the highest cabinet officials and tended to chill open discussion.[150] Cheney could bulldoze his way into any process and intervene at any level because officials had to assume that the positions advocated by OVP staff had presidential approval, whether or not this was actually the case.[151]

The consequences of OVP going operational played out in a variety of barely believable ways. OVP began running the legal side of the war against terror, thus contributing to the torture memo fiasco.[152] Cheney bypassed a preexisting interagency review in obtaining an executive order to establish military commissions as the administration's way of handling terrorist detainees.[153] If the commissions were meant as trials to punish these detainees, they were not effective. The OVP was also intimately involved with initiating the NSA's domestic surveillance program, thus circumventing the preexisting law embodied in FISA.[154] An internal administration controversy over the legality of this program nearly caused a constitutional crisis in 2004 when Bush and Cheney decided to go forward in the face of the uniform opposition of the DOJ. When it became apparent that the entire top leadership of the DOJ and FBI would resign rather than carry out the president's apparently illegal policy, President Bush backed down at the last moment.[155] Once again, the wages of the jerry-built post-1945 order had manifested themselves.

To carry out their sole responsibility for protecting the country, presidents tended to alter the structure of the executive branch in ways that increased the instability of the constitutional order.

The Office of Legal Counsel in the War on Terror

Empowered by presidential claims of wartime authority, the executive branch set into motion all of the questionable policies that would later come to light: indefinite detentions, military commissions, NSA surveillance outside of FISA, and harsh interrogation techniques.[156] Secrecy was essential to the creation of this new constitutional order.[157] The 9/11 War featured secret decisions, secret executive orders, and secret programs, not unusual in wartime.[158] However, these initiatives also had *secret constitutional rationales,* something that was crucial to getting them off the ground by shielding them from the normal processes of interagency review.[159] This was vital to the survivability of the extremely controversial opinions generated by John Yoo and others at OLC at the apparent instigation of the White House.[160] As I have already noted and discuss below, it has become apparent that the only reason Yoo's opinions were not discarded by more experienced government attorneys was that they were hidden from view.

As many commentators have pointed out, OLC functions as a Supreme Court for the executive branch. OLC opinions could be used to immunize executive branch officials for violations of federal law.[161] In addition, because OLC had the last word in disputes over constitutional interpretation, whoever controlled it had a decisive positional advantage in any legal debate within the executive branch.[162] Lawyers in Cheney's OVP and the White House Counsel's office sought to reduce the historically independent role of OLC in their effort to control interrogation policy.[163]

Lawyers in OLC responded to 9/11 with a series of opinions that took the executive branch out of the system of checks and balances during wartime.[164] These opinions were in a number of ways the apotheosis of the post-1945 constitutional order. They reflected the groundwork laid by the Reagan and Bush I administrations and by the Iran-contra Minority Report. But they were far more sweeping and systematic. At the same time, some elements were consistent with the claims of most post-1945 presidents and thus were familiar.

In a key September 2001 opinion summarizing presidential war powers in the "war on terror," John Yoo sounded many of the themes repeated by presidential administrations throughout the post–World War II period.[165] Yoo placed the president in the forefront of the government in foreign affairs and linked that status to war powers. He grounded presidential war powers firmly in the text of the Constitution. Citing the vesting and commander in chief provisions of Article II, Yoo stated that "these provisions vest full control of the military forces of the United States in the President."[166] By this, Yoo meant not simply that the president had the power to supervise the military, but to order it to initiate military conflicts.[167] Also consistent with earlier administrations, Yoo maintained that the "declare war" clause was not a check on presidential power. He argued that the context surrounding adoption of the clause showed "that Congress's power to declare war does not constrain the President's independent and plenary constitutional authority over the use of military force."[168]

Foreshadowing the position he would take in the "torture memo," Yoo picked up the Reagan administration's concern with exclusive presidential power described in Chapter 5. He contended that the President had "unilateral war powers" and thus could not be limited by congressional legislation.[169] Yoo thus treated the September 2001 AUMF as confirming (rather than authorizing) the power of President Bush to respond to the 9/11 attacks.[170] Because Yoo viewed presidential power so broadly, the AUMF was incapable of providing any additional legal authority. He treated it as a statement of opinion, saying that "congressional concurrence [on the nature of the terrorist threat] is welcome."[171] Other than mentioning congressional control over spending, Yoo did not acknowledge that the legislative branch had a single power that could constrain the executive in wartime.[172] The opinion was replete with overstatement, referring to the president's "broad constitutional power," "inherent executive power," "plenary authority," "full control of the military forces," "complete discretion," and "centralization of authority in the President alone."[173] Equally remarkable, Yoo did not acknowledge that there were *any* Supreme Court opinions placing constraints on presidential power during wartime. In particular, he ignored the clear relevance of Justice Jackson's concurring opinion in *Steel Seizure* in which Jackson specified that when the president acted against a law passed by Congress, his power was at its "lowest ebb."[174]

As we saw in Chapter 5, this concern with exclusive power was a relatively new element in the presidentialist position.[175] It illustrated the split between the parties on war powers that became evident in the 1980s. While conservatives tended to support the exclusive nature of presidential power in foreign affairs, including war powers, this position reminded liberals of former President Nixon's famous statement that "when the President does it, that means that it is not illegal."[176] Yoo's memo on presidential war powers was a de jure rendering of Nixon's position. The memo had the consequence of erecting a force field around the president that Congress could not penetrate. Presidential action in the war against terror thus could not be regulated by Congress and the Court under any circumstances.

The much criticized August 2002 "torture memo" used the exclusive power rationale to provide a kind of comprehensive constitutional insurance that the statute making torture a crime would never be applicable.[177] While this flawed constitutional analysis was not the only argument Yoo made, it was especially egregious in that he continued his refusal to recognize the relevance of the *Steel Seizure* case (other than when it favored his position).[178] The memo contended that "[a]ny effort by Congress to regulate the interrogation of battlefield combatants would violate the Constitution's sole vesting of the Commander-in-Chief authority in the President."[179] That is, the executive branch could determine for itself, outside of the judicial process, that the law making torture a crime was unconstitutional and refuse to enforce it.

With the incompetent torture memo, the executive branch reached its nadir. Other than Yoo, Bybee, and the White House, few prominent lawyers in the executive branch thought the analysis in the memo was sound. Daniel Levin told the DOJ's Office of Professional Responsibility that he had "the same reaction I think everybody who reads it has—'this is insane, who wrote this?'"[180] The claims of exclusive power in the torture memo were described by Goldsmith as having "no foundation in prior OLC opinions, or in judicial decisions, or in any other source of law."[181] These comments, along with earlier opposition to Yoo's memos among lawyers in the State Department and the DOD, show that the OLC memos survived only by being secret. Although the torture memo was withdrawn in 2004 the face of public criticism, the memo that replaced it simply dropped the analysis of executive power rather than rejecting it.[182] The struggle over interrogation policy continued after

Daniel Levin, the head of OLC after Goldsmith and the author of the new memo, left OLC.[183] White House and OVP lawyers continued in their efforts to influence OLC and the original analysis was reinstated secretly by the new OLC chief.[184]

An extensive investigation by the Senate Armed Services Committee found that the OLC opinions were critical to the creation of a lax interrogation policy in which abuses were all but inevitable. Sadly, it is evident that a number of detainees were cruelly mistreated, degraded, and tortured by U.S. personnel. In addition, the 2002 opinions played a role in the terrible mistreatment that occurred at Abu Ghraib prison during the Iraq War.[185] As Philip Zelikow, former counselor to Secretary of State Rice, summarized in 2009: "the U.S. Government over the past 7 years adopted an unprecedented program in American history of coolly calculated dehumanizing abuse and physical torment to extract information. This was a mistake—perhaps a disastrous one."[186] The Senate Armed Services Committee concluded:

> Legal opinions subsequently issued by the Department of Justice's Office of Legal Counsel (OLC) interpreted legal obligations under U.S. anti-torture laws and determined the legality of CIA interrogation techniques. Those OLC opinions distorted the meaning and intent of anti-torture laws, rationalized the abuse of detainees in U.S. custody and influenced Department of Defense determinations as to what interrogation techniques were legal for use during interrogations conducted by U.S. military personnel.[187]

With this discussion we have reached the end of the line with respect to executive branch legal opinions on war powers. I have reviewed every significant post–World War II opinion, beginning in Chapter 2 with the State Department's memorandum supporting President Truman's decision to intervene in Korea. It is disturbing to realize that none of them can be regarded as candid and forthright with respect to the state of the law. Certainly none of them can be regarded as meeting scholarly standards for the assessment of historical evidence. To be fair, some of the opinions were directed at evaluating minor military operations not involving significant hostilities. They were not typically concerned with the issue of the general allocation of war powers and their analyses often proceeded on narrow fronts, an approach appropriate for cautious government attorneys. It remains the case that, taken together, these opinions were more in the nature of advocates' briefs than fair-minded and well-researched attempts to reach sound legal conclusions.[188]

Afghanistan and Iraq: The Executive Branch at War

The Bush administration's OLC opinions often invoked Alexander Hamilton's insights on the nature of executive power. In *The Federalist* No. 70 Hamilton argued that "[e]nergy in the executive is a leading character in the definition of good government. It is essential to the protection of the community against foreign attacks."[189] John Yoo offered this further gloss on Hamilton's reasoning: "[t]he centralization of authority in the President alone is particularly crucial in matters of national defense, war, and foreign policy, where a unitary executive can evaluate threats, consider policy choices, and mobilize national resources with a speed and energy that is far superior to any other branch."[190]

This is an essential pillar of the reasoning behind presidential leadership in foreign policy. In addition, because of the military legacy of the Cold War, the president has not only the ability to make swift decisions, but also the resources available to actually have them visited rapidly on the enemy. There is little doubt that Yoo's somewhat Napoleonic portrayal of presidential decisionmaking is also part of the cultural legacy of the Cold War. It was certainly promoted in the early Cold War by presidents themselves as well as their congressional supporters.[191]

As a comparison of the relative ability of the executive and legislative branches to make speedy decisions, Hamilton's argument is certainly plausible as far as it goes, but in the kind of government we have had since the Cold War began, it does not take us very far. Swift decisionmaking has little to do with presidential determinations to initiate major wars, the kind of war that has occupied us in this book. Wars involving the potential of thousands of American casualties, millions of foreign casualties, and the expenditure of hundreds of billions of dollars are unlikely to be based on quick decisions. The wars in Korea, Vietnam, and Kuwait were enormous undertakings and required layers of complex interagency decisionmaking, not a single swift move. Indeed, this was part of why it was necessary to establish the NSC to coordinate the resources of the executive branch.

As we saw in Chapter 2, even Truman took some time to deliberate before he made the decision to intervene in Korea. Prior to Korea,

Truman had avoided using the NSC, believing it was an intrusion on his constitutional powers. Once Korea started, however, Truman found it necessary to work through the NSC. Moreover, his initial decision to intervene could inherently involve only a commitment to assist and defend South Korea. Simply getting the troops to Korea took weeks, creating additional time to deliberate not only over whether to continue participating in the war, but also over ultimate U.S. war aims and the strategy for accomplishing them.

The role of war aims warrants further comment and illustrates how deliberation, rather than speed, is of chief importance when we consider how the Constitution structures decisions for war. The distinction between deciding for war and determining war aims has not been appreciated in the enormous literature on war powers. Especially after a surprise attack, such as that experienced at Pearl Harbor and in Korea, Kuwait, or on 9/11, the decision to strike back seems easily made. Once the nation is committed to war, however, the issue becomes its ultimate purpose beyond the defeat of the enemy. Here we might consider that liberal democracies are not barbarians. We are not interested in exterminating the enemy or, in general, in military victory as our sole goal. Reducing the risk of future conflicts is desirable, of course. Surely standard aims of American wars have been to defend and increase national security and advance U.S. objectives in foreign affairs. This entails understanding the relationship between any given war and those broader objectives.

In understanding the policy difficulties that plagued the Bush administration with respect to the separate wars in Afghanistan and Iraq, we should focus our attention first on how the lack of meaningful interbranch deliberation meant that the executive branch never had to decide for itself what the omnibus 9/11 War was all about. This in turn contributed to the derangement of policy by allowing the conflicts and tensions that are part of any administration at war to go unmediated by outside democratic institutions. In other words, it turned out once again that the interagency process was a poor substitute for the interbranch process.

With the advantage of hindsight, we should pause to consider that some moves had been made on the policy chessboard prior to 9/11 and could not be unmade. As I have already observed, foreign policy is an ongoing process and it is impossible to start afresh even after an event that seems to "change everything."[192] So conservatives, including President Bush, tended to believe prior to 9/11 that the world was a dangerous place, full of threats the U.S. had to manage. Their views were amply confirmed by a nightmarish attack on the homeland.[193] Further, the U.S. had already fought one war with Iraq in 1991 and had maintained a close watch on its armed forces. Because of this experience, the U.S. had well-developed war plans for attacking Iraq. Perhaps most important, the uncertainty and risks that are part of any military venture had been reduced greatly by the outcome of the 1991 Gulf War. It was clear that the Iraqi army was no match for the U.S. military. For their part, congressional Democrats continued to be relatively uninvolved in military affairs and remembered well how they were roundly criticized for arguing that the 1991 war would be a disaster.[194]

Unfortunately, none of these experiences were directly relevant to formulating war aims and a strategy for combating al Qaeda. So apart from the CIA, which enjoyed a rare moment in the sun, the government floundered somewhat in coming up with a conventional military plan for addressing the situation in Afghanistan. Whereas the CIA had a plan for overcoming the Taliban and disrupting al Qaeda, the regular military did not.[195] There was confusion on war aims:

> The military operation lacked clarity of purpose. Was it to get Osama bin Laden? To destroy al Qaeda? Topple the Taliban? Ensure Afghanistan would never again be a terrorist haven? Send a message to other terrorist supporters? All of the above? Bush's war council had not given definitive answers to any of these questions.[196]

It is no accident that President Obama found much the same situation prevailing with respect to the War in Afghanistan upon assuming office in 2009.[197] The lack of policy direction Obama encountered was a direct consequence of the failure of Bush's "War Cabinet" to specify war aims for the 9/11 War. In general, one of the signal features of Bush's "war on terror" was the lack of a way to measure progress other than through successful terrorist attacks or failed attempts. Military historian Richard Kohn has argued insightfully that a lack of clear war aims meant there was no way for citizens to understand the war and whether it was achieving its objectives.[198]

Perhaps we should not be surprised at the irresolution and lack of expertise that prevailed in the executive branch in fall 2001. If we took seriously the notion that everything changed after 9/11, this would have meant in literal terms that no one had the necessary experience to cope with a fundamentally new policy environment. As there were by definition no experts, Bush had everything to gain by throwing the net for advice as wide as possible and including Congress in deliberation over war aims. The Bush administration followed the opposite approach.

If the bipartisan congressional leadership had been included, even in a minimal way in the crucial executive branch deliberations that occurred in fall 2001, they would have likely perceived how the War in Afghanistan was essentially an improvised operation. They would have noticed how there was no preexisting military (as opposed to CIA) plan for removing the Taliban from power and no concept for what to do after the Taliban were routed. The eventual lack of focus on Osama bin Laden himself might also have impressed them. In a controversial decision, the military decided to rely on local assistance rather than U.S. troops when al Qaeda was cornered in the cave complex of Tora Bora.[199] Members of Congress might also have realized there were already well-developed war plans to attack Iraq. While it would be too simple to say that Iraq was a target from late fall 2001 onward because the Pentagon had preexisting plans to attack Iraq but not Afghanistan, this certainly made planning the Iraq War easier.

It would have been harder for members of Congress to observe how Bush had made a regular interagency process all but impossible due to a number of key institutional decisions he made at the outset of his administration. The ordinary NSC process was undermined as Condoleezza Rice was surrounded by heavyweights such as Rumsfeld and Cheney, who resisted her efforts to coordinate policy. In addition, Rice was hampered by the fact that the OVP under Cheney had its own policy shop and that Rumsfeld had effectively silenced the independent voice of the JCS.[200] This administrative terrain made carrying out any national security effort unusually difficult.

It is by now conventional wisdom, confirmed by those who served in the Bush II administration, that the Iraq War was not preceded by any NSC-coordinated interagency process to study whether to go to war or the likely consequences of the war. Indeed, it appears there was never a NSC meeting or other session with principal officials to actually discuss and make the decision to go to war.[201] This makes Iraq unique among the major wars we have considered and supports the credibility of accounts that the administration viewed Iraq as a natural follow-on to what I have called the 9/11 War.[202] As former CIA intelligence officer Paul Pillar comments, "[t]he most extraordinary aspect of the George W. Bush administration's launching of a war in Iraq in March 2003 was the absence of any apparent procedure for determining whether the war was a good idea."[203]

This would be more of an interesting contrast if the lack of study given to the Iraq War decision was different from detailed studies that could have been done before Cold War administrations went to war. But as I discuss in more detail in Chapter 7, the stronger pattern both pre- and post-9/11 is that presidents tend to resist processes that are threats to the belief that they should have sole responsibility for making important decisions. So, for example, Truman initially resisted the new NSC and Johnson personalized the decisionmaking process in the run-up to the crucial 1965 Vietnam decisions. As Richard Haass, who led the State Department's Policy Planning Staff during the Bush II administration, has aptly commented, each president creates his own NSC process.[204]

To be fair, it is possible to argue that U.S. war aims became considerably clearer after Bush's 2002 State of the Union address, in which he highlighted the "axis of evil" that existed among the nuclear-bound states of North Korea, Iran, and Iraq. This represented a distinct shift from concentrating on the threat posed by al Qaeda. James Mann describes the administration's evolution:

> Thus over a period of less than five months the administration had progressively shifted the focus of the war on terrorism from (a) retaliating against the perpetrators of the September 11 attacks to (b) stopping terrorists from acquiring weapons of mass destruction to (c) preventing states from supplying terrorists with these weapons. Indeed, there were suggestions in Bush's speech that a link between the states and terrorism wasn't absolutely necessary; what mattered above all were (d) the axis-of-evil states and their weapons programs.[205]

Shifting the focus to the risks that terrorist groups might acquire weapons of mass destruction (WMD) on their own or from states promoting terrorism was certainly a logical outgrowth of 9/11. It also made the "war on terror" reminiscent of the Cold War. It was certainly understandable for officials post-9/11 to look to the early Cold War for inspiration in a general sense by identifying key states that were working to destabilize the global status quo. But this also made the war on terror similar to the Cold War in terms of policy. After all, state-sponsored terrorism had been a steady concern of the executive branch since at least the Reagan administration. Looking to the Cold War as a model cut many different ways.

For one thing, invoking the Cold War counted against the idea that we were in a totally new age in which everything had changed. In the early Cold War, the U.S. built alliances against the Soviet Union and worked to educate Congress on the worldwide strategy of the administration.[206] Neither approach was pursued by the Bush administration.[207] As I have already argued, it would have also meant confronting the legacy of the Cold War in realistic terms. The Cold War showed that public morale could not be sustained forever even in the face of consistently elevated threat levels. Americans would either attempt to eliminate the threat or they would begin to ignore it. But with respect to global terrorism, neither of these choices was necessarily realistic. The Cold War also demonstrated that fighting a war would inevitably distract the president from other crucial policy tasks. Secretary of State Powell warned President Bush that this would happen if the U.S. invaded Iraq, and subsequent experience showed Powell was correct.[208] Finally, American strategy in the Cold War was built in part on the containment and deterrence of aggressive states. The Bush administration never explained why the same strategy would not work against states which allowed terrorist groups to operate. It also could not explain why Iraq had to be invaded essentially immediately even though the nuclear programs of North Korea and Iran were far more advanced.[209]

Although the Bush II administration could claim consistency with respect to viewing Saddam Hussein as a threat both before and after 9/11, what it could not claim is that the failure to engage in a proper interagency decisionmaking process had no adverse effects. The most outstanding example, which stunned prominent officials in the administration, was Vice President Cheney's audacious August 2002 claim that Iraq had WMD it was readying to be used against the United States.[210] This claim, which was not cleared by the CIA, was nonetheless picked up by the rest of the administration in order to sell the war.[211] The public debate over whether to go to war was thus primarily based on the contention that Iraq not only possessed WMD in terms of chemical and biological weapons, but also was actively working to acquire nuclear weapons.[212] The lack of close attention to the intelligence showing uncertainties about the level of actual threat from Iraq subsequently created a monumental credibility problem that damaged U.S. foreign policy after it was discovered that Iraq had no WMD.[213]

In assessing the role of intelligence, we should avoid the tangled debate over whether the Bush administration politicized the intelligence process.[214] We should concentrate rather on the difference between how the Clinton and Bush administrations used intelligence in public. Foreign policy professionals have reminded us that the Clinton administration, indeed the international intelligence community, were convinced that Saddam Hussein had WMD.[215] Far from directing attention away from how the Bush administration sold the war, this reality exposes once again the fragile, if lasting, structure of the post-1945 constitutional order. For although much of the intelligence on Iraq predated 9/11, the Bush administration certainly did not tell the public that the war was justified on the basis of Clinton-era intelligence. In fact, Bush was distinctly unimpressed with the CIA's December 2002 summary of the evidence because it rested on obscure inferences from old data.[216] Cheney's speech illustrated the typical administration response to the difficulty posed by old intelligence—it went beyond the intelligence to oversell the war based on the perception of an imminent threat. In particular, Cheney's office and the DOD promoted a dubious link between al Qaeda's 9/11 attack and Saddam Hussein that proved to be a false trail.[217] The sense of an imminent threat was heightened by eliding the difference between the relatively slight danger posed by chemical and biological weapons and the far more serious prospect that Iraq would be able to brandish nuclear weapons in fairly short order.[218] After the invasion found no WMD, CIA Director Tenet was left to apologize repeatedly for the gap between what the uncertain intelligence actually showed and what the administration claimed.[219]

Beginning with the Truman administration, one consistent theme of the post-1945 order was that presidents oversold foreign threats in order to move the balky constitutional machinery. As we have seen, however, bypassing that machinery increased the risk of the derangement of policy. Presidents place themselves and their administrations on the line when they are convinced of a foreign threat. This means they must win the political decision to go ahead. This did not pose great difficulties for President Bush, as Congress devoted little time to examining the decision to go to war with Iraq. Congress requested a National

Intelligence Estimate from the CIA on the WMD threat from Iraq, but did not examine closely what it said.[220]

Another consequence of the derangement of the policy process was the failure to think through what would happen after the U.S. conquered Iraq. The interagency process completely broke down with respect to formulating a strategy to deal with the internal crisis and insurgency Iraq experienced after the fall of Saddam Hussein. This failure occurred apparently because the Pentagon, which was focused on winning the war and then removing troops as quickly as possible, was placed in charge of postwar Iraq. Postwar U.S. policy blunders such as dismissing all members of the Baath Party from their positions and disbanding the Iraqi army did not help. It is noteworthy once again that these key strategic decisions were not made through a proper review by the White House and the NSC.[221] These key failures plunged the U.S. into a second unforeseen war. The contrast between the casualties suffered up to May 1, 2003, when President Bush declared the war over, and the present is both remarkable and awful. When Bush made his announcement, 139 Americans had been killed and 542 wounded.[222] The current toll, as reflected by the table in Chapter 1, is over 36,000 U.S. casualties at a cost of nearly $800 billion. We should also consider Iraqi civilian deaths, which have been estimated at around 90,000.[223] Instead of a quick war settling accounts with Saddam Hussein, the Iraq War became one of the most devastating conflicts in U.S. history.

The poor record of the Bush administration in justifying and running the Iraq War was equaled by the pathetic lack of inquiry by Congress, a classic instance where a proposed war that should have demanded the legislative equivalent of strict scrutiny received the lightest examination possible.[224] Unlike his father, Bush asked Congress for a resolution prior to going to the Security Council, giving Congress roughly five weeks to come to grips with the decision to go to war. Like his father, Bush did not concede that such a resolution was constitutionally required. The historic weakness of Democrats on military matters finally caught up with them, as they feared basing the upcoming 2002 congressional elections on the war, trying to pivot instead to the economy.[225] Even if we imagine that Congress would have favored the war no matter what, it did not fulfill its role as a check on the executive. Congress did not push Bush to estimate casualties, the costs of the war, or the likely consequences of victory. The administration was allowed to evade such obvious issues until it was too late.[226]

Reflecting on his service in the Bush II administration, Richard Haass concluded:

> George W. Bush inherited a robust economy, a budgetary surplus, a rested military, and, even after 9/11, a world largely at peace and well-disposed toward the United States. He handed off to his successor a recession, a massive deficit and debt, a stretched and exhausted military, two wars, and a world marked by pronounced anti-Americanism.[227]

As the realities of the long and costly wars in Afghanistan and Iraq sank in, there were many comparisons to Vietnam.[228] The wars took place in countries Americans, especially American soldiers, knew little about and had little sympathy for. The real strength of the comparison was that once again the political leadership of the country, aided by a fundamentally flawed constitutional order, had failed the American people and their military.

7

A New Constitutional Order?

Like a clash of tectonic plates, the conflict between the original constitutional order and the post-1945 order in foreign affairs helped define the Cold War and post–Cold War periods. The persistence of the post-1945 order with its dependence on unilateral presidential leadership in national security matters and presidential decisions for war made outside of the cycle of accountability illustrates how in important respects we have not moved beyond the politics, diplomacy, and national security strategy of the Cold War.

Looking at the Cold War from a high altitude, we can see that Korea and Vietnam, the two major wars fought under its aegis, were followed by periods of reaction and slow recovery. In the immediate aftermath of Korea, for example, congressional leaders were not interested in intervening when President Eisenhower informed them that the French faced defeat at Dienbienphu.[1] Americans were simply unready for another major military commitment. Likewise, Americans were taken aback when, in the midst of winding down the U.S. commitment in Iraq, President Obama used military force to intervene in Libya in 2011. This shows the unique character of major wars. They require substantial national effort and have long-lasting consequences. In particular, they are very hard on ground forces, the Army and the Marines. The experience of the Cold War suggested that these forces cannot sustain a high level of action indefinitely and must be rebuilt after the war is over. Compared to the many other sorts of military action presidents have taken, major conventional wars have been relatively rare since 1945. At the same time, when they have occurred, they have usually lasted for much longer than originally anticipated by the executive branch.

This history suggests that the departure of U.S. troops from Iraq in December 2011 and the winding down of the War in Afghanistan will be followed by a similar period of reaction and recovery. Given the Republican Party's defeat in the 2012 presidential election, it is still too early to say whether Republicans have been affected by the Iraq War as the Democratic Party was by the Vietnam War. After Vietnam the Democratic Party, especially its congressional wing, never appeared to regain its equilibrium with respect to foreign affairs and the making of national security policy. Democrats in Congress never produced a coherent account of the place of America in the world after the Cold War ended for them in the 1970s. The post–Cold War position of the Republican Party in foreign affairs was built around what might be called an ideology of threat, the maintenance of military supremacy, and unilateral presidential leadership in foreign policy. If the Republicans imitate the 1970s Democrats, these commitments will be tested in the years ahead.

Perhaps the Cold War defense structure will be eroded by a faltering economy. Perhaps Americans will develop a sense of their place in the world that does not depend on being the sole military superpower. If this happens, the post-1945 order could come into question in a way that has not occurred since the 1970s, when both liberals and conservatives argued that the constitutional system had broken down with respect to war powers and foreign affairs. In the wake of the Iraq War in particular, it is possible to imagine a bipartisan agreement that the presidential power to initiate war must be checked in a more effective way than is possible through the War Powers Resolution.[2]

While all of this could happen, the course of history since the Cold War began argues against it. Despite budgetary challenges, the U.S. will likely maintain a defense structure that gives it the ability to intervene anywhere in the world. It will tend to define threats to national security in ways that suggest that they can be met primarily through military means, both conventional and covert. It will eventually recover from the debilitating wars in Iraq and Afghanistan and adopt new technologies to reduce the strains of war on the armed forces. Presidents will continue to claim that they must provide leadership in foreign affairs and American national security sometimes demands military intervention. The judiciary will continue its policy of nonintervention with respect to decisions for war and covert operations. This set of circumstances will likely guarantee the continued relevance of the post-1945 constitutional order.

Unfortunately, as long as the post-1945 constitutional order exists, the problems and tensions attendant to that order will persist. There will likely be another major war or significant covert operations that are based on insufficient deliberation. In the absence of a meaningful cycle of accountability, the results of the war will likely be unsatisfying, tragic, and possibly deadly to national security. To fulfill what it perceives as its duty to defend the country, the executive branch will again manipulate its institutional structure in defiance of the limits of the law and possibly cause another constitutional crisis. We thus have good reason to continue to be concerned with the post-1945 constitutional order.

Critiques that claim we have strayed from the Constitution are typically accompanied by calls for a return to the original constitutional order. This is not my position and I hope the theory presented in Chapter 1 at least planted the suspicion that this is not a reasonable alternative. Recall that a constitutional order involves reciprocal relationships between the text of the Constitution and the political and policy objectives of state officials, elites, and the public, as well as between each of these and the structure and capacity for action of state institutions. So we can no more return to the original constitutional order than we can return to the political and institutional world of the early republic and the first presidential administrations of Washington, Adams, Jefferson, and Madison. Without some sort of constitutional upheaval that is difficult to foresee, we are stuck with a constitutional order in foreign affairs that is an uncomfortable and even combustible mixture of past and present. In this book, what I have thought important is to understand where we are by looking back before having a discussion of how to move forward.

The discussion in this chapter thus assumes that the post-1945 constitutional order will continue to be relevant to government decision-making in foreign policy and national security. My purpose is to see whether there is a reasonable possibility of modifying the present situation so as to avoid the defects of the post-1945 order. To set up this inquiry, I first review and summarize the most salient points made in the previous chapters through a discussion of how the standard war powers debate should be redirected. I then strike out afresh by presenting an explanation of the problems presidents have experienced in making decisions for war. It then becomes plausible to take a closer look at Congress to evaluate its potential contributions to a new constitutional order. I conclude by arguing that we should move beyond both the critique of the "imperial presidency" and presidential triumphalism while also integrating the Constitution more closely into the history of government policymaking.

What the War Powers Debate Should Be About

Decisions for war are among the most serious any government can make. Yet few are satisfied with either the process or the outcome of those decisions. Since 1945 the United States has enjoyed many discrete successes in combat in the major military conflicts it has fought—the Korean War, the Vietnam War, the 1991 Gulf War, and the wars following 9/11 in Afghanistan and Iraq. These wars have cost the nation hundreds of thousands of casualties and trillions of dollars.[3] Yet few regard them as unalloyed successes because they have been wrapped in larger failures of political decisionmaking and national security strategy.

How these deliberative failures are connected to the Constitution has been obscured by the standard war powers debate. Congressionalist scholars who hold that Congress alone has the power to decide not only for "war" but also any sort of military action have tended to focus on the formal issue of whether wars are authorized rather than on whether robust interbranch deliberation took place before and during the war. In response, presidentialist scholars have contended that a Congress concerned largely with domestic issues has little to contribute to the president's responsibility to order military action as part of his conduct of foreign policy.

One reason the war powers debate has generated more heat than light is because recent major wars *have* been authorized by Congress. The 1991 Gulf War and the wars in Afghanistan and Iraq were all accompanied by congressionally approved "AUMFs"—Authorizations to Use Military Force. To this extent, the proponents of the War Powers Resolution were successful in getting the idea across that major military undertakings must be legislatively authorized. As we saw in Chapter 1, constitutional scholars agree that these authorizations are the legal equivalent of declarations of war.[4] Nonetheless, the debate has gone stale and has recently featured extreme claims. Presidentialists assert, essentially, that the "declare war" clause is obsolete and that there is therefore no check on presidential authority other than through the appropriations process. For their part, congressionalists have claimed that presidents should be impeached (!) when they fail to get congressional authorization for *any* military intervention, regardless of the circumstances.[5]

The most important constitutional issue posed by the wars fought since 1945 is not formal authorization but rather meaningful interbranch deliberation. Although presidents may have acquired the habit of going to Congress, this does not mean that any president ever truly acknowledged a constitutional requirement to do so, instead viewing such authorizations as politically convenient (although the case of President Obama is discussed below). Presidents thus have not based their decisionmaking around the assumption that Congress could effectively veto a military proposal. This accounts for the inadequate quality of the deliberation around the three AUMFs for the Gulf War, Afghanistan, and Iraq. Virtually no one believes, for example, that the deliberation both inside the executive branch and in Congress prior to the 2003 Iraq War was adequate, yet this is somehow *not* the issue to which constitutional scholars have devoted most of their attention.[6] This failure of analysis is similar to what happened with respect to Vietnam. Scholars focused so much on the 1964 Tonkin Gulf Resolution that they neglected inquiring into the adequacy of the deliberation that occurred in 1965, a far more significant and consequential issue.

While the question of authorization is always relevant, issues of deliberation and capacity deserve much greater scrutiny. The architects of the post-1945 order expected that once presidents were given the military capacity to advance the foreign policy and defend the national security of the United States on a global basis, they would have the ability to make effective decisions. As we have noticed, the implicit assumption was that the interagency process inside the executive branch would serve as an effective substitute for the interbranch process. The standard war powers debate, occupied with legalistic distinctions not suitable for a sphere of the Constitution unenforced by the Supreme Court, has rarely concentrated in detail on how presidents have decided for war. As I discuss below, retrospective analysis with respect to conflicts such as Vietnam has shown with notable clarity the substantial difficulties presidents have had with such decisions.

Another problem with the standard war powers debate is that the congressionalist position has rested on an account of presidential motivation drawn straight from the eighteenth century. In this telling, presidents go to war out of ambition and a vainglorious sense of America's place in the world. Yet we do live in a democracy. While it is unlikely that presidents start wars without considering the political consequences and public opinion, this is what the congressionalist position seems to assume. Congressionalists and critics of the "imperial presidency" lack a plausible account of presidential motivation. Even if it was true that presidents are solely responsible for starting wars and have engaged in massive abuses of power, it is surely relevant to know why they have done so. The congressionalist critique creates an unnecessary mystery by ignoring the link between presidential decisions for war and the president's responsibility for foreign policy.

Once we highlight this link, it makes more sense to begin with the idea of a constitutional order that was constructed deliberately in order to cope with the new circumstances of the Cold War. Presidents could not create this order entirely by themselves and so up to a point, the creation of the post-1945 order was democratic. As we saw in Chapter 2, presidents had plenty of assistance from members of Congress and the foreign policy elite. Throughout the early Cold War, Americans worried about a repetition of the appeasement at Munich and the domination of Europe and Asia by communist states. These were not unreasonable concerns. It was also hard to imagine an alternative to relying on the power of the presidency with Congress in the state it was at the beginning of the Cold War. Although Congress could be dynamited into action, leadership in foreign affairs was in short supply.

In contemporary times, presidents are motivated by the knowledge that the American people expect them to advance the foreign policy and defend the national security of the United States. As I develop further below, President Obama came to the realization that he was only the latest heir to this legacy.[7] No post-1945 president has ever run for office promising to make Congress an equal partner in foreign policy (nor have many members of Congress, for that matter). Try to recall when, after an attack on U.S. soil or against U.S. personnel abroad, the public responded by calling for an investigation into how *Congress* had failed in its responsibility to protect Americans from danger. Americans wanted "no more Vietnams," but this does not mean there was a corresponding permanent shift favoring Congress to run foreign policy.

For their part, presidentialists continue to embrace the profoundly mistaken notion that war can be subsumed under the conduct of foreign affairs. The creators of the post-1945 order appeared to believe that "long wars" could be maintained indefinitely in a constitutional democracy. Robert Beisner remarks that Secretary of State Acheson lacked "the ability to promise either Americans or Europeans when an end would come to the sacrifices he asked them to make."[8] We have had enough experience to know that this assumption was seriously flawed. Although former president Eisenhower supported the Vietnam War publicly, privately he wrote to Johnson in 1966 and "curtly dismissed the McNamarian notion that 'small wars' like Vietnam could go on indefinitely and society must be prepared to support them. Americans 'eventually get tired of supporting involvements of this kind,' the former president insisted, and the war must be ended as soon as possible."[9]

Wars cannot be treated as just another aspect of foreign policy because they are qualitatively different. The Korean and Vietnam wars both destabilized American politics the longer they lasted. All major conventional wars involve substantial burdens on the country and it is unlikely that any democratic state could sustain the morale necessary for a permanent state of war. Moreover, as Vietnam and Iraq illustrated, even limited wars tend to subordinate the rest of the nation's foreign policy to their requirements rather than the reverse. As Secretary of State Colin Powell warned President George W. Bush before the Iraq War, war takes all the oxygen out of the policy room.[10] In starting a major war, the president is almost literally betting the policy ranch.

The presidentialist position assumes that the executive branch's diplomatic and military expertise can be extended to decisions for war. Experience suggests rather powerfully, however, that the interagency process is not an adequate substitute for the constitutionally mandated interbranch process. The war powers debate thus should be centrally concerned with the ability of the executive branch to make decisions and how to ensure meaningful interbranch deliberation prior to decisions for war. The inability of the executive branch to deliberate and make effective decisions manifested itself in distinct patterns of dysfunctional and even deranged decisionmaking all connected to the lack of interbranch deliberation built into the post-1945 constitutional order.

As we have seen, the most prominent patterns have been a failure to engage in realistic war planning, a closely related failure to decide on war aims, and the misguided expectation that the president can carry the entire burden of decisionmaking. We should now look more closely at why these patterns have occurred.

From Vietnam to Iraq

These dysfunctional patterns of decisionmaking stem from the clash between the original constitutional order and the requirements of the post-1945 order. Under Article II, the president is the unitary head of the executive branch and holds his office based on the authority granted by a democratic election. Everyone in the executive branch is keenly aware of the president's unique status as chief officer and sole executive heir of the democratic authority conveyed by the people. The president's constitutional status makes it very unlikely that any system of checks and balances over time—a cycle of accountability—could evolve or be effective *within* the executive branch. Our experience with decisions for war after 1945 provides substantial evidence that this status is inimical to effective deliberation. Indeed, we might say that without the participation of Congress, the policy space around the president is inherently warped.

Especially during the Cold War, presidents appeared to be the victims of consistently poor policy advice with respect to decisions for war. Think of Truman's decision to move troops north of the 38th parallel, Kennedy's decision to let the Bay of Pigs operation go forward, and the failure of LBJ's advisers to probe more deeply into what it would take to prevail in Vietnam. But then we might reflect that presidents are often the true authors of the advice they receive. As Fredrik Logevall remarks, history shows that "no president is a prisoner to his advisers."[11] Presidents can have trouble receiving sound and candid advice because of careerism on the part of their subordinates. But they also sometimes deliberately avoid such advice out of concerns about becoming trapped.

The phenomenon of inadequate advice is symptomatic of a larger difficulty. The presidency is an inherently disruptive office which resists being captured in institutional forms.[12] We might say, for example, that in the nonlegalized Constitution, in the absence of regular judicial oversight, the president functions as his or her own Supreme Court.[13]

Certainly this was powerfully suggested by the experience of the Bush II administration. Congress can create entities such as the NSC, but presidents are subordinate to no one, and no agency or institution is ultimately in charge. Motivated by reelection, the desire to fulfill their office, accomplish their policy objectives, a concern to advance their historical reputations, and, in foreign affairs, the sense that they are ultimately responsible for advancing the foreign policy and defending the national security of the United States, presidents resist being tied down by institutions and reorganizations.

Each president thus creates his own national security structure.[14] With everyone in the executive branch, especially the White House, responsive to and subordinate to the president, there is no clear path to relying on internal checks and balances to promote deliberation. Given the president's overriding constitutional authority and responsibility for foreign policy and national security, it is not clear how Congress could encase any president in an institutional structure. It is also not clear whether Congress has the expertise to make such a project work. As I argue below, Congress has plenty of work to do simply to get its own house in order.

These lessons of experience are best illustrated by the Vietnam War. Yet historians might be surprised to learn that Vietnam has played a marginal role at best in the war powers debate in recent years. This is in part the legacy of the deliberation over the WPR, when both parties in Congress avoided inquiring into how the war came about. But it is also because presidentialists either simply bypass or will not engage seriously with the immense literature on the war. That is a shame because, as one might suspect, Vietnam is the most carefully documented post-1945 war from the standpoint of executive branch decisionmaking. Critical decisions made on Vietnam by presidents from FDR to Ford have received intense scrutiny and the resulting scholarship has generated many valuable insights.

Keeping Vietnam offstage might be regarded as a tribute to Nixon, Ford, and Kissinger's efforts to separate the Republican Party from the war and blame Democrats in Congress for its length and tragic outcome. Indeed, one background circumstance that has impaired the war powers debate from the beginning is the refusal by Republicans and conservative supporters of presidentialism to share any significant responsibility for this tragic conflict. They thus never had to confront the question of what went wrong in a suitably realistic spirit. Although LBJ held his decisionmaking cards close, sound historical scholarship has established that leading Republicans in the 1960s, including presidential contenders such as Nixon, shared Johnson's outlook that the war had to be fought.[15]

So no one who studies executive decisions for war in the post-1945 period can ignore Vietnam. George Herring has provided the best analysis of the Johnson administration's management of war decisionmaking inside the executive branch. He addresses "the curious phenomenon of why, although there was near universal dissatisfaction among Johnson's advisers with the way the war was being fought and the results that were being obtained, there was no change of strategy or even substantive discussion of a change."[16] He notices that from 1965 onward, "the entire system seems to have been rigged to prevent debate and adaptation."[17] Arguably, however, there wasn't much *system* to executive branch decisionmaking, which was held tightly at the very top of the administration without using the NSC to evaluate different courses of action.[18] There was also no effective civil-military relationship; rather, the command system operated in a "bureaucratic fog" that made it difficult for JCS recommendations to penetrate Johnson's inner circle.[19]

As we saw in Chapter 4, while there was plenty of interagency activity in the run-up to the crucial 1965 decisions to Americanize the war, there was no true interagency deliberation. Fearing the outcome of a no-holds-barred deliberative process, LBJ rigged the system to produce consensus.[20] The JCS was not fully engaged, while "the civilians did not provide the military strategic direction, set precise limits, or even define with clarity what they wanted done. National Security Adviser McGeorge Bundy later conceded that a 'premium [was] put on imprecision.'"[21] As a consequence, Johnson never had to make fundamental decisions on the relationship between means and ends—determining the objectives of the war and how best to accomplish them.[22] Herring observes that "[t]he president and his civilian advisers, on the other hand, did not question the military persistently enough to get answers they perhaps did not want to hear."[23] These answers most probably related to the military's belief that Vietnam would have to be fought with every resource in the American arsenal (save perhaps nuclear weapons), including mobilization of the reserves.[24]

Herring speaks of a persistent "bureaucratic and strategic gridlock" affecting the war, lasting into late 1966 and originating from Johnson's management style.[25] But it was broken to some extent when John Stennis, chair of the Senate Armed Services Committee, held hearings to criticize Secretary of Defense McNamara's handling of the war and prod the administration to take a more aggressive line.[26] To this point, beyond the hearings held in early 1966 by Senator Fulbright, Congress had played no role in generating a cycle of accountability that could have served the purpose of loosening the deadlock inside the administration. In an interesting observation supporting my argument, Herring states that "[i]n a strange, almost surreal way, the Stennis committee hearings of August 1967 became the forum for a debate that *could not take place* within the inner councils of the executive branch."[27] This showed, albeit in a minimal way, what Congress could accomplish in starting a cycle of accountability and what the checks and balances in the Constitution were really for. By this late stage, however, the strategic advice offered by the military had gone stale. It was too late for the Johnson administration to change course.[28]

With respect to more recent major wars such as Iraq, we of course lack the sort of detailed archival study of decisionmaking that Herring so ably provides. But Vietnam and Iraq were similar in terms of exhibiting the inherent deficiencies of executive branch decisionmaking. The defects that are most relevant here relate to managing the fraught civil-military relationship and the relative absence of interbranch and public deliberation. With respect to Vietnam, for example, Herring explains that "[i]n various ways, between July 1965 and August 1967, debate was stifled and dissent squelched. When Army Chief of Staff Harold Johnson warned in a speech that the war might last ten years, Barry Zorthian later recalled, 'he got his ass chewed out. That was denied awfully fast.'"[29] Johnson's prediction was roughly accurate. Likewise, in early 2003 as another round of deliberation was occurring in the run-up to the Iraq War, Army Chief of Staff Eric Shinseki accurately warned Congress that the coming conflict would require several hundred thousand troops. Civilians at the Pentagon, as well as Vice President Cheney, immediately disputed Shinseki and played down the troops and funding that would be required to prevail in the war.[30] It is striking that the deliberation required before the nation went to war had not improved in the four decades that had elapsed since Vietnam. Of the major wars fought after 1945, Vietnam and Iraq were certainly "wars of choice."[31] There was sufficient time for an adequate public debate if the president so wished. But it did not happen. The consequence was the pattern we have observed throughout this book—a lack of effective war planning, confusion over war aims, and overreliance on the president as the sole decisionmaker.

Vietnam and Iraq also point to the inherent lack of expertise on the civilian side of the executive branch with respect to making decisions for war. Of all the shibboleths of the Cold War, none have arguably done more harm than the idea that the executive branch's undoubted expertise with respect to foreign affairs has something to do with the knowledge necessary for planning and running a war. This was amply confirmed by the run-up to the Iraq War, as the Bush administration determinedly avoided expert advice. As described in Chapter 6 and summarized by former CIA intelligence officer Paul Pillar, "[t]he president reached his decision on Iraq without hearing the views of any of his senior advisers, save for the vice president and possible the national security adviser, about whether it was wise or not."[32] Pillar goes on to describe the Bush administration's decisionmaking process more generally:

> The nonuse of intelligence in making the decision to launch the Iraq War was part of a larger pattern of dismissing relevant sources of insight and expertise. Across the entire range of issues pertinent to the war, the war makers not only did not seek input from such sources, but also consciously excluded it. Insights from the civilian and military bureaucracy were ignored or rejected, as were the perspectives of experts outside government (except for a very few whose policy preferences already were safely in line with those of the war makers).[33]

Our experience with presidential administrations in the post-1945 period is clear—there is no such thing as a civilian "expert" and there is no such thing as a standard interagency process in making the policy choices and decisions necessary for war. Even if we accept the reasonable point that military leaders are expert in planning and running military operations, no post-1945 president except Eisenhower possessed the requisite experience (and we might notice that Eisenhower avoided starting a major conventional war). Consider also that the substantial experience FDR had acquired with respect to foreign policy by the time he was elected to a third term in 1940 is barred to any contemporary president by the Twenty-Second Amendment. Further, cabinet officials and advisers are rarely drawn from a pool of those knowledgeable about war. As we drew away from the World War II generation, the secretaries of state and defense have usually been different sorts of technocrats, careerists, or politicians. While there is nothing wrong with this, none of them had experience in making decisions for war.[34] Presidential decisions for war are grounded first and foremost in political values rather than foreign policy and national security expertise. After we examine the record so far of the Obama administration, this makes it all the more necessary to consider the proper role of Congress.

Obama's Way of War

When we situate Bush and Obama within the post-1945 constitutional order, the parallels with the positions occupied by Truman and Eisenhower respectively are striking. Like Truman, Bush initiated major military commitments, both overt and covert, in an atmosphere of emergency. Like Eisenhower, Obama had to wind down a war (the Iraq War) but at the same time maintain a commitment to a "long war" against a foreign threat. Obama even had his own version of Eisenhower's "Old Guard" Republicans—liberals suspicious of executive power who demanded criminal investigations of the excesses of the Bush administration. To cope with these varied national security challenges amid the reality of a war-weary public, Obama, also like Eisenhower, increasingly turned to "covert" means of war such as drone strikes, after initially expanding the conventional commitment in Afghanistan. As in the Eisenhower administration, this meant that the role of the CIA's clandestine service expanded significantly.

Obama in effect endorsed the post-1945 constitutional order in his widely noticed address accepting the 2009 Nobel Peace Prize. He declared: "Whatever mistakes we have made, the plain fact is this: the United States of America has helped underwrite global security for more than six decades with the blood of our citizens and the strength of our arms. The service and sacrifice of our men and women in uniform has promoted peace and prosperity from Germany to Korea, and enabled democracy to take hold in places like the Balkans."[35] The global commitment Obama invoked is of course one of the founding stones of the post-1945 constitutional order. That commitment, backed by the enormous post-World War II capacity of the U.S. to intervene worldwide, generates the problematic situation we have been analyzing.

Liberals who complained that Obama did not successfully break with all of the controversial policies of the Bush administration, much less the imperial presidency (discussed below), perhaps did not pay sufficient attention to what might be termed Obama's Eisenhower moment. Because the 9/11 Wars were such salient issues in the 2008 presidential election, Obama's decisions were underwritten by democratic deliberation. Obama opposed the Iraq War as a senator, a position that did not hurt him in the run-up to the election, as the public had soured on the war. At the same time, he gave clear indications in the presidential campaign that he would expand the nation's commitment in Afghanistan to prevent a resurgence of al-Qaeda. When Obama followed through on this commitment, sending tens of thousands of additional troops to Afghanistan to revive a moribund war effort, this should not have been a cause for great surprise.[36] This does underscore, however, that by the time Obama took office, critiques of excessive presidential power relied far more heavily on rule of law considerations than the kind of failure of democratic deliberation that had occurred in the Iraq War.

Yet Obama signaled that he was not necessarily comfortable with all of the elements of the post-1945 constitutional order. Obama did draw an important distinction with the Bush administration by declaring that all of his legal authorities for continuing the war against al-Qaeda came from the September 2001 AUMF or other acts of Congress.[37] As we saw in Chapter 6, Obama's OLC, like Clinton's, conceded that Congress has some role in authorizing war. On the other hand, Obama's position on his Article II power was not altogether clear, partly because he did not repudiate the Bush administration's position. In October 2011, for example, Obama ordered 100 armed military advisers to central Africa to combat the Lord's Resistance Army. While this was arguably in service of a policy previously adopted by Congress, the president noted that "he had decided to act because it was 'in the national security and foreign policy interests of the United States.'"[38] In invoking his authority under Article II, this rationale was of course expressive of the post-1945 order as I have defined it.

President Obama's intervention in Libya illustrated the continuing complexities of the president's role under the post-1945 constitutional order. Obama initiated military operations (largely air strikes and the provision of intelligence) against the Libyan regime of Muammar al-Qaddafi in 2011. These actions were first begun by the U.S. to enforce a U.N. Security Council resolution and then carried out under the aegis of NATO.[39] Obama's Libya operation was similar to Reagan's 1986 air strike on Qaddafi in that it was aimed more nearly at the Libyan leader himself and his military rather than the Libyan nation as a whole.[40] Arguably the U.S. and Libya were engaged throughout the 1980s in a low-intensity military conflict spurred by Qaddafi's claims over the Gulf of Sidra, aggressive U.S. naval responses to maintain freedom of navigation, and Qaddafi's subsequent sponsorship of terrorist attacks in Europe that killed and wounded a large number of American citizens. Reagan's strike on the cities of Tripoli and Benghazi was popular because Americans perceived a morally justifiable link between Qaddafi's earlier terrorist attacks and the administration's response.[41] Obama's operation, while taken with support from the international community and successful in helping to remove Qaddafi, received a far more equivocal public reaction.

But were these actions constitutional under the "declare war" clause? Debate over Obama's operation came to focus on the meaning of the word "hostilities" in the WPR in starting the sixty-day clock. While the Obama administration did not dispute the constitutionality of the WPR, it did claim that the Libya operation, which ran over the sixty-day limit, did not constitute hostilities and thus the WPR had not been violated.[42] Although widely derided, this argument was surely an example of a rather arcane dispute over statutory interpretation substituting for a discussion that should have engaged more meaningfully with constitutional values.[43] The issue is how that discussion should proceed.

One of my purposes in writing this book is to suggest that while asking the constitutional question with respect to every single presidential military action, including those clearly short of war, may not be wholly misguided, it is certainly not very helpful. Consider that the original constitutional order was designed to handle questions concerning *war,* not intermittent military operations short of war conducted on a global basis. Contrary to what originalists may think, there is no way to generate meaningful doctrine from the original constitutional order to answer every contemporary military contingency. There is also something slightly perverse in the way the war powers debate focuses on every presidential military action as if it might be a new Vietnam. This may be an outgrowth of a common misunderstanding about the key significance of the Johnson administration's decision to Americanize the war in 1965 as compared to the incremental decisions to aid South Vietnam taken before that time. But it is nonetheless odd. As the Obama administration observed, there was nothing about the Libya operation that made it close to a war or even remotely likely that it would become one.[44]

With respect to the WPR itself, there is a sense in which the close parsing of its terms misses the point its proponents were trying to make in 1973. Prior to its passage, Congress had spent nearly seven years practically begging the executive branch to take the initiative in establishing a sounder basis for interbranch deliberation on matters of war. The response from the Nixon administration was consistently negative, indeed, intransigently so. What Congress should be asking for today is for the executive branch to consistently engage with it on matters of foreign policy and national security strategy, not to file reports to start arbitrary clocks. As I discuss below, however, doing this in a meaningful way will require Congress to change its structure, much as the executive branch was reorganized after 1945.

One practical point we should take away from the Libya operation is the difficult nature of the task we have imposed on presidents. It eventually emerged that Britain and France, America's allies in the war against al-Qaeda and the Taliban in Afghanistan, sought U.S. involvement in Libya as a kind of quid pro quo, viewing the chaos engulfing the Qaddafi regime as a security threat in their region of the world.[45] Seen in this light, Libya was not an otherwise puzzling stand-alone operation to depose a leader, but part of a broader web of national security relationships that it is the president's job to manage, often within the boundaries of diplomatic discretion. In this sense, it turned out that the Libya operation was in fact related to the war Congress authorized in Afghanistan.

By the time Obama won reelection in 2012, it was evident that the true "long war" was not the Iraq War or, strictly speaking, the War in Afghanistan, but the war against al Qaeda and its affiliates. Particularly in the Obama administration, this war extended well beyond the borders of Afghanistan to encompass drone strikes or "targeted killings" in Pakistan, Somalia, and Yemen.[46] For various reasons, the war against al Qaeda, what perhaps should be called the 9/11 War rather than the War in Afghanistan, has been a continuing source of contention and unease.

This is despite the clear authority Congress granted in the September 2001 AUMF, which provided the substantive constitutional and legal framework for striking back at those responsible for the 9/11 attacks. It authorized the president as follows:

> Use all necessary and appropriate force against those nations, organizations, or persons he determines planned, authorized, committed, or aided the terrorist attacks that occurred on September 11, 2001, or harbored such organizations or persons, in order to prevent any future acts of international terrorism against the United States by such nations, organizations or persons.[47]

The AUMF was broad in several respects. It authorized all force necessary and appropriate and applied to nonstate entities and persons as well as states. It further applied not only to the organization directly responsible for the attacks (al Qaeda) but also to those who assisted or harbored them, with the goal of preventing all future acts of terrorism. It clearly contemplated military action in multiple jurisdictions at once. In enacting the AUMF, Congress, supported by the overwhelming majority of the American people, had done everything it could think of to authorize a war or, under the terms of international law, the use of armed force.[48] Yet one undisputable fact that will undoubtedly be studied by future historians is that many distinguished observers, both international and domestic, never accepted the resulting conflict as a war or, at least, an unconventional war occurring pursuant to the terms of the AUMF.[49] What I am interested in here is how the unconventional war against al Qaeda and the criticism it has received illustrate some important themes of this book.

We might observe first the relationship between the textual obligation to authorize the war through Congress and the broader, implied value of interbranch deliberation. Although the obligation was met, the value of interbranch deliberation was undermined. The potential of the AUMF to spur public discussion was frustrated by the Bush administration's inability or refusal to use the deliberative process to think through the unconventional war it was about to launch. This was true in several senses. The administration probably did not take the congressional process as seriously as it might have because acquiescence in a strong resolution was assured. Besides, the administration never believed its authority depended on that process. As we saw in the previous chapter, the Bush administration did not accept that presidential authority to prosecute the war depended wholly on congressional authorization. The administration always argued that it had an independent line of authority to prosecute the war based in Article II. In addition, Bush stoked public expectations for an all-out "war," without paying much attention to the obvious differences between the coming unconventional war against al Qaeda and the conventional wars the U.S. had fought previously. In particular, matters such as whether the war would be fought in multiple countries, what would be done with those captured, and whether the rules of wartime would apply inside the United States were never discussed.

The Bush administration undoubtedly clouded the waters further by referring to the conflict as the "war on terror" or the "global war on terror," implying to many informed observers that the target was terrorism itself rather than organizations and persons linked to 9/11 under the AUMF. Keeping what Congress had enacted firmly in mind would have spared the public many unproductive debates. Nevertheless, there was never any doubt that Bush and Obama had a public consensus behind them in waging a war, however unconventional its methods, against al Qaeda, as well as any affiliated support groups.[50] There was also no doubt that all three branches of the national government were on record as affirming that a war was being fought against al Qaeda.[51]

This surely helps explain why critics were unable to gain any traction in their disputes with both administrations, particularly with respect to detention policies at Guantanamo Bay and so-called "targeted killings." The objections to these policies were founded largely on international law and moral considerations.[52] Arguments have been made, for example, based on worries about reciprocity. What if another country used the same tactics against the United States?[53]

The history of the Cold War can help us understand why the critics won no favor with the public. During the early Cold War when there was a public consensus behind vigorous action against the threat of communism, Americans were not impressed by arguments based on reciprocity. Americans, then and now, had a tendency to see their country as on the right side of history, both in prudential and moral terms. In the run-up to the Cuban missile crisis, for example, Americans "saw their country in a mortal struggle against a ruthless enemy" and rejected arguments based on the theory that the Soviet Union and Cuba had an equal right to defend themselves.[54] This should have a familiar ring.

The Obama administration made promises to reverse Bush administration policies, but was unable to deliver in some notable respects. The facility at Guantanamo Bay remained open and the Obama administration acted even more aggressively than the Bush administration in pursuing targeted killings against terrorists when it had a solid basis in intelligence to believe they were dangerous. The arguments of critics that this contravened international law had little influence with the public. If anything, Congress stood to the right of the administration on these matters.[55] In saying this, I am not trying to dispute the relevance of international law and the possibility of reciprocity invoked by the critics. But to avoid what might be termed a democratic deficit, these arguments should be made as appropriate within the kind of domestic deliberation that attended the AUMF, not confined to an elite international discourse.

To be sure, resting the entire burden of settling the controversies arising from the war against al Qaeda on the AUMF would not be a fully satisfactory way to proceed. After all, the Tonkin Gulf Resolution was not regarded by many as fully effective in underwriting the Vietnam War. However, it cannot be shown easily that the AUMF had the same defects. The immediate aftermath of the 9/11 attacks left few doubts about the gravity of the situation. So understood, the basic problem pointed out by the critics was that the deliberation in September 2001 had not anticipated all the possible issues that might arise in the war. But this would be an unrealistic basis on which to ignore the legal authority provided by the AUMF.

A more promising line for criticism is that neither the Bush nor the Obama administration thought through what would happen after al Qaeda's ability to strike had been significantly degraded and Osama bin Laden was killed or captured. At that point, perhaps already reached in 2011, the nature of the conflict could well be said to have changed in terms that the public could understand, which might have been a wise time to go back to Congress for another resolution, possibly to terminate the war. This would appropriately invite a public debate.[56]

Critics also charged that a continuing endless war promised an unreasonable extension of broad executive power.[57] Yet as we have seen, general worries about increased executive power based in notions of the "imperial presidency" are misplaced. After 9/11, violations of civil liberties were minor in comparison with past wars. But they were also minor relative to where the true dangers of executive leadership lay—that without proper deliberative support from Congress, policy becomes deranged. Congress and the public agreed to back a war against al Qaeda and its affiliates. This meant that the policies pursued by the executive branch would in all likelihood be well adapted to those ends. They did not anticipate or discuss, however, a war against Iraq in September 2001. As we saw in the last chapter, public support for the Iraq War depended partly on the advocacy of a false link between 9/11 and Saddam Hussein. This demonstrates once again the importance of interbranch deliberation and the relationship between the executive branch and Congress.

Starting the Cycle of Accountability

We might say that from the perspective of the president, one of the founding stones of the post-1945 order was that seeking congressional approval for the use of military force, including war, was always secondary to the duty to defend the national security of the United States. As such, it is difficult to find examples of presidents thinking of Congress *first* in the process of decisionmaking for war, except in the immediate aftermath of Korea and Vietnam. As noted earlier, Eisenhower did consult congressional leaders in the 1954 Dienbienphu crisis, and President Ford met with the leadership and called on Congress to approve a final aid package to Vietnam in 1975, because he believed he had no other choice.

Under the influence of the post-1945 order, it has been hard for presidents to visualize what useful role Congress can play in their decisionmaking process, other than of course lending unquestioning political support in the manner expected by presidents such as Johnson and Nixon. Then again, it is worth considering that this difficulty, shared by many in the foreign policy elite, is partly due to the history of presidential war making that has created a reality in which we all find it hard to imagine a way forward. This is one reason I have presented an internal critique of the post-1945 order, proceeding as if many of its assumptions, such as presidential leadership in foreign affairs, were largely sound. We must work from the inside out, as it were, in understanding how Congress could have developed a meaningful role in the genuinely new circumstances that prevailed after World War II. However odd it may seem to congressionalists, this means we must be able to articulate a place for Congress that at least in principle could make sense to presidents. Congressionalists are correct to stress the unavoidable role of Congress in the original constitutional design. But congressionalist analyses tend to be unhelpful in focusing solely on the decision for war, rather than addressing how Congress can contribute with respect to foreign policy generally, especially in light of its own institutional problems.

It has long been clear to many commentators that the real work necessary to improve the post-1945 order has to do with the structure of Congress. If the original constitutional design was premised on inter-branch deliberation, what sort of process are the branches supposed to create? This question must be answered in the context of our own time, rather than the eighteenth century. Understanding the role of constitutional orders in implementing the Constitution helps us perform this task by underscoring the relevance of the distinctive circumstances of American foreign policy after 1945. But as the previous chapters have demonstrated, the defects of the post-1945 constitutional order are manifest. Experience has shown that the executive branch is incapable of handling the deliberation necessary for decisions about war on its own. Perhaps this is what we should expect, given the tidal pull of the original constitutional order. Yet it is still striking how consistently poor executive decisionmaking for war has been in the post-1945 period.

Defenders of the presidency often stress its unitary character. With a single person at the helm, the executive branch can act quickly to address foreign crises. We can now see more clearly that when the executive branch is not subject to oversight it is too easy either for presidents to dominate their advisers, thus suppressing valuable policy input (Johnson and Nixon), or to so rearrange the White House and the executive branch that an effective policy process becomes nearly impossible (Reagan, Bush II, and possibly Kennedy, Carter, and Clinton in his first term). This supports the surprising conclusion that *a chief purpose of inter-branch deliberation is to ensure that the executive branch makes decisions for war based on a sound interagency process.* A "sound" interagency process is one that enables the president and his advisers to defend their proposal for war publicly. As we saw in the example of the Stennis hearings, congressional oversight also has the potential to counter the LBJ scenario in which the president dominates his advisers. Although this is obviously a more difficult case, such hearings can provide a public forum in which advisers have an opportunity to speak out.

This conclusion may strike some as simply a logical consequence of a system of checks and balances. Yet it is still surprising, given the overwhelming emphasis in the post-1945 order on unilateral presidential decisionmaking amid the inadequacies of Congress. But without oversight, policy in the executive branch becomes deranged. One pathway to policy disaster, seen in the Bay of Pigs and Vietnam, is along a course in which the various agencies responsible for war are never compelled to agree on a unified set of goals and the means necessary to achieve those goals. Without strong external compulsion it is too easy for the different parts of the executive branch to fall into quarreling without ever resolving their differences. When the State Department, DOD, and CIA fail to agree, the NSC process has been insufficient to create a consensus on a proposed course of policy.

While it is reasonable to assume that the nation requires a unified foreign policy, nothing in the internal architecture of the executive branch guarantees unity. This can sound surprising, because the executive branch is a hierarchy and we expect presidents to have the ability to lead. Experience shows, however, that leadership with respect to decisions for war is usually expressed either through domination involving the suppression of dissident views or by the president's unwillingness or inability to manage the many different parts of the executive branch, with their often strong-willed department heads, in a sufficiently unified manner. Striking the appropriate balance has been difficult for presidents who, after all, are expert politicians, not expert managers.

Another pathway to disaster occurs through the proven difficulty for the executive branch of determining war aims. Understandably the president and his advisers tend to respond to the exigencies of the moment, rather than concerning themselves with how a given military operation relates to the grand strategy of the U.S. in foreign affairs. The executive branch does not have any inherent or unique ability to relate short-term responses to long-term goals. George Kennan's hope that the State Department's Policy Planning Staff would perform this function for the executive branch as a whole never came to fruition.[58] As we saw with the 1991 Gulf War, this inability to justify a war in terms of long-term goals can even run contrary to the president's own political interests, which would seem to give presidents a good reason for paying attention to the role of interbranch deliberation.

One purpose of the cycle of accountability is thus to test the executive branch's claims with respect to war and foreign affairs in a way that works to the advantage of both branches and the nation as a whole. As noted in Chapter 4, it is not necessary to assume anything about the policy knowledge of members of Congress or the quality of congressional hearings to appreciate that a world in which the executive branch is required to regularly justify itself in public provides a significant incentive for the president to insist on a unified approach to policy.[59] In the Iran-contra affair, the obligation of Reagan administration principals to testify before Congress at a crucial stage of the scandal made officials realize that they did not have the full story.[60] It is not hard to see how repeated iterations of oversight would build up congressional expertise in foreign policy and thus begin a meaningful cycle of accountability whereby each branch would learn over time.

There is another way to understand the purpose of congressional oversight. There is a reasonable amount of evidence that presidents have made decisions for war based in part on considerations of domestic politics. This is the "intermestic" dimension or relationship between the international and domestic highlighted by Campbell Craig and Fredrik Logevall in Chapter 5.[61] Examples are not hard to find. Truman's decision to go north of the 38th parallel is one.[62] Historians have argued persuasively that LBJ was concerned with various consequences for his domestic political standing if he failed to make a commitment to Vietnam and became responsible for "losing" a war.[63] If presidents are concerned with domestic matters when they make decisions for war, no one would argue that Congress, as the most representative institution in government, is ill-equipped to help them make those decisions.

Despite the sense in which everyone accepts oversight as a traditional function of Congress, it is noteworthy that there was no strong tradition of external review established in the early Cold War. As discussed in Chapter 3, the situation with respect to the CIA eventually became notorious, with a small group of senators handling oversight on a basis akin to a private club.[64] But the situation with respect to foreign affairs in general was little better, with many hearings and exchanges held in executive session or off the books in private gatherings. While it is a mistake to think that the congressional leadership had no influence over foreign policy, the lack of *public* oversight meant that the proper incentives were never provided to executive branch agencies. As Robert Johnson recounts, later in the Cold War the influence of the Senate Foreign Relations Committee waned in comparison with the growing power of the Armed Services Committee.[65] This further undermined executive accountability and was emblematic of the dominant militarized approach to the Cold War.

Although the executive branch was retooled to a certain extent for Cold War duty after 1947, nothing was done to the structure of Congress. Members of Congress assumed that the existing committee structure would suffice. Eventually the costs of this approach became apparent, at least with respect to intelligence policy. The intelligence reforms of the 1970s established committees to oversee the intelligence community. The subsequent difficulties with implementing this oversight have been well analyzed by a number of scholars and presidential commissions, including the 9/11 Commission. Some of the ignored proposals of the 9/11 Commission had to do with changes to congressional oversight of intelligence.[66] What oversight exists has been rendered less effective by the use of term limits for service on the intelligence committees and the fact that budgetary authority is located elsewhere.[67] As Amy Zegart concluded in her study of Congress, the intelligence community, and 9/11:

> It was no secret that this fragmented oversight system desperately needed fixing. Restructuring the Congress was recommended in seven of the twelve intelligence and terrorism studies between 1991 and 2001. Yet Congress never acted. In fact, Congress was the only government entity that failed to implement a single recommendation for reform during the decade—a record worse than either the CIA's or the FBI's.[68]

If Congress can reform itself, the major wars since 1945 show that effective interbranch deliberation is pragmatically possible. Despite advances in technology, the advice given to FDR highlighted in Chapter 2 is still sound—only land armies win wars. Because American armies have been fighting far from home in the post–World War II period, considerable time has been required to transport them to the theatre of conflict and assemble the necessarily enormous amount of supply material. Aside from true surprises such as the Cuban missile crisis, there has always been plenty of time for interbranch deliberation over the decision to go to war.

This has not always been highlighted by presidents. In Korea, many weeks were required before the Inchon landing and break-out from the Pusan perimeter became possible. In Vietnam, it took two years for General Westmoreland to assemble the supply chain necessary to support the conventional military operations he envisioned in 1965.[69] The buildup required to simply provide an effective defense for Saudi Arabia (Operation Desert Shield) in the Gulf War took seventeen weeks. Additional weeks were required to attain an offensive capability. Months were required after 9/11 before there were sufficient regular armed forces in Afghanistan to conduct meaningful operations, and the same was true for the Iraq War. The fact of a crisis or apparent emergency that arguably requires a military response does not mean that there is little time for proper deliberation. For a major war, the time is always there if we wish to use it.

The Difference Parties Make

Many analyses of presidential war power end here, with the author exhorting Congress to reclaim its proper place in the constitutional order. But we should mistrust being satisfied with the sort of analysis the founding generation would have found familiar, by speaking only of the president and Congress and their separate responsibilities. We must take into account modern political parties, which did not exist in the eighteenth century. Constitutional scholars have attempted to describe the difference political parties make to the eighteenth-century system of separation of powers, with specific reference to periods of unified and divided government.[70] Periods of unified government presumably give the president as party leader greater leeway in domestic and foreign affairs.[71] At the same time, they have noticed that in foreign affairs Congress seems to avoid responsibility regardless of which party controls Congress or whether government is unified or divided. Daryl Levinson and Richard Pildes have argued that this avoidance presumably reflects "the relatively low material stakes of congressional constituencies and the high level of risk aversion among incumbent legislators. Since World War II, Congress has preferred to let the President lead the country into war, eventually either jumping on the bandwagon or turning critical depending on how events played out."[72] Levinson and Pildes observe that the existence of unified government after 9/11 helped explain the striking lack of congressional action with respect to the war on terror.[73]

The analysis would be easier if the parties' views on presidential war powers were symmetrical. But they are not. As we saw in Chapter 5, when the Cold War "consensus" broke up, the party consensus on presidential power did as well. Elements in the congressional wing of the Democratic Party still defend the WPR and warn of the dangers of the "imperial presidency." While some Republicans attempted to wield the WPR as a club against President Obama when he launched his Libya operation in 2011, it should be recalled that House Republicans attempted to repeal the WPR in 1995. Scholars have shown that the Republicans made their peace with executive power in the 1970s. This consensus on strong presidential leadership was only solidified by the Iran-contra affair, which was seen as a partisan attack on President Reagan. By contrast, unified government in the first two years of the Obama administration did not spare the president from critics in his own party who wanted him to move faster on ending the wars in Iraq and Afghanistan, investigating the abuses of the Bush II presidency, and closing the detainee prison at Guantanamo Bay.[74]

This suggests that unified Republican government means broad support for the exercise of presidential power, including the war power. This was clearly demonstrated by the Bush II presidency. Republicans seemed to resist the very idea of holding the president accountable, perhaps partly out of a loss of institutional identity in Congress.[75] By contrast, government unified under the Democrats does not give the president the same open field. As discussed in Chapter 6, the Clinton and Obama administrations featured OLC opinions which accepted that congressional approval was constitutionally mandated in the case of a "real" war. To be sure, this was a rather minimal concession on the part of the executive branch. Yet there is no evidence that a future Republican administration would agree that presidential authority is so limited.

One additional problem in starting the cycle of accountability is that to the extent members of Congress accept the notion, they interpret it in partisan terms. Accountability is appropriate only when an opposition president has failed. Thus, congressional Democrats were more willing to consider war powers measures while the Vietnam War was still ongoing when Republicans controlled the White House. Nixon was not entirely wrong to think that some of the high-minded "constitutional" concerns about his use of presidential power were motivated by partisanship.

Once we introduce the variable of party competition into foreign affairs, imagining how to start the cycle of accountability thus becomes considerably more difficult. But the true difficulty is that it has been hard for congressionalist critics to accept that creating a cycle of accountability in the new circumstances of the Cold War would have required not only changes to executive branch behavior, but also significant alterations to the structure of Congress to create a joint decisionmaking process.

Here we do not have to stipulate that the structure of Congress would have to be made over to resemble the unitary structure of the executive branch. Yet without some acceptance of centralized decision-making in foreign policy, there is unlikely to be a path forward. As we observed in Chapter 5, President Ford had a sound point when he asked who he was supposed to consult with in responding to the requirements of the WPR. To provide effective advice to the executive branch in the Cold War would have meant centralizing control over foreign affairs in the congressional leadership and one committee in each house (possibly one joint committee), sustaining the commitment to centralization over decades of inevitable ups and downs in foreign policy, and sharing the political success and pain with the president. Because members of Congress would naturally not want to share the pain, this sort of institutional architecture implies (1) a much greater degree of centralization of authority in the leadership than has ever been possible combined with (2) a widespread commitment to a norm that foreign policy and national security, including decisions for war, are part of every member's portfolio of responsibilities. It is emblematic of Congress's view of its role in foreign policy in both the Cold War and post–Cold War periods that no member of either party has ever proposed such measures.

Suppose in the future a cooperative president and Congress created a minimally effective cycle of accountability. The president would reject the "Korea precedent" and accept that he or she has no Article II authority to order the nation into war. The president would know that a decision for war must be approved by Congress in advance *and* that this decision is binding. What this means is that presidents would have to conduct diplomacy and carry out national security strategy with the knowledge that they always have to maintain their position with Congress. In turn, this would require Congress to so organize itself to be able to give the president the assurance of support such a strategy would require. We might observe that post-1945 conditions in foreign policy suggested the desirability of a quasi-parliamentary style of government.

In the war powers debate what congressionalists have really wanted is to preserve Congress's option to say no and have that decision stick. While that option would formally exist under the system we are imagining, Nicholas Katzenbach, the former attorney general and under secretary of state whose Vietnam War testimony we examined in Chapters 1 and 4, suggests the practical problems with such an approach. Because there is no clear way to relieve presidents of their duty to lead in foreign affairs and defend the national security of the

United States, a threat assessed by the executive branch as genuine would mean the issue of war would immediately become the administration's most important policy priority. In these circumstances, Katzenbach points out that the administration has every unfortunate incentive to exaggerate the evidence of the threat and minimize the risks of military action.[76] Indeed, the administration *must* win the policy battle. An administration that did not prevail on a war vote might well be crippled politically in the aftermath. Even in a world where parties did not exist or the president could not count on the ready support of his own party, there is an obvious asymmetry between the time, energy, and information available to key members of an administration as compared to members of Congress.

This reasoning suggests that the congressionalist position in the war powers debate has been based implicitly on the assumption that ordinary politics can be removed from decisions to go to war. Nothing in the American experience suggests this is correct. Once we allow parties back into the picture, Katzenbach's analysis applies with greater force. The president's party will typically support him or her in arguing for war. The opposition is likely to be divided and confused. If the executive branch had conceded throughout the Cold War that Congress had a right of first refusal on whether to go to war, it is hard to know what would have occurred other than the president would have had the support of his party.

Where it would have made a difference is in terms of the acceptance of responsibility and a reckoning with the burdens of history. The idea of a cycle of accountability is about process, not outcome. No process can be devised to avoid all policy mistakes or even policy disasters. Besides locating accountability where it belongs—in both branches—the idea of a cycle is to build expertise over time so that appropriate lessons are learned by both branches and both parties. While making it more difficult for members of Congress to shirk responsibility, the cycle should have this effect on the public as well. As we saw with Korea in Chapter 2, the conflict could be written off as "Truman's war." This meant it was easier for the public to simply forget about it. A cycle of accountability would bring to the forefront the hidden assumption of the WPR we observed in Chapter 5—that the president should not be able to go to war unless conditions are favorable in Congress. This would create a situation in which the president would be carefully cultivating Congress throughout his or her administration in order to preserve the political capital necessary in case a threat to national security arose. This process would naturally tend to increase congressional awareness and knowledge of the administration's foreign policy in general. And it is worth noting that building experience is easier for members of Congress—unlike presidents, members are not term-limited.

At present, this vision is likely to be more appealing to Democrats than Republicans. The approach of the Bush II administration was to assume that their conservative-dominated party in Congress would support the president down the line. But both parties have a role to play if we are to increase the role of interbranch deliberation in foreign affairs. There may be some Republicans who appreciate that the costs of deference to executive power include a lack of feedback that accentuates the problems that inherently afflict the decisionmaking process in the executive branch. On the other side, the inadequate scrutiny the Bush II administration received in the run-up to the Iraq War showed that congressional Democrats made the country pay a heavy price for their almost instinctive aversion to foreign policy and the use of armed force, their limited knowledge about military matters, and their lack of credibility on national security issues. Change on all of these fronts is desirable before congressional Democrats can play the role of a steady balance wheel in the constitutional order.

Beyond the Imperial (Triumphal) Presidency

Despite referring to the concept of the "imperial presidency" throughout this book, I have not engaged with it directly, save for the discussion in Chapter 2. However, I have provided a narrative and analysis of presidential decisionmaking with respect to war and allied matters in foreign affairs in the post-1945 period. I regard this account as an improvement and an alternative to the somewhat stale critique of the imperial presidency. To the extent that concerns about the imperial presidency are driven by accurate analysis of presidential violations of civil liberties and abuses of power, there is little to criticize. Otherwise the critique is played out and of little help in understanding presidential power in foreign affairs. In this section I will contrast the account I have provided with some leading critiques as well as celebrations of executive power. This will serve to clarify and advance further the arguments I have made in the preceding chapters.

Executive Doubters

In 1967, reflecting on the governmental crisis caused by the Vietnam War, liberal historian Arthur Schlesinger remarked in his journal:

> The irony is that all of us for years have been defending the presidential prerogative and regarding the Congress as a drag on policy. It is evident now that this delight in a strong presidency was based on the fact that, up to now, all strong Presidents in American history have pursued policies of which one has approved. We are now confronted by the anomaly of a strong President using these arguments to pursue a course which, so far as I can see, can lead only to disaster.[77]

Schlesinger meant that liberals had favored a strong presidency not only from the example of effective leadership provided by FDR, but also to defend the Roosevelt and Truman administrations against the critique of presidential power advanced by the "Old Guard" of the Republican Party. Schlesinger later wrote the well-received book *The Imperial Presidency,* which joined together Vietnam and Watergate, the two most prominent crises of presidential power in the post–World War II era.[78] Schlesinger's critique of the imperial presidency has been a durable part of our constitutional culture for several decades, so much so that the controversial exercises of power in the Bush II administration were widely discussed within this framework.[79]

It may not be remembered that Schlesinger, who served in the Kennedy administration, began his book by endorsing "presidential primacy" as "indispensable to the political order."[80] No one who had seen Cold War episodes such as the Cuban missile crisis up close could doubt the essential role of the president in providing leadership in foreign affairs. Nevertheless, he maintained that the constitutional order was badly out of balance and that this was as much the fault of Congress as of imperial presidents.[81] He argued for a middle ground between the imperial presidency and a weakened presidency: "we need a strong Presidency—but a strong Presidency *within the Constitution.*"[82]

Schlesinger drew a number of distinctions that demonstrated he was not making a wholesale case against the exercise of presidential power in time of danger. He believed Presidents Lincoln and Roosevelt had acted properly in the crises that led to the Civil War and World War II.[83] In fact, Schlesinger *opposed* the WPR on policy grounds because he thought it would have prevented presidents such as FDR from taking actions necessary to preserve national security.[84] Perhaps it is not surprising that, apart from some discussion of Korea and the *Steel Seizure* case, he said relatively little about Truman, Eisenhower, and Kennedy's use of war powers and covert action. By contrast, Schlesinger reserved special treatment and scorn for Johnson and Nixon.[85] In Schlesinger's view only Lyndon Johnson qualified as an imperial president. Richard Nixon had gone beyond even the imperial, and was denominated a "revolutionary" president because of his abuses of power and for moving to a "plebiscitary Presidency."[86]

How had this happened? Schlesinger explained the rise of the imperial presidency after observing that Eisenhower, a president opposed to the accumulation of power in the executive, was forced to act in an imperial way. Schlesinger therefore posited that deeper forces were at work. While his explanation was not systematic, it touched on a number of the aspects of what I have called the post-1945 constitutional order. Schlesinger argued that the traditional separation of powers was overcome after World War II by concern about the communist threat.[87] In the 1950s "American foreign policy called on the American government to do things no American government had ever tried to do before."[88] There was a sense of "omnipresent crisis."[89] The very fact of a permanent standing army increased presidential power. Nuclear weapons and the necessity of covert operations seemed to dictate presidential leadership in war.[90] The Constitution began to totter under the unceasing burden of "indiscriminate globalism."[91] He concluded: "This vision of the American role in the world unbalanced and overwhelmed the Constitution."[92]

Schlesinger's attempt to explain the imperial presidency raised many questions. If these were in fact changes to the Constitution, how exactly had they occurred? Of course, no amendments had been adopted and there was no judicial doctrine to study. Evidently, Schlesinger was referring to the *practice* of the separation of powers. But if these changes were made as matters of practice by Congress and presidents acting in good faith, how could Schlesinger be sure that they violated the Constitution? Paradoxically, Schlesinger endorsed the living Constitution and downplayed the relevance of the original constitutional order.[93] This created an analytical difficulty. Why couldn't these developments be considered reasonable adaptations of the Constitution to new circumstances? In addition, if these changes had been set in motion by the Cold War, why would they have not affected all post-1945 presidencies starting with

Truman? Why hadn't the presidency turned imperial before Vietnam? These methodological problems afflicted Schlesinger's account because he lacked a systematic account of constitutional change.

Moreover, by focusing so much attention on Johnson and Nixon, Schlesinger left no room for understanding why the imperial presidency might last beyond them. He sailed with the consensus prevailing in the early 1970s that the presidency had acquired too much power.[94] Had Schlesinger extended his account to the Ford administration, he would have had a difficult time accounting for its attempt to reinvigorate executive power, including the maneuvering by conservatives recounted in Chapter 5 that undermined the 1975 intelligence investigations. Schlesinger thought Watergate had terminated Nixon's revolutionary presidency and "reinvigorated the constitutional separation of powers."[95] He asserted that Vietnam had destroyed the idea, influential after World War II, that "foreign policy must be trusted to the executive"[96] and "it was hard to see why any future President would ever wish to go to war without Congress beside him as a genuine and definite partner in the decision."[97] Events would soon show that conservatives and Republican presidents did not agree with this quintessentially liberal analysis of the lessons of Vietnam and Watergate.

Schlesinger was right to identify the early Cold War as a period of key significance for the Constitution. Because there were extraordinary uses of presidential power that he was willing to defend, however, his account left it unclear how "presidential primacy" had morphed into the imperial presidency. How had the Constitution changed in such a short span of time? It was inherently difficult for Schlesinger to provide an answer given his interpretive methodology, which emphasized the centrality of the living Constitution. As a consequence, he could not provide a stable normative baseline by which to judge the actions of post-1945 presidents. The promising structural explanation Schlesinger advanced was overwhelmed in the end by his disagreements with Johnson and Nixon over foreign policy and his revulsion at their abuses of power.

There is surely nothing wrong with calling attention to abuses of power committed by the executive branch. But the analysis Schlesinger did not provide has also eluded his legions of followers—how we are to understand claims that the presidency is *too* powerful. The question can always be asked: relative to what baseline? The failure to address this conundrum meant that subsequent critiques of the imperial presidency were reduced to long lists of how presidents have supposedly increased or abused their power without much analysis of why or attention to the appropriate baseline for comparison.

What the many critiques of the imperial presidency lack is a sufficiently rich historical context. Almost every critique, including Schlesinger's, lacks a forthright account of how the presidency became more powerful in World War II and the early Cold War. As I argued in Chapter 2, any reasonable history would make clear that presidents had plenty of help in making the presidency supreme in matters of foreign policy and national security, including war. The increase in the power of the presidency that was an essential part of the post-1945 constitutional order had a democratic basis. Presidents Truman, Eisenhower, and Kennedy, who Schlesinger thought had generally made defensible national security decisions, were just as "imperial" in this respect as their successors. As I argued in Chapter 4, there is something to the idea that Johnson and Nixon were uniquely undemocratic in their approach to foreign affairs. Yet the assumptions behind their exercise of presidential power in foreign policy were little different from those of their predecessors.

In 1973, Schlesinger believed that Watergate had terminated the imperial presidency. But how could that be the end of the post-1945 order if the president had not been relieved of his duty to lead in foreign affairs and defend the national security of the United States? Perhaps liberal Democrats like Schlesinger believed that henceforth Congress and the president would cooperate in foreign policy. But this ignored the asymmetrical position of the parties with respect to the lessons of Vietnam. As we saw in Chapter 5, Democrats believed there were important lessons to be learned. Republicans in the Ford and Reagan administrations did not agree, at least not with respect to presidential power.

Contemporary critiques of the imperial presidency strike a wrong note in ignoring the solid base of the post-1945 constitutional order in concerns about threats to national security. They also ignore the obvious inability of Congress to contribute meaningfully to national security policy, at least without major structural reforms. It is noteworthy that regardless of their political commitments, diplomatic historians agree that the congressional "resurgence" in foreign policy of the 1970s pretty much ended in a number of telling fiascos, although they are little remembered today.[98] It turned out that giving an unreconstructed Congress a greater role in foreign policy meant furnishing individual

headstrong members great leeway, a situation providing little improvement over existing executive branch efforts. Obsessing over the imperial presidency turned out to be a good way to avoid thinking seriously about foreign policy, which not surprisingly has been a near-constant issue for liberals and Democrats since Vietnam. In turn, this failure meant that when decisions for war came along, such as the Iraq War decision in 2002, Democrats in Congress were unprepared. While I hope that this book has demonstrated that significant and very troubling constitutional issues are posed by the exercise of presidential war powers, there is little in the contemporary critiques of the imperial presidency that helps us understand the origins of these problems or how we might address them in the future.

Executive Enthusiasts

The deeply problematic legacy of the post-1945 constitutional order cannot be addressed solely through a critique of presidential power. At the same time, that legacy cannot be wished away by exalting the presidency. As we have seen, one common reaction to the extraordinary exercise of presidential power by the Bush II administration was a revival of concern about the imperial presidency. Yet the novel threat posed by al Qaeda impelled some legal scholars in the opposite direction.[99]

In *Crisis and Command* John Yoo, discussed in previous chapters as a presidentialist scholar and author of the "torture memo," has compiled a narrative of the Cold War that covers the same ground I analyzed in the preceding chapters, although his discussion is more limited. I say limited because Yoo's account of the Cold War is at best partial. The significance of the book is in showing what has to be emphasized or omitted in order to provide a consistently pro-executive view of recent history. What changes have to be made in order to support the claim that presidents have performed well in war and foreign affairs?

We should note first that Yoo treats the Cold War as one continuous period of "existential threat," running together many different developments.[100] In particular he ignores the substantial differences distinguishing the early Cold War, the era of détente, and the twilight of the Cold War in the 1980s. Among Yoo's omissions, like many legal scholars, he emphasizes the primacy of presidential decisionmaking, discounting entirely Congress's role in the early Cold War.[101] But the reality is that

Congress was there for the entire ride and, as we noticed in Chapters 2 and 3, Truman and Eisenhower had to work hard to bring its members along. Tellingly, Yoo does not mention Eisenhower's consultation with congressional leaders during the 1954 Dienbienphu crisis or that it limited the options he and Secretary of State Dulles were developing.[102] He does not discuss the Vietnam War or Watergate in any detail, thus missing the foreign policy connections between them identified in Chapter 4.[103] Not surprisingly, the overall effect of these omissions is one-sided history.

Consistent with the presidentialist position we have explored throughout this book, Yoo states that "cooperation between the President and Congress on national security policy is politically desirable, but it has never been constitutionally necessary."[104] This is an accurate summary of one element of the post-1945 constitutional order and it has been the stance of all presidents since Truman. Indeed, Lyndon Johnson and Richard Nixon could not have put it better. It is this stance that directly conflicted with the original constitutional order and thus has produced the policy disasters of the post-1945 period. Presidential leadership in foreign policy has been read as primacy in the powers of war. Presidents have believed that it was their sole duty to defend the United States and that the commander in chief power gave them the power to go to war. This belief has had the effect of imposing the weaknesses of the executive branch on the rest of the government as well as the polity as a whole. Referring to the Tonkin Gulf Resolution, Yoo argues that Vietnam shows that "[c]ongressional participation is no guarantee against poor judgment, ineffective tactics, or just bad luck."[105] Amazingly, Yoo bypasses Johnson's deliberate concealment of the Americanization of the war from Congress and the public in 1965. With no effective democratic participation in these decisions, the Johnson administration eventually suffered from a "credibility gap." As the discussion in Chapter 4 demonstrated, Nixon was no better. This undemocratic approach with respect to crucial foreign affairs decisions makes no impression on Yoo.

Yoo and I agree that the Korean War was justified as a matter of policy and that the public opposed the expansion of communism.[106] But Yoo's presidentialist bias renders invisible the real costs that Truman incurred by making the decision to intervene without Congress. Those costs, explored at length in Chapter 2, were both constitutional and political. Yoo contends that the U.S. avoided another great power conflict similar to World War II through "the stewardship of Presidents from Truman through George H. W. Bush." The favorable end of the Cold War "was not produced by a system where Congress generally controls foreign and national security policy."[107] We should take cover from this hailstorm of non sequiturs. While there were periods when American officials feared that another general war would break out, no reputable scholar argues that this was likely during the entire period of the Cold War. Similarly, few argue that Congress does or should control foreign policy. What responsible commentators did argue during the Cold War and after was that policymaking under the Constitution must be a joint process and that Congress is the gatekeeper with respect to decisions for war.

In contrast to Yoo's historical argument, Eric Posner and Adrian Vermeule have recently provided a provocative theoretical grounding for executive enthusiasm.[108] They present a tightly woven argument that challenges what they describe as the "Madisonian" understanding of separation of powers. Their target, which they call "liberal legalism," is the idea that the executive can be constrained primarily through legal means, including the constitutional law promulgated by judges as well as statutes passed by Congress.[109] While their argument is wide-ranging, extending to administrative law and "global liberal legalism," my comments here are directed at the parts of their argument most nearly relevant to war and foreign affairs.

Posner and Vermeule's basic approach is well illustrated by their treatment of the WPR. Here was a statute passed by Congress in order to constrain the power of the executive to go to war. Posner and Vermeule dismiss the WPR as a dead letter and point out that it can hardly be said to have fulfilled its purpose.[110] Although the discussion of the WPR in Chapters 5 and 6 (and its invocation in the Libya controversy) shows that the picture is more complicated than Posner and Vermeule allow, there is no doubt that the political constraint of "no more Vietnams" was far more effective at limiting presidential options. This is a good example of the point Posner and Vermeule are trying to make. Because Congress is always behind the rapid decisionmaking of the president and the light-footedness of the executive branch when it comes to thinking up rationales for avoiding laws like the WPR, it is bootless to attempt to tie down the executive through legal means. Their examples of effective constraints on the executive all relate to politics and public opinion rather than fundamental law and interbranch interaction.[111] This is what they mean by the failure of the "Madisonian" republic.

Somewhat oddly, while Posner and Vermeule have plenty to say about how constitutions and laws fail to constrain the executive, they offer little about whether and how constitutions constitute the government. This is not a play on words, as scholars in many disciplines have contributed to our understanding of how constitutions make a government.[112] To take a simple point, Posner and Vermeule refer to "the executive," but how do they know who that is? The executive is constituted by the Constitution itself, through an election system specified in the text, which has been filled out by statutes. The executive is also constituted by its powers. We have seen how crucial the textual power of "commander in chief" has been to post-1945 presidents, who have used this power along with new capacities for action (created by law) to gain additional power for the executive branch. As we have seen, starting with Korea presidential power was built on *legal* claims, not solely on political maneuvering.

This straightforward point can be turned on Posner and Vermeule. If presidents have exercised powers given to them by the Constitution, that leaves them vulnerable to charges that they have exceeded their power. Impeachment is a constraint specified in the Constitution, available when presidents abuse their power. To be sure, it was not thought to be effective prior to the Nixon impeachment. But no one can doubt in the wake of the Nixon and Clinton impeachments that Congress can use this power. Posner and Vermeule do not say much about the effect the Nixon impeachment had on subsequent presidents.[113] Reagan's supporters worried about the prospect of impeachment during the Iran-contra affair, for example.[114] This shows that a constraint specified in the Constitution can have lasting effects. But Posner and Vermeule's model does not allow for this.

There is arguably a subtle bias in the Posner and Vermeule analysis. They criticize the eighteenth-century "Madisonian" view of how an executive should be constrained. But why constrain the executive at all? Here Posner and Vermeule confine themselves to critiquing what might be called an eighteenth-century view of the dangers posed by the executive—chiefly the threat to civil liberties and the possibility, which they rightly discount, that the term-limited democratically elected president might somehow become a tyrant.[115] But they do not consider reasons for caution about the executive branch connected with our twentieth-century experience in war and foreign affairs. They believe one fatal problem with liberal legalism is that Congress can never catch up with emergencies. By the very nature of emergencies, rules cannot be created in advance to handle them. By contrast, the executive is well suited to handling fast-changing situations—"in emergencies, only the executive can supply new policies and real-world action with sufficient speed to manage events."[116]

While this is superficially plausible, it will have a strange ring to anyone who lived through Hurricane Katrina in 2005. Of course, this does not mean Congress somehow would have done better. Posner and Vermeule's analysis is appropriately comparative. The fact that the executive inevitably makes mistakes and fails sometimes does not show that liberal legalism is a workable alternative. What Posner and Vermeule do not consider is the steady tidal influence, amply demonstrated by the analysis I have presented, of the original constitutional order. That order both constitutes the executive and legislative branches and constrains their actions and arguments. Of course, my argument has been that the original order was altered substantially by the post-1945 constitutional order, an order at variance with the original design. But the influence of the original order remains.

Because Posner and Vermeule do not consider how constitutional orders work, they miss the significance of the original Constitution. My argument has concerned war and foreign affairs. But it supports the general inference that the original design made it difficult for either branch to devise good policy on its own. Sound policy with respect to war requires the branches to cooperate. Although political parties have made such cooperation more difficult in times of divided government, parties are an example of how constitutional change tends to add to rather than completely replace the original constitutional order.[117] The discussion in this book has shown that policymaking in the executive branch becomes deranged without the oversight and input of Congress. Posner and Vermeule have no way to account for this because they assume that the executive branch is generally competent not only to execute the law in a narrow sense, but also to make policy on its own. Strangely, they do not consider the generally poor record of the executive branch with respect to war in the post-1945 period. This period is littered not simply with mistakes, but with policy catastrophes, some of which undermined the stability of the government as a whole.

It is also noteworthy that Posner and Vermeule focus on the *executive branch* without managing to say much about the person of the *president* or how the president runs the White House. Whether you describe Watergate and Iran-contra as scandals or constitutional crises, these episodes make no impression on the Posner-Vermeule analysis. That cannot be right. As I have shown, these crises were closely related to the unstable nature of the post-1945 order, as the government struggled to reconcile its new global responsibilities with the original constitutional order. Moreover, the post–World War II experience showed that the president was incapable of managing the tasks of war without the support of Congress.

Briefly stated, the biggest problem with the arguments of these executive enthusiasts is that they reflect pre-Vietnam understandings of how the executive branch makes decisions in foreign policy. It is as if the substantial and closely documented historical scholarship on the Vietnam War (not to mention Iraq as well) has made no impression. These scholars continue to treat the executive branch as if it were a black box full of the "best and the brightest"—knowledgeable experts willing to make hard choices and swift, yet measured and effective decisions.[118] History shows differently.

Writing the Constitution into History

At the beginning of the book I noted that one could read many pages of Cold War history without encountering a discussion of the influence of the Constitution upon events. How does the Constitution influence history in the absence of judicial decisions? We should now have a better understanding. Even in the nonlegalized sphere, without the benefit of Supreme Court decisions, the Constitution retains its power as supreme law. As such, it exerts a causal effect, the influence I have referred to as "tidal." The tidal influence of the Constitution comes from the persistence of the original constitutional order. At the formation of this order, we might say that the Constitution was ineluctably imprinted on the structure of the state. Certainly members of the founding generation such as Hamilton, Madison, and Jefferson cared deeply about ensuring that the Constitution was implemented. That is one of the reasons they argued so often, sometimes bitterly, about what it meant.

What of today?

During the Cold War, the question whether the United States should use the tactics of the enemy came up repeatedly. We should recall the

Doolittle report quoted in Chapter 2 that warned Americans they had to stand ready to violate long-held principles and beliefs in order to win the struggle against communism. In this sense, the debate after 9/11 over the use of torture to fight terrorism was nothing new. But the Cold War provided overlooked evidence that Americans are simply not very good at using the tactics of the enemy because they live in the country the Constitution helped create. Growing up in the United States does not typically harden or desensitize citizens to legal and moral considerations in the way that would be necessary to routinely use brutal tactics. At the height of the Cold War, during a period of extreme tension, even agents of the CIA, often assumed to operate on the far side of the law, expressed moral and legal qualms about what they were asked to do in service of their country. As we saw in Chapter 3, once CIA personnel began running sabotage operations against Cuba from Florida, they began to wonder whether such operations were truly, well, constitutional. After 9/11, it was FBI agents and JAG officers who stepped forward and expressed opposition to the use of torture.[119]

The Constitution has always been an available text which ordinary citizens believe they can understand. Most citizens and certainly most government personnel know that the Constitution is a law that the government must respect, not merely a list of aspirations. They worried about its requirements and raised their hands to object even when they were ordered to do otherwise during periods commonly regarded as genuine emergencies. That is some comfort amid occasional misguided efforts to turn the United States into another kind of country.

When reviewing the record of the United States in world affairs since 1945, we should consider the tragedy of the constitutional order left to us by the Cold War. Presidents made many indefensible decisions ordering the armed forces to war. But they had a lot of help. They made such decisions under the aegis of the post-1945 constitutional order in foreign affairs. That order did have a democratic foundation. While responsibility runs principally to the presidents and their advisers, it runs also to Congress and to us.

Imagine crossing the Potomac toward Arlington after visiting the war memorials on the Mall. What should we say to those silent markers? Surely we can rise up tomorrow and do better.

Appendix

Executive Branch War Powers Opinions since 1950

U.S. Dept. of State, "Authority of the President To Repel the Attack in Korea" (July 3, 1950), in 23 *Dep't St. Bull.* 173 (1950).

Staff of Joint Committee Made Up of Committee on Foreign Relations and Committee on Armed Services of the Senate, 82d Cong., "Report on the Powers of the President to Send the Armed Forces outside the United States" (1951).

Memorandum from Legal Adviser Leonard Meeker, June 25, 1964, on file at Lyndon Baines Johnson Library and Museum, Austin, TX, NSF Country File: Vietnam 7B 1965–1968, Legality Considerations.

Memorandum from Legal Adviser Leonard Meeker, February 11, 1965, on file at Lyndon Baines Johnson Library and Museum, Austin, TX, NSF Country File: Vietnam 7B 1965–1968, Legality Considerations.

Memorandum from Legal Adviser Leonard Meeker, April 6, 1965, on file at Lyndon Baines Johnson Library and Museum, Austin, TX, NSF Country File: Vietnam 7B 1965–1968, Legality Considerations.

Memorandum from Attorney General Katzenbach to President Johnson, June 10, 1965, U.S. Dept. of State, *Foreign Relations of the United States, Vietnam: January-June 1965* 751 (1996).

Memorandum from Legal Adviser Leonard Meeker, June 11, 1965, on file at Lyndon Baines Johnson Library and Museum, Austin, TX, NSF Country File: Vietnam 7B 1965–1968, Legality Considerations.

U.S. Dept. of State, "The Legality of United States Participation in the Defense of Viet-Nam," 54 *Dep't State Bull.* 474 (1966), *reprinted in* "Symposium, Legality of United States Participation in the Viet Nam Conflict," 75 *Yale L.J.* 1084 (1966).

Memorandum fromWilliam H. Rehnquist, Assistant Att'y Gen., Office of Legal Counsel, "The President and the War Power: South Vietnam and the Cambodian Sanctuaries," to Charles W. Colson, Special Counsel to the President, May 22, 1970, on file at Nixon Presidential Library and Museum, Yorba Linda, CA, White House Special Files: Staff Member and Office Files: Charles W. Colson; Box 42; Cambodia, Accordion Folder II: Cambodia Legal Briefs [1 of 2].

Memorandum from Elliot Richardson, Attorney General, to Roy L. Ash, Oct. 18, 1973, on file at Nixon Presidential Library and Museum, Yorba Linda, CA, White House Central Files, Subject Files, FE (Federal Government) 4-1, 10/1/73–11/30/73, Box 6.

Veto of the War Powers Resolution, 1973 *Public Papers of the Presidents* 893 (Oct. 24, 1973).

Statement of Monroe Leigh, State Department Legal Adviser, *War Powers: A Test of Compliance Relative to the Danang Sealift, the Evacuation at Phnom Penh, the Evacuation of Saigon and the Mayaguez Incident: Hearings before the Subcommittee on International Security and Scientific Affairs of the H. Committee on International Relations*, 94th Cong. 95 (1975).

"Presidential Power to Use the Armed Forces Abroad without Statutory Authorization," 4A Op. O.L.C. 185 (1980).

"Overview of the War Powers Resolution," 8 Op. O.L.C. 271 (1984).

Memorandum from C. Boyden Gray to President George Bush, Aug. 7, 1990, on file at George Bush Presidential Library and Museum, College

Station, TX, John Sununu Files, OA/ID 29166-008, Persian Gulf War 1991 [6].

Memorandum from C. Boyden Gray to Governor John Sununu, Dec. 6, 1990, on file at George Bush Presidential Library and Museum, College Station, TX, John Sununu Files, OA/ID CF 00472, File: Persian Gulf War 1991 (11).

"Authority to Use United States Military Forces in Somalia," 16 Op. O.L.C. 6 (1992).

"Deployment of United States Armed Forces into Haiti," 18 Op. O.L.C. 173 (1994).

"Proposed Deployment of United States Armed Forces into Bosnia," 19 Op. O.L.C. 327 (1995).

"Authorization for Continuing Hostilities in Kosovo," 24 Op. O.L.C. 327 (2000).

Memorandum from John Yoo to Timothy Flanigan, Deputy Counsel to the President, Sept. 25, 2001, reprinted in *The Torture Papers: The Road to Abu Ghraib* 3 (Karen J. Greenberg and Joshua Dratel eds., 2005).

"Authority of the President under Domestic and International Law to Use Military Force against Iraq," 26 Op. O.L.C. 1 (Oct. 23, 2002), available at www.justice.gov/olc/2002/iraq-opinion-final.pdf.

"Authority to Use Military Force in Libya," 35 Op. O.L.C. 1 (Apr. 1, 2011), available at www.justice.gov/olc/2011/authority-military-use-in-libya.pdf.

Notes

Introduction

1. This is a major theme in Jack Goldsmith, *Power and Constraint: The Accountable Presidency after 9/11* 3–22 (2012).

2. Id. at 23–29.

3. See, e.g., Benjamin Wittes, *Law and the Long War* (2008).

4. See, e.g., Harold H. Bruff, *Bad Advice: Bush's Lawyers in the War on Terror* (2009); William N. Eskridge Jr. and John Ferejohn, *A Republic of Statutes: The New American Constitution* 389–392 (2010); Jack Goldsmith, *The Terror Presidency* (2007).

5. For collections that do focus on the Cold War, see Mary L. Dudziak ed., *September 11 in History: A Watershed Moment?* (2003); Ellen Schrecker ed., *Cold War Triumphalism: The Misuse of History after the Fall of Communism* (2004). See also Mary L. Dudziak, *War Time: An Idea, Its History, Its Consequences* (2012).

6. This approach differs from the methodology followed in two notable recent studies by political scientists. See William G. Howell and Jon C. Pevehouse, *While Dangers Gather: Congressional Checks on Presidential War Powers* (2007); Douglas L. Kriner, *After the Rubicon: Congress, Presidents, and the Politics of Waging War* (2010). These studies employ a dataset that, at least originally, was limited to political uses of military force short of war. See Howell and Pevehouse at 53–54. The original dataset thus excluded Korea and Vietnam because they were wars involving sustained hostilities. See Barry Blechman and Stephen Kaplan, *Force without War: U.S. Armed Forces as a Political Instrument* 12–16 (1978). Minor uses of the military, such as force deployments without hostilities, have not caused the sort of systemic problems with the constitutional order which is my concern in this book. It should be noted, however, that Kriner's study includes Korea and Vietnam. See Kriner at 89–91.

1. War Powers and Constitutional Change

1. See Louis Henkin, *Foreign Affairs and the U.S. Constitution* 4 (2d ed. 1996).

2. See Neal Devins and Louis Fisher, *The Democratic Constitution* (2004); William Michael Treanor, "The War Powers outside the Courts," in *The Constitution in Wartime* 143 (Mark Tushnet ed., 2005) [hereinafter Treanor, "War Powers"].

3. See respectively *Brown v. Board of Education*, 347 U.S. 483 (1954); *Youngstown Sheet & Tube Co. v. Sawyer*, 343 U.S. 579 (1952); *Dennis v. United States*, 341 U.S. 494 (1951). For the relevance of *Brown* to the Cold War, see Mary L. Dudziak, *Cold War Civil Rights: Race and the Image of American Democracy* (2000).

4. The historiography of the Cold War is unusually complex and contested. See, e.g., Michael J. Hogan ed., *America in the World: The Historiography of American Foreign Relations since 1941* (1995). General histories of the Cold War include Campbell Craig and Fredrik Logevall, *America's Cold War: The Politics of Insecurity* (2009); John Lewis Gaddis, *Strategies of Containment: A Critical Appraisal of American National Security Policy during the Cold War* (rev. ed. 2005) [hereinafter Gaddis, *Containment*]; *The Cold War: A New History* (2005) [hereinafter Gaddis, *Cold War*]; George C. Herring, *From Colony to Superpower: U.S. Foreign Relations since 1776* (2008); Walter Isaacson and Evan Thomas, *The Wise Men: Six Friends and the World They Made* (1986); Thomas G. Paterson, *On Every Front: The Making and Unmaking of the Cold War* (rev. ed. 1992); James T. Patterson, *Grand Expectations: The United States, 1945–1974* (1996); Julian E. Zelizer, *Arsenal of Democracy: The Politics of National Security—From World War II to the War on Terrorism* (2010). In addition, the recently published volumes in the Cambridge history of the Cold War are wonderfully helpful. See 1 *Cambridge History of the Cold War: Origins* (Melvyn P. Leffler and Odd Arne Westad eds., 2010).

Works of special relevance to the Truman administration include Robert L. Beisner, *Dean Acheson: A Life in the Cold War* (2006); Michael J. Hogan, *A Cross of Iron: Harry S. Truman and the Origins of the National Security State, 1945–1954* (1998); Melvyn P. Leffler, *A Preponderance of Power: National Security, the Truman Administration, and the Cold War* (1992).

5. See Arthur M. Schlesinger Jr., *The Imperial Presidency* (1973).

6. Patterson at 105, 169, 176–178.

7. Isaacson and Thomas at 509, 519–520; Patterson at 241–242; Eugene V. Rostow, "Great Cases Make Bad Law: The War Powers Act," 50 *Tex. L. Rev.* 833, 871, 883 (1972).

8. Gaddis, *Cold War*, at 171–176.

9. Treanor, "War Powers," at 143.

10. See, e.g., Raoul Berger, "War-Making by the President," 121 *U. Pa. L. Rev.* 29 (1972); Alexander M. Bickel, "Congress, The President and the Power to Wage War," 48 *Chi-Kent L. Rev.* 131 (1971); Henry P. Monaghan, "Presidential War-Making," 50 *B.U. L. Rev.* 19 (1970).

11. For accounts that stress the importance of multiple institutions implementing the Constitution, as well as constitutional orders, see Bruce Ackerman, *We The People: Foundations* (1991); *We The People: Transformations* (1998); "Oliver Wendell Holmes Lectures: The Living Constitution," 120 *Harv. L. Rev.* 1737 (2007); Philip Bobbitt, *The Shield of Achilles: War, Peace and the Course of History* (2002); *Terror and Consent: The Wars for the Twenty-First Century* (2008); Keith Whittington, *Constitutional Construction: Divided Powers and Constitutional Meaning* (1999); Mark Tushnet, *Why the Constitution Matters* (2010). To a degree I find hard to estimate, the theory offered here has also been influenced by the school of thought known as "American political development" in political science. See, e.g., Karen Orren and Stephen Skowronek, *The Search for American Political Development* (2004).

12. For a valuable account of the difference between these constitutional norms, see Jack M. Balkin, *Living Originalism*, 14–16, 41–49 (2011).

13. See, e.g., Philip Bobbitt, *Constitutional Fate* (1982); *Constitutional Interpretation* (1991).

14. Compare constitutional scholar Edward Corwin's dictum that the Constitution "is an invitation to struggle for the privilege of directing American foreign policy." Edward S. Corwin, *The President: Offices and Powers, 1787–1984* 201 (5th rev. ed. 1984).

15. See, e.g., Neal Devins and Louis Fisher, "The Steel Seizure Case: One of a Kind?," 19 *Const. Comm.* 63 (2002).

16. Bruce Ackerman, *We The People: Foundations* (1991); *We The People: Transformations* (1998); "Oliver Wendell Holmes Lectures: The Living Constitution," 120 *Harv. L. Rev.* 1737 (2007).

17. See, e.g., William R. Casto, *Foreign Affairs and the Constitution in the Age of Fighting Sail* 178 (2006); H. Jefferson Powell, *The President's Authority over Foreign Affairs* (2002); Michael D. Ramsey, *The Constitution's Text in Foreign Affairs* (2007).

18. On the importance of interbranch deliberation, see Mariah A. Zeisberg, *War Powers: A Political Theory of Constitutional Judgment* 57–63 (Princeton University Press, forthcoming 2013).

19. See Jack Goldsmith, *Power and Constraint: The Accountable Presidency after 9/11* 182 (2012).

20. *Youngstown Sheet & Tube Co. v. Sawyer*, 343 U.S. 579, 634 (1952) (Jackson, J., concurring).

21. Id.

22. Casto at 178.

23. Id. at 178–179.

24. See Ramsey at 88–89.

25. See, e.g., Robert A. Katzmann, "War Powers: Toward a New Accommodation," in *A Question of Balance: The President, the Congress, and Foreign Policy* 35, 36–38 (Thomas E. Mann ed., 1990); David B. Rivkin Jr. and Lee A. Casey, "'Presidential Wars': An Exchange," *N.Y. Rev. Books*, Nov. 21, 1991.

26. See, e.g., John Hart Ely, *War and Responsibility: Constitutional Lessons of Vietnam and Its Aftermath* 148 n.54 (1993).

27. For the Pacificus essays, see 15 *The Papers of Alexander Hamilton, June 1793–January 1794* (Harold C. Syrett et al. eds., 1969) [hereinafter Hamilton's *Papers*].

28. See Gordon S. Wood, *Empire of Liberty: A History of the Early Republic, 1789–1815* 181–184 (2009) [hereinafter Wood, *Empire*].

29. See "Pacificus No. I," Hamilton's *Papers*, at 33–43.

30. See id. at 37–38.

31. Id. at 38.

32. Id. at 39.

33. Id. at 42. In presenting the "Little Sarah" incident as evidence that President Washington's administration believed that it had "some power to take military action without congressional sanction in order to achieve the executive's goals," Jefferson Powell seems to ignore Hamilton's sound point that, in so acting, the administration was justified in trying to implement the Proclamation and so keep the U.S. out of the European war. Powell at 61.

34. 15 *The Papers of James Madison, 24 March 1793–20 April 1795* 66 (Robert A. Rutland et al. eds., 1985) [hereinafter Madison's *Papers*].

35. Id. at 67. For Jefferson's approval of the Helvidius essays, see id. at 65. For his agreement with Madison that the war power rested with Congress, see David N. Mayer, *The Constitutional Thought of Thomas Jefferson* 231–233 (1994).

36. Madison's *Papers* at 68.

37. Id. at 69 (emphasis in original).

38. Id. at 70.

39. Id. at 71 (emphasis in original).

40. Id. at 72 (emphasis in original).

41. Casto at 69 (noting the "disconnect" between Helvidius and Pacificus). As Casto states, "Hamilton did not dispute Madison's assertion that the president lacks constitutional authority to make war." Id. See also Powell at 49–51.

42. Casto at 68–69 (describing Madison's "technical and complex reply" and "relatively narrow" goals).

43. Id. at 69–79. See also Ramsey at 85–89; Saikrishna Prakash, "Unleashing the Dogs of War: What the Constitution Means by 'Declare War,'" 93 *Cornell L. Rev.* 45, 91 (2007).

44. Casto at 69–79.

45. Id. at 77.

46. "Helvidius No. 4," Madison's *Papers*, at 108.

47. Casto at 181.

48. See Wood, *Empire*, at 143–145.

49. Id. at 276–277.

50. Id. at 90–94.

51. John Brewer, *The Sinews of Power: War, Money and the English State, 1688–1783* xix (1989).

52. Wood, *Empire*, at 93–94, 100–104.

53. Id. at 104.

54. Id. at 149. See also id. at 272 for the similar views of President John Adams.

55. Id. at 189.

56. Alexander DeConde, *The Quasi-War: The Politics and Diplomacy of the Undeclared War with France 1797–1801* 17–18, 31, 60–61, 67–77 (1966).

57. Id. at 103–108, 235, 246, 281–282, 329–330.

58. Id. at 31, 90–91, 106.

59. Id. at 126, 329–330. See *Bas v. Tingy*, 4 U.S. 37 (1800).

60. DeConde at 112; Wood, *Empire*, at 262–267. See also Richard H. Kohn, *Eagle and Sword: The Federalists and the Creation of the Military Establishment in America, 1783–1802*, 224–273 (1975).

61. Frank Lambert, *The Barbary Wars* 103, 125–126 (2005).

62. "The Examination No. 1," in 25 Hamilton's *Papers*, at 444–456 (Dec. 17, 1801).

63. Lambert at 131–133.

64. The editor of Hamilton's *Papers* notes that Hamilton's criticisms of Jefferson in "The Examination" attracted little attention as Hamilton was a spent force in national politics. 25 Hamilton's *Papers* at 452–453.

65. Lambert at 189.

66. With respect to presidential power, see David K. Nichols, *The Myth of the Modern Presidency* (1994), for a valuable presentation of this perspective.

67. See David Gray Adler and Larry N. George eds., *The Constitution and the Conduct of American Foreign Policy* (1996) [hereinafter Adler and George]; Ely; Louis Fisher, *Presidential War Power* (2d ed. 2004); Michael J. Glennon, *Constitutional Diplomacy* (1990); Powell; Ramsey; W. Taylor Reveley III, *War Powers of the President and Congress* (1981); Abraham D. Sofaer, *War, Foreign Affairs and Constitutional Power: The Origins* (1976); Donald L. Westerfield, *War Powers: The President, the Congress, and the Question of War* (1996); Francis D. Wormuth and Edwin B. Firmage, *To Chain the Dog of War: The War Power of Congress in History and Law* (2d ed. 1989); John Yoo, *The Powers of War and Peace: The Constitution and Foreign Affairs after 9/11* (2005).

68. For an insightful summary of the presidentialist position, see Zeisberg at 20–27.

69. Jide Nzelibe and John Yoo, "Rational War and Constitutional Design," 115 *Yale L.J.* 2512, 2516 (2006); William Michael Treanor, "Fame, the Founding, and the Power to Declare War," 82 *Cornell L. Rev.* 695, 698 (1997) [hereinafter Treanor, "Fame"].

70. For examples of this approach, see Reveley; Sofaer.

71. See, e.g., Powell at 114–115.

72. See, e.g., *U.S. Commitments to Foreign Powers: Hearing before the Sen. Comm. on Foreign Relations*, 90th Cong. 71–82 (1967) (testimony of Nicholas Katzenbach, Under Secretary of State) [hereinafter *Commitments Hearing*]. See also John

N. Moore, "The National Executive and the Use of the Armed Forces Abroad," in *Congress, the President, and the War Powers: Hearing before the Subcomm. on National Security, Policy and Scientific Developments of the H. Comm. on Foreign Affairs,* 91st Cong. 505 (1970) [hereinafter 1970 *Hearings*]; *War Powers Legislation: Hearing before the Sen. Comm. on Foreign Relations,* 92nd Cong. 501 (1971) (testimony of William P. Rodgers, Secretary of State) [hereinafter 1971 *Hearings*]; Memorandum from William H. Rehnquist, Assistant Att'y Gen., Office of Legal Counsel, "The President and the War Power: South Vietnam and the Cambodian Sanctuaries," to Charles W. Colson, Special Counsel to the President, May 22, 1970 [hereinafter Rehnquist OLC opinion]. See also Rostow at 833.

For a statement of the "one instrument among others" view in the Reagan administration, see Ivo H. Daalder and I. M. Destler, *In the Shadow of the Oval Office* 151 (2009) (views of Secretary of State George Shultz).

73. See, e.g., Yoo at 2–9.

74. For example, Eugene Rostow, who ardently defended a broad presidential war power and opposed the WPR after serving in the Johnson administration, began government service under Secretary of State Dean Acheson in the Truman administration. See Beisner at 17.

75. In this vein, see Louis Fisher, *The Constitution and 9/11: Recurring Threats to America's Freedoms* 364–365 (2008); Theodore Draper, "Presidential Wars," *N.Y. Rev. Books,* Sept. 26, 1991, at 64.

76. Quoted in William Stueck, *Rethinking the Korean War* 193 (2002).

77. See Peter Raven-Hansen, "The Gulf War: Collective Security, War Powers, and Laws of War," Proceedings of the 85th Annual Meeting, Am. Soc. Int'l Law 8, 9 (1991). See also Powell at 18.

78. Henkin at 109.

79. George Bush and Brent Scowcroft, *A World Transformed* 397–398, 441 (1998). See also James A. Baker, *The Politics of Diplomacy: Revolution, War and Peace, 1989–1992* 338–339 (1995); Bob Woodward, *The Commanders* 325 (1991).

80. Woodward at 285 (views of Brent Scowcroft, the national security adviser). See also Daalder and Destler at 151.

81. Zelizer at 370–371.

82. On the relevance of the 1950 thesis to war powers scholarship, see Zeisberg at 127–128. Gordon Silverstein's well-researched account of the growth of executive prerogative power is broadly consistent with the 1950 thesis. Gordon Silverstein, *Imbalance of Powers: Constitutional Interpretation and the Making of American Foreign Policy* 43–82 (1997).

83. See Fisher, *The Constitution and 9/11,* at 364–365; Draper at 64.

84. For a relatively early example, see Raoul Berger, "War-Making by the President," 121 *U. Pa. L. Rev.* 29, 66–67 (1972). See also Treanor, "Fame," at 702. For criticism of the 1950 thesis, see Robert F. Turner, "Truman, Korea, and the Constitution: Debunking The 'Imperial President' Myth," 19 *Harv. J.L. & Pub. Pol'y* 533 (1995).

85. Fisher, *Presidential War Power,* at xi.

86. Id. at 97–100.

87. Ely at 10. See also Wormuth and Firmage at 151 (endorsing the 1950 thesis).

88. Glennon at 80 (footnote omitted). In a Foreword, former Senator J. William Fulbright argued that the Korean War had changed a historical pattern of executive-legislative partnership in foreign policy. Id. at x–xi. He stated that before Truman, "no president had ever asserted a right to commit the United States to war on his own authority." Id. at xi. This repeated a claim Fulbright had made in an important Senate report. See "National Commitments Report," S. Rep. No. 91–129, 18–19 (1969) [hereinafter "National Commitments Report"].

89. Credibility was a key to the doctrine of containment. See Gaddis, *Containment,* at 142, 211. Because perceptions of strength, resolve, and decisiveness were crucial to credibility, this key concept also led in the direction of increased and unilateral presidential power.

90. William Bundy, *A Tangled Web: The Making of Foreign Policy in the Nixon Presidency* 396 (1998) (emphasis in original).

91. See *Commitments Hearing* at 71–82.

92. Id. at 72.

93. Id.

94. Id. at 73.

95. Id. at 170–171.

96. Id. at 171.

97. Id.

98. Id.

99. Id.

100. My inquiry is narrow by design in that it takes the crucial question to be presidential war-initiating authority, rather than authority to, say, repel a sudden attack, defend American lives and property abroad, carry out rescue operations, and otherwise engage in actions short of war. The "declare war" clause self-evidently identifies "war" as a relevant focus for interpretive inquiry. But the actions of post-1945 presidents have done the same. For an example of this sort of interpretive approach, see "Deployment of United States Armed Forces into Haiti," 18 Op. O.L.C. 173, 177–179 (1994).

101. Rehnquist OLC opinion at 12–13. See also "Presidential Power to Use the Armed Forces Abroad without Statutory Authorization," 4A Op. O.L.C. 185, 187–188 (1980) [hereinafter OLC Presidential Power].

102. Wormuth and Firmage at 20, 23–25, 27–28, 30–31, 60–63, 77–78, 112.

103. See 2 *Records of the Federal Convention of 1787* 318–319 (Max Farrand ed. 1967) [hereinafter FC]. For the commentary, see, e.g., Charles A. Lofgren, *"Government From Reflection and Choice": Constitutional Essays on War, Foreign Relations, and Federalism* 7 (1986); Powell at 115–118; Treanor, "War Powers."

104. For reliable accounts that illustrate the application of the standard forms of argument, see Ely at 3–10; Reveley; Wormuth and Firmage at 17–18.

105. 1 FC at 64. For a good discussion of the pre-August debates, see Reveley at 74–79.

106. Id. at 64–65.

107. Id. at 65.

108. Id.

109. Fisher, *Presidential War Power*, at 1–2.

110. 1 FC at 65–66. James Madison apparently agreed with Wilson. See id. at 70 (notes of Rufus King).

111. See Articles of Confederation, Art. III, VI, VII, VIII, IX.

112. Presidentialists have claimed that the Continental Congress was an "executive branch." Yoo at 73. Historians have more accurately noted that the status of the Congress was unclear, although it was said to exercise executive power. Jack N. Rakove, *The Beginnings of National Politics: An Interpretive History of the Continental Congress* 383–385 (1979). Presidentialists have generally missed the practical point that under the Articles, the war power was assigned to a multimember body. That would not have suggested to the framers that it was desirable to assign the war power to the unitary (by which I mean simply not plural) executive created by the Constitution. Such an executive did not exist under the Confederation and raised all sorts of new issues at the Philadelphia Convention.

113. Articles of Confederation at Art. V. The Confederation Congress was considered to have both legislative and executive rights. See the "Virginia Plan" submitted to the Philadelphia Convention. 1 FC at 21.

114. Articles of Confederation at Art. IX. See also the commentary in Reveley at 101–102 (ratifiers equated Congress's power under Confederation with power granted in Constitution).

115. Richard Beeman, *Plain, Honest Men: The Making of the American Constitution* 190 (2009) ("[t]hirty of the fifty-five men serving in the Convention had engaged in active military service during the Revolutionary War").

116. Kohn at 77.

117. Allan R. Millett and Peter Maslowski, *For the Common Defense: A Military History of the United States of America* 79 (1984).

118. See Beeman at 54–56.

119. Ramsey at 448 n.45.

120. 2 FC at 318–319.

121. Id. at 318.

122. Id.

123. Id. Philip Bobbitt argues that it is implausible to think Gerry was responding to Butler as Butler did not make a motion. Philip Bobbitt, "War Powers: An Essay on John Hart Ely's *War and Responsibility: Constitutional Lessons of Vietnam and Its Aftermath*," 92 *Mich. L. Rev.* 1364, 1379–1380 (1994). This is one of those times when we should regret that we have Madison's summary of the

debate, rather than a transcript. I doubt whether much turns on Madison's use in his notes of the word "motion" to describe what Gerry said, as Madison could have used it in the sense of "Butler made an argument in support of an apparent motion." Gerry is most naturally taken to be referring to Butler's advocacy of placing the power to make war "in the President." 2 FC at 318. Bobbitt proposes Gerry was answering Roger Sherman, who favored retaining the draft language of "make." Bobbitt at 1380–1381. But Bobbitt's argument applies with equal force to Sherman, as Sherman made no motion and did not need to, as he was supporting the original committee language. This leaves Bobbitt without a way to explain this exchange among the delegates. The standard reading, which I follow in the text, does allow for a reasonable explanation.

124. Prakash at 84–94; Treanor, "War Powers," at 144; Wormuth and Firmage at 19–20.

125. 2 FC at 319.

126. Bobbitt; Ramsey at 218–219; Treanor, "War Powers," at 151–152. For the reference to the early debate, see "National Commitments Report" at 10.

127. Bobbitt at 1375–1377; Treanor, "War Powers," at 150.

128. See Reveley at 100–106 for a review of the evidence as to ratification.

129. Ramsey at 235–238; Treanor, "War Powers," at 151–152.

130. It should be noted that a number of originalist scholars largely endorse the conclusions I reach about the meaning of the "declare war" clause. See Michael Stokes Paulsen, "The War Power," 33 *Harv. J.L. & Pub. Pol'y* 113 (2010); Prakash; Michael D. Ramsey, "Textualism and War Powers," 69 *U. Chi. L. Rev.* 1543 (2002).

131. 2 *The Documentary History of the Ratification of the Constitution* 583 (Merrill Jensen ed., 1976). Wilson had exceptional judgment and insight into the substance of the new constitutional order. Beeman at 266, 380–381. For additional evidence from the ratification debates supporting Wilson, see David Gray Adler, "The Constitution and Presidential Warmaking," in Adler and George, at 183, 186–187.

132. For an early study often cited by presidentialist scholars see Charles C. Thach Jr., *The Creation of the Presidency 1775–1789: A Study in Constitutional History* (1923). Thach's conclusions were supported to a degree in Jack N. Rakove, *Original Meanings: Politics and Ideas in the Making of the Constitution* (1996).

133. Saul Cornell, *The Other Founders: Anti-Federalism and the Dissenting Tradition in America, 1788–1828* 31 (1999); Pauline Maier, *Ratification: The People Debate the Constitution, 1787–1788* 372, 392, 416 (2010). See also the comments in the ratification conventions on the commander in chief clause cited in Adler at 193–195. For an argument that Anti-Federalists agreed that Congress had the war power and believed that it was a bad idea to place the war power unilaterally either with Congress or the executive, see Cameron O. Kistler, "The Anti-Federalists and Presidential War Powers," 121 *Yale L.J.* 459 (2011).

134. Bobbitt contends that "the power to make war is not an enumerated power." Bobbitt at 1365. This suggestion, intended to undermine the standard

reading of the "declare war" clause, is not consistent with evidence from the ratification and post-ratification periods.

135. Casto at 189 (footnote omitted).

136. Powell at 115–116; Treanor, "War Powers," at 151–152.

137. On the usefulness of purposive interpretation for American constitutionalism and government, see the wonderful presentation in Stephen Breyer, *Making Our Democracy Work: A Judge's View* (2010).

138. "Documents Relating to the War Power of Congress, the President's Authority as Commander-In-Chief and the War in Indochina," Sen. Comm. on Foreign Relations, 91st Cong. (July 1970). Similarly, the committee's report cited the following sparse authority for its view that the Constitution gave Congress the power to initiate war: (1) records of the Philadelphia Convention; (2) one paper from *The Federalist*; (3) statements from Thomas Jefferson in 1789 and as president in 1801; (4) 1824 statement from Secretary of State John Quincy Adams; (5) Lincoln's statement as a member of the House of Representatives during the Mexican War. See "National Commitments Report."

139. It was cited by Senator Sam Ervin in the hearings. See *Commitments Hearing* at 192–193.

140. See Edward S. Corwin, *The President: Office and Powers, 1787–1984* (5th ed. 1984). The fifth edition left the text of the 1957 edition intact. Id. at xi–xii.

141. Id. at 224–234.

142. Id. at 228–234.

143. Id. at 232–234.

144. Jane E. Stromseth, "Understanding Constitutional War Powers Today: Why Methodology Matters," 106 *Yale L.J.* 845, 852–853 (1996).

145. *Dellums v. Bush*, 752 F. Supp. 1141 (1990). The brief filed by eleven eminent scholars was reprinted in "Memorandum, *Amicus Curiae* of Law Professors," 27 *Stanford J. Int'l L.* 257 (1991). See also *The Constitutional Roles of Congress and the President in Declaring and Waging War: Hearing before the S. Comm. on the Judiciary*, 102nd Cong. (1991).

146. Sofaer at 56 (footnote omitted).

147. Id. Like Reveley, Sofaer moved to a discussion of practice to elicit the meaning of presidential war powers.

148. For similar analyses, see the distinguished roster of witnesses who supported the congressionalist interpretation in the hearings held during the Persian Gulf War. *The War Power after 200 Years:—Congress and the President at a Constitutional Impasse: Hearings before the Special Subcomm. on War Powers, Sen. Comm. on Foreign Relations*, 100th Cong. 1 (1988).

149. Yoo at 9 ("Practice as it has developed over the last few decades generally falls within the range of permissible outcomes allowed by the Constitution"). He concludes that "the practice of unilateral presidential warmaking falls within the permissible bounds of discretion granted to the political branches." Id. at 294. Yoo thus would reject the 1950 thesis.

150. Id. at 144–152.

151. Id. at 24–25.

152. Id. at 27–29.

153. See the comprehensive critiques of Yoo's use of history in Janet Cooper Alexander, "John Yoo's *War Powers:* The Law Review and the World," Stanford Public Law and Legal Theory Working Paper Series, March 31, 2012, available at http://ssrn.com/abstract=2024138; Julian Davis Mortenson, "Executive Power and the Discipline of History," 78 *U. Chi. L. Rev.* 377 (2011).

154. Gordon S. Wood, *The Creation of the American Republic, 1776–1787* (1969) [hereinafter Wood, *Creation*]. For Yoo's citations to Wood, see Yoo at 29, 36, 38.

155. Wood, *Creation,* at 523–524. See also Wood, *Empire,* at 407.

156. See Mortenson at 391–399.

157. John Yoo, "Clio at War: The Misuse of History in the War Powers Debate," 70 *U. Colo. L. Rev.* 1169, 1189–1191 (1999).

158. Yoo at 22, 27–28.

159. Yoo's qualification concerning total war is ad hoc because it is unrelated to his account of the nature of executive power. It is also unsupported by historical evidence.

160. Id. at 31.

161. Id. at 86.

162. Id. at 73. Compare Beeman: "The Articles of Confederation neglected to provide for an executive branch altogether." Beeman at 125.

163. Yoo at 75.

164. Id. at 90–93.

165. Id. at 91–92, 96–100.

166. Id. at 100.

167. See Mortenson at 395–399.

168. For a description of what a contextual approach involves relevant to executive power, see Martin S. Flaherty, "The Most Dangerous Branch," 105 *Yale L.J.* 1725, 1751–1753 (1996).

169. See Flaherty's discussion of the lack of consensus over the nature of executive power at 1755–1774.

170. Yoo at 99, 120–121.

171. See Wormuth and Firmage; Treanor, "Fame," at 723–727. As noted earlier, Hamilton and Madison agreed on this point during their debate as Pacificus and Helvidius. See Ramsey at 218.

172. Yoo at 28.

173. See, e.g., Flaherty at 1774–1810; Curtis A. Bradley and Martin S. Flaherty, "Executive Power Essentialism in Foreign Affairs," 102 *Mich. L. Rev.* 545 (2004).

174. Beeman at 136, 233–234.

175. 1 FC at 65–66. See also Bradley and Flaherty at 593–594.

176. See Wood, *Creation,* at 523–524.

177. Beeman at 233–234, 238–239. See also Wood, *Creation*, at 525.

178. Beeman at 233. See also Treanor, "Fame," at 729–756.

179. See Mortenson at 395–399. For doubts about whether the U.S. Constitution tracked the British, see Wood, *Creation*, at 560–561.

180. For a recent example of a commentator ignoring the significance of authorized wars, see Max Boot, *The Savage Wars of Peace: Small Wars and the Rise of American Power* 14 (2002).

181. I should note here that while some regard the Philippine-American War as separate from the 1898 Spanish-American War, both were authorized by Congress. The Philippine-American War can be regarded as authorized by either the declaration of war against Spain or the subsequent treaty with Spain, ratified by the Senate, in which the U.S. annexed the Philippines. See David J. Silbey, *A War of Frontier and Empire: The Philippine-American War, 1899–1902* 34, 58, 65, 88–95 (2007).

182. See Dean Alfange Jr., "The Quasi-War and Presidential Warmaking," in Adler and George, at 274; Gerhard Casper, "The Washington Administration, Congress, and Algiers," in Adler and George, at 259.

183. Curtis A. Bradley and Jack L. Goldsmith, "Congressional Authorization and the War on Terrorism," 118 *Harv. L. Rev.* 2047, 2059 (2005). See also Saikrishna Bangalore Prakash, "Exhuming the Seemingly Moribund Declaration of War," 77 *Geo. Wash. L. Rev.* 89 (2008).

184. Bradley and Goldsmith at 2059–2060.

185. Id. at 2060.

186. Id. at 2061.

187. Id.

188. See, e.g., 1970 *Hearings* at 214–215 (Rehnquist testimony), 506–507 (Moore statement). See also Rehnquist OLC opinion at 2.

189. For an especially clear example of the bypassing of constitutional requirements in favor of basing arguments entirely on subsequent practice, see OLC Presidential Power at 186–187. This move has the effect of treating the text and original intent or meaning as irrelevant. The opinion stated, "We believe that the substantive constitutional limits on the exercise of these inherent powers by the President are, at any particular time, a function of historical practice and the political relationship between the President and Congress." Id. at 187. To the same effect, see "Proposed Deployment of United States Armed Forces into Bosnia," 19 Op. O.L.C. 327, 330–331 (1995).

190. Wormuth and Firmage at 141.

191. See the comments of Senators Albert Gore and Clifford Case in *Commitments Hearing* at 187.

192. Scholars like Garry Wills are not wrong to think that the advent of nuclear weapons made a difference to how public officials regarded executive power, but it is not the major part of the story. See Garry Wills, *Bomb Power: The Modern Presidency and the National Security State* (2010).

193. See Anne Leland and Mari-Jana Oboroceanu, "American War and Military Operations Casualties: Lists and Statistics," Congressional Research Service (Feb. 26, 2010).

2. Truman and the Post-1945 Constitutional Order

1. For general histories, see Campbell Craig and Fredrik Logevall, *America's Cold War: The Politics of Insecurity* (2009); John Lewis Gaddis, *Strategies of Containment: A Critical Appraisal of American National Security Policy during the Cold War* (rev. ed. 2005) [hereinafter Gaddis, *Containment*]; *The Cold War: A New History* (2005) [hereinafter Gaddis, *Cold War*]; George C. Herring, *From Colony to Superpower: U.S. Foreign Relations since 1776* (2008); Robert J. McMahon, *The Cold War* (2003); Thomas G. Paterson, *On Every Front: The Making and Unmaking of the Cold War* (rev. ed. 1992); James T. Patterson, *Grand Expectations: The United States, 1945–1974* (1996); Julian E. Zelizer, *Arsenal of Democracy: The Politics of National Security* (2010). See also 1 *Cambridge History of the Cold War: Origins* (Melvyn P. Leffler and Odd Arne Westad eds., 2010) [hereinafter 1 *Cambridge History*]. Regarding the beginning of the Cold War and the importance of the events of 1946, see Craig and Logevall at 66–73; Patterson at 113–117.

For works of special relevance to the Truman administration, see Robert L. Beisner, *Dean Acheson: A Life in the Cold War* (2006); Michael J. Hogan, *A Cross of Iron: Harry S. Truman and the Origins of the National Security State, 1945–1954* (1998); Walter Isaacson and Evan Thomas, *The Wise Men: Six Friends and the World They Made* (1986); Melvyn P. Leffler, *A Preponderance of Power: National Security, the Truman Administration, and the Cold War* (1992).

2. Herring at 650.

3. For the beginnings of such an assessment, see Craig and Logevall at 79–82.

4. Hogan at 40. See also id. at 327–328 (referring to the Korea decision).

5. Id. at 1.

6. Several examples from the twentieth century will be presented in the discussion below. For some examples from the nineteenth century additional to the ones reviewed in Chapter 1, see David S. Heidler and Jeanne T. Heidler, *Henry Clay: The Essential American* 93–95 (2010) (views of Speaker of the House Clay on the eve of the War of 1812); Arthur M. Schlesinger Jr., *The Imperial Presidency* 42–43 (1973) (views of Abraham Lincoln in 1848); Joseph Story, 3 *Commentaries on the Constitution of the United States* 59–62 (1970) (1833 edition); *The Prize Cases*, 67 U.S. 635, 668 (1863). Various presidential statements from the nineteenth century are collected in Albert H. Putney, "Executive Assumption of the War Making Power," 7 *Nat'l U.L. Rev.* 1 (1927).

7. See generally Herring at 1–10, 482–483. There are many histories that discuss the age of American empire. For two recent accounts that highlight military involvements, see Greg Grandin, *Empire's Workshop* (2006); Michael H.

Hunt and Steven I. Levine, *Arc of Empire: America's Wars in Asia from the Philippines to Vietnam* (2012).

8. See Bruce Ackerman, *We The People: Foundations* (1991); *We The People: Transformations* (1998).

9. Works helpful in understanding the pre–Pearl Harbor constitutional order and President Roosevelt's diplomacy include Robert Dallek, *Franklin Roosevelt and American Foreign Policy, 1932–1945* (1979); Robert A. Divine, *The Reluctant Belligerent: American Entry into World War II* (2d ed. 1979); Patrick J. Hearden, *Roosevelt Confronts Hitler: America's Entry into World War II* (1987); Waldo Heinrichs, *Threshold of War: Franklin D. Roosevelt and American Entry into World War II* (1988); David M. Kennedy, *Freedom from Fear: The American People in Depression and War, 1929–1945* (1999); Warren F. Kimball, *The Juggler: Franklin Roosevelt as Wartime Statesman* (1991); David Reynolds, *From Munich to Pearl Harbor: Roosevelt's America and the Origins of the Second World War* (2001).

10. Dallek at 222–224, 229–232, 256–257, 263–268, 277–278, 290–292, 299–300, 312–313.

11. Kennedy at 496–500, 524.

12. Reynolds at 78. It should be noted that the Navy was in a far better position than the Army, which was why Pearl Harbor was perceived as such a devastating blow.

13. Hearden at 156–157, 194–206.

14. See Dallek at 313; Herring at 587–588; Reynolds at 184–185.

15. John Yoo, *Crisis and Command* 289–310 (2009). Curiously, Yoo bases his argument concerning Roosevelt on many of the same secondary works cited here. For criticisms of the adequacy of Yoo's analysis, see Julian Davis Mortenson, "Executive Power and the Discipline of History," 78 *U. Chi. L. Rev.* 377, 402–404 (2011).

16. Dallek at 222–224, 229–232, 256–257, 263–268, 277–278, 290–292, 299–300, 312–313.

17. See id.

18. Kennedy at 432.

19. Divine at 69; Reynolds at 115.

20. Divine at 88–89; Reynolds at 78.

21. Divine at 88–89 (footnote omitted).

22. Kennedy at 493.

23. Reynolds at 130.

24. Craig and Logevall at 24–27.

25. See Heinrichs for the best account of FDR's 1941 campaign to win public support.

26. See id. at 11. It is worth noting that Hitler considered Lend-Lease a "declaration of economic war against Germany." Hearden at 194.

27. Heinrichs at 83–85, 151, 167–168. Probably too much has been made of casual comments Roosevelt made to Churchill during the Atlantic conference of

August 1941. Churchill picked up the idea that FDR was going to use an incident to compel Congress to give him a declaration of war: "The President had said he would wage war, but not declare it, and that he would become more and more provocative." Reynolds at 149. FDR was presumably referring to causing an incident between U.S. and German naval forces. For a presidentialist interpretation that stresses these remarks, see Yoo at 307. For a more balanced account, see Kimball at 207 n.34.

28. Kennedy at 490–493.

29. Id. at 497–500.

30. Warren F. Kimball, "The Sheriffs: FDR's Postwar World," in *FDR's World: War, Peace, and Legacies* 91, 94–95 (David B. Woolner, Warren F. Kimball, and David Reynolds eds., 2008) [hereinafter *FDR's World*].

31. See, e.g., Dallek at 313; Herring at 587–588; Reynolds at 184–185.

32. Kennedy at 460–461.

33. Id. at 487. For a similar cogent argument, see John J. Mearsheimer, *The Tragedy of Great Power Politics* 83–85 (2001).

34. Mark A. Stoler, "FDR and the Origins of the National Security Establishment," in *FDR's World*, at 63, 71.

35. Reynolds at 155–157.

36. Id. at 164.

37. Quoted in Reynolds at 103–104.

38. Patterson at 103.

39. Id. See also Michael H. Hunt, *Ideology and U.S. Foreign Policy* 150–151 (2009).

40. Divine at 66.

41. Id.

42. Id. at 59.

43. Schlesinger at 97–99, 122–126.

44. On the importance of the foreign policy elite or "Establishment," see Patterson at 98–104. On the "wise men," see Isaacson and Thomas.

45. Gaddis, *Cold War*, at 254.

46. Id. at 262–263.

47. Id. at 206.

48. See Melvyn P. Leffler, "The Emergence of an American Grand Strategy, 1945–1952," in 1 *Cambridge History*, at 67.

49. Leffler at 16–17, 142–146, 157–164.

50. Leffler, 1 *Cambridge History*, at 81.

51. Gaddis, *Containment*, at 112.

52. Leffler at 15–19. See also Leffler, 1 *Cambridge History*, at 73–88.

53. Gaddis, *Containment*, at 34.

54. Id. at 34–36.

55. Id. at 35–38.

56. Paterson at 143–144.

57. Leffler, 1 *Cambridge History*, at 80.

58. Craig and Logevall at 61–62.

59. Gaddis, *Containment*, at 50. In particular, Kennan was skeptical that Congress could ever play a responsible role in foreign policy. Id. at 50–52.

60. Id. at 88. For the text of NSC-68, see U.S. Dept. State, 1 *Foreign Relations of the United States, 1950: National Security Affairs* 235–292 (1977) [hereinafter FRUS 1950].

61. Beisner at 317, 654; Gaddis, *Containment*, at 97–98. For discussions of the importance of NSC-68, see Gaddis, *Containment*, at 90–91, 95, 124–125; Hogan at 12 (referring to NSC-68 as the "bible of American national security policy" and the "fullest statement" of the "new ideology" of national security). It was not declassified until the mid-1970s.

62. Gaddis, *Containment*, at 91.

63. FRUS 1950 at 240.

64. Gaddis, *Containment*, at 92, 94–95.

65. FRUS 1950 at 252–253.

66. Gaddis, *Containment*, at 90.

67. FRUS 1950 at 238.

68. See, e.g., Eugene V. Rostow, "Great Cases Make Bad Law: The War Powers Act," 50 *Tex. L. Rev.* 833 (1972).

69. See Douglas T. Stuart, *Creating the National Security State: A History of the Law That Transformed America* 7, 29 (2008).

70. Gaddis, *Containment*, at 83.

71. Id. at 95 (emphasis supplied).

72. Quoted in John Ranelagh, *The Agency: The Rise and Decline of the CIA* 277 (1987).

73. For general comments, see Leffler at 20–21.

74. Hogan at 16; Paterson at 101–102.

75. Ted Galen Carpenter, "United States' NATO Policy at the Crossroads: The 'Great Debate' of 1950–1951," 8 *Int'l History Rev.* 345, 400–401 (1986) ("By precept and example, administration leaders demonstrated their belief that congress occupied a distinctly inferior status in foreign policymaking").

76. Hogan at 60, 288–289; Stuart at 40–42.

77. Gaddis, *Containment*, at 123. When Acheson was asked after he left office about the failure to obtain congressional authorization for the Korean intervention, he stated that "the thing to do was to get on and do what had to be done as quickly and effectively as you could, and if you stopped to analyze what you were doing . . . [a]ll you did was to weaken and confuse your will and not get anywhere." Quoted in id.

78. See Casto; Powell; Ramsey.

79. 299 U.S. 304 (1936).

80. Id. at 320.

81. See id. at 319–320. Justice Sutherland's opinion for the Court in *Curtiss-Wright* was based in part on a controversial theory of the relationship of the

foreign affairs power exercised by the U.S. government during the Revolutionary and Confederation periods to its power under the Constitution. See id. at 315–319. For discussion and criticism, see Sarah H. Cleveland, "Powers Inherent in Sovereignty: Indians, Aliens, Territories, and the Nineteenth Century Origins of Plenary Power over Foreign Affairs," 81 *Tex. L. Rev.* 1 (2002); David M. Levitan, "The Foreign Relations Power: An Analysis of Mr. Justice Sutherland's Theory," 55 *Yale L.J.* 467 (1946); Charles A. Lofgren, "United States v. Curtiss-Wright Export Corporation: An Historical Reassessment," 83 *Yale L.J.* 1 (1973).

82. For this argument by Katzenbach (invoking *Curtiss-Wright*), see U.S. Dept. State, *Foreign Relations of the United States, 1964–1968: Vietnam: January–June 1965* 751 (1996) (Memorandum from Attorney General Katzenbach).

83. This is the sense conveyed in J. William Fulbright, "American Foreign Policy in the 20th Century Under an 18th-Century Constitution," 47 *Cornell L.Q.* 1 (1961). Senator Fulbright later repudiated these views concerning the necessity of expanding presidential power in foreign affairs.

84. Gaddis, *Containment*, at 26–28.

85. Id. at 55–56, 63.

86. Id.

87. Gaddis, *Containment*, Id. at 120–121.

88. Hogan at 1.

89. Id. at 40.

90. Id. at 18, 69–71, 93, 266, 289.

91. Id. at 8–9.

92. The limitations of the National Security Act in this respect are discussed in Chapter 3.

93. Hogan at 369; David R. Kepley, "The Senate and the Great Debate of 1951," *Prologue*, Winter 1982, at 226; Leffler at 407–408. See also Duane Tananbaum, *The Bricker Amendment Controversy: A Test of Eisenhower's Political Leadership* (1988).

94. Gaddis, *Cold War*, at 317; Isaacson and Thomas at 33.

95. Gaddis, *Containment*, at 108; Isaacson and Thomas at 395; Patterson at 128.

96. Patterson at 127–128.

97. Gaddis, *Cold War*, at 351–352; Isaacson and Thomas at 397–398.

98. Gaddis, *Cold War*, at 341; Leffler at 141–146.

99. Beisner at 66–69, 642–643; Leffler at 157–164, 188–192; Leffler, 1 *Cambridge History*, at 74–80. See also the valuable discussion in Tony Judt, *Postwar: A History of Europe since 1945* 86–99 (2005).

100. In assessing the record of the Nixon administration, Gaddis makes a point that is worth bearing in mind concerning all administrations in the post-1945 period: "One must distinguish between situations Nixon and Kissinger inherited, and those they created. One must differentiate between events within and beyond their capacity to control. One must consider alternatives to courses of action actually followed. One must in particular avoid ex post facto

judgments: the fairer procedure is to evaluate the strategy according to the goals its architects set for it, not by some external frame of reference they themselves did not impose." Gaddis, *Containment*, at 310.

101. See the discussion in Craig and Logevall at 76–82.

102. Beisner at 63; Isaacson and Thomas at 432–433.

103. Isaacson and Thomas at 434, 439–441; Patterson at 132.

104. Leffler, 1 *Cambridge History*, at 80.

105. For the relevant views of Acheson on Congress, see Beisner at 22, 61–63.

106. See the discussion in Stephen M. Griffin, *American Constitutionalism: From Theory to Politics* 37–40 (1996).

107. Patterson at 103–104. See also the discussion of the early Cold War in Robert David Johnson, *Congress and the Cold War* 11–68 (2006).

108. Isaacson and Thomas at 466, 475, 494–495; Patterson at 169–173.

109. See the discussions of NSC-68 in Beisner at 224, 241–243, 250; Hogan at 12–13, 26–27.

110. Hogan at 26. He remarks that national security needs were starting "to dissolve the usual distinction between war and peace in the minds of American policy makers." Id. For evidence as to the undermining of the war-peace distinction during the Truman administration, see id. at 26, 66, 134, 179, 195, 207, 296, 318–319, 342. For evidence that members of Congress agreed the distinction no longer existed, see id. at 287, 319, 330, 363. With respect to the public, see id. at 465.

111. Id. at 60. For a study of the later significance of this concept in the Eisenhower administration, see Kenneth Osgood, *Total Cold War: Eisenhower's Secret Propaganda Battle at Home and Abroad* (2006).

112. Hogan at 12.

113. Id. at 13 (footnote omitted).

114. Id. at 265–418.

115. Id. at 267, 367, 415.

116. Id. at 284, 305–306, 312–313, 367–368, 392–393, 415–416.

117. Id. at 287–288.

118. Quoted in id. at 319.

119. Quoted in id. at 343.

120. Id. at 363.

121. Id. at 330.

122. Id.

123. On Johnson, see id. at 319.

124. Id. at 415.

125. Reynolds at 157.

126. As Reynolds discusses, by late fall 1941 FDR had agreed that if Japan attacked British possessions in Asia, the U.S. would help defend them. He continues: "On November 28 Roosevelt had already agreed on this position with

his principal military and naval advisers. But he could only propose war; the Congress had to declare it. From a purely diplomatic point of view, Pearl Harbor was therefore a godsend." Id. at 164.

127. As Kennedy comments, if Hitler had not declared war on the U.S. after the U.S. declared war on Japan, FDR would have found it much more difficult to wage war in Europe: "In the absence of such a legal declaration, Roosevelt might well have found it impossible to resist demands to place the maximum American effort in the Pacific, against the formally recognized Japanese enemy, rather than in the Atlantic, in a nondeclared war against the Germans." Kennedy at 524.

128. For pertinent and very interesting commentary, see Mariah A. Zeisberg, *War Powers: A Political Theory of Constitutional Judgment* 149–154 (Princeton University Press, forthcoming 2013).

129. See, e.g., "National Commitments Report," S. Rep. No. 91-129 at 22–23 (1969) [hereinafter "National Commitments Report"].

130. President Truman's decision to intervene in Korea has been the subject of numerous studies, and the origins of the Korean War continue to be the subject of scholarly debate. The works most relevant to my inquiry into the Korea decision are Beisner; Rosemary Foot, *The Wrong War: American Policy and the Dimensions of the Korean Conflict, 1950–1953* (1985); Gary R. Hess, *Presidential Decisions for War* (2d ed. 2009); Hunt and Levine; Burton I. Kaufman, *The Korean War: Challenges in Crisis, Credibility, and Command* (2d ed. 1997); Leffler; Glenn D. Paige, *The Korean Decision* (1968); William Stueck, *The Korean War: An International History* (1995) [hereinafter Stueck, *Korean War*]; *Rethinking the Korean War: A New Diplomatic and Strategic History* (2002) [hereinafter Stueck, *Rethinking*]; Jane E. Stromseth, "Rethinking War Powers: Congress, the President, and the United Nations," 81 *Geo. L.J.* 597 (1993).

For biographical accounts sympathetic to Truman, see Alonzo L. Hamby, *Man of the People: A Life of Harry S. Truman* (1995); David McCullough, *Truman* (1992). For more critical accounts, see Bruce Cumings, 2 *The Origins of the Korean War: The Roaring of the Cataract, 1947–1950* (1990); Arnold A. Offner, *Another Such Victory: President Truman and the Cold War, 1945–1953* (2002). In particular, Cumings suggested that the U.S. wanted an opportunity to roll back communism and may have attempted to provoke the North Koreans into attacking. Cumings at 431–432, 615–621. As Cumings grants, however, this argument deserves considerable skepticism. See id. For a critical assessment of the idea that the Korean War should be regarded as a "civil war," see Stueck, *Rethinking*, at 61–83.

131. Hess at 9–11; Hunt and Levine at 128–135.

132. Hamby at 534–537; Hess at 17.

133. Hess at 17–32.

134. Id. at 8, 24–25.

135. See, e.g., Donald R. McCoy, *The Presidency of Harry S. Truman* 229 (1984).

136. Kaufman at 45; McCullough at 779.

137. For a relevant discussion, see Stromseth at 622–625.

138. See, e.g., Robert F. Turner, "Truman, Korea, and the Constitution: Debunking The 'Imperial President' Myth," 19 *Harv. J.L. & Pub. Pol'y* 533 (1995).

139. Patterson at 212–213. Connally was not regarded as a reliable member of Congress. See Johnson at 1, 15, 42.

140. Hess at 26, 31.

141. Hamby at 524, 538–539, 550, 560.

142. At a meeting of the Cabinet including members of Congress on June 30, for example, Senator Wherry repeatedly raised the issue of congressional authorization, only to be put off by Truman's comment "that if any large scale actions were to take place, he would tell the Congress about it." Truman thus committed himself only to providing information, not giving Congress a deciding role. Memorandum of Meeting of Cabinet and Members of Congress, Subject File: Korea-June 30, 1950, Papers of George M. Elsey, HST Administration, Harry S. Truman Presidential Library. The memorandum was apparently authored by Elsey, Truman's aide.

143. For an example of a claim of precedent by the executive branch, see William H. Rehnquist, Assistant Att'y Gen., Office of Legal Counsel, "The President and the War Power: South Vietnam and the Cambodian Sanctuaries," Memorandum to Charles W. Colson, Special Counsel to the President, May 22, 1970 12–13 [hereinafter Rehnquist OLC opinion].

144. Hess at 18.

145. Hess at 12–15; Isaacson and Thomas at 508.

146. Beisner at 327–330; Leffler at 368; Zelizer at 100.

147. Beisner at 327–330; Kaufman at 16–17; McCullough at 543–549. See also Hogan at 13 on the Clifford-Elsey report.

148. Beisner at 328–329.

149. Hess at 39–40; Kaufman at 23. In his biography of Acheson, Robert Beisner comments: "Because the administration was the first after World War II to face this intermediate kind of conflict, uncertainty about how to gain legal authority for waging it is understandable and so was the state department's concern about a declaration of war, which might set off popular passions, extinguishing the chance to wage the limited war Acheson and his advisers favored." Beisner at 347.

150. William Stueck, "The Korean War," in 1 *Cambridge History*, at 276. See also Hunt and Levine at 135–136.

151. See Beisner at 345; Hamby at 537–538; McCullough at 782. In addition, Truman was concerned to avoid escalating the Korean situation into a general war with the Soviet Union. This might have led Truman to avoid "war" talk. Hess at 23, 28–29. Hamby believes Truman was talking of police actions and describing the North Korean army as bandits because he was unwilling to admit he was taking the nation to war. Hamby at 537–538.

152. Hess at 21–22.

153. Beisner at 348; Hess at 26.

154. As a practical matter, members of the cabinet such as Acheson did not deny that Korea was a war. See Louis Fisher, "The Korean War: On What Legal Basis Did Truman Act?," 89 *Am. J. Int'l L.* 21, 34 (1995).

155. Beisner at 347–349; Herring at 641; Hess at 34–36; McCullough at 789; Offner at 376–377; Patterson at 212–213. See also McCullough's comments on Truman's decision to seize the steel mills in 1952. McCullough at 896–897. This is also suggested by Acheson's account. Dean Acheson, *Present at the Creation* 415 (1969).

156. The decision is sometimes attributed to Acheson's advice, based on the account in his memoirs. Acheson at 414–415. For examples of this attribution, see David J. Barron and Martin S. Lederman, "The Commander in Chief at the Lowest Ebb—A Constitutional History," 121 *Harv. L. Rev.* 941, 1056 (2008); Stromseth at 631–633. However, Acheson's most recent biographer notes that he made efforts throughout the month that followed the Korea decision to get Truman to engage with Congress through a formal address and resolution of support. Beisner at 347–349. Truman biographer Hamby comments that Acheson's assertion claiming sole responsibility for not taking the matter to Congress was exaggerated. Hamby at 539. Beisner's account is supported by memorandums prepared by Truman's aide George Elsey. See Memorandum of July 1950, Subject: Congressional Action; Memorandum for Mr. Smith, July 16, 1950, both in Subject File: Korea-July 1950, George M. Elsey Papers, Box 71, HST Presidential Library. See also Memorandum for File, Subject: Preparation of President's Message to Congress on Korea, July 19, 1950, Korea-July 19, 1950 Message Folder, George M. Elsey Papers, Box 71, Harry S. Truman Presidential Library.

157. Hamby at 539.

158. Gordon Silverstein, *Imbalance of Powers: Constitutional Interpretation and the Making of American Foreign Policy* 67 (1997).

159. For an example of an originalist scholar driven to this conclusion, see Michael Stokes Paulsen, "The War Power," 33 *Harv. J. L. & Pub. Pol'y* 113 (2010). However, I do not claim the Korean War was illegal. Conclusions about legality are best reserved for situations where we have judicial doctrine to guide us.

160. Hess at 32; McCullough at 780–781; Patterson at 213–214.

161. Beisner at 347–348; McCullough at 813–816, 847, 860; Patterson at 232.

162. Hess at 38–39; Hunt and Levine at 176–177.

163. Id. at 28.

164. Beisner at 393–401; Kaufman at 55–57; Leffler at 377–380; Patterson at 219–220.

165. Beisner at 410–416; Kaufman at 67–68.

166. Kaufman at 25; Leffler at 366.

167. Hess at 67–70.

168. Hamby at 560; Hunt and Levine at 159.

169. David Halberstam, *The Coldest Winter: America and the Korean War* 150 (2007).

170. Stueck, *Korean War*, at 361.

171. Id.

172. See the table in Chapter 1, pp. 46–47.

173. Beisner at 445; Hess at 72–74; Kaufman at 215–216; Patterson at 236.

174. U.S. Dept. State, "Authority of the President To Repel the Attack in Korea (July 3, 1950)," in 23 *Dep't St. Bull.* 173 (1950) [hereinafter *Bulletin*]. Acheson was confident of the memorandum's conclusions, saying "[t]here has never, I believe, been any serious doubt—in the sense of non-politically inspired doubt—of the President's constitutional authority to do what he did." Acheson at 414. See also Beisner at 349.

175. An additional 27-page defense of executive power to send troops abroad was prepared by the executive branch in the context of the debate over sending several divisions to support NATO. See Staff of Joint Comm. Made Up of Comm. on Foreign Relations and Comm. on Armed Services of the Senate, 82d Cong., 1st Sess., Report on the Powers of the President to Send the Armed Forces outside the United States (1951).

176. *Bulletin* at 174.

177. Id. at 176.

178. Id. at 176–177.

179. Id. at 177–178. In defending the legality of the Vietnam War, the legal adviser for the Department of State advanced a similar claim that there were "at least 125 instances in which the President has ordered the armed forces to take action or maintain positions abroad without obtaining prior Congressional authorization." Office of the Legal Adviser, "The Legality of United States Participation in the Defense of Viet Nam," 75 *Yale L.J.* 1085, 1101 (1966). These arguments have had a long life in the executive branch. The Korea and Vietnam memorandums were cited with approval by the Office of Legal Counsel in the Clinton administration. See "Proposed Deployment of United States Armed Forces into Bosnia," 19 Op. O.L C. 327, 331 (1995).

180. For notable attempts to sort through the conceptual mess created by such arguments, see Curtis A. Bradley and Trevor W. Morrison, "Historical Gloss and the Separation of Powers," 126 *Harv. L. Rev.* 411 (2012); Peter J. Spiro, "War Powers and the Sirens of Formalism," 68 *N.Y.U. L. Rev.* 1338, 1355–1356 (1993).

181. For a relevant discussion, see Bradley and Morrison at 466.

182. For an account of some of the incidents in the nineteenth century, see Putney.

183. John Hart Ely, *War and Responsibility: Constitutional Lessons of Vietnam and Its Aftermath* 147–150 n.54 (1993). For an account of the shifting numbers over the years see Wormuth and Firmage at 142–151. Their effective critique is still worth reading (as is Ely's).

184. See, e.g., H. Jefferson Powell, *The President's Authority over Foreign Affairs* 119–120 (2002).

185. See, e.g., Rostow.

186. See David Golove, "From Versailles to San Francisco: The Revolutionary Transformation of the War Powers," 70 *U. Colo. L. Rev.* 1491 (1999).

187. John Milton Cooper Jr., *Breaking the Heart of the World: Woodrow Wilson and the Fight for the League of Nations* 10–11 (2001).

188. Id. at 11.

189. Id. at 52.

190. Margaret Macmillan, *Peacemakers: The Paris Conference of 1919 and Its Attempt to End War* 102–103 (2001). See also Thomas J. Knock, *To End All Wars: Woodrow Wilson and the Quest for a New World Order* 205 (1992) (objections of Secretary of State Lansing to proposed treaty along similar lines).

191. Cooper at 118.

192. Id. at 194, 226.

193. Id. at 142.

194. Herring at 430.

195. Cooper at 131.

196. Id. at 389.

197. See Robert A. Divine, *Second Chance: The Triumph of Internationalism in America during World War II* 222–225 (1967); Robert C. Hilderbrand, *Dumbarton Oaks: The Origins of the United Nations and the Search for Postwar Security* 149–151 (1990).

198. Divine, *Second Chance*, at 192, 222–225.

199. James Grafton Rogers, *World Policing and the Constitution* (1945).

200. See id. at 7.

201. For a use of Rogers's work as authority by the Office of Legal Counsel, see "Authority to Use United States Military Forces in Somalia," 16 Op. O.L.C. 6, 9 (1992).

202. Rogers at 11–12.

203. Id. at 18.

204. Id. at 45, 54–55.

205. Id. at 92–123.

206. Id. at 56.

207. Stromseth at 608.

208. See the discussion in id. at 607–612.

209. Id. at 618.

210. During Senate hearings on the Charter, Senator Vandenberg stated his view that the president had acquired authority based on practice to intervene in circumstances short of war. See Divine, Second Chance, at 305–306.

211. Stromseth at 616–618.

212. See the discussion in id. at 618–619.

213. Office of the Legal Adviser at 1106.

214. With respect to Wilson, see Herring at 398–410; Knock at 105–122. For FDR, see Dallek at 199–313; Herring at 517–537.

215. David Gartner, "Foreign Relations, Strategic Doctrine and Presidential Power," 63 *Ala. L. Rev.* 499 (2012).

216. Henry P. Monaghan, "Presidential War-Making," 50 *B.U. L. Rev.* 19, 26–27 (1970).

217. Herring at 299–398.

218. Id. at 331–333.

219. Id. at 299–305, 335. See also Hunt at 58–91; Lars Schoultz, *Beneath the United States: A History of U.S. Policy Toward Latin America* 177 (1998) (ideology of jingoism in relation to Latin America).

220. Herring at 331–333.

221. Id. at 369–371; Schoultz at 183–192.

222. Herring at 369–370.

223. Id. at 497–501; Schoultz at 290–292; Gaddis Smith, *The Last Years of the Monroe Doctrine, 1945–1993* 26 (1994).

224. Grandin at 27–28, 31–35; Herring at 497; Schoultz at 302–306. In saying this, I am not denying that the U.S. retained considerable influence in Latin American countries through nonmilitary means. See the account of the Good Neighbor policy in Walter LaFeber, *Inevitable Revolutions: The United States in Central America* 80–85 (2d ed. 1993). I am also not denying that the U.S. intervened in Latin America and the Caribbean multiple times during the Cold War on anticommunist grounds. Some of these interventions are discussed in later chapters. But because these interventions occurred after 1950, they do not affect the argument here that pre-1950 incidents were not regarded as precedents for the kind of broad war powers presidents claimed in the post-1945 period.

225. Fisher at 37–38.

226. William Howard Taft, *Our Chief Magistrate and His Powers* 95–96 (1916). When the Mexican Revolution threatened U.S. interests, Taft dispatched troops to Texas for maneuvers, saying that he would not order them into Mexico "without express Congressional approval." Lewis L. Gould, *The William Howard Taft Presidency* 145 (2009).

227. Taft at 94. Further evidence that no one rested arguments for broad presidential power on lists of past military interventions prior to deliberations over the U.N. comes from two reasonably comprehensive reviews of presidential power in foreign affairs published between the world wars. These scholars were concerned with the practical and political issue of which branch had the initiative in proposing or starting a war rather than the issue of which branch had the proper constitutional authority. See Clarence A. Berdahl, *War Powers of the Executive in the United States* 78–98 (1920); Charles P. Howland, *Survey of American Foreign Relations, 1928* 97–112 (1928) (published for the Council on Foreign Relations).

228. See 117 Cong. Rec. 14334 (daily ed. May 11, 1971).

229. See Wormuth and Firmage at 142–143 on the pre-1950 lists which were either not produced by the executive branch or not directed at showing a presidential authority to engage in war.

230. Some scholars believe the Mexican War of 1846 is an additional precedent for a broad presidential war power. The reality behind this contention is

that the War, although declared, was in truth initiated by President James Polk when he ordered the army across a disputed border to occupy Mexican territory. The problems with Polk's actions do not end there. Historians have argued that Polk misrepresented his actions and played fast and loose with legislative procedure to rush Congress to approve the war. All in all, an early example of the imperial presidency in action! For a thoughtful historical account that advances these criticisms, see Amy S. Greenberg, *A Wicked War: Polk, Clay, Lincoln, and the 1846 U.S. Invasion of Mexico* (2012).

The question for my account of how presidents exercise power within constitutional orders is what Polk's actions meant for the future. Although the Mexican War raises many fascinating issues, it has served more as a negative precedent for future presidents than one that underwrote a broader view of presidential authority. Certainly no president cited Polk's actions favorably in the same way post-1950 presidents cited Korea. In fact, the force of its negative example perhaps explains why early twentieth century commentators thought it important to concentrate on which branch had the practical initiative in starting a war. Polk's actions powerfully suggested that the president could put Congress in a position where it had to go to war. Nevertheless, because there was no permanent change in the capacity of the government to wage war, Polk's actions did not alter the original constitutional order.

The example of the Mexican War contains further complexities that are not often highlighted. I have emphasized the value of democratic deliberation before starting a war. But even historians critical of Polk agree that the public wanted war in order to expand the country. See id. at 96–97, 103, 105, 108. As I will discuss in Chapter 7, the Constitution provides processes without generally dictating policy outcomes. So complying with the "declare war" clause does not protect the country from making mistakes. The advantage of authorized wars within the original constitutional order, as Greenberg's history amply shows, is that they provided the opportunity to learn the lessons of history through the cycle of accountability. This is an opportunity we do not have today.

231. *U.S. Commitments to Foreign Powers: Hearing before the S. Comm. on Foreign Relations*, 90th Cong. 80 (1967) (testimony of Nicholas Katzenbach, Under Secretary of State).

232. Id.

233. Id. at 80–81.

234. Id. at 81, 161–162.

235. Id. at 174–175, 179–180 (remarks of Senator Fulbright), 187 (remarks of Senators Gore and Case), 192–193 (remarks of Senator Ervin).

236. Id. at 174–175.

237. The contemporary opinions are discussed in detail in Chapters 5 and 6.

238. Paul Kennedy, *The Parliament of Man: The Past, Present, and Future of the United Nations* 73–74, 85–86 (2006).

239. Thomas M. Franck and Faiza Patel, "U.N. Police Action in Lieu of War: 'The Old Order Changeth,'" 85 *Am. J. Int'l L.* 63 (1991). For critical examinations

of this thesis, see Michael J. Glennon, "The Constitution and Chapter VII of the United Nations Charter," 85 *Am. J. Int'l L.* 74 (1991); Stromseth.

240. Beisner at 46.

241. Id. at 51–52.

242. Id. at 155, 529–530.

243. Beisner at 56, 59; Paterson at 71.

244. Gaddis, *Containment*, at 56.

245. See the discussion in Chapter 5.

246. The most comprehensive legal memo written for Bush during the Gulf War was by White House Counsel C. Boyden Gray. Memorandum for President from C. Boyden Gray, Aug. 7, 1990, John Sununu Files, OA/ID 29166-008, Persian Gulf War 1991 [6], George Bush Presidential Library.

247. This lack of approval was one of the reasons commentators believed the Iraq War violated the U.N. Charter. See Thomas M. Franck, "What Happens Now? The United Nations after Iraq," 97 *Am. J. Int'l L.* 607 (2003).

248. Fisher at 37–38.

249. See Herring at 657–658; Johnson at 23–61; Zelizer at 81–124.

250. Beisner at 299–320; Zelizer at 103.

251. Beisner at 319.

252. See Patterson at 169–205; Zelizer at 81–120.

253. See Patterson at 236–242.

254. Zelizer at 112–113.

255. Id. at 94–95.

256. Ellen Schrecker, *Many Are the Crimes: McCarthyism in America* 371–373 (1998).

257. Id. at 372. See also Hunt and Levine at 180–181.

258. *Youngstown Sheet & Tube Co. v. Sawyer*, 343 U.S. 579 (1952).

259. See id. at 634–655 (Jackson, J., concurring).

260. Harold Hongju Koh, *The National Security Constitution: Sharing Power after the Iran-Contra Affair* 105–113 (1990). Koh's analysis of the Iran-contra affair is considered in Chapter 5.

261. For commentary on the poor legal handling of the case, see Harold H. Bruff, *Bad Advice: Bush's Lawyers in the War on Terror* 49–52 (2009).

262. See Maeva Marcus, *Truman and the Steel Seizure Case* (1994) (originally published 1978).

263. Id. at 58–129.

264. See Hamby at 595.

265. Allan R. Millett and Peter Maslowski, *For the Common Defense: A Military History of the United States of America* 497 (1984) (summarizing state of forces in Korea in 1951).

266. See McCullough at 902.

267. Millett and Maslowski at 502.

268. Marcus at 75–76.

269. In fact, such histories typically do not mention the case at all. See, e.g., Millett and Maslowski. But see McCullough, citing an observation on the negative effect of the strike by Secretary of Defense Lovett. McCullough at 901–902. For doubts about whether the strike had any impact on the war effort, see Hamby at 597.

270. See, e.g., Amy B. Zegart, *Flawed by Design: The Evolution of the CIA, JCS, and NSC* 96–97 (1999).

271. Isaacson and Thomas at 555–556; Marcus at 74–75.

272. Harry S. Truman, 2 *Memoirs: Years of Trial and Hope* 472–473 (1956).

273. Truman at 478. Truman also displayed some impatience with the idea that Korea was not a declared war. "It is not very realistic for the justices to say that comprehensive powers shall be available to the President only when a war has been declared or when the country has been invaded. We live in an age when hostilities begin without polite exchanges of diplomatic notes." Id.

274. See McCullough at 899.

275. Id. at 495.

276. Id. at 498–499.

277. Id. at 501.

278. Id. at 503.

279. Id. at 504–506.

280. For the steel strike, see Marcus at 225–227.

281. McCullough at 897.

282. Id. at 859–860, 872–874; Hamby at 595.

283. Marcus at 224, 258.

284. Id. at 136, 146, 150. During oral argument, Justices Frankfurter and Jackson specifically disputed whether the nation was at war. Id. at 173.

285. McCullough at 900–901.

286. The detainee cases made it clear that Jackson's concurrence remains influential. See *Boumediene v. Bush,* 553 U.S. 723, 743 (2008); *Hamdan v. Rumsfeld,* 548 U.S. 557, 638–639 (2006); *Hamdi v. Rumsfeld,* 542 U.S. 507, 552 (2004).

287. See Louis Henkin, *Foreign Affairs and the U.S. Constitution* 95, 378 n.24 (2d ed. 1996); Koh at 106–107; Schlesinger at 143–144; Patricia L. Bellia, "Executive Power in *Youngstown*'s Shadows," 19 *Const. Comm.* 87, 117 (2002).

288. Jackson had served as solicitor general and attorney general in the Roosevelt administration and chief prosecutor for the U.S. in the Nuremberg trials in 1945–1946.

289. 343 U.S. 635 (Jackson, J., concurring).

290. Id.

291. Id. at 637.

292. Id.

293. Id.

294. Id.

295. Id. at 638.

296. Id. at 640.
297. Id. at 640–647.
298. Id. at 641.
299. Id. at 642–643.
300. Id. at 642.
301. Id.
302. Id. at 645.
303. See id. at 642–643, 649–653.
304. Id. at 653.
305. See Rostow at 836, 841.

3. War and the National Security State

1. Pub. L. No. 80-235, 61 Stat. 495 (1947) (codified at 50 U.S.C. ch. 15 (2006)).

2. On the evolution of the National Security Act, see Douglas T. Stuart, *Creating the National Security State* 143 (2008); Amy B. Zegart, *Flawed by Design: The Evolution of the CIA, JCS, and NSC* 10–11 (1999).

3. See James T. Patterson, *Grand Expectations: The United States, 1945–1974* 133 (1996).

4. Stuart at 52.

5. See Mark A. Stoler, *Allies and Adversaries: The Joint Chiefs of Staff, The Grand Alliance, and U.S. Strategy in World War II* 64–65, 103–104 (2000).

6. Stuart at 94.

7. Michael J. Hogan, *A Cross of Iron: Harry S. Truman and the Origins of the National Security State, 1945–1954* 194 (1998); Stuart at 105–108.

8. Hogan at 206; Stuart at 188–191, 196, 199–200. Further centralization was required under Eisenhower and accomplished in the Department of Defense Reorganization Act of 1958, Pub. L. No. 85-599, 72 Stat. 514 (1958). Stuart at 227.

9. Patterson at 133.

10. Stuart at 129, 239.

11. See John Ranelagh, *The Agency: The Rise and Decline of the CIA* 21 (1987). For other useful histories of the CIA, see Stuart; Thomas F. Troy, *Donovan and the CIA* (1981) (originally a classified CIA internal history); Tim Weiner, *Legacy of Ashes: The History of the CIA* (2007); Zegart; Anne Karalekas, "History of the Central Intelligence Agency," in *The Central Intelligence Agency: History and Documents* (William M. Leary ed., 1984). See also U.S. Dept. State, *Foreign Relations of the United States, 1945–1950: Emergence of the Intelligence Establishment* (1996) [hereinafter FRUS: *Emergence*]; U.S. Dept. State, *Foreign Relations of the United States: The Intelligence Community 1950–1955* (2007) [hereinafter FRUS: *Intelligence*].

12. Karalekas at 19; Ranelagh at 55; Stuart at 2, 7, 42.

13. Stuart at 72.

14. See, e.g., Roberta Wohlstetter, *Pearl Harbor: Warning and Decision* (1962).

15. Karalekas at 24.

16. Ranelagh at 112; Zegart at 167–168.

17. Ranelagh at 11, 18.

18. Id. at 279.

19. Zegart at 210.

20. Ranelagh at 119–121, 169, 279, 486.

21. Id. at 535.

22. Ranelagh at 116; Stuart at 141; Troy at 375–376, 381, 394–395, 408.

23. See, e.g., Frank J. Donner, *The Age of Surveillance* 8 (1981); Harold Hongju Koh, *The National Security Constitution* 103 (1990); Thomas Powers, *The Man Who Kept the Secrets: Richard Helms and the* CIA 29 (1979); Zegart at 186–187.

24. FRUS: *Emergence* at 521.

25. Id. at 521–522, 538–548.

26. Id. at 522.

27. Id.

28. Id. at 713.

29. Stuart at 268–269.

30. Id.

31. Ranelagh at 193–195; Weiner at 40.

32. For a useful discussion of the types of covert operations, see Gregory F. Treverton, *Covert Action: The Limits of Intervention in the Postwar World* 12–28 (1987).

33. Id. at 25–28.

34. See generally Jules Lobel, "Covert War and Congressional Authority: Hidden War and Forgotten Power," 134 *U. Pa. L. Rev.* 1035 (1986).

35. Ranelagh at 558–559.

36. Id. at 106.

37. Id. at 194.

38. Id. at 106, 119, 168, 179, 183–184, 211–212.

39. Id. at 227, 353; Stuart at 264–265.

40. See NSC Directive 10/2, June 18, 1948, in FRUS: *Emergence*, at 713, 714; NSC Directive 5412/1, March 12, 1955, in FRUS: *Intelligence*, at 622, 624.

41. Robert P. Joyce, Memorandum, Jan. 26, 1953, in FRUS: *Intelligence*, at 400.

42. Id. at 402.

43. Id. at 402–403.

44. Ranelagh at 281–283; Stuart at 271.

45. Ranelagh at 282–283.

46. Id. at 571–577.

47. Id. at 550 (emphasis in original).

48. Id. at 574.

49. Id. at 485–486, 511, 554.

50. See, e.g., Louis Fisher, *Presidential War Power* 117–125 (2d ed. 2004); Jane E. Stromseth, "Rethinking War Powers: Congress, the President, and the United Nations," 81 *Geo. L.J.* 597, 638 (1993); "Understanding Constitutional War Powers Today: Why Methodology Matters," 106 *Yale L.J.* 845, 869–870 (1996).

51. On the foreign policy and national security strategy of the Eisenhower presidency, see Robert R. Bowie and Richard H. Immerman, *Waging Peace: How Eisenhower Shaped an Enduring Cold War Strategy* (1998); Campbell Craig and Fredrik Logevall, *America's Cold War: The Politics of Insecurity* (2009); John Lewis Gaddis, *Strategies of Containment: A Critical Appraisal of American National Security Policy during the Cold War* (rev. ed. 2005) [hereinafter Gaddis, *Containment*]; *The Cold War: A New History* (2005) [hereinafter Gaddis, *Cold War*]; George C. Herring, *From Colony to Superpower: U.S. Foreign Relations since 1776* (2008); Robert David Johnson, *Congress and the Cold War* (2006); James Ledbetter, *Unwarranted Influence: Dwight D. Eisenhower and the Military-Industrial Complex* (2011); Fredrik Logevall, *Embers of War: The Fall of an Empire and the Making of America's Vietnam* (2012); Robert J. McMahon, *The Cold War* (2003); Gregory Mitrovich, *Undermining the Kremlin: America's Strategy to Subvert the Soviet Bloc, 1947–1956* (2000); David A. Nichols, *Eisenhower 1956: The President's Year of Crisis* (2011); Patterson; Julian E. Zelizer, *Arsenal of Democracy: The Politics of National Security* (2010); Robert J. McMahon, "U.S. National Security Policy from Eisenhower to Kennedy," in 1 *The Cambridge History of the Cold War: Origins* 288 (Melvyn P. Leffler and Odd Arne Westad eds., 2010) [hereinafter McMahon, *Cambridge History*]. For an informative presidential biography, see Stephen E. Ambrose, *Eisenhower: The President* (1984).

52. Zelizer at 85.

53. Herring at 656–657.

54. See Duane Tananbaum, *The Bricker Amendment Controversy: A Test of Eisenhower's Political Leadership* 199–200 (1988).

55. Craig and Logevall at 192–196.

56. Johnson at 56; Zelizer at 126–127.

57. Johnson at 56.

58. President's News Conference of March 10, 1954, 1954 Public Papers 306 (March 10, 1954). See also Logevall at 458.

59. Quoted in Tananbaum at 200 (footnote omitted).

60. Id. at 200–202, 208–209.

61. Nichols at 62, 136, 138–139, 148, 161–162, 167.

62. Ambrose at 232; Hogan at 452; Tananbaum at 200. See also George C. Herring and Richard H. Immerman, "Eisenhower, Dulles, and Dienbienphu: 'The Day We Didn't Go to War' Revisited," 71 *J. Am. Hist.* 343, 352 (1984).

63. Logevall at 466–467; Tananbaum at 201–202, 208–209; Herring and Immerman at 352.

64. Ambrose at 232; Johnson at 65; Patterson at 300; Zelizer at 130.

65. Fisher at 118–120.

66. In the Dienbienphu crisis, for example, it appears that congressional consultation was meaningful in that it influenced administration policy. Members of Congress insisted that there could be no American intervention without the cooperation of allies and this constituted a check on Eisenhower's desire to aid the French. See Logevall at 467–480, 494.

67. Zelizer at 130–131.

68. Herring and Immerman at 351, 363.

69. Logevall at 459–461.

70. Nichols at 250; Tananbaum at 201.

71. Zelizer at 83–85.

72. Id. at 83–84; Johnson at 35, 61.

73. Zelizer at 85, 123; Johnson at 27–28.

74. Tananbaum at 199–200, 218.

75. Id.

76. Zelizer at 120–121.

77. Johnson at 52.

78. Craig and Logevall at 175; Zelizer at 145.

79. Ambrose at 172, 226.

80. Rosemary Foot, *The Wrong War: American Policy and the Dimensions of the Korean Conflict, 1950–1953* 214, 230 (1985).

81. John Lewis Gaddis, *The Long Peace: Inquiries into the History of the Cold War* 136–137 (1987); McMahon at 81.

82. Gaddis, *Cold War,* at 73.

83. Logevall at 697.

84. Herring at 685; Tananbaum at 218; Douglas Little, "Mission Impossible: The CIA and the Cult of Covert Action in the Middle East," 28 *Diplomatic Hist.* 663 (2004).

85. Zelizer at 120–121.

86. Ambrose at 584.

87. Ledbetter at 216; Patterson at 440–441.

88. Hogan at 383–384.

89. For an interesting commentary on Eisenhower, see Ambrose at 561, 594. See also McMahon, *Cambridge History,* at 288–289.

90. McMahon, *Cambridge History,* at 304.

91. See Stephen G. Rabe, *Eisenhower and Latin America* 129–130, 166–167, 170–171 (1988).

92. Interview with General Andrew J. Goodpaster, June 26, 1975 at 7 (available from Eisenhower Presidential Library at http://eisenhower.archives.gov/research/oral_histories/oral_history_transcripts/Goodpaster_Andrew_378.pdf

93. Id.

94. On U.S. policy toward Cuba during this period, including the Bay of Pigs intervention and the October 1962 missile crisis, see Graham Allison and Philip Zelikow, *Essence of Decision: Explaining the Cuban Missile Crisis* (2d ed. 1999);

Hal Brands, *Latin America's Cold War* (2010); Michael Dobbs, *One Minute to Midnight: Kennedy, Khrushchev, and Castro on the Brink of Nuclear War* (2008); Lawrence Freedman, *Kennedy's Wars* (2000); Aleksandr Fursenko and Timothy Naftali, *"One Hell of a Gamble": Khrushchev, Castro, and Kennedy, 1958–1964* (1997); James N. Giglio, *The Presidency of John F. Kennedy* (2d ed. 2006); Howard Jones, *The Bay of Pigs* (2008); G. Calvin Mackenzie and Robert Weisbrot, *The Liberal Hour: Washington and the Politics of Change in the 1960s* 266 (2008); Lars Schoultz, *That Infernal Little Cuban Republic: The United States and the Cuban Revolution* (2009); Rabe; Robert Weisbrot, *Maximum Danger: Kennedy, the Missiles, and the Crisis of American Confidence* (2001); James G. Hershberg, "The Cuban Missile Crisis," in 2 *The Cambridge History of the Cold War: Crises and Détente* 65 (Melvyn P. Leffler and Odd Arne Westad eds., 2010).

95. See generally Weisbrot.

96. Fursenko and Naftali at 83.

97. Freedman at 125.

98. Fursenko and Naftali at 9, 16, 83; Jones at 39–40.

99. Freedman at 126; Jones at 37, 54–55, 75.

100. Freedman at 129.

101. Jones at 58–59, 70–71, 125–126, 141–142; Schoultz at 164–165.

102. Id. at 52–53, 55, 58, 127.

103. Freedman at 130; Jones at 51; Schoultz at 145.

104. Jones at 50–51, 55, 58, 66–67.

105. Fursenko and Naftali at 85, 93; Jones at 94.

106. Jones at 114–122.

107. Jones at 3. Jones argues that the CIA projects to assassinate Castro were an integral element of the operation to change his regime. Id. at 35–36.

108. Id. at 5.

109. See the discussion in Chapter 2 and Ranelagh at 277.

110. Kathryn S. Olmsted, *Challenging the Secret Government: The Post-Watergate Investigations of the CIA and FBI* 88–89, 109–110 (1996).

111. Jones at 61; Schoultz at 158; Weiner at 165.

112. Jones at 53, 150.

113. Freedman at 128; Fursenko and Naftali at 85; Jones at 58.

114. Freedman at 128.

115. Schoultz at 152.

116. Jones at 52; Ranelagh at 372–373; Schoultz at 162–164. See also Gordon M. Goldstein, *Lessons in Disaster: McGeorge Bundy and the Path to War in Vietnam* 39–40 (2008).

117. Freedman at 138.

118. Weiner at 351.

119. Jones at 67.

120. Here I refer to the use of CIA-trained Cuban operatives in the Watergate burglary, discussed in Chapter 4. See J. Anthony Lukas, *Nightmare: The Underside of the Nixon Years* 95–96 (1988).

121. Schoultz at 171.

122. Dobbs at 8; Jones at 154; Schoultz at 175–176.

123. Lukas at 95–96.

124. Quoted in Fursenko and Naftali at 148. See also Brands at 36.

125. Powers at 136.

126. Id. at 96.

127. Weisbrot at 7, 11. See also Gaddis Smith, *The Last Years of the Monroe Doctrine, 1945–1993* 97–98, 104–109 (1994).

128. Weisbrot at 11.

129. Id. at 44–45, 87–89.

130. Id. at 85.

131. Id. at 143.

132. Id. at 119–120.

133. Brands at 49–50; Dobbs at 344; Fursenko and Naftali at 73, 182–183; MacKenzie and Weisbrot at 266; McMahon at 90–91. See also James G. Blight and Janet M. Lang, "How Castro Held the World Hostage," *N.Y. Times*, Oct. 26, 2012, at A27.

134. Hershberg at 66.

135. Id. at 65.

136. Id. at 77.

137. Fursenko and Naftali at 244–245; Hershberg at 73; Zelizer at 166.

138. See *The Kennedy Tapes: Inside the White House during the Cuban Missile Crisis* 290 (Ernest R. May and Philip D. Zelikow eds., 1997).

139. Freedman at 194.

140. Weisbrot at 136–146.

141. Freedman at xii; Hershberg at 66.

142. Ledbetter at 213.

143. Id.

144. Jones at 21–22, 26.

145. Ambrose at 609; Rabe at 172.

146. Jones at 159.

147. James Bamford, *Body of Secrets* 82–91 (2002); Kathryn S. Olmsted, *Real Enemies: Conspiracy Theories and American Democracy, World War I to 9/11* 227 (2009).

148. Freedman at xi.

149. Quoted in Little at 680.

150. Weiner at 178.

151. Ranelagh at 211.

152. Id.

153. Jones at 48–49.

154. Quoted in id. at 49.

155. Ranelagh at 485–486, 511, 554.

156. See Kenneth Osgood, *Total Cold War: Eisenhower's Secret Propaganda Battle at Home and Abroad* (2006).

157. Zegart at 45.

158. Ambrose at 225, 561; Ledbetter at 98–99.

159. Hogan at 85, 97; Zegart at 11, 45, 131–132, 139–140, 142–145.

160. Ledbetter at 193.

161. Ambrose at 225.

162. See Freedman at 19; David Halberstam, *The Best and the Brightest* 142 (1972) (views of Matthew Ridgway); Stuart at 185.

163. George C. Herring, *LBJ and Vietnam: A Different Kind of War* 27 (1994).

164. Fursenko and Naftali at 156–157.

165. Weisbrot at 189.

166. Freedman at 219 (footnotes omitted).

167. Ledbetter at 98–99.

168. Patterson at 285.

169. See Ellen Schrecker, *Many Are the Crimes: McCarthyism in America* 359–415 (1998).

170. Patterson at 291.

171. Weisbrot at 15–16.

172. Id. at 28–29.

4. Vietnam and Watergate

1. The Vietnam War is one of the most studied conflicts in twentieth-century American history. Relevant general histories include Campbell Craig and Fredrik Logevall, *America's Cold War: The Politics of Insecurity* (2009); George C. Herring, *America's Longest War: The United States and Vietnam, 1950–1975* (4th ed. 2002) [hereinafter Herring, *America's Longest*]; Michael H. Hunt, *Lyndon Johnson's War* (1996); Stanley Karnow, *Vietnam: A History* (1983); Robert Mann, *A Grand Delusion: America's Descent into Vietnam* (2001); Robert D. Schulzinger, *A Time for War: The United States and Vietnam, 1941–1975* (1997); Marilyn B. Young, *The Vietnam Wars, 1945–1990* (1991). In addition, the four-volume work of William Conrad Gibbons, *The U.S. Government and the Vietnam War*, is essential. Individual volumes of this work are cited in the notes below.

For more specialized works focusing on the crucial Kennedy-Johnson decisions of 1963–1965, as well as other matters, see Lawrence Freedman, *Kennedy's Wars* (2000); Andrew L. Johns, *Vietnam's Second Front: Domestic Politics, the Republican Party, and the War* (2010); George McT. Kahin, *Intervention: How America Became Involved in Vietnam* (1986); David Kaiser, *American Tragedy: Kennedy, Johnson, and the Origins of the Vietnam War* (2000); Fredrik Logevall, *Choosing War: The Lost Chance for Peace and the Escalation of War in Vietnam* (1999); Gary Stone, *Elites for Peace: The Senate and the Vietnam War, 1964–1968* (2007); Brian VanDeMark, *Into the Quagmire: Lyndon Johnson and the Escalation of the Vietnam War* (1991).

Useful memoirs and biographies include Clark Clifford, *Counsel to the President* (1991); Robert Dallek, *Flawed Giant: Lyndon Johnson and His Times, 1961–1973*

(1998) [hereinafter Dallek, *Flawed Giant*]; Gordon M. Goldstein, *Lessons in Disaster: McGeorge Bundy and the Path to War in Vietnam* (2008); Nicholas deB. Katzenbach, *Some of It Was Fun: Working with RFK and LBJ* (2008); Robert S. McNamara, *In Retrospect: The Tragedy and Lessons of Vietnam* (1995); Deborah Shapley, *Promise and Power: The Life and Times of Robert McNamara* (1993).

Key revisionist accounts include H. R. McMaster, *Dereliction of Duty* (1997); Mark Moyar, *Triumph Forsaken: The Vietnam War, 1954–1965* (2006); Lewis Sorley, *A Better War* (1999); Harry G. Summers Jr., *On Strategy: A Critical Analysis of the Vietnam War* (1982). Works helpful in sorting out the various controversies over the war include Gary R. Hess, *Vietnam: Explaining America's Lost War* (2009) [hereinafter Hess, *Vietnam*]; Michael Lind, *Vietnam: The Necessary War* (1999); John Prados, *Vietnam: The History of an Unwinnable War, 1945–1975* (2009).

2. Dallek, *Flawed Giant*, at 156.

3. Kaiser at 409–410, 435–436.

4. Id. at 486–487.

5. Herring, *America's Longest*, at 358.

6. See the informed discussions in William Bundy, *A Tangled Web: The Making of Foreign Policy in the Nixon Presidency* 396–397 (1998); Dallek, *Flawed Giant*, at 153–156; Gary R. Hess, *Presidential Decisions for War* 84 (2d ed. 2009) [hereinafter Hess, *Presidential*]; Gordon Silverstein, *Law's Allure* 211 n.4 (2009).

7. For the origins of the resolution, see Karnow at 344–345; Andrew L. Johns, "Opening Pandora's Box: The Genesis and Evolution of the 1964 Congressional Resolution on Vietnam," 6 *J. American-East Asian Relations* 175 (1997) [hereinafter Johns, "Opening"].

8. William Conrad Gibbons, *The U.S. Government and the Vietnam War, Pt. 3* 240, 283–284 (1989) [hereinafter Gibbons 1989]; Johns, "Opening," at 178–179.

9. Kaiser at 304.

10. Herring, *America's Longest*, at 141–147; Hess, *Presidential*, at 85–86.

11. Dallek, *Flawed Giant*, at 153.

12. See *U.S. Commitments to Foreign Powers, Hearings before the S. Comm. on Foreign Relations*, 90th Cong. 71 (1967) [hereinafter *Commitments Hearing*].

13. William Conrad Gibbons, *The U.S. Government and the Vietnam War, Pt. 4* 808 (1995) [hereinafter Gibbons 1995].

14. See Katzenbach, *Some of It Was Fun*.

15. *Commitments Hearing* at 80–81.

16. Id. at 81, 161–162.

17. Id. at 82.

18. U.S. Dept. State, *Foreign Relations of the United States, Vietnam: January–June 1965* 751 (1996) (Memorandum from Attorney General Katzenbach) [hereinafter FRUS 1965].

19. Id. at 751–752.

20. Id. at 752.

21. Id.

22. Id.

23. Id. at 752–753. Katzenbach made the same point in *Commitments Hearing* at 161, 174.

24. FRUS 1965 at 752.

25. Id. at 753. Katzenbach cited the *Steel Seizure* case, *Youngstown Sheet & Tube Co. v. Sawyer*, 343 U.S. 579 (1952), and *Little v. Barreme*, 6 U.S. 170 (1804).

26. Johnson's statement was reprinted in *Commitments Hearing* at 121, 126. For Johnson's 1965 statement, see Gibbons 1989 at 283–284.

27. Stone at 61.

28. Mann at 354, 398.

29. *Commitments Hearing* at 130, 141.

30. William Conrad Gibbons, *The U.S. Government and the Vietnam War, Pt. 2* 306 (1986) [hereinafter Gibbons 1986]. The legal adviser provided the same advice to then–Under Secretary of State George Ball for testimony before Congress in April 1965. See Gibbons 1989 at 215.

31. Gibbons 1986 at 306. Somewhat ironically in light of the later commitment of over 500,000 troops to Vietnam, the adviser distinguished situations that would require a declaration of war, saying "[a] declaration of war, however, has always been thought of as implying a massive commitment of U.S. forces. That is not the case here." Id.

32. Gibbons 1989 at 79 n.97.

33. Leonard Meeker, Legal Advisor, Memorandum, April 6, 1965, LBJ Presidential Library, NSF Country File: Vietnam 7B 1965–1968 Legality Considerations.

34. See U.S. Dept. State, "The Legality of United States Participation in the Defense of Viet-Nam," 54 *Dep't State Bull.* 474 (1966), reprinted in Symposium, "Legality of United States Participation in the Viet Nam Conflict," 75 *Yale L.J.* 1084 (1966) [hereinafter cited as Vietnam Memorandum]. The memorandum was mostly devoted to justifying the war under international law. Vietnam Memorandum at 1085–1100.

35. Id. at 1100.

36. See Gibbons 1989 at 281–283, 460; Logevall at 402; Mann at 335.

37. See Gibbons 1986 at 308. See also Dallek, *Flawed Giant*, at 154; Young at 120.

38. See Gibbons 1989 at 281–282.

39. See, e.g., George C. Herring, *From Colony to Superpower: U.S. Foreign Relations since 1776* 87, 534 (2008) (referring to undeclared wars in American history); Hess, *Vietnam*, at 105–106; David Reynolds, *From Munich to Pearl Harbor: Roosevelt's America and the Origins of the Second World War* 185 (2001).

40. See John Hart Ely, *War and Responsibility: Constitutional Lessons of Vietnam and Its Aftermath* 26 (1993) (endorsing Katzenbach's "functional equivalent" assertion).

41. See Curtis A. Bradley and Jack L. Goldsmith, "Congressional Authorization and the War on Terrorism," 118 *Harv. L. Rev.* 2047, 2057–2066 (2005).

42. For the recent AUMFs, see S.J. Res. 23, 107th Cong. (2001); Pub. L. No. 107–40, 115 Stat. 224 (2001).

43. Ely at 12–30.

44. Stone at 25; Fredrik Logevall, "A Delicate Balance: John Sherman Cooper and the Republican Opposition to the Vietnam War," in *Vietnam and the American Political Tradition: The Politics of Dissent* 237, 245–248 (Randall B. Woods ed., 2003).

45. Gibbons 1995 at 549; Gibbons 1989 at 280–281; Hess, *Presidential*, at 142.

46. Gibbons 1989 at 238–239, 242–250.

47. Id. at 281–283.

48. This is suggested by Dallek, *Flawed Giant*, at 153.

49. Gibbons 1989 at 391–392.

50. Logevall at 171.

51. Herring, *America's Longest*, at 140–141.

52. See, e.g., Merlo J. Pusey, *The Way We Go to War* ix (1969).

53. Craig and Logevall at 236.

54. See Herring, *America's Longest*, at 147 (citing Kaiser, Logevall, and McMaster). For continuing doubts about the early decision thesis, see Johns; Stone. For an important discussion that supports Herring, see Goldstein at 204–219.

55. Craig and Logevall at 236.

56. See Herring, *America's Longest*, at 147.

57. See, e.g, Andrew J. Polsky, *Elusive Victories: The American Presidency at War* 211–212, 215 (2012).

58. For the best analysis of this issue, see generally Logevall.

59. George C. Herring, *LBJ and Vietnam: A Different Kind of War* 3–6 (1994) [hereinafter Herring, *LBJ and Vietnam*].

60. Herring, *America's Longest*, at 204–223.

61. Bundy at 6; Herring, *America's Longest*, at 158, 272; Logevall at 76, 306. For Nixon, see also Walter Isaacson, *Kissinger: A Biography* 206–209 (2005).

62. See Arthur M. Schlesinger Jr., *The Imperial Presidency* 177–182, 187–193 (1973).

63. Gibbons 1989 at 431.

64. Id. at 281–282.

65. Herring, *America's Longest*, at 104, 144, 158, 358. See also McNamara at 173–174, 191–192.

66. Freedman at 396–397; Shapley at 293.

67. Freedman at 371; McNamara at 101.

68. Freedman at 371.

69. Kaiser at 116.

70. Hess, *Presidential*, at 107.

71. Young at 137.

72. For a balanced discussion, see James N. Giglio, *The Presidency of John F. Kennedy* 255–270 (2d ed. 2006). For sophisticated cases that Kennedy had a

distinctly different approach than Johnson to foreign policy and diplomacy, see Craig and Logevall at 226–228; Freedman generally; Kaiser at 284–290; Logevall at 395–400.

73. Hess, *Presidential,* at 82; Logevall at 76–78; Shapley at 291.

74. See Craig and Logevall at 232–236; Herring, *America's Longest,* at 147; Kaiser; Logevall.

75. Logevall at 108–109, 230–231, 235.

76. Dallek, *Flawed Giant,* at 246–247; Kaiser at 355, 392–393, 400–401; Logevall at 252–280, 318–319.

77. Goldstein at 186–228; Kaiser at 410–411, 440–441, 473; Logevall at 268–272, 310–319, 369–374, 383–384.

78. Dallek, *Flawed Giant,* at 248, 252–253, 257; Kaiser at 5, 381, 400–403, 408–409, 413, 418–419, 435–436; Logevall at 272–274, 303–315, 331–336.

79. Kaiser at 400–402; McNamara at 172.

80. Logevall at 304.

81. Dallek, *Flawed Giant,* at 276.

82. See, e.g., Robert A. Caro, *The Years of Lyndon Johnson: Master of the Senate* (2002).

83. Logevall at 297–298.

84. See, e.g., Goldstein at 178–185; Herring, *America's Longest,* at 147–151; Logevall. I discuss this point further in Chapter 7.

85. Goldstein at 178–185.

86. Kaiser at 368.

87. Logevall at 119.

88. Goldstein at 204–219. See also Cyrus R. Vance, "Striking the Balance: Congress and the President under the War Powers Resolution," 133 *U. Pa. L. Rev.* 79, 91 (1984). Vance served in the DOD in the Johnson administration.

89. Logevall at 295.

90. Mann at 103, 387.

91. McNamara at 32–33.

92. Kaiser at 179.

93. Dallek, *Flawed Giant,* at 102; Kaiser at 179, 482; Logevall at 91–92; Mann at 172–173.

94. Logevall at 402.

95. Id. at 169–170.

96. Quoted in id. at 346–347.

97. See the discussion in Chapter 2.

98. Dallek, *Flawed Giant,* at 253.

99. Id.

100. Id.

101. Herring, *LBJ and Vietnam,* at 158–159.

102. Id. at 159; Mann at 585–586.

103. See McNamara at 205; Shapley at 347, 368–369.

104. Schulzinger at 233.

105. Craig and Logevall at 236–240; Stone at xxvi–xxvii.

106. Logevall at 387–395.

107. On the "credibility gap," see Dallek, *Flawed Giant*, at 449; Schulzinger at 180.

108. McNamara at 192.

109. Freedman at 293–304.

110. Robert D. Putnam, *Bowling Alone: The Collapse and Revival of American Community* 47 (2000).

111. Id. (emphasis in original).

112. Here I draw on my own analysis. See Stephen M. Griffin, "California Constitutionalism: Trust in Government and Direct Democracy," 11 *U. Pa. J. Const. L.* 551, 571–575 (2009).

113. Gary Orren, "Fall from Grace: The Public's Loss of Faith in Government," in *Why People Don't Trust Government* 77, 80 (Joseph S. Nye Jr. et al. eds., 1997).

114. Id.

115. Margaret Levi and Laura Stoker, "Political Trust and Trustworthiness," 3 *Ann. Rev. Pol. Sci.* 475, 480–481 (2000).

116. Joseph S. Nye Jr., "Introduction: The Decline of Confidence in Government," in *Why People Don't Trust Government*, at 1, 15.

117. Dallek, *Flawed Giant*, at 344–345.

118. Id. at 291.

119. Id. at 284.

120. Id. at 345; McNamara at 224–225.

121. Logevall at 369–370, 393.

122. Dallek, *Flawed Giant*, at 103, 356–357, 377–378, 388; Kaiser at 460–461; Logevall at 370–372.

123. Dallek, *Flawed Giant*, at 470; Kaiser at 462; Logevall at 389.

124. Kaiser at 462.

125. Quoted in Young at 206 (footnote omitted).

126. Dallek, *Flawed Giant*, at 494–495.

127. Id. at 352.

128. Id. at 366–367.

129. Id. at 486–487.

130. On Johnson, see id. at 489. For Nixon, see Melvin Small, *The Presidency of Richard Nixon* 70 (1999).

131. Herring, *America's Longest*, at 300; Mann at 687; Young at 238, 260–261.

132. For histories of Nixon's administration and foreign policy, see Bundy; Robert Dallek, *Nixon and Kissinger: Partners in Power* (2007) [hereinafter Dallek, *Nixon*]; Raymond L. Garthoff, *Détente and Confrontation: American-Soviet Relations from Nixon to Reagan* (rev. ed. 1994); David Greenberg, *Nixon's Shadow: The History*

of an Image (2003); Jeffrey Kimball, *Nixon's Vietnam War* (1998); Rick Perlstein, *Nixonland* (2008); Small.

Useful memoirs and biographies include Walter Isaacson, *Kissinger: A Biography* (2005); Richard Nixon, *RN: The Memoirs of Richard Nixon* (1978).

On Watergate, see Fred Emery, *Watergate: The Corruption of American Politics and the Fall of Richard Nixon* (1995); Ken Gormley, *Archibald Cox: Conscience of a Nation* (1997); Stanley I. Kutler, *The Wars of Watergate* (1990) [hereinafter Kutler, *Watergate*]; *Abuse of Power* (1997) [hereinafter Kutler, *Abuse*]; J. Anthony Lukas, *Nightmare: The Underside of the Nixon Years* (1988); Michael Schudson, *Watergate in American Memory* (1992).

133. See generally Kimball.

134. Id. at 166.

135. Dallek, *Nixon*, at 118; Kimball at 131.

136. Kimball at 136.

137. Id. at 160.

138. Id.

139. Dallek, *Nixon*, at 132–133; Kimball at 169–170.

140. Kimball at 197.

141. Id. at 213.

142. Dallek, *Nixon*, at 198–200, 205; Isaacson at 260–262.

143. Kimball at 203–204.

144. Id. at 221.

145. Kutler, *Watergate*, at 98.

146. Small at 56.

147. Id. at 70.

148. Dallek, *Nixon*, at 208; Greenberg at 82–83.

149. Kimball at 225.

150. Kutler, *Watergate*, at 96–101.

151. Lukas at 33.

152. Id. at 35–37.

153. See generally Perlstein.

154. For an example of the standard understanding from a member of the foreign policy establishment, see Bundy at 470.

155. For a relatively full accounting, see Lukas.

156. Garthoff at 30; Small at 60–62, 156.

157. John Ranelagh, *The Agency: The Rise and Decline of the CIA* 546 (1987); Schulzinger at 332.

158. Bundy at 44; Howard Jones, *The Bay of Pigs* 14 (2008).

159. Small at 64–65.

160. Id. at 61–62.

161. Id. at 55.

162. Dallek, *Nixon*, at 84–85; Small at 51–52. For the CIA, see Ranelagh at 499–501, 538, 540–541.

163. Ranelagh at 546, 552. See also Kimball at 33.

164. Kimball at 76–77.

165. Bundy at 517; Isaacson at 45, 67; Kimball at 2, 148; Small at 61–62.

166. Isaacson at 206–207, 327, 486–487; Kimball at 189; Small at 61–62, 242.

167. Dallek, *Nixon,* at 208.

168. See Kutler, *Abuse,* at 3–37.

169. Id. at 8 (emphasis in original). John Mitchell was the attorney general.

170. Id. (emphasis in original).

171. Kutler, *Watergate,* at 111–112.

172. Kutler, *Abuse,* at 28–30.

173. Small at 238, 276. See also Nixon's remarks in his memoirs. Nixon at 841–842.

174. Ranelagh at 521.

175. Kutler, *Abuse,* at 3–6, 27–28.

176. Lukas at 94–97.

177. Small at 255.

178. Kutler, *Abuse,* at 61–62, 67–70.

179. Id. at 67–70. See also Kutler, *Watergate,* at 218.

180. Kutler, *Watergate,* at 221; Ranelagh at 522–530; Small at 277.

181. Lukas at 94–101, 190–193, 196–200.

182. Id. at 94–96.

183. Kutler, *Watergate,* at 254.

184. Id. at 249.

185. This appears to be the view of a number of diplomatic historians with experience in government. See Bundy at 470; Garthoff.

186. Kimball at 62; Small at 64–66.

187. See, e.g., Greenberg at 333–334; Harry P. Jeffrey and Thomas Maxwell Long eds., *Watergate and the Resignation of Richard Nixon: Impact of a Constitutional Crisis* (2004); Kutler, *Watergate,* at 209, 316; Thomas E. Mann and Norman J. Ornstein, *The Broken Branch* 118–119 (2008); Sean Wilentz, *The Age of Reagan* 8 (2008).

188. See Sanford Levinson and Jack M. Balkin, "Constitutional Crises," 157 *U. Pa. L. Rev.* 707, 712, 742 (2009); Keith E. Whittington, "Yet Another Constitutional Crisis?," 43 *Wm. & Mary L. Rev.* 2093, 2131 n.175 (2002).

189. Kutler, *Watergate,* at 247–254.

190. Small at 282.

191. Kutler, *Watergate,* at 263.

192. Id. at 290–320.

193. Dallek, *Nixon,* at 544–545; Kutler, *Watergate,* at 324–325; Small at 271. See also Nixon's revealing comments in his memoirs. Nixon at 848–849.

194. Bundy at 433, 440; Dallek, *Nixon,* at 522, 528; Isaacson at 514, 531.

195. Garthoff at 458–459.

196. Nixon at 761–762.

197. Isaacson at 474.

198. Nixon at 850.

199. Dallek, *Nixon*, at 433–434.

200. Bundy at 359; Herring, *America's Longest*, at 317; Isaacson at 440.

201. See, e.g., Jonathan Schell, *The Time of Illusion* 257–259 (1975).

202. Isaacson at 206–209.

203. This list is suggested especially by the accounts in Dallek, *Nixon*; Herring, *America's Longest*; Kimball.

204. Dallek, *Nixon*, at 429; Isaacson at 484–485; Kimball at 190–192; Schulzinger at 304. See also the discussion in John Lewis Gaddis, *Strategies of Containment* 337–339 (rev. ed. 2005).

205. Dallek, *Nixon*, at 107, 196.

206. Bundy at 152–153; Dallek, *Nixon*, at 118; Kimball at 127, 131–133, 160, 165; Small at 78.

207. Bundy at 72.

208. Bundy at 149; Isaacson at 177, 272; Kimball at 199.

209. Bundy at 159–160; Isaacson at 270.

210. See William H. Rehnquist, Assistant Att'y Gen., Office of Legal Counsel, "The President and the War Power: South Vietnam and the Cambodian Sanctuaries," Memorandum to Charles W. Colson, Special Counsel to the President, May 22, 1970 [hereinafter Rehnquist OLC opinion].

211. Id. at 2.

212. Id.

213. Id. at 12–13.

214. Id. at 13.

215. Id. at 26.

216. Isaacson at 264; Kimball at 208.

217. Rehnquist OLC Opinion at 17.

218. Kimball at 368–371.

219. Id. at 368–369.

220. Id. at 369.

221. Id.

222. Id. at 370.

223. Id. at 90.

224. Bundy at 517.

225. Isaacson at 642–644; Mann at 721. See also P. Edward Haley, *Congress and the Fall of South Vietnam and Cambodia* 80–93, 107–115, 154–156 (1982).

226. U.S. Dept. State, *Foreign Relations of the United States: Vietnam, January 1973–July 1975* 761 (2010) (Memorandum of Conversation, April 8, 1975).

227. Address before a Joint Session of the Congress Reporting on United States Foreign Policy, Public Papers of the Presidents 459, 461 (April 10, 1975).

228. Herring, *America's Longest*, at 347.

5. The Constitutional Order in the Post-Vietnam Era

1. Stanley I. Kutler, *The Wars of Watergate* 377 (1990).

2. Works that are helpful in understanding the post-Vietnam era include Lou Cannon, *President Reagan: The Role of a Lifetime* (2000); Ivo H. Daalder and I. M. Destler, *In the Shadow of the Oval Office* (2009); John Lewis Gaddis, *Strategies of Containment: A Critical Appraisal of American National Security Policy during the Cold War* (rev. ed. 2005) [hereinafter Gaddis, *Containment*]; Raymond L. Garthoff, *Détente and Confrontation: American-Soviet Relations from Nixon to Reagan* (rev. ed. 1994); George C. Herring, *From Colony to Superpower: U.S. Foreign Relations since 1776* (2008); Robert J. McMahon, *The Cold War* (2003) [hereinafter McMahon, *Cold War*]; Yanek Mieczkowski, *Gerald Ford and the Challenges of the 1970s* (2005); Gaddis Smith, *Morality, Reason, and Power: American Diplomacy in the Carter Years* (1986); Odd Arne Westad, *The Global Cold War* (2007); Sean Wilentz, *The Age of Reagan: A History, 1974–2008* (2008); Julian E. Zelizer, *Arsenal of Democracy: The Politics of National Security* (2010) [hereinafter Zelizer, *Arsenal*].

3. Mieczkowski at 292–293.

4. Herring at 864; Westad at 331; James Kurth, "Variations on the American Way of War," in *The Long War: A New History of U.S. National Security Policy since World War II* 53, 71–72 (Andrew J. Bacevich ed., 2007) [hereinafter *Long War*].

5. See, e.g., Michael J. Glennon, "Too Far Apart: Repeal the War Powers Resolution," 50 *U. Miami L. Rev.* 17, 18 (1995). On the divided Democrats, see Wilentz at 268.

6. War Powers Resolution of 1973, Pub. L. No. 93-148, 87 Stat. 555 (1973) (codified at 50 U.S.C. §§ 1541–1548 [2006]). While there is no standard scholarly history of the WPR, there are some helpful studies. See Ann-Marie Scheidt, "The Origins and Enactment of the War Powers Resolution, 1970–73" (Ph.D. diss., SUNY Stony Brook, 1989); John H. Sullivan, "The War Powers Resolution: A Special Study of the Committee on Foreign Affairs," House Committee on Foreign Affairs (1982).

7. See, e.g., Gregory Mitrovich, *Undermining the Kremlin: America's Strategy to Subvert the Soviet Bloc, 1947–1956* (2000).

8. Id. at 134–151. See also H. W. Brands, "The Age of Vulnerability: Eisenhower and the National Insecurity State," 94 *Am. Hist. Rev.* 963, 966–968 (1989).

9. On Ford, see Wilentz at 32.

10. On Truman, see Michael J. Hogan, *A Cross of Iron: Harry S. Truman and the Origins of the National Security State, 1945–1954* 265–275 (1998). For Eisenhower see Robert J. McMahon, "US National Security Policy from Eisenhower to Kennedy," in 1 *The Cambridge History of the Cold War: Origins* 288, 288–289 (Melvyn P. Leffler and Odd Arne Westad eds., 2010) [hereinafter 1 *Cambridge History*]; Stephen E. Ambrose, *Eisenhower: The President* 225, 561 (1984).

11. McMahon, 1 *Cambridge History*, at 304.

12. Id. at 289. See also Melvyn P. Leffler, *A Preponderance of Power: National Security, the Truman Administration, and the Cold War* 497–498 (1992).

13. See Robert Dallek, *Nixon and Kissinger: Partners in Power* 214–216 (2007).

14. Gaddis, *Containment*, at 277–278.

15. See, e.g., Marilyn B. Young, *The Vietnam Wars, 1945–1990* 134–135 (1991).

16. See U.S. Dept. State, *Foreign Relations of the United States 1969–1976: Vietnam, January 1973–July 1975* 827, 828 (2010) (Minutes of Cabinet Meeting, April 16, 1975).

17. See Fredrik Logevall, "The Indochina Wars and the Cold War, 1945–1975," in 2 *The Cambridge History of the Cold War: Crises and Détente* 281, 302 (Melvyn P. Leffler and Odd Arne Westad eds., 2010) [hereinafter 2 *Cambridge History*].

18. For an illuminating review of the evidence, see Ole R. Holsti, *American Public Opinion on the Iraq War* 76–84 (2011).

19. Daalder and Destler at 100–101.

20. McMahon, *Cold War*, at 116; Zelizer, *Arsenal*, at 204. This sense that the early Cold War period belonged to another era of history can be glimpsed in Arthur Schlesinger's journal. In early 1971, Schlesinger finds himself insisting against Kennedy's critics that "[t]he Cold War was hardly a figment of someone's imagination." Arthur M. Schlesinger Jr., *Journals: 1952–2000* 334 (2007).

21. Nancy Mitchell, "The Cold War and Jimmy Carter," in 3 *The Cambridge History of the Cold War: Endings* 66, 68 (Melvyn P. Leffler and Odd Arne Westad eds., 2010) [hereinafter 3 *Cambridge History*].

22. Herring at 828–830; Mieczkowski at 287–288.

23. Olav Njolstad, "The Collapse of Superpower Détente, 1975–1980," in 3 *Cambridge History*, at 135, 139.

24. Holsti at 83.

25. See Mieczkowski at 273–274; Melvin Small, *The Presidency of Richard Nixon* 61 (1999). For Reagan, see Cannon at 162, 262–263.

26. Campbell Craig and Fredrik Logevall, *America's Cold War: The Politics of Insecurity* 10 (2009).

27. On the bipartisan support for the WPR, see the helpful discussion in Charles O. Jones, *The Presidency in a Separated System* 234–236 (1994).

28. Herring at 828.

29. Julian E. Zelizer, "How Conservatives Learned to Stop Worrying and Love Presidential Power," in *The Presidency of George W. Bush: A First Historical Assessment* 15, 17 (Julian E. Zelizer ed., 2010) [hereinafter Zelizer, *Bush*].

30. Mieczkowski at 281–282; Zelizer, *Arsenal*, at 262.

31. Wilentz at 49, 61; Zelizer, *Bush*, at 33. For Cheney's views on war powers, see Dick Cheney, "Congressional Overreaching in Foreign Policy," in *Foreign Policy and the Constitution* 101 (Robert A. Goldwin and Robert A. Licht eds., 1990).

32. On these investigations, see Loch K. Johnson, *A Season of Inquiry: Congress and Intelligence* (1988) [hereinafter Johnson, *Inquiry*]; Kathryn S. Olmsted,

Challenging the Secret Government: The Post-Watergate Investigations of the CIA and FBI (1996); John Ranelagh, *The Agency: The Rise and Decline of the CIA* (1987).

33. See Olmsted at 81–82, 88–89.

34. Johnson, *Inquiry*, at 112.

35. Robert David Johnson, *Congress and the Cold War* 225 (2006).

36. Quoted in Johnson, *Inquiry*, at 113. Mathias was Senator Charles "Mac" Mathias, a Republican senator from Maryland.

37. Olmsted at 109–110.

38. Id. at 88–91.

39. See, e.g., U.S. Dept. State, *Foreign Relations of the United States, 1961–1963: Cuban Missile Crisis and Aftermath* 837–838 (1996) (Memorandum for the Record, June 19, 1963: "higher authority" shows interest in "external sabotage operations" against Cuba).

40. Olmsted at 109–110.

41. Quoted in Ranelagh at 277.

42. See Schlesinger; L. Gordon Crovitz and Jeremy A. Rabkin eds., *The Fettered Presidency: Legal Constraints on the Executive Branch* (1989); John G. Tower, "Congress versus the President: The Formulation and Implementation of American Foreign Policy," *Foreign Affairs*, Winter 1981–1982, at 229.

43. Olmsted at 124, 160–161, 166–167.

44. Id. at 177, 182–183. For Bush, see Tim Weiner, *Legacy of Ashes: The History of the CIA* 348 (2007).

45. Zelizer, *Arsenal*, at 301.

46. Zelizer, *Bush*, at 27.

47. Id. at 28.

48. For example, the recently published and extremely useful three-volume *Cambridge History of the Cold War* (Melvyn P. Leffler and Odd Arne Westad eds., 2010) (all volumes cited in the notes in this chapter) is a global history of the Cold War divided loosely into three periods: 1945 to 1962 (the year of the Cuban missile crisis), 1962 to 1975, and 1975 to 1991. The editors and authors do not attempt to provide a periodization that would capture how American citizens perceived the conflict over time.

49. This is the impression given by histories such as Gaddis, *Containment*.

50. Tami Davis Biddle, "Shield and Sword: U.S. Strategic Forces and Doctrine since 1945," in *Long War*, at 137, 163.

51. Michael Dobbs, *One Minute to Midnight: Kennedy, Khrushchev, and Castro on the Brink of Nuclear War* 349 (2008).

52. Biddle at 171–172.

53. Lawrence Freedman, *The Evolution of Nuclear Strategy* 234 (3d ed. 2003).

54. Garthoff at 595.

55. Cannon at 133. See also Garthoff at 872–873.

56. See Frances Fitzgerald, *Way Out There in the Blue: Reagan, Star Wars, and the End of the Cold War* 117–118 (2000).

57. Id. at 16–17.

58. Freedman at 233–234.

59. This is suggested by the accounts in McGeorge Bundy, *Danger and Survival: Choices about the Bomb in the First Fifty Years* 556–583 (1988); Fitzgerald at 79–97; Walter Isaacson and Evan Thomas, *The Wise Men: Six Friends and the World They Made* 722–729 (1986); Nicholas Thompson, *The Hawk and the Dove: Paul Nitze, George Kennan, and the History of the Cold War* 250–275 (2009).

60. Garthoff at 60–61.

61. Ambrose at 563–564.

62. William Burr and David Alan Rosenberg, "Nuclear Competition in an Era of Stalemate, 1963–1975," in 2 *Cambridge History*, at 88, 89–92.

63. Garthoff at 857–858.

64. Cannon at 254; McMahon, *Cold War*, at 158.

65. Cannon at 133–140.

66. Id. at 139–140, 279; Fitzgerald at 156, 187–194; McMahon, *Cold War*, at 146.

67. The best account of the hidden 1983 nuclear crisis is David E. Hoffman, *The Dead Hand* 60–100 (2009).

68. McMahon, *Cold War*, at 146, 148.

69. Christopher Andrew, "Intelligence in the Cold War," in 2 *Cambridge History*, at 417, 432–433.

70. Beth A. Fischer, "US Foreign Policy under Reagan and Bush," in 3 *Cambridge History*, at 267, 272.

71. Fitzgerald at 228–229; Hoffman at 94–95; Zelizer, *Arsenal*, at 325.

72. Fitzgerald at 238; Hoffman at 95–96.

73. McGeorge Bundy at 565.

74. For examples of Reagan's lack of knowledge in foreign affairs, see Cannon at 140, 250.

75. See, e.g., Robert D. Schulzinger, *A Time for War: The United States and Vietnam, 1941–1975* 278, 288 (1997); Gordon Silverstein, *Law's Allure* 209–212 (2009).

76. Sullivan at 43.

77. Id. at 26–28, 31–41, 43, 71–72.

78. Scheidt at 75, 89–90.

79. See Henry A. Kissinger, Memorandum for Bill Timmons, Subject: War Powers Resolution, Aug. 22, 1970, FE 4-1 Presidential Powers 1969–1970, White House Central Files, Subject Files, FE (Federal Government) Box 6, Nixon Presidential Library. In a 1972 memorandum, Kissinger reported that the Javits-Stennis bill on war powers, which provided for the termination of U.S. involvement after thirty days, had passed the Senate. Kissinger commented that the bill was "unconstitutional and unwise." He continued: "The Zablocki bill has twice passed the House with our tacit support. It is a moderate sense of the Congress resolution that provides that the President should consult with Congress before acting—if circumstances permit. If that is not possible then the President must

report to Congress promptly. Justice, State, and NSC agree that this bill presents no problem." Henry A. Kissinger, Memorandum for the President, Subject: War Powers Legislation, June 22, 1972, White House Central Files, Staff Member Office Files, William E. Timmons, Series I: Subject Files 1973–1974, Box 50, War Powers (1 of 3), Nixon Presidential Library.

80. See, e.g., Silverstein at 214–215.

81. Scheidt at 102.

82. Sullivan at 75–77. See also James N. Giglio, *Call Me Tom: The Life of Thomas F. Eagleton* 102–103 (2011).

83. Keith E. Whittington, *Constitutional Construction: Divided Powers and Constitutional Meaning* 184 (1999).

84. Sullivan at 52–53.

85. Id. at 148. The sixty-day period could be extended to ninety days as a practical matter as the president was allowed thirty days to extract the troops.

86. WPR Sec. 3.

87. Scheidt at 80.

88. Sullivan at 125, 130.

89. See David J. Barron and Martin S. Lederman, "The Commander in Chief at the Lowest Ebb—A Constitutional History," 121 *Harv. L. Rev.* 941, 1070 (2008) [hereinafter Barron and Lederman, "History"].

90. For the invocation of the necessary and proper clause, see WPR Sec. 2(b).

91. *Youngstown Sheet & Tube Co. v. Sawyer*, 343 U.S. 579, 635–637 (1952) (Jackson, J., concurring).

92. For articulation of general separation of powers principles, see *Morrison v. Olson*, 487 U.S. 654 (1988). For a defense of the constitutionality of the WPR, see Stephen L. Carter, "The Constitutionality of the War Powers Resolution," 70 *Va. L. Rev.* 101 (1984).

93. In June 2011, the Obama administration defended against a concerted congressional attack its assistance of a NATO operation designed to support rebels opposing Col. Muammar al-Qaddafi, the leader of Libya. Charlie Savage and Mark Landler, "White House Defends Continuing U.S. Role in Libya Operation," *N.Y. Times*, June 15, 2011, at A1. The administration argued that the WPR did not apply to the operation but, unlike Republican administrations, was willing to affirm that the WPR was constitutional. This stance is discussed in Chapter 6.

94. Elliot Richardson, Office of the Attorney General, to Roy L. Ash, Oct. 18, 1973, White House Central Files, Subject Files, FE (Federal Government) 4-1, 10/1/73–11/30/73, Box 6, Nixon Presidential Library.

95. Id. at 3–4.

96. Id. at 4–5 (emphasis in original).

97. Veto of the War Powers Resolution, 1973 Public Papers 893–895 (Oct. 24, 1973) [hereinafter Nixon Public Papers].

98. For the State Department's drafting, see Scheidt at 174.

99. Nixon Public Papers at 893.

100. Id.

101. Scheidt at 180.

102. For relevant commentary by President Reagan's secretary of state, see George P. Shultz, *Turmoil and Triumph* 294 n.3 (1993).

103. For a critique of the WPR, see Robert F. Turner, *The War Powers Resolution: Its Implementation in Theory and Practice* (1983).

104. See, e.g., Barry M. Blechman, *The Politics of National Security: Congress and U.S. Defense Policy* 6, 181 (1990).

105. 136 Cong. Record 27808 (Oct. 5, 1990)(statements of Sen. Nunn).

106. Sullivan at 166.

107. See U.S. Dept. State, *Foreign Relations of the United States, 1969–1976: Vietnam, January 1973–July 1975* 775–776, 818 (2010). See also Duane Tananbaum, "Gerald Ford and the War Powers Resolution," in 2 *Gerald R. Ford and the Politics of Post-Watergate America* 523, 529 (Bernard J. Firestone and Alexej Ugrinsky eds., 1993).

108. Sullivan at 190–191. See also P. Edward Haley, *Congress and the Fall of South Vietnam and Cambodia* 101 (1982).

109. Sullivan at 198–199.

110. They are collected in id. at 205–254.

111. See "Presidential Power to Use the Armed Forces Abroad without Statutory Authorization," 4A Op. O.L.C. 185, 186–188 (1980).

112. Sullivan at 247–248 (relating nomination hearing of Secretary of State Alexander Haig in 1981).

113. Tananbaum at 532–534.

114. See Blechman at 190; John Hart Ely, *War and Responsibility: Constitutional Lessons of Vietnam and Its Aftermath* 120–121 (1993).

115. See 141 Cong. Rec. 15191 (June 7, 1995). The repeal was sponsored by Rep. Henry Hyde and supported by Speaker Newt Gingrich. With respect to Ford, see Tananbaum at 529–530. Curiously, no president has been willing to expend political capital while in office to either repeal or reform the WPR.

116. Cannon at 346–348; Herring at 873.

117. Barron and Lederman, "History," at 1079–1080; Stuart Taylor Jr., "Questions Raised Again on Reagan's Limits under War Powers Act," *N.Y. Times*, Oct. 24, 1983, at A1.

118. See Steven R. Weisman, "President v. Congress," *N.Y. Times*, April 7, 1984, at A1.

119. This is reflected in newspaper stories of the period. See Wayne King and Warren Weaver Jr., "Briefing; Dept. of Hostilities," *N.Y. Times*, March 29, 1986; Steven V. Roberts, "War Powers? What War Powers?," *N.Y. Times*, Oct. 6, 1987.

120. Barron and Lederman, "History," at 1070 n.529.

121. See the discussion in James E. Baker, *In the Common Defense: National Security Law for Perilous Times* 185–189 (2007).

122. Blechman at 3–7, 170–174, 181, 186. Blechman argues that the episode so discomfited the Senate that the administration was forced to consult with Congress about the operation on a more regular basis. See id. at 174–177.

123. William Bundy, *A Tangled Web: The Making of Foreign Policy in the Nixon Presidency* 399 (1998). See also Whittington at 173, 184–185.

124. For an interesting and readable, if somewhat flawed attempt to describe the forest post-Vietnam, see Rachel Maddow, *Drift: The Unmooring of American Military Power* (2012).

125. Herring at 875.

126. James Mann, *Rise of the Vulcans: The History of Bush's War Cabinet* 43–44, 53, 119–120 (2004); Kurth at 74–75.

127. On the Bush presidency and the Gulf War, see James A. Baker, *The Politics of Diplomacy* (1995); George Bush and Brent Scowcroft, *A World Transformed* (1998); Michael R. Gordon and General Bernard E. Trainor, *The Generals' War* (1995); Richard N. Haass, *War of Necessity, War of Choice: A Memoir of Two Iraq Wars* (2009); Mann; Bob Woodward, *The Commanders* (1991) [hereinafter Woodward, *Commanders*]; Zelizer, *Arsenal.*

128. Bush and Scowcroft at 338; Garthoff at 521–523.

129. Zelizer, *Arsenal,* at 292.

130. For a discussion documenting this aggressive defense, see Barron and Lederman, "History," at 1083–1087.

131. Chuck Alston, "Bush Crusades on Many Fronts to Retake President's Turf," *CQ Weekly Report,* Feb. 3, 1990, at 291.

132. Zelizer, *Arsenal,* at 369.

133. Zelizer, *Arsenal,* Id. at 361–362.

134. Bush and Scowcroft at 324–325, 330, 335–336.

135. Id. at 327.

136. Id. at 371.

137. Id. at 358. Bush stated in his memoirs, "Some wanted me to deliver fireside chats to explain things, as Franklin Roosevelt had done. I am not good at that. I was convinced that the best way was to shape opinion not by rhetoric but by action." Id. See also Woodward, *Commanders,* at 267–268.

138. Bush and Scowcroft at 340–341.

139. Id. at 358, 374–375; Woodward, *Commanders,* at 302–303.

140. Baker at 333.

141. Baker at 335; Bush and Scowcroft at 382; Woodward, *Commanders,* at 281–287.

142. Gordon and Trainor at 135–141, 153–155.

143. Daalder and Destler at 199.

144. Bush and Scowcroft at 398–399; Woodward, *Commanders,* at 300–302, 308–312; Zelizer, *Arsenal,* at 364–365.

145. Baker at 336. See also Woodward, *Commanders,* at 308–312.

146. Baker at 332–333, 338–339, 344; Gordon and Trainor at 154.

147. On the need to accept the risk of a public debate with respect to war, see Robert S. McNamara, *In Retrospect: The Tragedy and Lessons of Vietnam* 192 (1995).

148. Bush and Scowcroft at 354–355, 399–400; Mann at 194–195; Zelizer, *Arsenal,* at 364, 376–379.

149. "Crisis in the Persian Gulf Region: U.S. Policy Options and Implications," *Hearing Before the Sen. Comm. on Armed Services,* 101st Cong. 701–702 (1990) (testimony of Richard B. Cheney, Dept. of Defense Sec'y).

150. For Bush's appeal to the example of the Tonkin Gulf Resolution as an expression of Congress's political support, see Bush and Scowcroft at 371.

151. Baker at 334; Bush and Scowcroft at 397–398, 441; Haass at 112–114.

152. C. Boyden Gray, Memorandum for President, Aug. 7, 1990, GBPL, John Sununu Files, OA/ID 29166-008, Persian Gulf War 1991 (6).

153. Id. Gray made an interesting comment in a later memo to Bush's chief of staff John Sununu: "We believe that the War Powers Resolution is unconstitutional insofar as it purports to allow Congress to compel the withdrawal of U.S. forces through inaction, but no President has wanted to jeopardize congressional support for his actions by defying the Resolution. It often falls to Executive branch lawyers to develop a legal theory permitting the President to avoid triggering the clock. Congress also has been reluctant to permit the President to act in defiance of its interpretation of the Resolution." C. Boyden Gray, Memorandum for Governor Sununu, Dec. 6, 1990, GBPL, John Sununu Files, OA/ID CF 00472, File: Persian Gulf War 1991 (11).

154. Bush and Scowcroft at 397–398, 441.

155. Zelizer, *Arsenal,* at 370.

156. Id. at 446. See also Baker at 338–339; Wilentz at 300.

157. Baker at 334.

158. Bush and Scowcroft at 417.

159. See Derek Chollet and James Goldgeier, *America between the Wars* 14–16 (2008).

160. Kurth at 77–80 (commenting on the Gulf War as an application of the Army's new Air-Land battle doctrine).

161. See, e.g., Bob Woodward, *Plan of Attack* 21–22 (2004).

162. Cannon at 659–660; Zelizer, *Arsenal,* at 354. For how Bush felt about Walsh's action, see the suggestive account in his son's memoir. George W. Bush, *Decision Points* 49–50 (2010).

163. The various threads of the Iran-contra affair are not easily untangled, as they involve separate events in Central America and the Middle East that came together in Washington. For works on Iran-contra and U.S. policy in Latin America generally, see Hal Brands, *Latin America's Cold War* (2010); Theodore Draper, *A Very Thin Line: The Iran-Contra Affairs* (1991); Greg Grandin, *Empire's Workshop* (2006); Harold Hongju Koh, *The National Security Constitution: Sharing Power after the Iran-Contra Affair* (1990); Walter LaFeber, *Inevitable Revolutions: The United States in Central America* (2d ed. 1993); William M. LeoGrande, *Our*

Own Backyard: The United States in Central America, 1977–1992 (1998); Jane Mayer and Doyle McManus, *Landslide: The Unmaking of the President, 1984–1988* (1988); Gaddis Smith, *The Last Years of the Monroe Doctrine, 1945–1993* (1994)[hereinafter Smith, Monroe Doctrine]; Lawrence E. Walsh, *Firewall: The Iran-Contra Conspiracy and Cover-Up* (1997); *Final Report of the Independent Counsel for Iran/Contra Matters*, submitted to the U.S. Court of Appeals for the District of Columbia Circuit, Aug. 4, 1993 [three volumes, hereinafter Walsh, *Final Report*]; Bob Woodward, *Veil: The Secret Wars of the CIA, 1981–1987* (1987) [hereinafter Woodward, *Veil*]; "Report of the Congressional Committees Investigating the Iran-Contra Affair," H.R. Rep. No. 100-433, S. Rep. No. 100-216 (1987) [hereinafter Iran-Contra Congressional Investigation].

164. Cannon at 290–291, 302–303; Shultz at 294; Westad at 331, 338–339.

165. These views on Reagan and their sources among journalists and former officials are reviewed in Cannon at 36, 59, 141–171, 262–263, 293–295; Daalder and Destler at 128–130, 140–141, 151–155; Fitzgerald at 158, 171–172, 218–219; Mayer and McManus at 24–30, 51–56.

166. See Fitzgerald at 175, 205–209; Robert C. Rowland and John M. Jones, *Reagan at Westminster: Foreshadowing the End of the Cold War* (2010).

167. Cannon at 749.

168. Id. at 109.

169. Fitzgerald at 74, 79; Cannon at 241–242, 540.

170. Daalder and Destler at 141; LeoGrande at 113–114; Woodward, *Veil*, at 181, 446–447, 462.

171. Brands at 200; Cannon at 303, 554–555; Draper at 219; LeoGrande at 300, 337.

172. Herring at 889; LaFeber at 301, 307; LeoGrande at 285–287, 308–311; Smith, *Monroe Doctrine*, at 154, 187.

173. Brands at 198–199; Cannon at 162–163, 291; LeoGrande at 80–86.

174. Smith, *Monroe Doctrine*, at 187.

175. Cannon at 306–309, 312, 320, 330–331, 334–335; Fitzgerald at 230–231; LaFeber at 297–304; LeoGrande at 314–320, 328–332; Smith, *Monroe Doctrine*, at 190; Zelizer, *Arsenal*, at 311–312. See also Richard Sobel, *The Impact of Public Opinion on U.S. Foreign Policy since Vietnam* 236–237 (2001).

176. Fitzgerald at 67. Reagan had the same impression with respect to his own experience in Iran-contra. See Zelizer, *Arsenal*, at 345.

177. These observations are suggested by Cannon at 111, 338, 627.

178. Cannon at 335–336, 559–560, 639; Mayer and McManus at 80, 168, 179; Wilentz at 212.

179. LeoGrande at 201–202, 213–215.

180. LeoGrande at 345, 347–349, 378; Mayer and McManus at 3–7.

181. Brands at 215; Grandin at 115–117; LeoGrande at 413–417.

182. Cannon at 332–333, 335–336, 639; Majority Report, Iran-Contra Congressional Investigation, at 37.

183. LeoGrande at 532, 548.

184. Cannon at 639; LeoGrande at 483; Zelizer, *Arsenal*, at 347–348, 354.

185. Cannon at 540, 543; Mayer and McManus at 107–108, 115–116.

186. Draper at 225–229; Mayer and McManus at 179.

187. Draper at 247–249; Mayer and McManus at 183–184; Majority Report, Iran-Contra Congressional Investigation, at 203.

188. Draper at 464–470; Fitzgerald at 382–387; Mayer and McManus at 296–299, 302, 307–312; Shultz at 838.

189. Mayer and McManus at 356–358, 370–372.

190. Cannon at 524; Mayer and McManus at 331; Wilentz at 227–228, 230; Zelizer, *Arsenal*, at 344.

191. Smith, Monroe Doctrine, at 187; Zelizer, *Arsenal*, at 334, 343.

192. LeoGrande at 503; Wilentz at 234.

193. Wilentz at 236–238; Zelizer, *Arsenal*, at 349.

194. Shultz at 908–909.

195. Id. at 908.

196. See Minority Report, Iran-Contra Congressional Investigation, at 437.

197. Heidi Kitrosser, "It Came from beneath the Twilight Zone: Wiretapping and Article II Imperialism," 88 *Tex. L. Rev.* 1401, 1408 (2010).

198. See, e.g., Zelizer, *Arsenal*, at 348.

199. See Kitrosser at 1408–1409.

200. Barron and Lederman highlight an OLC opinion that advanced these claims in response to one aspect of the Iran-contra affair. Barron and Lederman, "History," at 1082–1083.

201. The leading scholarly discussion is David J. Barron and Martin S. Lederman, "The Commander in Chief at the Lowest Ebb: Framing the Problem, Doctrine, and Original Understanding," 121 *Harv. L. Rev.* 689 (2008).

202. See the discussion in Barron and Lederman, "History," at 1058–1078.

203. Minority Report, Iran Contra Congressional Investigation, at 469.

204. Id. at 472.

205. *Youngstown*, 343 U.S. at 637 (Jackson, J., concurring).

206. Memorandum of Law of the United States Filed by the Department of Justice as *Amicus Curiae* with Respect to the Independent Counsel's Opposition to the Defendant's Motions to Dismiss or Limit Count One, *United States v. Oliver L. North*, U.S.D.C. (D.C. Crim. No. 88-0080-02-GAG) [hereinafter DOJ Memorandum]. The brief was written by Edward S. G. Dennis Jr. of the Criminal Division and Douglas W. Kmiec of the Office of Legal Counsel. For discussion, see Koh at 28–29.

207. DOJ Memorandum at 7–18.

208. Id. at 19.

209. Id. at 20.

210. Id. at 21–22. See *United States v. Curtiss-Wright Export Corp.*, 299 U.S. 304 (1936). The broad rationale for presidential power offered in *Curtiss-Wright* has been heavily criticized by scholars. See, e.g., Koh at 93–95.

211. DOJ Memorandum at 22.
212. Id. at 28.
213. LeoGrande at 501.
214. See Koh.
215. Id. at 72.
216. Id. at 67–100.
217. Id. at 105–113.
218. Id. at 113–116.
219. Id. at 157, 166–184.
220. In doctrinal terms, this counter-tradition was founded on *Curtiss-Wright*.
221. See Minority Report, Iran Contra Congressional Investigation, at 437.
222. See id.
223. See Koh at 101–105.
224. See the discussion in Zelizer, *Arsenal*, at 354.
225. LaFeber at 362.
226. Id. See also Brands at 221–222.
227. John H. Coatsworth, "The Cold War in Central America, 1975–1991," in 3 *Cambridge History*, at 201, 221.
228. Brands at 189–195.
229. Herring at 892–893.

6. The 9/11 Wars and the Presidency

1. See, e.g., Bruce Ackerman, *The Decline and Fall of the American Republic* (2010) [hereinafter Ackerman, *Decline*]; Gabriella Blum and Philip B. Heymann, *Laws, Outlaws, and Terrorists: Lessons from the War on Terrorism* (2010); Harold H. Bruff, *Bad Advice: Bush's Lawyers in the War on Terror* (2009); David Cole and Jules Lobel, *Less Safe, Less Free: Why America Is Losing the War on Terror* (2007); Matthew Crenson and Benjamin Ginsberg, *Presidential Power: Unchecked and Unbalanced* (2007); Louis Fisher, *The Constitution and 9/11: Recurring Threats to America's Freedoms* (2008); Benjamin A. Kleinerman, *The Discretionary President: The Promise and Peril of Executive Power* (2009); Joseph Margulies, *Guantanamo and the Abuse of Presidential Power* (2006); Scott M. Matheson Jr., *Presidential Constitutionalism in Perilous Times* (2009); James P. Pfiffner, *Power Play: The Bush Presidency and the Constitution* (2008); Christopher H. Pyle, *Getting Away with Torture: Secret Government, War Crimes, and the Rule of Law* (2009); Andrew Rudalevige, *The New Imperial Presidency* (2005); Frederick A. O. Schwarz Jr. and Aziz Z. Huq, *Unchecked and Unbalanced: Presidential Power in a Time of Terror* (2008); Peter M. Shane, *Madison's Nightmare: How Executive Power Threatens American Democracy* (2009). For a critique by a knowledgeable journalist, see Charlie Savage, *Takeover: The Return of the Imperial Presidency and the Subversion of American Democracy* (2007).

2. For an observation that the public did not generally agree with the criticisms from the human rights community, see Jack Goldsmith, *Power and Constraint: The Accountable Presidency after 9/11* 194–196 (2012) [hereinafter Goldsmith,

Power and Constraint]. For a general defense of Bush's record, see Stephen F. Knott, *Rush to Judgment: George W. Bush, The War on Terror, and His Critics* (2012).

3. See, e.g., James Fallows, *Blind into Baghdad: America's War in Iraq* 114–115 (2006).

4. On the Bush-Truman comparison, see Jacob Weisberg, *The Bush Tragedy* 234–236 (2008).

5. Works helpful in understanding the period after the Cold War with respect to foreign affairs, war, and covert war include Derek Chollet and James Goldgeier, *America between the Wars* (2008); Ivo H. Daalder and I. M. Destler, *In the Shadow of the Oval Office* (2009); Ivo H. Daalder and James M. Lindsay, *America Unbound: The Bush Revolution in Foreign Policy* (2005); Richard N. Haass, *War of Necessity, War of Choice: A Memoir of Two Iraq Wars* (2009); George C. Herring, *From Colony to Superpower: U.S. Foreign Relations since 1776* (2008); James Mann, *Rise of the Vulcans: The History of Bush's War Cabinet* (2004) [hereinafter Mann, *Rise*]; Tim Weiner, *Legacy of Ashes: The History of the CIA* (2007); Odd Arne Westad, *The Global Cold War* (2007); Sean Wilentz, *The Age of Reagan: A History, 1974–2008* (2008); Julian E. Zelizer, *Arsenal of Democracy: The Politics of National Security* (2010)[hereinafter Zelizer, Arsenal].

6. See the discussion of defense strategy at the end of the Bush I administration in Mann, *Rise*, at 199–200, 214.

7. Herring at 876; Weiner at 388–389; Zelizer, *Arsenal*, at 335–336, 408.

8. Beth A. Fischer, "US Foreign Policy under Reagan and Bush," in 3 *The Cambridge History of the Cold War: Endings* 267 (Melvyn P. Leffler and Odd Arne Westad eds., 2010) [hereinafter 3 *Cambridge History*].

9. See Robert L. Beisner, *Dean Acheson: A Life in the Cold War* 185–189 (2006).

10. James G. Hershberg, "The Cuban Missile Crisis," in 2 *The Cambridge History of the Cold War: Crises and Détente* 65, 86 (Melvyn P. Leffler and Odd Arne Westad eds., 2010) [hereinafter 2 *Cambridge History*].

11. See generally Raymond L. Garthoff, *Détente and Confrontation: American-Soviet Relations from Nixon to Reagan* (rev. ed. 1994).

12. Westad at 336.

13. Nancy Mitchell, "The Cold War and Jimmy Carter," in 3 *Cambridge History*, at 66.

14. Fischer at 275–276.

15. See Chollet and Goldgeier at 8–9; Frances Fitzgerald, *Way Out There in the Blue: Reagan, Star Wars and the End of the Cold War* 438–439, 461, 467–468 (2000); James Mann, *The Rebellion of Ronald Reagan: A History of the End of the Cold War* 48–51, 324–325 (2009) [hereinafter Mann, *Rebellion*].

16. Fitzgerald at 443–446.

17. See David E. Hoffman, *The Dead Hand* 294–295, 315–319, 361–362 (2009); Mann, *Rebellion*, at 99–100.

18. Campbell Craig and Fredrik Logevall, *America's Cold War: The Politics of Insecurity* 345–350 (2009); Alex Pravda, "The Collapse of the Soviet Union, 1990–1991," in 3 *Cambridge History*, at 356, 361.

19. Chollet and Goldgeier at 8–9.

20. See the suggestive discussion in Thomas G. Paterson, *On Every Front: The Making and Unmaking of the Cold War* 192 (rev. ed. 1992).

21. Craig and Logevall at 345–350.

22. Daalder and Lindsay at 81.

23. Chollet and Goldgeier at 145, 173, 309; Daalder and Lindsay at 41–42.

24. See his discussion of the development of conservative internationalism during the early Cold War in Zelizer, *Arsenal*, at 83–96.

25. Id. at 379.

26. See the analysis in Lori Fisler Damrosch, "The Clinton Administration and War Powers," 63 *L. & Contemp. Prob.* 125, 131–138 (2000).

27. "Deployment of United States Armed Forces into Haiti," 18 Op. O.L.C. 173, 176 (1994) [hereinafter Haiti opinion]. While not contesting the constitutionality of the WPR in this opinion, OLC specifically reserved the issue of whether the sixty-day clock was constitutional. See id. n.2.

28. Chollet and Goldgeier at 97.

29. Haiti opinion at 177 (footnote omitted).

30. "Proposed Deployment of United States Armed Forces into Bosnia," 19 Op. O.L.C. 327, 332 (1995) [hereinafter Bosnia opinion].

31. "Authority to Use Military Force in Libya," , 35 Op. O.L.C. 1, 13 (2011) [hereinafter Libya opinion].

32. Id. at 8.

33. Bosnia opinion at 330–331.

34. Id. at 331.

35. The argument from practice in the Bosnia opinion was cited with approval by the OLC in the Obama administration in justifying U.S. intervention in Libya. See Libya opinion at 7.

36. *H. Con. Res. 82, Directing the President to Remove Armed Forces from Operations against Yugoslavia, and H.R.J. Res. 44, Declaring War Between the U.S. and Yugoslavia, Hearing Before the H. Comm. On Int'l Relations,* 106th Cong. 32 (1999) (statement of Barbara Larkin, Assistant Sec'y of State).

37. Id. at 32–33. See also Chollet and Goldgeier at 229 (Clinton did not ask permission for military action in Kosovo because he wanted to preserve presidential power to intervene).

38. *Applying the War Powers Resolution to the War on Terrorism, Hearing Before the Subcomm. on the Constitution, Federalism, and Property Rights of the Sen. Comm. on Judiciary,* 107th Cong. 8 (2002) (testimony of John C. Yoo).

39. Id. at 9.

40. Id.

41. See *Libya and War Powers, Hearing Before the Sen. Comm. on Foreign Relations,* 112th Cong. 53 (2011) (responses of Legal Adviser Harold Koh to questions submitted by Senator Richard G. Lugar).

42. Works useful in understanding 9/11 and the wars thereafter include Peter L. Bergen, *The Longest War: The Enduring Conflict between America and al*

Qaeda (2011); Philip Bobbitt, *Terror and Consent* (2008); Thomas E. Ricks, *Fiasco: The American Military Adventure in Iraq* (2006); Gregory F. Treverton, *Intelligence for an Age of Terror* (2009); Bob Woodward, *Bush at War* (2002); *Plan of Attack* (2004); *State of Denial* (2006); *The War Within* (2008); *Obama's Wars* (2010); Amy B. Zegart, *Spying Blind: The CIA, the FBI, and the Origins of 9/11* (2007). See also National Commission on Terrorist Attacks upon the United States, *The 9/11 Commission Report* (2004) [hereinafter *9/11 Commission Report*].

Useful biographies and memoirs include Elisabeth Bumiller, *Condoleezza Rice: An American Life* (2007); George W. Bush, *Decision Points* (2010); Karen DeYoung, *Soldier: The Life of Colin Powell* (2006); Bradley Graham, *By His Own Rules: The Ambitions, Successes, and Ultimate Failures of Donald Rumsfeld* (2009); George Tenet, *At the Center of the Storm: My Years at the CIA* (2007).

On the Pearl Harbor analogy, see the useful discussion in Elaine Tyler May, "Echoes of the Cold War: The Aftermath of September 11 at Home," in *September 11 in History: A Watershed Moment?* 35, 41 (Mary L. Dudziak ed., 2003).

43. Bush at 137; Daalder and Lindsay at 81.

44. See, e.g., Bush at 140, 368.

45. See, e.g., Tenet at 170.

46. Bergen at 252.

47. Weisberg at 105, 231–232.

48. Bush at 141–142.

49. With respect to detainee abuse and allied problems in the Bush administration, see the following governmental inquiries: "Inquiry into the Treatment of Detainees in U.S. Custody," Sen. Comm. Armed Services, 110th Cong. (2008) [hereinafter Senate Report]; *What Went Wrong: Torture and the Office of Legal Counsel in the Bush Administration, Hearing Before Sen. Comm. on the Judiciary,* 111th Cong. (2009) [hereinafter Senate Torture Hearing]; U.S. Dep't of Justice, Office of Prof'l Responsibility, "Investigation into the Office of Legal Counsel's Memoranda Concerning Issues Related to the Central Intelligence Agency's Use of 'Enhanced Interrogation Techniques' on Suspected Terrorists" (2009) [hereinafter OPR Report]; David Margolis, Associate Deputy Attorney General, Memorandum of Decision Regarding the Objections to the Findings of Professional Misconduct in the Office of Professional Responsibility's Report (2010) [hereinafter Margolis Memo].

For relevant legal commentary and journalism, see David Cole, *The Torture Memos* (2009) [hereinafter Cole, *Torture Memos*]; Barton Gellman, *Angler: The Cheney Vice Presidency* (2008); Jack Goldsmith, *The Terror Presidency* (2007) [hereinafter Goldsmith, *Terror Presidency*]; Jane Mayer, *The Dark Side* (2008); Kathleen Clark, "Ethical Issues Raised by the OLC Torture Memorandum," 1 *J. Nat'l Security L. & Pol'y* 455 (2005); David Luban, "Liberalism, Torture, and the Ticking Bomb," 91 *Va. L. Rev.* 1425 (2005); Michael D. Ramsey, "Torturing Executive Power," 93 *Geo. L.J.* 1213 (2005); Jeremy Waldron, "Torture and Positive Law: Jurisprudence for the White House," 105 *Colum. L. Rev.* 1681 (2005).

50. Bergen at 39.

51. Chollet and Goldgeier at 55–57.

52. Garthoff at 1121.

53. See Goldsmith, *Power and Constraint,* at 3–22.

54. Fitzgerald at 467–468.

55. Chollet and Goldgeier at 57–59, 90–91; Daalder and Destler at 212.

56. Zegart at 143–144, 154; Zelizer, Arsenal, at 400–401, 405–408.

57. Bergen at 45–47. Seventeen sailors were killed and thirty-nine injured. The explanations of the Clinton and Bush II administrations as to why there was no response are unconvincing. This was reviewed in the *9/11 Commission Report* at 190–197, 201–202, 212–214.

58. Bergen at 43–44; Chollet and Goldgeier at 278–279, 306–308, 310–311, 321–323, 326–327; Daalder and Destler at 261–262; DeYoung at 324–335; Tenet at 138–139.

59. Daalder and Destler at 262–267; Tenet at 150–154.

60. Chollet and Goldgeier at 261–262; Tenet at 108; Zegart at 62–69, 96–97.

61. Weiner at 440; Zegart at 71.

62. Weiner at 348; Woodward, *State of Denial,* at 286.

63. Daalder and Lindsay at 158.

64. Mayer at 4–5.

65. Goldsmith, *Terror Presidency,* at 165–168; Mayer at 33.

66. Goldsmith, *Terror Presidency,* at 11–12, 71–75, 79. Goldsmith summarized the views of OVP lawyer David Addington and the administration: "Since the President would be blamed for the next homeland attack, he must have the power under the Constitution to do what he deemed necessary to stop it, regardless of what Congress said." Id. at 79.

67. Id. at 75 (commenting on effect of 9/11 Commission on administration).

68. John Ashcroft, *Never Again: Securing America and Restoring Justice* 130 (2006). For the impact this message had on Ashcroft and his subordinates, see Goldsmith, *Terror Presidency,* at 75 (Bush told Ashcroft "to stop the next attack, period—whatever it takes").

69. Id. See also Bruff at 126–127.

70. See, e.g., Savage at 311–314.

71. See, e.g., Crenson and Ginsberg at 356–357.

72. This is also suggested by the account in Goldsmith, *Terror Presidency.*

73. Weiner at 481 (CIA had operated secret interrogation centers in the 1950s and had participated in torture of suspects in Vietnam).

74. On the CIA volunteering after 9/11, see Mayer at 143–146.

75. OPR Report at 11.

76. Margolis Memo at 2.

77. Id. Margolis developed this argument at length in id. at 16–21.

78. Quoted in id. at 19. For other comments in this vein, see Cole, *Torture Memos,* at 2.

79. Bush at 137; Woodward, *Bush at War*, at 283.

80. For an excellent short account of the Japanese-American internment, see David M. Kennedy, *Freedom from Fear: The American People in Depression and War, 1929–1945* 748–760 (1999). For more extensive treatments, see, e.g., Peter Irons, *Justice at War* (1983); Eric L. Muller, *American Inquisition: The Hunt for Japanese-American Disloyalty in World War II* (2007); Greg Robinson, *A Tragedy of Democracy: Japanese Confinement in North America* (2009).

81. Quoted in Kennedy at 752.

82. Irons at 271–273; Kennedy at 754–756.

83. *Korematsu v. United States*, 323 U.S. 214 (1944); *Hirabayashi v. United States*, 320 U.S. 81 (1943).

84. Eugene V. Rostow, "The Japanese American Cases—A Disaster," 54 *Yale L.J.* 489 (1945). The article appeared in the June 1945 issue.

85. Id. at 490.

86. Id. at 491.

87. Id. at 514–520.

88. Id. at 524. See *Ex parte Milligan*, 71 U.S. 2 (1866).

89. Rostow at 525–528.

90. Irons at 25–28, 30–31, 38–39, 48–52, 58–64, 206–212; Robinson at 69–71.

91. Robinson at 87–93, 221–225.

92. Irons at 32, 280–287.

93. Of Bendetsen, Irons remarks, "The crucial role of this recently mobilized Army officer and lawyer illustrates the power exercised by lower-echelon but strategically placed officials in affecting the decisions of superiors who are distracted by other duties and who are dependent on their subordinates for information and advice." Id. at 49. This remark has obvious applicability to Yoo.

94. For relevant comments by Margolis, see Margolis Memo at 67.

95. See Karen Greenberg, *The Least Worst Place: Guantanamo's First 100 Days* 50–54, 91–92, 120–123, 153–157 (2009).

96. See, e.g., Cole, *Torture Memos*, at 19–35; Goldsmith, *Terror Presidency*, at 106; David D. Cole, "The Sacrificial Yoo: Accounting for Torture in the OPR Report," 4 *J. Nat'l Security L. & Pol'y* 455, 455–456 (2010); Neal Kumar Katyal, "Internal Separation of Powers: Checking Today's Most Dangerous Branch from Within," 115 *Yale L.J.* 2314, 2335–2342 (2006).

97. See Cole, *Torture Memos*, at 1.

98. See Walter LaFeber, *Inevitable Revolutions: The United States in Central America* 228 (1993); Gaddis Smith, *The Last Years of the Monroe Doctrine, 1945–1993* 71 (1994).

99. See Treverton at 240, 261.

100. Compare George Bush and Brent Scowcroft, *A World Transformed* 374–375 (1998) with Bush at 171 (Americans had not committed unlawful torture because senior legal officers had reviewed interrogation methods).

In deciding not to apply the Geneva Conventions to detainees, Bush also appeared to be influenced by the fact that terrorists used brutal tactics and did not apply the Conventions to their hostages. Id. at 166–167 (discussing Daniel Pearl killing).

101. Jack Goldsmith argues to the contrary, largely on the basis of a review conducted by the CIA's inspector general. Goldsmith, *Power and Constraint,* at 95–108.

102. Michael Nelson, "Presidential Power," *Chron. of Higher Educ.,* March 21, 2008. Nelson was referring to Richard E. Neustadt's classic work, *Presidential Power and the Modern Presidents* 11 (1990) ("Presidential power is the power to persuade"). Bush left office as the most unpopular president ever, according to a CNN poll. See "Belief That Country Heading in Right Direction Is at All-Time Low," CNNPolitics.com, Nov. 11, 2008, available at http://www.cnn.com/2008/POLITICS/11/10/bush.transition.poll/index.html.

103. Daalder and Lindsay at 12–15, 201–202.

104. See Jonathan Mahler, "After the Imperial Presidency," *N.Y. Times Mag.,* Nov. 9, 2008, at 42, 44 ("The assertion of expansion of presidential power is arguably the defining feature of the Bush years").

105. See Jeffrey Rosen, "Power of One," *The New Republic,* July 24, 2006, at 8. For a useful discussion on the Republicans and presidential power, see Julian E. Zelizer, "The Conservative Embrace of Presidential Power," 88 *B.U. L. Rev.* 499 (2008).

106. Goldsmith, *Terror Presidency,* at 132.

107. Stuart Taylor Jr., "Law Should Trump Loyalty," *Nat. J.,* Sept. 1, 2007, at 14, 15.

108. See generally Savage.

109. See Schwarz and Huq.

110. Id. at 7.

111. See generally id. at 65–150.

112. See generally Fisher.

113. Pfiffner at 4.

114. That the support of Congress yielded greater constitutional power was something Bush remarked on in his memoirs. See Bush at 175.

115. To be sure, it is much easier to analyze this pattern for past presidential administrations in the light of multiple reliable historical accounts. Carrying forward this approach into the Bush II administration on the basis of memoirs, government investigations, and journalistic accounts poses obvious difficulties and the account here is limited by the evidence currently available.

116. For an insightful discussion, see Mary L. Dudziak, *War Time: An Idea, Its History, Its Consequences* 100–105 (2012).

117. For Bush's account in his memoirs, see Bush at 137–141.

118. See *9/11 Commission Report* at 326, 330–338.

119. Bush at 142 (emphasis in original).

120. For these concerns, see Bruff at 129. Bush showed no awareness in his memoirs of the importance of separation of powers principles (beyond those that support presidential authority) and Congress almost never appears. For references to Congress in the context of the renewal of FISA and the Military Commissions Act, see Bush at 177–179.

121. See Bruce Ackerman, *We The People: Foundations* (1991); *We The People: Transformations* (1998); "Oliver Wendell Holmes Lectures: The Living Constitution," 120 *Harv. L. Rev.* 1737 (2007); Keith Whittington, *Constitutional Construction: Divided Powers and Constitutional Meaning* (1999).

122. Matheson at 87.

123. For a careful study of these framing effects, see W. Lance Bennett, Regina G. Lawrence, and Steven Livingston, *When the Press Fails: Political Power and the News Media from Iraq to Katrina* (2007).

124. See Ole R. Holsti, *American Public Opinion on the Iraq War* 92 (2011); Paul R. Pillar, *Intelligence and U.S. Foreign Policy* 43–45 (2011).

125. See S.J. Res. 23, 107th Cong. (2001); Pub. L. No. 107-40, 115 Stat. 224 (2001). In signing the AUMF, the President stated, "In signing this resolution, I maintain the longstanding position of the executive branch regarding the President's constitutional authority to use force, including the Armed Forces of the United States and regarding the constitutionality of the War Powers Resolution." See "President Signs Authorization for Use of Military Force Bill," September 18, 2001, available at http://georgewbush-whitehouse.archives.gov/news/releases/2001/09/20010918-10.html. On the interpretation of the AUMF, see Curtis A. Bradley and Jack L. Goldsmith, "Congressional Authorization and the War on Terrorism," 118 *Harv. L. Rev.* 2047 (2005).

126. See President's Letter to Congress on American Campaign against Terrorism (Sept. 24, 2001), available at http://z22.whitehouse.gov/news/releases/2001/09/20010924-17.html; President's Letter to Congress on American Response to Terrorism (Oct. 9, 2001), available at http://georgewbush-whitehouse.archives.gov/news/releases/2001/09/20010924-17.html. The quotation comes from the Sept. 24 letter.

127. Zelizer, *Arsenal*, at 442. Note this was consistent with the statement of administration policy given by John Yoo in 2002 reviewed earlier.

128. Bush at 154–155.

129. DeYoung at 409.

130. President George W. Bush, The President's State of the Union Address (Jan. 29, 2002), available at http://z22.whitehouse.gov/news/releases/2002/01/20020129-11.html (referring to the "axis of evil").

131. President George W. Bush, Address to the Nation, President Discusses War on Terrorism (Nov. 8, 2001), available at http://z22.whitehouse.gov/news/releases/2001/11/20011108-13.html.

132. Daalder and Lindsay at 118–119.

133. This was a point made in John Yoo's OLC memo in the immediate aftermath of the 9/11 attacks. See Memorandum from John Yoo to Timothy

Flanigan, Deputy Counsel to the President (Sept. 25, 2001), in *The Torture Papers: The Road to Abu Ghraib* 3, 5, 21 (Karen J. Greenberg and Joshua Dratel eds., 2005) [hereinafter *Torture Papers*].

134. Goldsmith, *Terror Presidency*, at 68.

135. For the story of this suggestion from former attorney general William Barr, see Goldsmith, *Terror Presidency*, at 109. The unlawful combatants language comes from *Ex parte Quirin*, 317 U.S. 1 (1942).

136. See Gellman at 31–60, 132–133.

137. Savage at 7.

138. Goldsmith, *Terror Presidency*, at 27, 76–90, 124–129; Mayer at 51–54, 63–64, 265, 308–311, 321–324. See also Dana Milbank, "In Cheney's Shadow, Counsel Pushes the Conservative Cause," *Wash. Post*, Oct. 11, 2004, at A21.

139. See Savage at 9, 43.

140. See Gellman at 99–102; Mayer at 59–61; Weisberg at 150–182.

141. See Gellman at 51; Goldsmith, *Terror Presidency*, at 76–79; Mayer at 63.

142. Gellman at 50. Gellman remarks, "Cheney was the nearest thing there was to an antipolitician in elected office." Id. at 325. See also Weisberg at 168–170.

143. Gellman at 16, 44, 49, 51–53, 87.

144. See David Ignatius, "Cheney's Enigmatic Influence," *Wash. Post*, Jan. 19, 2007, at A19. See also Gellman at 390.

145. This is a central theme of Gellman's book on Cheney. See Gellman at 50–55, 127–128, 131–154. See also Mayer at 52–53, 323.

146. Compare the useful discussion in Bruff at 116–117.

147. Stanley I. Kutler, *The Wars of Watergate* 101 (1990).

148. Theodore Draper, *A Very Thin Line: The Iran-Contra Affairs* 3–6, 558–579 (1991). See also Karen DeYoung, "Naming National Security Team Will Be a Priority for Obama," *Wash. Post*, Nov. 19, 2008, at A8.

149. Gellman at 50–55, 127–128, 131–154.

150. DeYoung at 415–417; Gellman at 168, 173; Mayer at 264–265; Tenet at 138.

151. Woodward, *The War Within*, at 194–195.

152. Gellman at 134–139, 350–352, 377–378.

153. DeYoung at 364–372; Gellman at 162–168; Mayer at 80–87.

154. Bruff at 145–160; Gellman at 139–154, 277–293.

155. Blum and Heymann at 47–62; Gellman at 299–326.

156. Mayer at 33.

157. Id. at 268–269.

158. The meetings held by the president with his top advisers in 2003 to approve "enhanced" interrogation methods are an example. See Mayer at 39–43; Anthony Lewis, "Official American Sadism," *N.Y. Rev. Books*, Sept. 25, 2008, at 45, 45; Eric Schmitt and Mark Mazzetti, "Secret Order Lets U.S. Raid Al Qaeda in Many Countries," *N.Y. Times*, Nov. 10, 2008, at A1; Joby Warrick, "CIA Tactics Endorsed in Secret Memos," *Wash. Post*, Oct. 15, 2008, at A1.

159. See Blum and Heymann at 18–19; Bruff at 285; Goldsmith, *Terror Presidency*, at 166–167; Mayer at 268–269; David Johnston and Scott Shane, "Memo Sheds New Light on Torture Issue," *N.Y. Times*, Apr. 3, 2008, at A15; Scott Shane, David Johnston, and James Risen, "Secret U.S. Endorsement of Severe Interrogations," *N.Y. Times*, Oct. 4, 2007, at A1.

160. See Goldsmith, *Terror Presidency*, at 24 (remarking that "in practice" John Yoo worked for the White House rather than OLC).

161. Gellman at 177.

162. Goldsmith, *Terror Presidency*, at 23; Mayer at 65.

163. Gellman at 133–139, 174–184.

164. See Goldsmith, *Terror Presidency*, at 97–98. I examine only two of the OLC opinions here. For a thorough review, see Bruff.

165. *Torture Papers* at 3.

166. Id. at 5.

167. Bruff at 135.

168. *Torture Papers* at 7.

169. Id. at 21.

170. Id. at 20–23.

171. Id. at 23.

172. Id. at 8. For Congress's war powers, see U.S. Const. Art. I., § 8, cl. 14 (power "to make rules for the government and regulation of the land and naval forces"); id. cl. 11 (power to "make rules concerning captures on land and water"); id. cl. 10 ("define and punish . . . offenses against the law of nations"); id. cl. 18 (necessary and proper clause); and "declare war" clause. For a relevant discussion see Ramsey at 1240–1243.

173. *Torture Papers* at 3–4, 5, 7.

174. See *Youngstown Sheet & Tube Co. v. Sawyer*, 343 U.S. 579, 637 (1952) (Jackson, J., concurring). Yoo cited Jackson's concurrence to show that the president was "acting at the apogee of his powers" in responding to the 9/11 attacks on the basis of his Article II authority plus the September 2011 AUMF. *Torture Papers* at 21. This argument was sound so far as it went. Yoo was never willing to acknowledge that Jackson's concurrence was equally relevant when the president exercised his Article II authority against a congressional statute.

175. The exclusive power argument is examined in detail and rejected in David J. Barron and Martin S. Lederman, "The Commander in Chief at the Lowest Ebb—Framing the Problem, Doctrine, and Original Understanding," 121 *Harv. L. Rev.* 689 (2008); "The Commander in Chief at the Lowest Ebb—A Constitutional History," 121 *Harv. L. Rev.* 941 (2008).

176. Quoted in Henry P. Monaghan, "The Protective Power of the Presidency," 93 *Colum. L. Rev.* 1, 7 (1993). This article considers Nixon's position in detail and is one of the best general treatments of the issue of whether the president can violate the law.

177. See Memorandum from Jay S. Bybee, Assistant Attorney General, Office of Legal Counsel, to Alberto R. Gonzales, Counsel to the President, in *Torture Papers*, at 172, 204–206.

178. See Bruff at 250–252. Bruff comments, "Of all the legal opinions provided to President Bush during the war on terrorism, Interrogation [the "torture memo"] is the most deficient in legal right and moral conscience. Its legal conclusions are almost wholly antithetical to existing bodies of law and their manifest purposes." Id. at 252.

179. *Torture Papers* at 207. For the statute prohibiting torture, see 18 U.S.C. §§ 2340–2340A.

180. OPR Report at 124.

181. Goldsmith, *Terror Presidency*, at 149.

182. Gellman at 190–191. See Memorandum from Daniel Levin, Acting Assistant Attorney General, Office of Legal Counsel, "Legal Standards Applicable under 18 U.S.C. secs.2340–2340A" to James B. Comey, Deputy Attorney General (Dec. 30, 2004), available at http://www.usdoj.gov/olc/18usc23402340a2.htm.

183. Mayer at 308–312.

184. See the important article by Shane, Johnston, and Risen. See also Mayer at 309–310. After Bybee, no subsequent head of OLC was confirmed by Congress until the Obama administration.

185. Bergen at 107–115; Cole, *Torture Memos*, at 4–6, 13–18. Much of Cole's analysis is based on the Senate report. The relationship between the interrogation techniques used on al Qaeda prisoners and the abuses at Abu Ghraib is one John Yoo was especially concerned to deny as a "partisan smear." John Yoo, *War by Other Means* 168 (2006). Unfortunately, later detailed investigations established a link as noted in the text. See also James P. Pfiffner, *Torture as Public Policy* (2010).

186. Senate Torture Hearing at 16.

187. Senate Report at xxvi–xxvii. On the abuses at Abu Ghraib and the Bush administration's failure to insist on accountability, see Ricks at 197–199, 291–292, 379.

188. For an incisive discussion of the problems with OLC, see Ackerman, *Decline*, at 95–110.

189. *The Federalist* No. 70 at 471 (Jacob E. Cooke ed., 1961).

190. *Torture Papers* at 7.

191. This was the sense conveyed in J. William Fulbright, "American Foreign Policy in the 20th Century under an 18th-Century Constitution," 47 *Cornell L.Q.* 1 (1961). Fulbright of course later changed his views on executive power during the Vietnam War.

192. See Dudziak at 108.

193. Daalder and Lindsay at 40–42, 78–79.

194. Ricks at 60–64.

195. Woodward, *Bush at War*, at 80, 97.

196. Daalder and Lindsay at 106.

197. Bergen at 193–196; Woodward, *Obama's Wars*, at 34, 42, 71, 80–81, 127, 176, 207.

198. Richard H. Kohn, "The Danger of Militarization in an Endless 'War' on Terrorism," 73 *J. Military Hist.* 177, 180 (2009).

199. Daalder and Lindsay at 109; Graham at 306–308.

200. Daalder and Lindsay at 58–59; DeYoung at 334–335, 394–396, 477–478; Haass at 183; Weisberg at 171–172; Woodward, *State of Denial*, at 108–110, 403–404.

201. Daalder and Destler at 278–279; DeYoung at 375, 394–396, 399, 428–429; Haass at 216, 234.

202. Bush at 228–229; Woodward, *Plan of Attack*, at 27.

203. Pillar at 13.

204. Haass at 33.

205. Mann, *Rise*, at 318.

206. Daalder and Lindsay at 9, 80.

207. The Bush administration was not interested in coalition warfare with respect to Iraq. DeYoung at 457–458.

208. Woodward, *Bush at War*, at 332; Woodward, *State of Denial*, at 329.

209. Tenet at 319.

210. Haass at 218–220; Mann, Rise, at 340–341; Ricks at 49–51; Woodward, *Plan of Attack*, at 163–164.

211. Pillar at 37–39.

212. Bergen at 172; Daalder and Lindsay at 145–156; Ricks at 58, 101; Wilentz at 445.

213. Daalder and Lindsay at 148, 154, 158. This point was acknowledged by President Bush in his memoir. Bush at 262.

214. For sophisticated discussions, compare the following to Pillar: Richard K. Betts, *Enemies of Intelligence: Knowledge and Power in American National Security* (2007); Robert Jervis, *Why Intelligence Fails: Lessons from the Iranian Revolution and the Iraq War* (2010).

215. Chollet and Goldgeier at 178–209; Daalder and Lindsay at 153.

216. Woodward, *Plan of Attack*, at 249.

217. Bergen at 138–139; Daalder and Lindsay at 156–167; Woodward, *Plan of Attack*, at 292; Tenet at 342–344, 346–348, 349–350, 354–355. See also Frank Rich, *The Greatest Story Ever Sold* 40, 60–61, 68, 185–190 (2006).

218. Tenet at 305. As a number of commentators have noted, the only genuine weapons of "mass destruction" are nuclear weapons. See Bergen at 225; John Mueller, *Overblown* 13–23 (2006).

219. Tenet at 327, 338–339, 375–376, 383; Woodward, *Plan of Attack*, at 439–440.

220. Tenet at 337.

221. Bumiller at 202–206, 213–226; Fallows at 91–94, 101–106, 221–223; Graham at 345–359, 377–386, 400–407; Ricks at 102, 110–111, 156, 169;

Woodward, *State of Denial*, at 103–104, 108–110, 129–130, 146, 190, 197–198, 240–241, 318, 379–380, 384.

222. Graham at 394.

223. Bergen at 159.

224. Andrew J. Bacevich, *Washington Rules: America's Path to Permanent War* 184–185 (2010); Thomas E. Mann and Norman J. Ornstein, *The Broken Branch* 220–224 (2008); Ricks at 60–64, 385, 387; Woodward, *Plan of Attack*, at 170.

225. Fallows at 138; Mann, Rise, at 343; Rich at 63; Zelizer, Arsenal, at 458–459, 471.

226. Fallows at 80–85, 97–99; Ricks at 86–88.

227. Haass at 270.

228. Fallows at 224–229; Marvin Kalb, "The Other War Haunting Obama," *N.Y. Times*, Oct. 8, 2011.

7. A New Constitutional Order?

1. See George C. Herring and Richard H. Immerman, "Eisenhower, Dulles, and Dienbienphu: 'The Day We Didn't Go to War' Revisited," 71 *J. Am. Hist.* 343, 351–354 (1984).

2. See the recent exchange concerning the National War Powers Commission Report, Miller Center of Public Affairs, University of Virginia (2008) [hereinafter Miller Center Report]. The report recommended repealing the War Powers Resolution of 1973 and substituting a new War Powers Consultation Act. Id. at 27–41. It was immediately attacked by congressionalists. See Louis Fisher, "When the Shooting Starts," *Legal Times*, July 28, 2008.

3. See the table in Chapter 1, pp. 46–47.

4. Curtis A. Bradley and Jack L. Goldsmith, "Congressional Authorization and the War on Terrorism," 118 *Harv. L. Rev.* 2047 (2005).

5. See, e.g., a recent debate between John Yoo and Louis Fisher using President Obama's Libya intervention as a point of departure in "Patriots Debate: The Meaning of the Constitution in a Time of Terror," 98 *ABA J.* 29–39 (Feb. 2012).

6. This point is well made in Mariah A. Zeisberg, *War Powers: A Political Theory of Constitutional Judgment* 66–67 (Princeton University Press, forthcoming 2013). Arguing for her own theory, she makes a pertinent comment: "No other war powers theory on offer can account for the common intuition that legislative processes may sometimes be so deficient as to actually impair the constitutional authority of legislative assent." Id. at 67.

7. See Jack Goldsmith, *Power and Constraint: The Accountable Presidency after 9/11* 3–22 (2012).

8. Robert L. Beisner, *Dean Acheson: A Life in the Cold War* 654 (2006).

9. George C. Herring, *LBJ and Vietnam: A Different Kind of War* 140 (1994) (footnote omitted).

10. Richard N. Haass, *War of Necessity, War of Choice: A Memoir of Two Iraq Wars* 215 (2009).

11. Fredrik Logevall, *Choosing War: The Lost Chance for Peace and the Escalation of War in Vietnam* 390 (1999).

12. See Stephen Skowronek, *The Politics Presidents Make: Leadership from John Adams to George Bush* 3–32 (1993).

13. Bruce Ackerman proposes the establishment of a "Supreme Executive Tribunal" to provide the constitutional guidance the Supreme Court cannot. Bruce Ackerman, *The Decline and Fall of the American Republic* 143 (2010). If what I argue here makes sense, however, I doubt Ackerman's proposal to cabin the president would work.

14. See, e.g., Haass at 33.

15. See Andrew L. Johns, *Vietnam's Second Front: Domestic Politics, the Republican Party, and the War* (2010).

16. Herring at xii.

17. Id. at 44.

18. Id. at 8–9, 13–14.

19. Id. at 41. See also id. at 49–50.

20. Id. at 30–36, 47–48.

21. Id. at 33 (footnote omitted).

22. Id. at 33, 37, 42–43, 47–48, 51, 54, 56–57.

23. Id. at 32 (footnote omitted).

24. Id. at 33–34.

25. Id. at 47.

26. Id. at 54–55.

27. Id. at 55 (emphasis added).

28. Id. at 57–62.

29. Herring at 50 (footnote omitted). Zorthian was head of the Joint Public Affairs Office in Vietnam from 1964–1968, the chief press officer for the U.S. government.

30. Haass at 255; Thomas E. Ricks, *Fiasco: The American Military Adventure in Iraq* 96–98 (2006); Bob Woodward, *State of Denial* 151 (2006).

31. See Haass.

32. Paul R. Pillar, *Intelligence and U.S. Foreign Policy* 52 (2011) (footnote omitted).

33. Id. at 51.

34. See the discussion in Walter Isaacson and Evan Thomas, *The Wise Men: Six Friends and the World They Made* 722–729 (1986).

35. President Barack H. Obama, "A Just and Lasting Peace," available at http://www.nobelprize.org/nobel_prizes/peace/laureates/2009/obama-lecture_en.html.

36. See James Mann, The Obamians: The Struggle Inside the White House to Redefine American Power xiv–xv, 86, 120, 130–131 (2012).

37. See Daniel Klaidman, *Kill or Capture: The War on Terror and the Soul of the Obama Presidency* 57–60 (2012).

38. Thom Shanker and Rick Gladstone, "Armed U.S. Advisers to Help Fight African Renegade Group," *N.Y. Times*, Oct. 14, 2011, at A1.

39. "Recent Administrative Interpretation," 125 *Harv. L. Rev.* 1546, 1547 (2012).

40. See Lou Cannon, *President Reagan: The Role of a Lifetime* 580 (2000).

41. See Jane Mayer and Doyle McManus, *Landslide: The Unmaking of the President, 1984–1988* 222–223 (1988).

42. There was a dispute within the Obama administration on this issue, with OLC on the side of invoking the sixty-day clock and the White House counsel and the State Department saying it did not apply. See Richard H. Pildes, "Law and the President," 125 *Harv. L. Rev.* 1381, 1389 (2012).

43. See "Recent Administrative Interpretation" at 1546, 1550–1553.

44. See *Libya and War Powers, Hearing before the Sen. Comm. on Foreign Relations*, 112th Cong. 7–8 (2011) (testimony of Harold Koh, Legal Adviser, U.S. Dept. of State).

45. Mann at 290.

46. See Klaidman; Claire Finkelstein, Jens David Ohlin, and Andrew Altman eds., *Targeted Killings: Law and Morality in an Asymmetrical World* (2012).

47. "Authorization for Use of Military Force," Pub. L. No. 107-40, 115 Stat. 224 (2001).

48. For a useful constitutional and legal discussion of the AUMF, see Bradley and Goldsmith.

49. On this point, see Mann at 217; Anna Stolley Persky, "Lethal Force," *Wash. Lawyer* 22, 28 (March 2012); Jimmy Carter, "A Cruel and Unusual Record," *N.Y. Times*, June 25, 2012, available at http://www.nytimes.com/2012/06/25/opinion/americas-shameful-human-rights-record.html?ref=todayspaper; Mary L. Dudziak, "This War Is Not Over Yet," *N.Y. Times*, Feb. 16, 2012, at A27; John Fabian Witt, "The Legal Fog between War and Peace," *N.Y. Times*, June 11, 2012, available at http://www.nytimes.com/2012/06/11/opinion/the-legal-fog-between-war-and-peace.html.

50. Ole R. Holsti, *American Public Opinion on the Iraq War* 84 (2011).

51. Bradley and Goldsmith at 2070–2072, 2083–2084.

52. For the debate based in international law, see the contrasting perspectives on targeted killings presented by Special Rapporteur on Extrajudicial, Summary, or Arbitrary Executions, *Study on Targeted Killings*, Human Rights Council, U.N. Doc. A/HRC/14/24/Add.6 (May 28, 2010)(by Philip Alston) and Harold Koh, Legal Adviser, Department of State, "The Obama Administration and International Law," Keynote Address at the Annual Meeting of the American Soc'y of Int'l Law, Mar. 25, 2010.

53. See generally the essays in Finkelstein, Ohlin, and Altman.

54. Robert Weisbrot, *Maximum Danger: Kennedy, the Missiles, and the Crisis of American Confidence* 90 (2001).

55. See Klaidman at 88–91, 104–111, 145–172.

56. This may have been one purpose of a speech by Jeh Johnson, as he was leaving the position of General Counsel of the Department of Defense in the Obama administration. See Jeh C. Johnson, "The Conflict Against Al Qaeda and Its Affiliates: How Will It End?," Speech to the Oxford Union, Nov. 30, 2012, available at http://www.lawfareblog.com/2012/11/jeh-johnson-speech-at-the-oxford-union.

57. See, e.g., Mary L. Dudziak, *War Time: An Idea, Its History, Its Consequences* (2012).

58. For discussion, see John Lewis Gaddis, *George F. Kennan: An American Life* 169, 245, 276–308 (2011).

59. See the suggestive discussion regarding the CIA in Goldsmith at 92.

60. Mayer and McManus at 318–319.

61. Campbell Craig and Fredrik Logevall, *America's Cold War: The Politics of Insecurity* 10 (2009).

62. William Stueck, *Rethinking the Korean War: A New Diplomatic and Strategic History* 215 (2002).

63. See the review of the literature presented in Gary Stone, *Elites for Peace: The Senate and the Vietnam War, 1964–1968* xxvi–xxvii (2007).

64. See, e.g., Robert David Johnson, *Congress and the Cold War* 130 (2006).

65. Id. at 242–286.

66. See National Commission on Terrorist Attacks upon the United States, *The 9/11 Commission Report* 419–421 (2004).

67. See Amy B. Zegart, "The Domestic Politics of Irrational Intelligence Oversight," 126 *Pol. Sci. Q.* 1, 14–25 (2011).

68. Amy B. Zegart, *Spying Blind: The CIA, the FBI, and the Origins of 9/11* 154 (2007).

69. David Kaiser, *American Tragedy: Kennedy, Johnson, and the Origins of the Vietnam War* 110 (2000).

70. See, e.g., Daryl J. Levinson and Richard H. Pildes, "Separation of Parties, Not Powers," 119 *Harv. L. Rev.* 2311 (2006).

71. Political science studies have shown that military interventions increase in periods of unified party government. See William G. Howell and Jon C. Pevehouse, *While Dangers Gather: Congressional Checks on Presidential War Powers* 63–74 (2007).

72. Levinson and Pildes at 2352 (footnote omitted).

73. Id.

74. See Douglas L. Kriner, *After the Rubicon: Congress, Presidents, and the Politics of Waging War* 27–34 (2010).

75. See Thomas E. Mann and Norman J. Ornstein, *The Broken Branch* 155–158 (2008).

76. Nicholas deB. Katzenbach, *Some of It Was Fun: Working with RFK and LBJ* 256–260 (2008).

77. Arthur M. Schlesinger Jr., *Journals: 1952–2000* 260 (2007).

78. Arthur M. Schlesinger Jr., *The Imperial Presidency* (1973) [hereinafter Schlesinger, *Imperial*].

79. See, e.g., Andrew Rudalevige, *The New Imperial Presidency* (2005); Charlie Savage, *Takeover: The Return of the Imperial Presidency and the Subversion of American Democracy* (2007).

80. Schlesinger, *Imperial*, at viii.

81. Id. at viii–ix.

82. Id. at x (emphasis in original).

83. See his discussion of Lincoln in id. at 58–67 and Roosevelt id. at 105–119.

84. See *War Powers, Hearings before the House Subcomm. on Nat'l Security Pol'y and Scientific Developments*, H. Comm. on Foreign Affairs, 93rd Cong. 163–175 (1973) (statement of Arthur Schlesinger Jr.).

85. Schlesinger, *Imperial*, at 143–150, 185–187.

86. Id. at 254. For the discussion of Nixon's abuses of power, see id. at 216–277.

87. Id. at 163–170.

88. Id. at 164.

89. Id.

90. Id. at 165–167.

91. Id. at 169.

92. Id.

93. Id. at 1.

94. For a relevant discussion, see Lewis L. Gould, *The Modern American Presidency* 171, 178 (2003).

95. Schlesinger, *Imperial*, at 277.

96. Id. at 282.

97. Id. at 307.

98. See William Bundy, *A Tangled Web: The Making of Foreign Policy in the Nixon Presidency* 343, 346–347 (1998); Raymond L. Garthoff, *Détente and Confrontation: American-Soviet Relations from Nixon to Reagan* 505–516 (rev. ed. 1994); George C. Herring, *From Colony to Superpower: U.S. Foreign Relations since 1776* 810–829 (2008); Robert David Johnson, *Congress and the Cold War* 186 (2006); Yanek Mieczkowski, *Gerald Ford and the Challenges of the 1970s* 275–280 (2005).

99. See Eric A. Posner and Adrian Vermeule, *Terror in the Balance: Security, Liberty, and the Courts* (2007); *The Executive Unbound: After the Madisonian Republic* (2010) [hereinafter Posner and Vermeule, *Executive Unbound*]; John Yoo, *Crisis and Command* (2009).

100. Yoo at 330.

101. Id. at 335. Later, Yoo concedes that "a high level of cooperation among the branches was necessary to prevail" in the Cold War, but that Congress could not have been left in charge of policy. Id. at 361.

102. See Herring and Immerman.

103. Yoo at 351–352.

104. Id. at 405.

105. Id. at 350–351.

106. Id. at 362.

107. Id. at 361.

108. Posner and Vermeule, *Executive Unbound.*

109. Id. at 3–4.

110. Id. at 85–86.

111. Id. at 113–153.

112. See, e.g., Pildes at 1409.

113. For their discussion of impeachment, see Posner and Vermeule, *Executive Unbound,* at 68–69.

114. Cannon at 626, 654.

115. Posner and Vermeule, *Executive Unbound,* at 176–205.

116. Id. at 7.

117. Posner and Vermeule have a complex theory of constitutional change not considered here that depends on interbranch conflicts, which they term "constitutional showdowns." Id. at 62–83.

118. See David Halberstam, *The Best and the Brightest* (1972).

119. See Goldsmith at 115, 174–177.

Acknowledgments

My thanks go first to the many librarians who helped me along the road. This includes Director James Duggan of the Tulane Law Library and his capable staff as well as the archivists at presidential libraries caring for the papers of Presidents Truman, Eisenhower, Johnson, Nixon, and George H. W. Bush. My scholarly research has always been generously supported by my deans, first Lawrence Ponoroff and now David Meyer. Tulane Law students Elizabeth Howard, Andrea Albright, and Lindsay Calhoun assisted at early and late stages of the project. My greatest thanks go of course to my family for giving me the time to research and write the book over a three-year period.

Early versions of some of the chapters were presented at the 2009 meeting of the American Political Science Association and in colloquia at the Tulane University Murphy Institute, Tulane Law School, Cornell Law School, the University of Texas School of Law, and the University of Kansas Law School. I am grateful for the comments I received on those occasions from Julie Novkov, Mike Dorf, Josh Chafetz, Sandy Levinson, Adeno Addis, Rex Martin, and all of the Tulane, Cornell, Texas, and Kansas participants. A later talk at Case Western Reserve School of Law hosted by Jonathan Entin was helpful in the last stages. Thanks also to my Tulane colleagues who gave me advice on research sources, including Adeno Addis and Gunther Handl; two anonymous reviewers for Harvard University Press; John Barrett for sharing his extensive knowledge of Iran-contra; and Mariah Zeisberg, who carefully reviewed the entire manuscript and made many valuable suggestions. My gratitude goes to Michael Aronson for seeing the project through.

I was fortunate to be invited to three extraordinary conferences at which I presented material from the book. The first was convened in September 2010 by the Office of the Historian at the U.S. Department of State on "The American Experience in Southeast Asia, 1946–1975." The conference featured many leading historians of the war, and I was grateful for the chance to talk to David

Anderson, George Herring, and Fredrik Logevall. It was fascinating to hear from diplomats such as former secretary of state Henry Kissinger, the late Richard Holbrooke, and John Negroponte.

I am similarly grateful to William Eskridge and John Ferejohn for graciously inviting me to participate at a conference on their impressive work, *A Republic of Statutes*, at Yale Law School in December 2010. Finally, I presented part of Chapter 4 at a January 2012 conference at Chapman University School of Law on the occasion of the fortieth anniversary of Watergate. I extend my thanks to Ronald Rotunda, Dean Tom Campbell, and the able staff of the *Chapman Law Review*.

After I graduated from law school, my mother, Marianne Lynch Griffin, began to tell me of her work in the early Cold War as an employee of the new National Security Agency. She told of seeing messages from French troops trapped at Dienbienphu and stories of her life in Washington. She saw Vice President Nixon presiding over the Senate, sat in on the Army-McCarthy hearings, and stood in a movie line in Georgetown with young Senator John F. Kennedy and his wife, Jacqueline. Her stories brought that period in Washington alive for me, and I deeply regret she just missed being able to read this book. She would have really enjoyed it.

Index

Able Archer, 165
Abu Ghraib, 210, 226
Acheson, Dean, 63, 66, 70–72, 74, 77, 86, 88, 91, 194–195, 197, 213, 242
Ackerman, Bruce, 17
Adams, John, 24–25, 236
Addington, David, 221
Afghanistan, 175, 182, 196, 198, 229, 249, 251, 260–261; Soviet invasion of, 175, 182, 198
Afghanistan War, 6, 30, 45, 47, 50, 126, 218, 228–230, 235, 237, 239–240, 248–249, 251, 260–261; and President Obama, 249, 251, 261; Operation Enduring Freedom, 47
Africa, 249
Algeria, 151–152
al Qaeda, 45, 194–196, 204, 208–209, 218–219, 229–231, 233, 249, 251–254, 269; and bombing of U.S. embassies, 196; and 9/11, 204, 218–219, 229–230, 233, 251–254; and USS *Cole* attack, 208–209
Arab-Israeli War, 146
Arbenz, Jacobo, 108, 110
Articles of Confederation, 37, 42
Ashcroft, John, 210
Asia, 51, 54, 59, 83, 89, 131–133, 137, 151, 155, 241; "Asia First" policy, 89; containment in, 59, 137; presidential use of force abroad, 83
Atlantic Charter, 57
Authorizations to Use Military Force (AUMF), 45, 126, 220, 224, 239–240, 249, 251–254
authorized wars, 45–51, 126, 239–240

Baath Party, 234
Baker, James, 178–180
Barbary Wars, 25, 45, 46
Bas v. Tingy, 24
Batista, Fulgencio, 109
Bay of Pigs operation, 2, 100, 108–117, 128, 144, 160, 183, 243, 257
Beisner, Robert, 88, 242
Bendetsen, Karl, 214
Benghazi, Libya, 250
Berlin, 114, 154, 156, 198
Berlin Wall, 197
Biddle, Francis, 212–214
Bin Laden, Osama, 204, 208–209, 230, 254
Bissell, Richard, 116
Boland Amendments, 185, 189–190
Borah, William, 58
Bosnia, 195, 200–202
Bowling Alone (Putnam), 136
Boxer Rebellion, 83
Bradley, Curtis, 48
Brandt, Willy, 156
Brezhnev, Leonid, 198
Bricker Amendment, 65, 107
British constitution, 44
Brookings Institution, 143

Brown v. Board of Education, 12
Bundy, McGeorge, 133, 135, 245
Bundy, William, 33, 151, 174
Burlamaqui, Jean-Jacques, 21
Bush, George H. W., 31, 87, 154, 160, 172, 174–181, 199, 208–217, 234; and Gulf War, 31, 87, 175–181, 215
Bush, George H. W., administration (Bush I), 9, 11, 87, 173, 175–176, 179, 195–196, 199, 206, 208, 223, 249
Bush, George W., 1, 87, 89, 150, 154, 181, 188, 194–195, 205–212, 215–226, 228, 234, 242, 247–248, 252–253, 256, 261, 269, 271; "Axis of Evil," 220, 231; defiance of Foreign Intelligence Surveillance Act (FISA), 217, 222–223; and "imperial presidency," 1, 217–218; and Iraq War, 87, 219–220; and torture controversy, 215–217, 223, 225–226
Bush, George W., administration (Bush II), 1, 2, 9, 11, 41, 192–195, 203–222, 227–235, 244, 247, 248, 252–254, 261, 264–265
Butler, Pierce, 38
Bybee, Jay, 212, 214, 225

Cambodia, 139–140, 148–150, 165–166; and Rehnquist memo, 149–150; U.S. bombing of, 139, 148–150, 165
Carter, Jimmy, 172, 175, 198, 207, 256
Carter administration, 162–164, 172, 182
Casey, William, 183–184, 187
Casto, William, 19, 39
Castro, Fidel, 99–100, 107–113, 115–117, 144–145, 160; U.S. plan to assassinate, 109, 115–117
Central America, 154, 165, 182–185, 193, 198; "covert" war against, 165
Central Intelligence Agency (CIA), 11, 62, 99, 100–104, 110–113, 115–116, 118, 138, 140, 142, 144, 147, 157, 159–160, 183–184, 187, 197, 209–211, 222, 229–234, 247–248, 257–259, 275; CIA Act, 102–103; estimate on Iraq's possession of WMDs, 234
Cheney, Dick, 159, 179, 186, 188, 208, 216, 221–223, 230, 232–233, 246
China, 62, 67, 75–76, 83–84, 89, 99, 108, 120, 129, 139, 141, 147, 153, 155, 157, 196–198; Eisenhower's plan to use nuclear weapons against, 108; Korean War intervention, 75–76, 99, 129; "loss" of, 62, 67, 89, 120, 157, 197; "opening" of, 139, 153; Soviet Union, conflict with, 141, 155, 198; U.S. involvement in, 84
China-Formosa (Taiwan) war scare, 105–106, 108
Church, Frank, 134, 159–161
Churchill, Winston, 56
Civil War, 5, 37, 204–205, 212, 265; 9/11 comparison, 204–205, 212
Clark, Tom, 92
Clifford, Clark, 135
Clinton, William Jefferson, 195–196, 200–203, 208–209, 256, 272; impeachment, 272
Clinton administration, 9, 154, 173, 195–196, 200–201, 203, 207–208, 233, 261
Colby, William, 104
Cold War, 2–12, 15, 24, 26, 31–33, 40–41, 45, 49–50, 52, 54, 56, 59–61, 63, 65, 67, 69–70, 73, 76–77, 79, 83, 85–86, 90, 92, 96, 98, 100, 102–107, 109–111, 114–119, 121–123, 125, 129–130, 132, 137, 142, 145, 147, 153–161, 165–166, 174–177, 179, 183–185, 187, 192, 195–200, 203, 205–206, 209–211, 215–216, 218–220, 227, 231–232, 236, 241, 243, 247, 253, 259–263, 265, 267–269, 271, 274–275; and Central Intelligence Agency, 102–103, 114–116, 118, 258; China's involvement in, 77; and Cuba, 109-110, 114; end of, 196–201; foreign policy, 15, 52; militarization of, 59; need for reassessment, 155–162; 9/11, 205–206, 209, 218–220; "Project Solarium," 155; relationship to torture controversy, 215; unilateral presidential military interventions during, 79, 85; United Nations Charter, effects on, 86; and Vietnam War, 122, 125, 132, 137; and Watergate, 142, 145, 147, 153
Communist Party, 12
Congress, 1–3, 13, 17, 23–25, 27, 30–31, 33–38, 40, 42, 45, 47, 50, 52, 54–59, 62, 64–69, 71, 74–80, 82–96, 101–108, 111–112, 114, 116–117, 121–128, 130–138, 140, 143–144, 147–151, 153–154, 158, 161, 163–164, 166–180, 183–186, 188–191, 194–196, 200–201, 203–205, 207, 209–210, 218–219, 221, 224–225, 230, 232–234, 237, 239, 241–244, 246,

248–249, 251–265, 268–274; appropriations authority, 52, 185; approval to go to war, 3–4, 17, 25, 27, 36–38, 50, 54, 56–58, 78–80, 82–83, 87, 94, 96, 104–107; and atomic weaponry, 163–164; Castro, opposition to operation to depose, 111; Central America, U.S. operations within, 184; and Central Intelligence Agency, 101–103, 183, 209–210; "Great Debate," 88; and Gulf War, 175-180; and Iran-contra affair, 183–186, 188, 258; Korean War, 74–77, 89–90, 132; 9/11, 205, 218–219, 224, 230, 251–252; Philippine War approval, 83; *Steel Seizure* case, 93, 224; U.S. peacekeeping missions under Clinton, 200–201, 203; and Vietnam War, 13, 121–128, 132–138, 140, 147–149, 166, 172, 268, 270; "War on Terror," 253–254; Watergate, 144, 153
congressionalists, 2–3, 7, 27–30, 240, 255–256, 261–263
constitutional crisis, 10, 119; Watergate as crisis, 141–147
constitutional orders, 4, 14–17, 54–55, 61, 218-219; and legalized and non-legalized Constitution, 11, 15–16, 72–74, 243, 274; original constitutional order, 17–18, 61, 97, 236, 266, 273–274; and state capacity, 24, 72. *See also* post-1945 (Cold War) constitutional order
Convention against Torture, 211
Connally, Tom, 72
Corwin, Edward, 40, 84
covert war, 4, 6, 97, 99–105; against Cuba, 109–113; against Nicaragua, 181–188
Cox, Archibald, 146–147 , 166
Cox, James, 80
Craig, Campbell, 128, 158, 199, 258
Creation of the American Republic (Wood), 41
Crisis and Command (Yoo), 269–271
Cuba, 6, 83, 99–100 , 107–115, 117, 121, 128, 144, 154, 157, 160–161, 183, 253, 275; Cuban brigade, 110–112; U.S. involvement in, 6, 83, 99–100, 109–115, 117, 121, 128, 144, 160, 275; U.S. quarantine of, 114
Cuban missile crisis, 9, 100, 110–114, 121, 157, 163, 165, 183, 197, 253, 259, 265
cycle of accountability, 5, 18, 50, 74–75, 97, 103–104, 106, 116, 128, 176–177, 243, 255–264
Czechoslovakia, 67

Dallek, Robert, 134
Darkness at Noon (Koestler), 215
Daschle, Tom, 219
declarations of war, 85–86, 123–126, 239
declared wars, *see* authorized wars
Democratic Party, 9, 126–127, 129, 134, 141, 146, 154, 158, 160–161, 163, 172–175, 180–181, 185, 187, 191, 200–202, 206, 209, 229, 237, 244, 260–261, 264, 268–269; and atomic weaponry, 163, 234; Cold War doubts, 9, 160–161; and concerns of "imperial presidency," 158, 160, 260, 269; and Iran-contra affair, 186, 191; and Iraq War, 234, 264, 269; Johnson, support for, 126–127; Kennedy, support for, 161, 187; Nixon, conflict with, 146–147; Truman, defense of, 107; unilateral presidential power support, 108; and Vietnam War, 130, 134, 154, 237, 244; and War Powers Resolution, 172–175 , 180, 200–201, 260; and Watergate, 141, 268
Dienbienphu, 105–107, 236, 255, 270
Dominican Republic, 83
Doolittle Report, 62, 111, 115–116, 160, 275
"Duck Hook," 139
Dulles, John Foster, 105–106, 115, 270

East Asia, 54, 83
Egypt, 115
Ehrlichman, John, 146
Eisenhower, Dwight, 9, 13, 30, 68–69, 95–96, 99–100, 104–112, 115, 117–118, 121, 128, 155, 160, 162, 164, 182, 187, 195, 199, 211, 236, 242, 247–249, 255, 266 268, 270; Cuba, 110; Korean War, 30, 182; and "Project Solarium," 155; and Vietnam War, 13, 236, 242, 255; views on congressional role in war, 104–109
Eisenhower administration, 9, 33, 45, 65, 68, 88, 99–100, 105, 107, 109–110, 116, 118, 134, 141–142, 144–145, 153, 156–157, 160, 165, 183, 192, 248; and "New Look" defense policy, 105, 108, 117–118
El Salvador, 182–183, 193

Ellsberg, Daniel, 143–144
Ellsworth, Oliver, 38
Ely, John Hart, 32, 126
Europe, 51, 59, 65–66, 70, 137, 156, 174, 192, 196, 198, 212, 240, 250; containment policy, 59, 137; post-World War II, 156, 192; terrorism in, 250; U.S. wars in, 51, 174; and World War II, 70, 212
Ex parte Milligan, 213

Federal Bureau of Investigation (FBI), 138–141, 144, 159, 214, 222, 259, 275
Federal Communications Commission (FCC), 214
The Federalist 70 (Hamilton), 227
Federalist Republic, 23
Federalists, 24–25
The Fettered Presidency (Crovitz and Rabkin), 160
Firmage, Edwin, 32
Fischer, Beth, 165
Fisher, Louis, 32, 217
Ford, Gerald, 151–153, 155–160, 171–172, 216, 244, 255, 262, 268; and Vietnam War, 255
Ford administration, 9, 155, 216, 221, 267
Foreign Intelligence Surveillance Act (FISA), 217, 222–223
Foreign Relations Committee, 40
Formosa Resolution, 106
France, 20, 23–24, 55–56, 105, 236, 251; and Dienbienphu, 105, 236; initiation of naval hostilities against U.S., 23–24; "War on Terror," 251; World War II, 55–56
Freedman, Lawrence, 112, 117, 131
Fulbright, J. William, 39, 86, 123, 137–138, 246

Gaddis, John Lewis, 59–60, 62
garrison state, 64–65
Garthoff, Raymond, 207
Gaulle, Charles de, 142, 151, 152
George III, 37
Geneva Convention, 217
Germany, 40, 55–59, 63, 70, 95, 120, 156, 248; and World War II, 55–58, 63, 70, 95, 120
Gerry, Elbridge, 38
Glennon, Michael, 32
Goldsmith, Jack, 48, 210, 212, 216, 225–226
Goldwater, Barry, 123, 159
"Good Neighbor" policy, 84
Goodpaster, Andrew, 109
Gorbachev, Mikhail, 199, 208
Gray, C. Boyden, 179–180
Great Britain, 20, 23, 55, 57, 69, 100, 251; and "War on Terror," 251; and World War II, 55, 57, 69, 100
"Great Debate" of 1951, 65
Greece, 59, 66, 86, 195
Greenland, 57
Grenada, 173, 184
Guantanamo Bay, 1, 115, 217, 253, 261; detention, 217, 253, 261
Guatemala, 108, 110, 112–113; CIA involvement in, 110; U.S. paramilitary operations in, 108
Gulf of Sidra, 250
Gulf War, 6, 11, 30–31, 40, 45, 47, 50, 171, 174–181, 195, 229, 239–240, 257, 259

Haass, Richard, 231, 235
Haig, Alexander, 173, 183–184
Haiti, 83, 195, 200–202; U.S. involvement in, 83; U.S. peacekeeping mission in, 195, 200–202
Haldeman, H. R., 144, 146, 153
Hamby, Alonzo, 73
Hamilton, Alexander, 19–23, 25–26, 35–36, 37, 44, 54–55, 94, 227, 274; "Pacificus" exchange with Madison, 19–22, 37, 44; view on president's power to act, 25
Harvey, William, 116
Helms, Richard, 144
Helsinki accords, 156, 198
Henkin, Louis, 31
Herring, George, 52, 245–246
Herter, Christian, 115
Hickenlooper, Bourke, 34
Hirabayashi v. United States, 213
Hiss, Alger, 143
Hitler, Adolf, 55–56, 63, 95, 119–120, 177, 204
Hogan, Michael, 52, 64–65, 67–69
Honduras, 83, 183–184
Hoover, J. Edgar, 138–141
Hughes, Charles Evans, 80
Hull, Cordell, 58, 81
Humphrey, Hubert, 68, 134, 165

Hunt, E. Howard, 144–145
Huq, Aziz Z., 217
Hurricane Katrina, 194, 273
Hussein, Saddam, 176–177, 180–181, 204, 209–210, 215, 219–220, 232–234, 255; and relation to 9/11, 219–220, 233, 255
Huston plan, 141, 144

Iceland, 57
imperial presidency, 2, 4
The Imperial Presidency (Schlesinger), 98, 160, 265
interbranch deliberation, 4, 8, 50, 55–56, 73, 97, 218, 255–256; and Gulf War, 175–176; and Vietnam, 130
interbranch synthesis, 17
Iran, 108, 182, 186–188, 206, 220, 231–232; "Axis of Evil," 220, 231; Iran-contra affair, 186–188; Iran-Iraq War, 173; U.S. covert operations against, 108
Iran-contra affair, 2, 13, 154, 161, 181–188, 191–193, 200, 206, 216, 222–223, 258, 261, 272, 274; Majority Report on, 191; Minority Report on, 188–189, 223
Iran-Iraq War, 173, 186
Iraq, 87, 176–179, 181, 186, 195, 220, 229–237, 239–240, 242–243, 246–249, 255, 260–261, 264, 269, 274; "Axis of Evil," 220, 231; invasion of Kuwait, 87, 176–179, 181; Iran-Iraq War, 173, 186; U.S. airstrikes in, 195
Iraq War, 6, 11, 30, 45, 47, 50, 87, 126, 174, 194–195, 206, 210, 218–221, 226, 228–237, 239–240, 242–243, 246–249, 251, 255, 260–261, 264, 269, 274; and Abu Ghraib scandal, 210, 226; comparison to Vietnam, 243–248; weapons of mass destruction, 232–234
isolationism, 54, 58, 63, 95

Jackson, Andrew, 73
Jackson, Robert, 18–19, 90, 92–95, 168, 189, 191, 218, 224
Japan, 58, 60, 63, 70, 72–73, 101, 120, 156; Pearl Harbor, 101; post–World War II, 156; World War II, 58, 63, 70, 72, 120
Japanese-American internment, 212–215
Jaworski, Leon, 146
Jefferson, Thomas, 20–21, 23, 25, 35, 94, 274; views on Congress's "declare war" power, 25
Jefferson administration, 19, 236
Jeffersonian Revolution of 1800, 23
Jeffersonians, 23–24, 26
Jieshi, Jiang (Chiang Kai-shek), 197
Johnson, Harold, 246
Johnson, Lyndon B., 33, 68, 89, 120–138, 140, 147, 150, 155, 174, 206, 211, 231, 242–243, 245–246, 255–256, 258, 266–268, 270; and Vietnam War, 120–138, 140, 242–243, 258
Johnson, Robert, 258
Johnson, Lyndon B., administration, 9, 33, 45, 118, 122, 127–129, 131–132, 134–137, 143, 155, 162, 165, 169, 174, 204, 245–246, 250
Joint Chiefs of Staff (JCS), 100, 112, 117–118, 135, 148, 230, 245
Jones, Howard, 111
Joyce, Robert, 103–104
Judge Advocate General (JAG), 275

Kaiser, David, 120
Katzenbach, Nicholas, 33–34, 47, 64, 85–87, 123–126, 150, 170, 204, 262
Kennan, George, 59–61, 64, 155, 257
Kennedy, John F., 8, 100, 107, 109–112, 114, 117–118, 120–121, 128, 131–132, 134, 136, 155, 160–161, 164, 174, 187, 198, 206, 211, 243, 256, 266, 268; as hero-president, 161, 187; CIA involvement in Cuba, 110–112, 128, 160; Cuban missile crisis, 121; on Vietnam, 132
Kennedy, John F., administration, 8, 33, 45, 99–100, 109, 112, 115, 117–118, 123, 131, 134, 144–145, 153, 156, 159–161, 165, 169, 174, 183, 192, 265
Kennedy, Robert, 113
Kenya, 196
Kerr, Philip (Lord Lothian), 58
Khrushchev, Nikita, 113–114, 198
Kimball, Jeffrey, 140, 142, 150
Kissinger, Henry, 140, 142–143, 147, 149, 151, 153, 156–158, 162, 166, 172, 244
Koestler, Arthur, 215
Koh, Harold, 90, 191–192
Kohn, Richard, 229
Korean War, 6, 8, 11, 12, 13, 28–32, 35, 45, 47–50, 52–53, 59, 72–79, 83, 88–90, 92, 96, 101, 103, 105–106, 108–109, 115, 117, 121, 123–125, 128–129, 132,

Korean War *(continued)*
134, 145, 149–150, 155, 182, 201–203, 226–228, 236, 239, 242, 248, 255, 259, 262–263, 266, 270, 272; Inchon landing, 259; "Korea decision" as precedent for future presidential action, 96, 106, 262
Korean War Veterans Memorial, 76
Korematsu v. United States, 213
Kuwait, 87, 173, 175–180, 215, 227–228; Iran-Iraq War, 173; Iraq invasion, 87, 176, 180; torture of citizens by Saddam Hussein, 215

LaFeber, Walter, 193
Laos, 114, 136
Larkin, Barbara, 203
Latin America, 11, 54, 80, 83–84, 109, 215; CIA interventions in, 11; torture, 215; U.S. military involvement in, 54, 80, 83–84
League of Nations, 63, 79–81
Lebanon, 173, 175, 182, 185–186, 204; U.S. hostages held in, 182, 185–186
Leffler, Melvyn, 59
Levi, Margaret, 136
Levin, Daniel, 225–226
Levinson, Daryl, 260
Libya, 197, 202, 204, 236, 249–251, 260, 271; U.S. bombing of, 197, 249–250; U.S. intervention in, 202, 204, 236, 249–251, 260, 271
Lincoln, Abraham, 5, 204–205, 265
living constitution, 2, 61, 266–267
Locke, John, 21
Lodge, Henry Cabot, 80
Lofgren, Charles, 40
Logevall, Fredrik, 108, 128, 133, 158, 199, 243, 258
long war, 5, 60, 62, 116, 118, 195, 242, 251
Lord's Resistance Army, 249
Lovett, Robert, 91

MacArthur, Douglas, 75, 89
Madison, James, 19–23, 25, 28, 35–38, 41-42, 94, 274; "Helvidius" exchange with Hamilton, 19, 21–22, 37, 44; views on Congress's "declare war" power, 25
Madison administration, 19, 236
Mann, James, 231
Mansfield, Mike, 113, 134
Margolis, David, 212, 214–215
Marshall, John, 169
Marshall Plan, 59, 66–67, 86, 156, 195
Mason, George, 38, 44
Matsu, 105
McCarthyism, 67, 88, 118, 138
McCord, James, 144
McCulloch v. Maryland, 169
McFarlane, Robert, 185
McKinley, William, 83–84
McNamara, Robert, 131, 134, 135, 138, 143, 155, 162, 242, 246
McNaughton, John, 138
Meese, Edwin, 186–187
Mexican War of 1846, 45–46
Mexico, 83
Miami, 113, 275
Middle East, 11, 51, 106, 108, 128, 146, 175–176; Arab-Israeli War, 146; CIA interventions in, 11, 108, 128; 1957 congressional resolution, 106
Mitchell, John, 143
Monaghan, Henry, 83
Monroe Doctrine, 84
Montesquieu, 21
Mossadegh, Mohammed, 108
Munich, 119–120, 240

Nasser, Abdel, 115
National Commitments Resolution, 39, 123
National Election Studies, 136
National Security Act, 12, 65, 100–102, 117, 192
National Security Agency (NSA), 138, 159, 217, 222–223; Shamrock program, 159; wiretapping under Bush (G. W.), 217, 222–223
National Security Council, 101, 114, 149, 164, 185, 187, 222, 227–228, 230–231, 234, 244–245, 257; "ExComm" in Cuban missile crisis, 114
national security state, 49, 99–119 *passim*
Nelson, Michael, 216
Neutrality Acts, 58, 63
Neutrality Proclamation, 20, 22
Nevada, 163
New Deal, 67
"New Look" defense policy, 105, 108, 117
New York Times, 143
Ngo Dinh Diem, 131

Nicaragua, 6, 83, 182–185, 185, 189–190, 198; U.S. involvement in, 6, 83, 182, 189–190, 198
1984 (Orwell), 215
Nixon, Richard, 10, 13, 121–122, 129–130, 136, 138–151, 153, 155–158, 162, 165–166, 168-170, 173-174, 184, 196–198, 206, 211, 222, 225, 244–245, 255–256, 261, 266–268, 270, 272; and Huston plan, 141, 144; impeachment of, 146–147, 272; and Vietnam War, 13, 139–142, 145–150, 153, 166, 244–245; and Watergate, 13, 122, 141, 144–147, 151, 165–166, 184, 222
Nixon administration, 2, 9, 129, 140, 145, 156, 162, 169, 251
North, Oliver, 185–188, 190, 222
North Atlantic Treaty Organization, 12, 52, 59, 68, 134, 156, 165, 195, 202, 249
North Korea, 12, 71, 75, 89, 132, 206, 220, 231–232; "Axis of Evil," 220, 231
North Vietnam, 123, 125, 127–128, 132, 137–140, 147–148, 150
NSC-68, 12, 60–62, 103, 115–117, 155
nuclear triad, 162–164
nuclear war, 99–100, 114, 127
nuclear weapons, 162–165, 266
Nunn, Sam, 171, 181
Nye, Joseph, 137

Obama, Barack, 1, 195–196, 202, 216, 229, 236, 240–241, 248–251, 253, 260; CIA, 248; Libya intervention, 236, 249–251, 260; Nobel Peace Prize speech, 248; position on war powers, 248–250
Obama administration, 1, 2, 9, 90, 154, 191, 195–196, 202–204, 207, 248, 251, 253 254, 261; and targeted killings, 253–254
Office of Legal Counsel (OLC), 123, 149, 172–173, 201–202, 210–212, 214, 223, 227, 249, 261; Bush (G. W.) OLC opinion on presidential war powers, 224–226; Bush (G. W.) OLC "torture memo," 211–212, 223–225; Carter OLC opinion, 173; Clinton OLC opinion on WPR, 201–203, 249, 261; Obama OLC opinion on Libya, 202, 249, 261
Office of the Vice President (OVP), 221–223, 226, 230, 233; and Cheney, Dick, 221–226, 230, 233
Operation Desert Shield, 176
Operation Enduring Freedom. *See* Afghanistan War
Operation Mongoose, 113
Operation Northwoods, 115
OPLAN 34A, 127
Orren, Gary, 136
Orwell, George, 215
Ostpolitik, 156
Our Chief Magistrate and His Powers (Taft), 84

Pakistan, 251
Panama, 83
Paris Peace Conference, 79
Pearl Harbor, 5, 6, 40, 53–54, 63, 70–72, 95, 101, 120, 204, 212, 214, 219, 228; 9/11 comparison, 204, 212, 214, 219
Pentagon, 109, 113, 115, 230, 234, 246
Pentagon Papers, 143, 166
Persian Gulf, 173, 175
Pfiffner, James, 217
Philadelphia Convention, 21, 28, 36–44
Philippine War, 83
Pildes, Richard, 260
Pillar, Paul, 231, 247
Pinckney, Charles, 36
Poindexter, John, 187, 222
Poland, 56, 58
Posner, Eric, 271–274
post-1945 (Cold War) constitutional order, 59–71, 89–92, 95–98, 114, 118–122, 127, 129–132, 154, 166–169, 175, 180–181, 185, 192, 194–201, 206, 216–222, 236–238, 241–243, 248–249, 255–256, 268–270, 273–275
Powell, Colin, 208, 232, 242
presidentialists and presidentialism, 2–3, 8, 27–30, 240, 270; "exclusive" presidency, 188–193; *Steel Seizure* case, 93–94
presidential power to initiate war, 71–77
presidential transitions and foreign affairs, 207–209
Project Solarium, 155
Putnam, Robert, 136

Qaddafi, Muammar, 197, 202, 249–251
Quasi-War with France, 19, 23–25, 45–46
Quemoy, 105

Ramsey, Michael, 37
Ranelagh, John, 102–104, 142

Reagan, Ronald, 153–154, 161–164, 167, 172–173, 182–190, 193, 196–200, 204, 206–208, 211, 222, 249–250, 256, 261, 272; antinomian tendencies, 184–185; as hero-president, 187; Berlin Wall, fall of, 197; Central America, 193; Iran-contra affair, 182–186, 222, 261, 272; Nicaragua, 182–185, 189–190; and Soviet Union, 165; Strategic Defense Initiative, 198–199
Reagan administration, 2, 9, 13, 162, 165, 172–175, 181–185, 188–189, 191–193, 196–198, 206, 223–224, 232, 258, 268; and nuclear weapons, 162–165
Rehnquist, William, 149–150
Republican Party, 9, 24, 31, 89, 105, 107–108, 151, 154, 158, 160–165, 173, 180–181, 183-184–188, 191–192, 196–197, 200, 203, 206–207, 209, 216, 237, 244–245, 260–261, 264–268; and atomic weaponry, 163–165; and Central America, 184; commitment to Cold War, 9, 160; conflict with Clinton over Serbia, 203; conservative internationalism, 107; "exclusive" presidency, 181, 188, 216; Gulf War, 31; Iran-contra affair, 184–188, 191, 200; Iraq War, 237; "Old Guard," 95, 105, 108, 248, 265; national security, 161; rejection of critique of imperial presidency, 154, 158, 192; and Truman, 89, 105, 197; and Vietnam War, 151, 244–245, 268; and War Powers Resolution, 173, 200–201, 260
Reveley, Taylor, 40
Revolutionary War, 37, 42
Reynaud, Paul, 56
Reynolds, David, 56
Rice, Condoleezza, 208, 226, 230
Richardson, Elliot, 169–170
Rogers, James Grafton, 81–82
Roosevelt, Franklin Delano, 5, 40, 49, 55–58, 60, 63, 69, 72, 79, 81, 83–84, 100, 120–121, 204–205, 213, 220, 244, 247, 259, 265; "Good Neighbor" Policy, 84; and World War II, 55–58, 81, 83–84, 120–121, 205, 213, 220
Roosevelt, Franklin, administration, 265
Roosevelt, Theodore, 83
Root, Elihu, 84
Rostow, Eugene, 213
Rumsfeld, Donald, 208, 212, 230
Rusk, Dean, 125, 135, 155
Russia, 208
Rutledge, John, 36

Saigon, 148
Sandinistas, 182, 185
Saudi Arabia, 176–177, 259
Savage, Charlie, 217
Schlesinger, Arthur, 98, 130, 192, 265–268
Schwartz, Frederick A.O., Jr., 217
Scowcroft, Brent, 31, 176, 179
Second Indochina War, 120. *See* Vietnam War
Secret Intelligence Service (M16), 103
Senate Armed Services Committee, 166, 226, 246, 258; investigation into OLC memos, 226
Senate Foreign Relations Committee, 258
September 11, 2001 terrorist attacks: and detainee cases, 92; and Iraq War, 219–220; and Japanese-American internment cases, 214; 9/11, 5, 9, 11, 13, 91, 92, 158, 175, 194, 204–207, 209–212, 214–220, 223–224, 228–233, 235, 251–255, 259–250, 275; and 9/11 Commission, 259; and United Flight 93, 205; and weapons of mass destruction, 231–233
Serbia, 196, 203, 248; U.S. support for Kosovo, 196, 203
Shamrock program, 159
Shinseki, Eric, 246
Shultz, George P., 186, 188
Silberman, Laurence, 104
Smith, Gaddis, 113
Smith, Walter Bedell, 116
Sofaer, Abraham, 40
Somalia, 195, 251; U.S. peacekeeping mission, 195
Somoza, Anastasio, 182–183
Southeast Asia, 122, 131–133, 151, 155
South Korea, 12, 70–71, 73, 134, 228
South Vietnam, 122–123, 127, 131, 138–139, 147–148, 150–151, 156–157, 164, 171–172, 250; Thieu government, 147–148, 150
Soviet Union, 5, 9, 29, 58–62, 64, 66–67, 71–73, 75, 86, 100, 103, 107–108, 111, 113–114, 119, 121, 123, 139, 142, 147, 153–158, 162–165, 175, 181–183, 192,

195–199, 206–208–209, 232, 253; and atomic weaponry, 62, 103, 114, 119, 155, 162–163; collapse of, 199; conflict with China, 141, 198; Cuba, influence in, 100, 108, 113, 121; Korean War involvement, 75; Middle East involvement, 175, 181–182, 198; Nixon's détente strategy, 139, 153, 157–158, 198; occupation of North Korea, 71
Spanish-American War, 45–46, 83
Special Investigative Unit (the Plumbers), 143
Stalin, Joseph, 52
Steel Seizure case, 12, 18–19, 90, 92–95, 168, 189–191, 218, 224–225, 266
Stennis, John, 85–86, 166, 246, 256
Stimson, Henry, 212–214
Stoker, Laura, 136
Stromseth, Jane, 82
Suez crisis, 106, 115
Sung, Kim Il, 71, 76
Supreme Court of the United States, 11–12, 14–15, 24, 34, 48, 53, 63–64, 72, 91, 124, 212, 225, 240, 274

Taft, Robert, 68, 72, 200
Taft, William Howard, 84
Taiwan war scare, 105
Taliban, 194, 229–230, 251
Tanzania, 196
Taylor, Stuart, 216–217
Tenet, George, 209, 233
Tet offensive, 135
Tonkin Gulf, 123, 125, 135
Tonkin Gulf Resolution, 33, 122–125, 127, 240, 254, 270
Tora Bora, 230
Tower, John, 159–160
Treaty of Versailles, 63, 79
Trinidad, 110
Tripoli, 25, 250
Truman, Harry S., 5, 7, 8, 13, 28, 30–33, 35, 49, 52–53, 59–60, 63, 65–76, 85, 87, 97, 99, 101, 106–109, 121, 123–124, 132, 135, 145, 149, 155, 194–195, 197, 203, 205, 210–211, 226–228, 231, 243, 248, 258, 263, 266–268, 270–271; "imperial" presidency, 88–95; "Korea decision" as precedent for future presidential action, 96, 106, 262; Korean War, 13, 31–32, 35, 49, 52–53, 70–71, 73–77, 88–92, 96, 99, 101, 106, 109, 121, 123–124, 132, 145, 149, 226–228, 243, 258, 263
Truman administration, 6, 32, 52–53, 62, 64, 70, 73, 86, 88, 90, 95, 102, 105, 107, 116–118, 147, 153, 155–156, 192, 195, 233, 265
Truman Doctrine, 12, 52, 59, 66, 86, 115, 155–156, 179
trust in government, 119, 122, 136–137
Tulane University, 153
Turkey, 59, 66, 86, 195

unitary presidency, 188, 256
United Flight 93, 205
United Kingdom, 103. *See also* Great Britain
United Nations, 12, 34, 64, 73, 76–79, 81–82, 84–87, 123–125, 134, 149, 176, 178, 249; Charter, 47, 53, 77, 79, 81–82, 84–87, 124–125, 149; Korean War, 76; Security Council, 71, 86–87, 176, 178, 249
United States Army, 51, 92, 101, 117, 138, 236; all-volunteer force, 180–181; casualties, 51; and Vietnam War, 138; World War II, 101
United States Constitution, 2–4, 11–18, 20–23, 25–30, 33–35, 38–44, 48–54, 61, 63–66, 69–71, 73, 75–76, 79, 81–82, 85, 87, 90–93, 95–96, 103–104, 111, 113–114, 116, 118–120, 122, 124–125, 129–130, 134, 136, 145–147, 149–150, 160, 168–171, 180, 188, 190, 192, 196, 201, 203, 205, 213–214, 220, 224–225, 228, 238, 243, 246, 249, 252, 256, 265–267, 271–275; Article I, 17, 33, 168, 170; Article II, 7, 20–21, 32, 49, 85, 90, 93, 125, 170, 180, 188, 190, 196, 203, 220, 224, 243, 249, 252, 262; Article V, 14, 16, 30; Fourteenth Amendment, 11, 213; Twenty-Second Amendment, 247
United States Department of Defense, 68–69, 101, 117–118, 142–143, 148, 175, 222, 225, 233, 257
United States Department of Justice, 31, 90, 104, 123, 161, 189–190, 201, 211–212, 214–215, 225; Office of Professional Responsibility, 211–212, 225; *Steel Seizure* case, 90. *See also* Office of Legal Counsel

United States Department of the Navy, 24, 100–102
United States Department of State, 31, 58, 68–69, 74, 77–79, 81–82, 85–87, 89–90, 101, 103, 110, 125, 133, 142, 148, 170, 179, 203, 213, 215, 225–226, 231, 257; memo on presidential war powers, 77–78, 81, 85, 87, 203, 226; participation in U.N. Charter, 79, 179; Policy Planning Staff, 257
United States Department of War, 100, 102, 212–214
United States Marines, 51, 236
United States Navy, 127
United States v. Curtiss-Wright Export, Corp., 63–64, 190
Utah, 163

Vandenberg, Arthur, 66–67
Vattel, Emerich de, 21
Vermeule, Adrian, 271–274
Vietnam War, 2, 6, 7, 9, 11, 13, 27, 29–31, 39, 47, 50–51, 78, 82, 86–87, 89, 95, 97, 108, 114, 118, 120–141, 143, 145, 147–150, 152–153, 155–158, 160–162, 165–167, 169, 172, 174–175, 181–183, 192, 196, 198–199, 201–203, 206, 227, 231, 236–237, 239–247, 250, 254–255, 257–259, 261–263, 265, 267, 269–271, 274; "Duck Hook," 139; Johnson's management of, 243–246; OPLAN 34A, 127; quagmire thesis, 128; Tet offensive, 135; and trust in government, 136–137; "Vietnam syndrome," 174, 183
Vinson, Carl, 68

Walsh, Lawrence, 181, 189–190
Walters, Vernon, 144
War of 1812, 45, 46
war powers debate, 6–7, 27–31, 39–40, 239–243; and 1950 thesis, 31–35; argument from historical practice, 77–85; OLC views, 201–204; position of political parties, 260–264; U.N. theory, 85–87
War Powers Resolution (WPR), 7, 13, 27–28, 39, 47, 85, 123, 154, 158, 165–175, 180–181, 189, 196, 200–201, 203–204, 213, 237, 239, 244, 250–251, 260–263, 265, 271; constitutionality of, 167–173; implementation of, 171–174
Washington, George, 20, 23, 25, 238
Watergate, 2, 13, 97, 113, 122, 136–137, 139, 141, 144–147, 151, 153, 166, 184, 187, 192, 206, 221–222, 265, 267–268, 270, 274; and Bay of Pigs, 144–145; as a constitutional crisis, 145–147; CIA involvement in, 113; "Saturday Night Massacre," 166
Weinberger, Caspar, 163, 181, 186, 207
Weinberger-Powell Doctrine, 175
Weisbrot, Robert, 113
Welles, Sumner, 56
Westmoreland, William, 132, 259
Wherry, Kenneth, 72
white supremacy, 83
Whittington, Keith, 166
Wilson, James, 36–38, 41, 43–44
Wilson, Woodrow, 79–81, 83; and Article X of Treaty of Versailles, 79–80
Wood, Gordon, 23, 41–42
World Trade Center bombing, 197
World War I, 45–46, 62–63, 79–81, 83, 134; evidence against presidential practice of unilaterally committing troops, 79
World War II, 2, 3, 5, 12, 13, 27, 32–33, 43, 45–46, 49–50, 54–55, 59, 62, 64, 71, 72, 74, 76, 79, 81, 83, 85, 100–101, 120, 124, 134, 159, 177, 192, 197–198, 203–205, 212–215, 220, 247, 260, 265–266, 268, 271; appeasement as cause of, 120; evidence against presidential practice of unilaterally committing troops, 79; Japanese-American internment, 205–206, 212–215; Nazi threat, 49, 58; 9/11, 204–205, 212, 220
Wormuth, Francis, 32

Year of Intelligence, 159
Yemen, 208, 251
Yoo, John, 41–44, 87, 150, 203–204, 212, 214–215, 223–225, 227, 269–271
Youngstown Sheet & Tube Co. v. Sawyer. See *Steel Seizure* case

Zablocki, Clement, 166
Zedong, Mao, 197
Zegart, Amy, 259
Zelikow, Philip, 226
Zelizer, Julian, 31, 107, 158, 161, 200
Zorthian, Barry, 246